You dont put
La-KWAH
in this
body

I DO NOT
COOK
I DO NOT
CLEAN
I DO NOT
FLY
COMMERCIAL

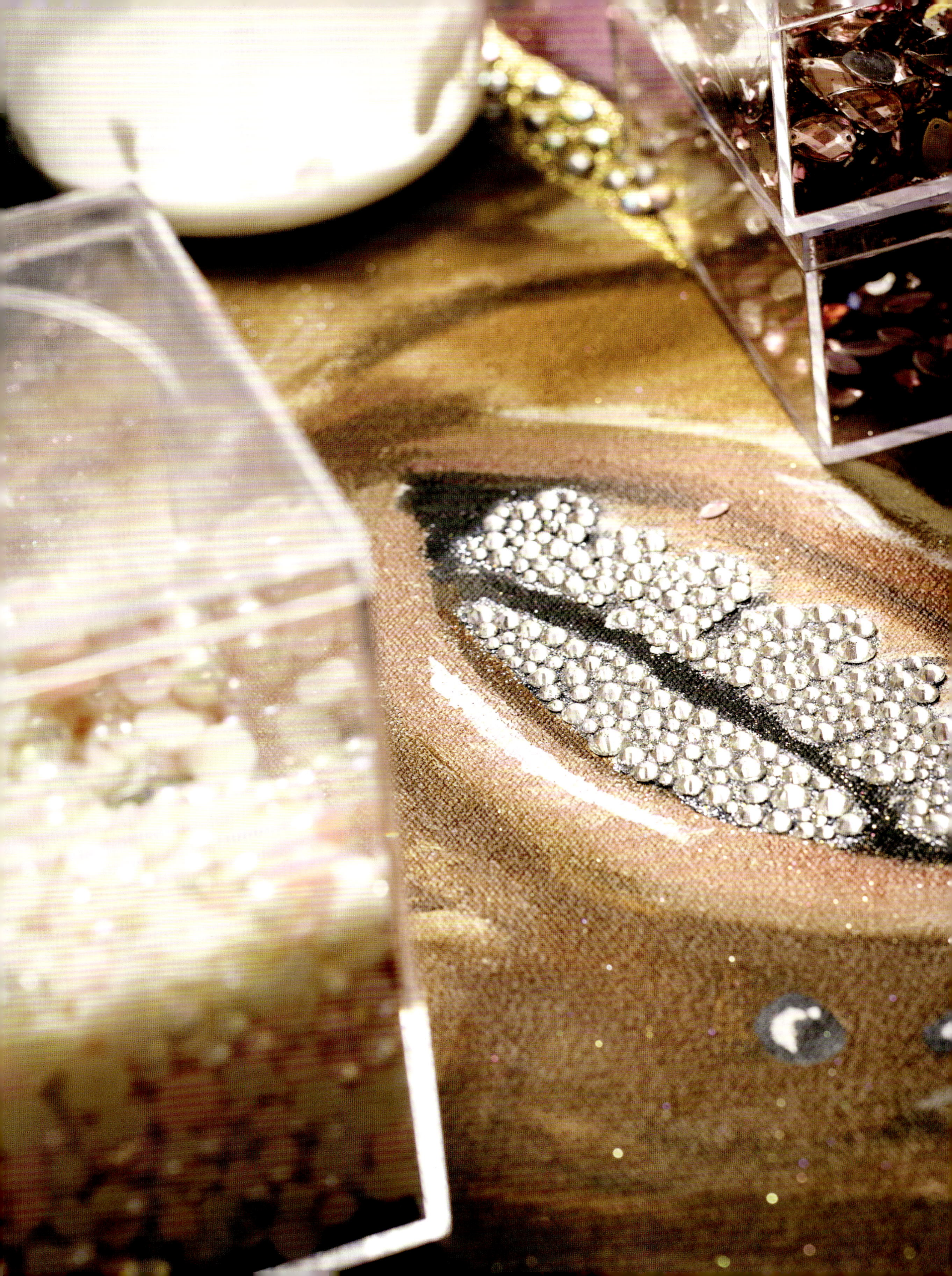

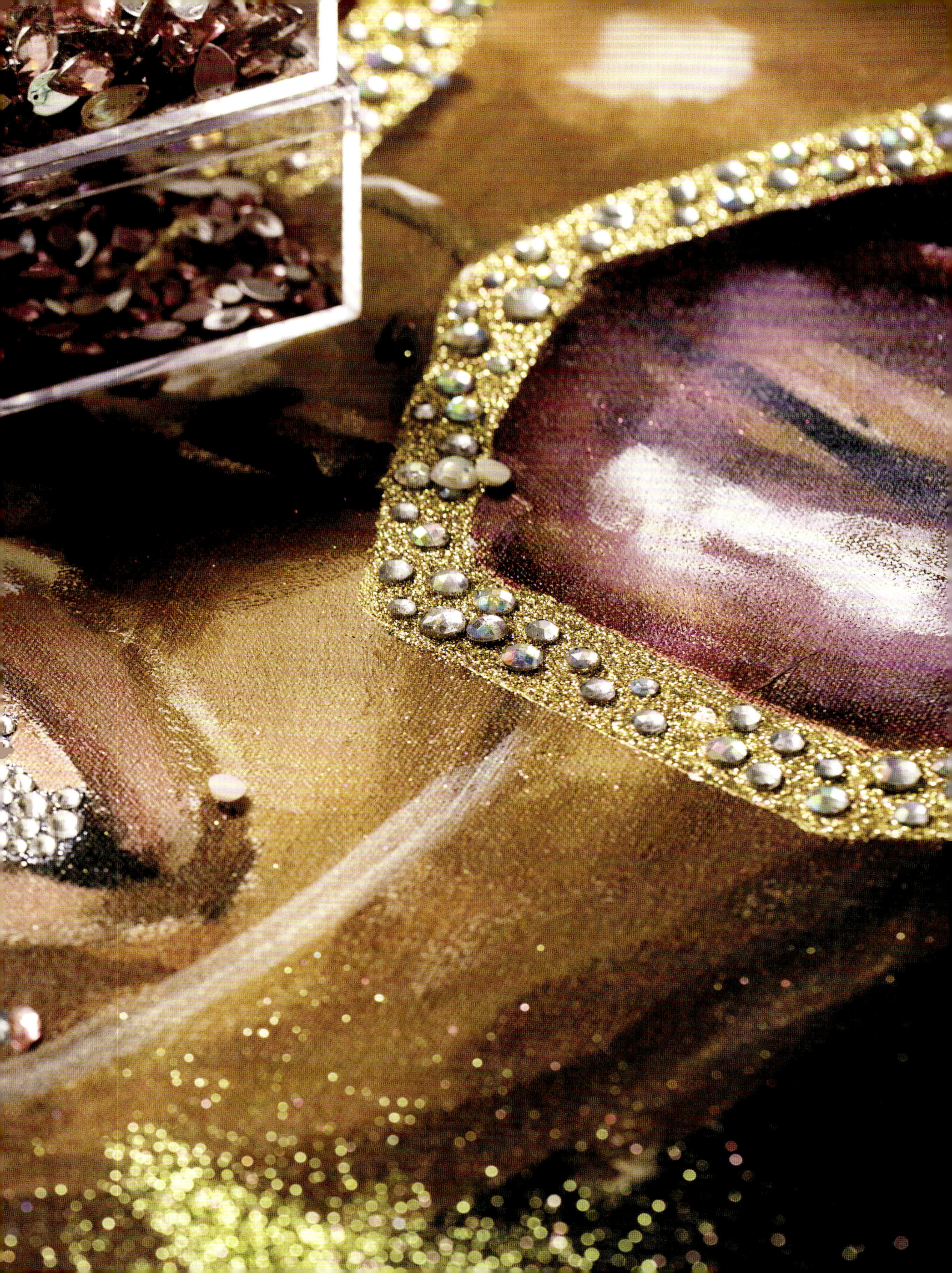

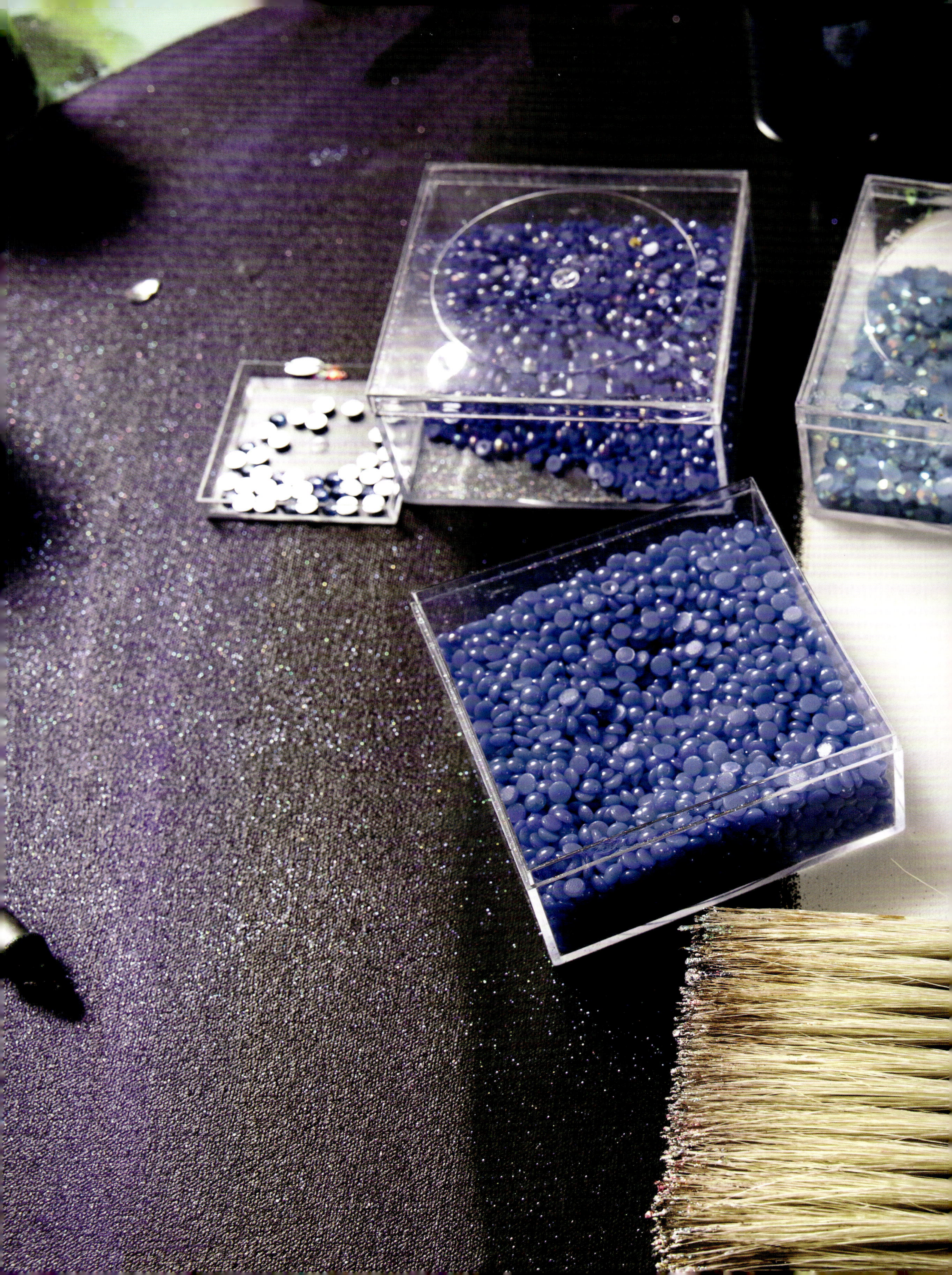

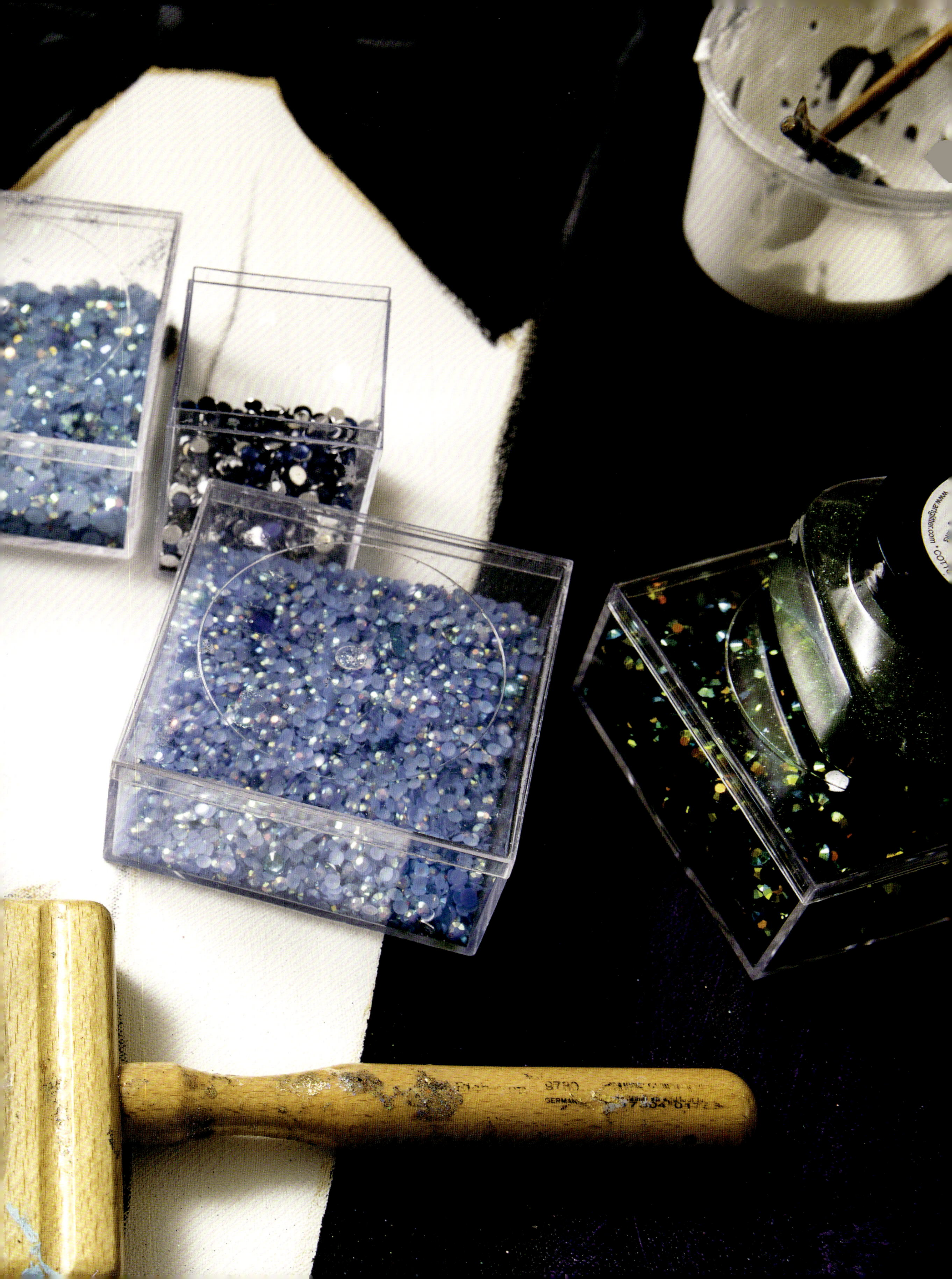
www.artglitter.com
8780

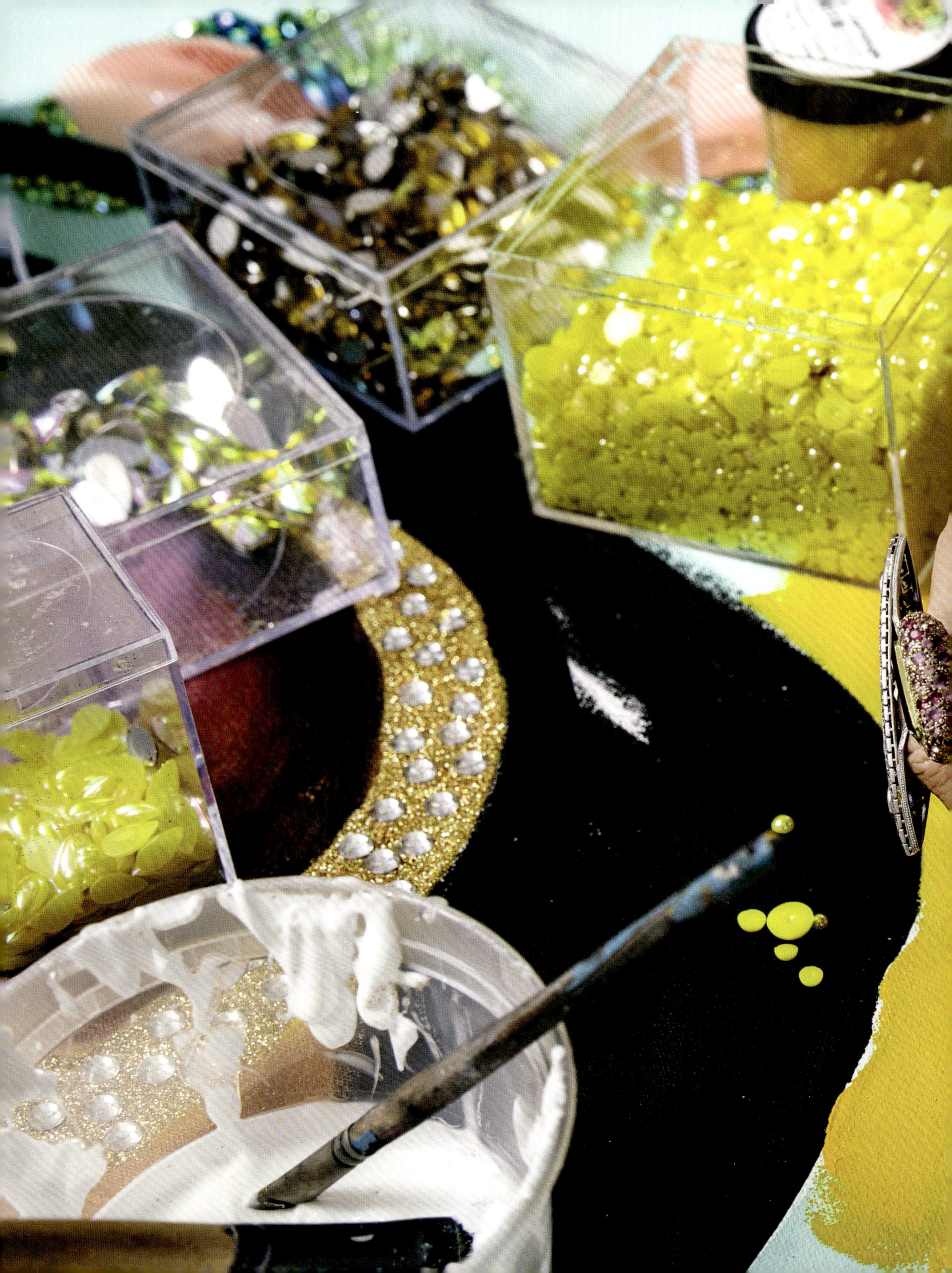

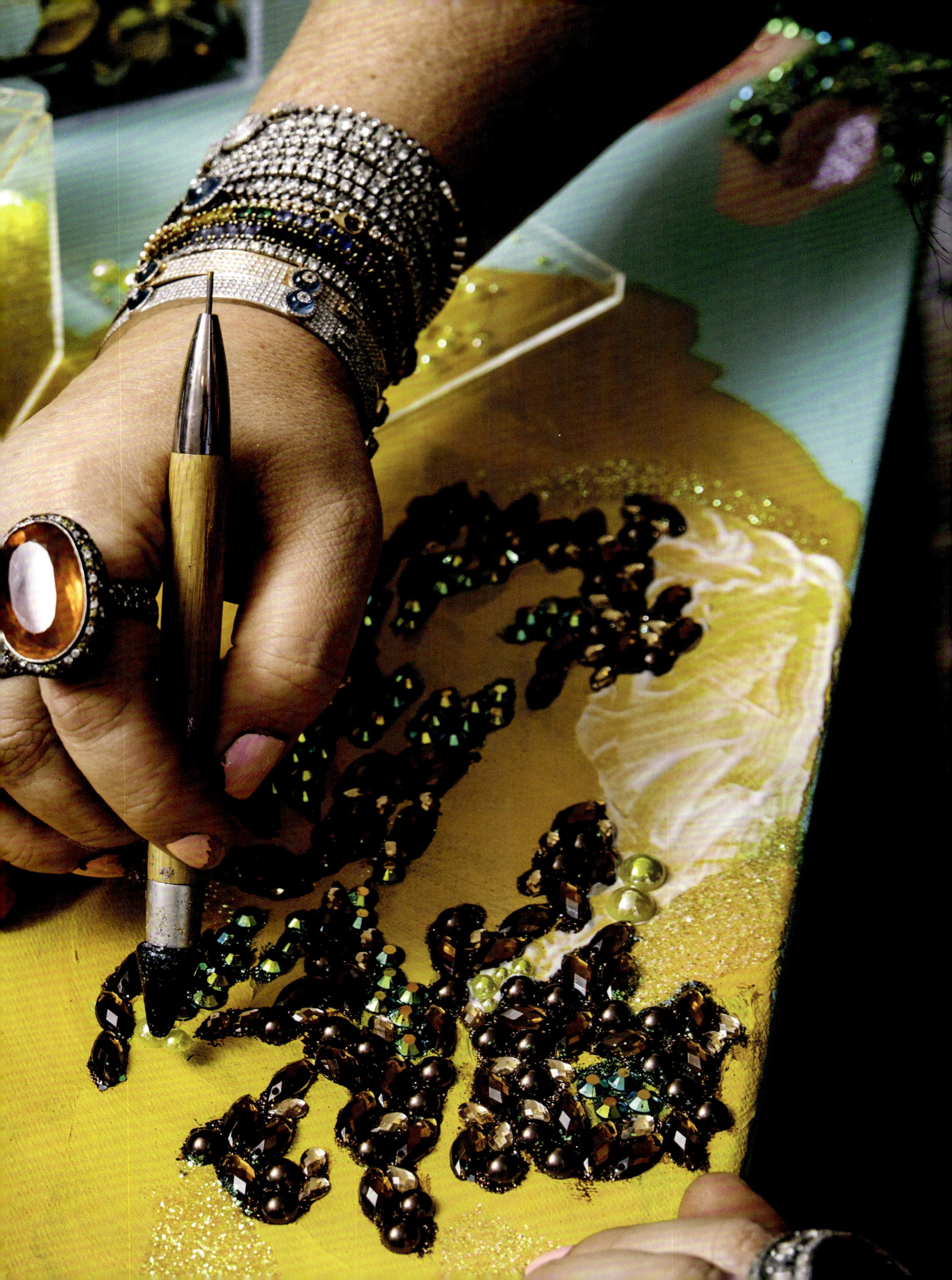

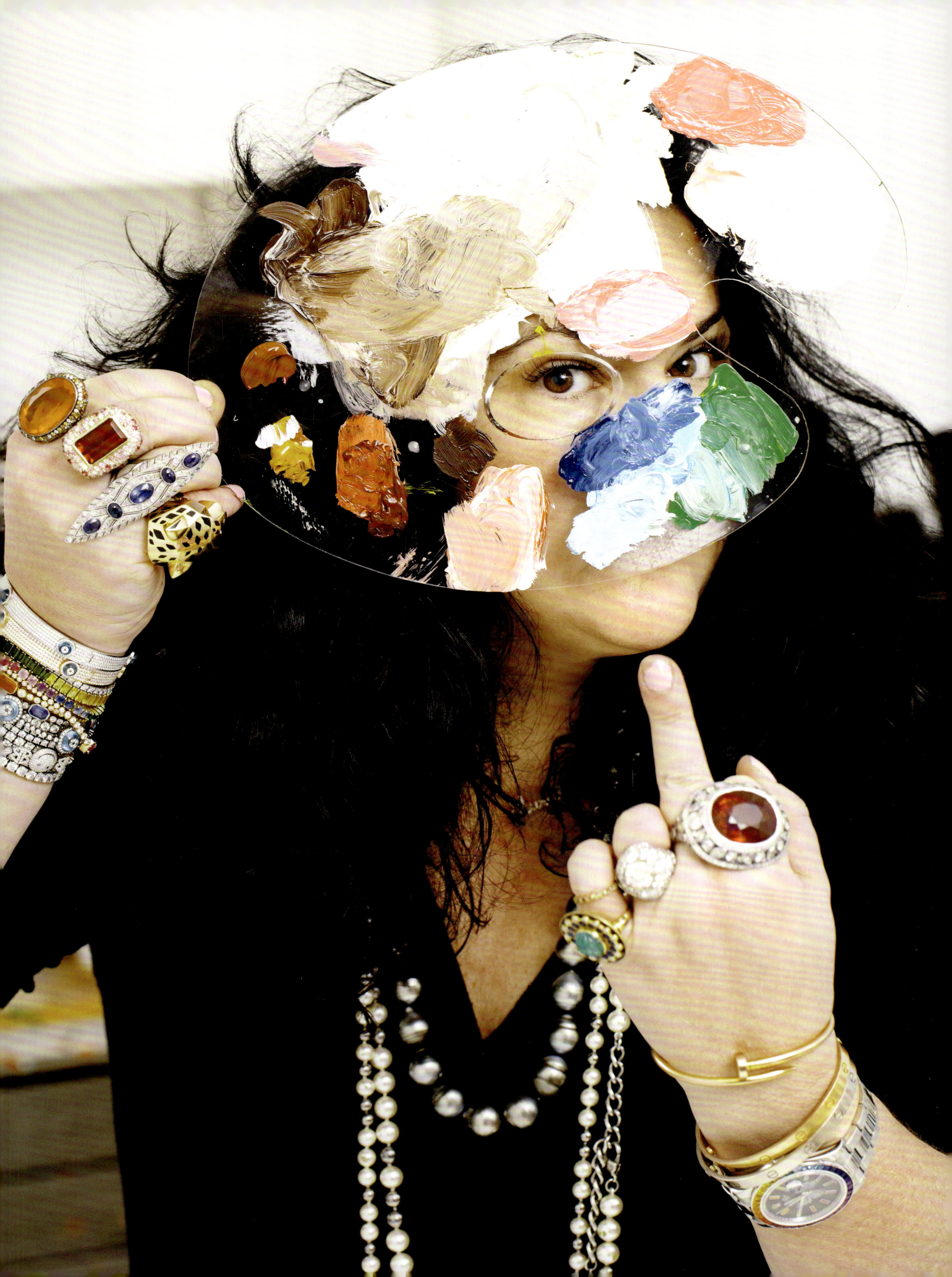

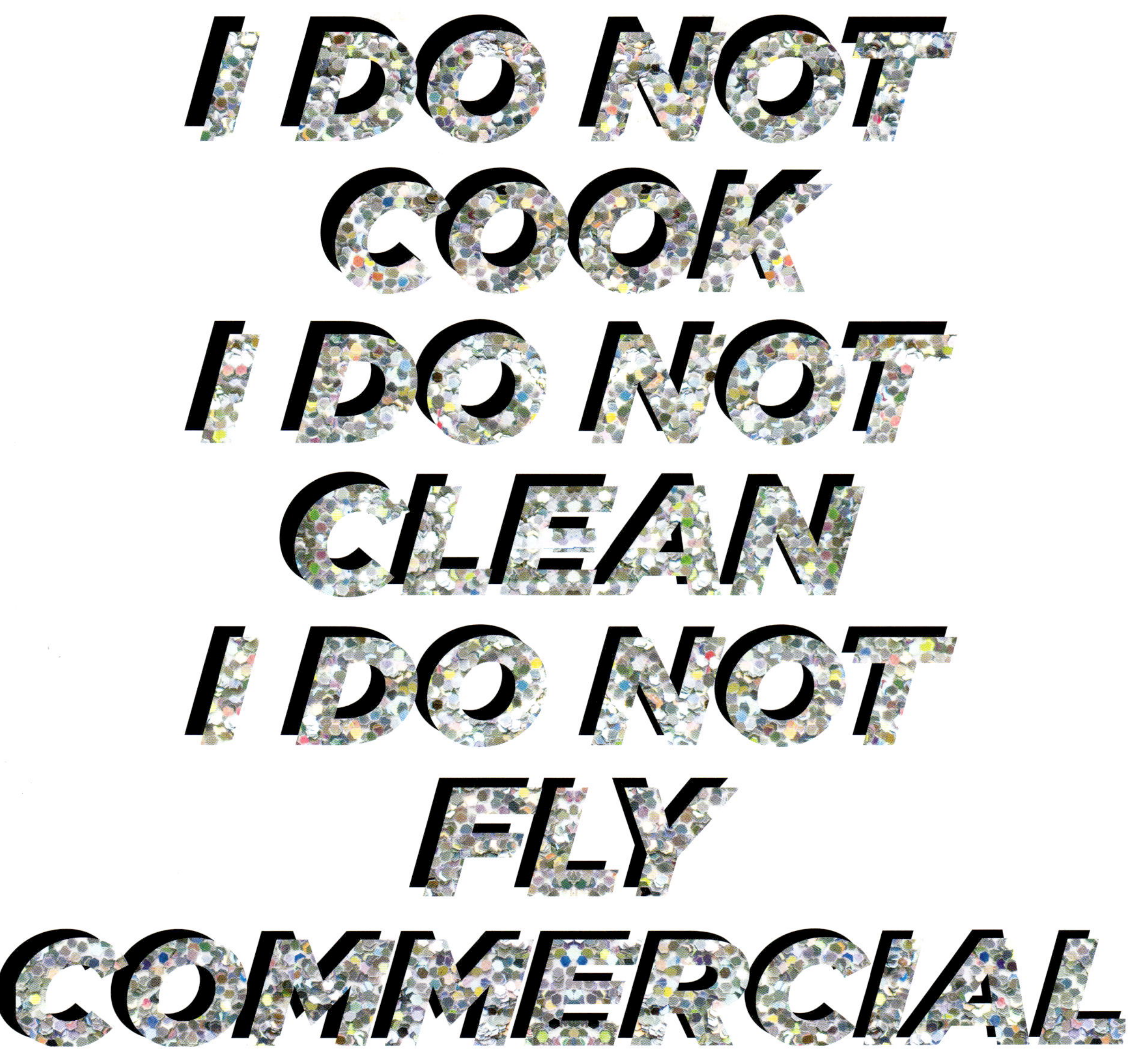

ASHLEY LONGSHORE

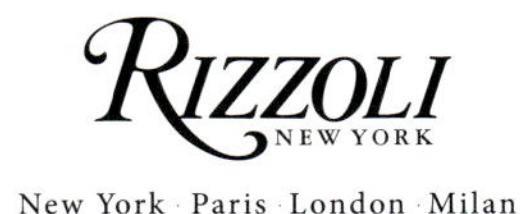

New York · Paris · London · Milan

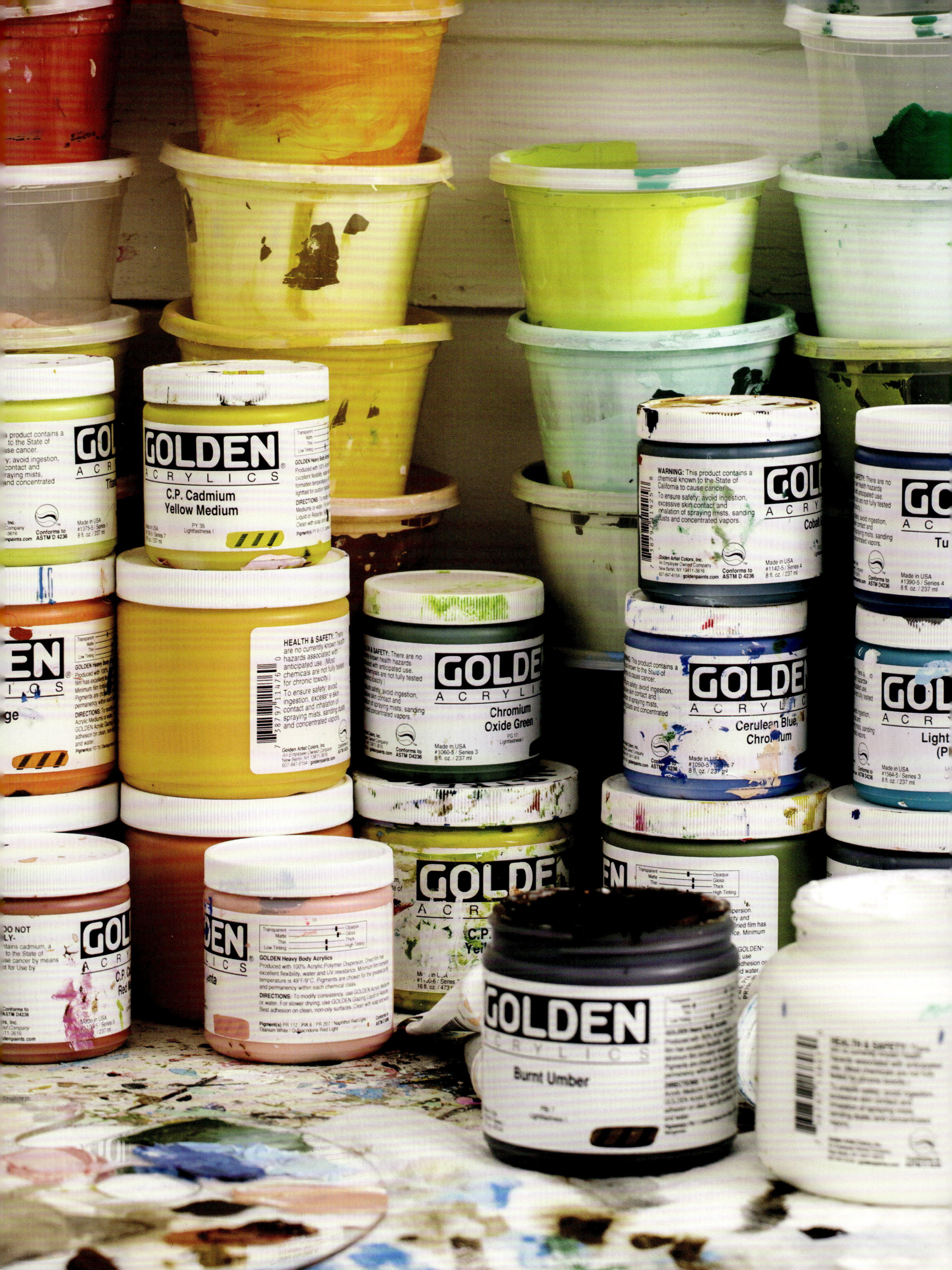
GOLDEN
ACRYLICS
C.P. Cadmium
Yellow Medium
GOLDEN
ACRYLIC
Chromium
Oxide Green
GOLDEN
Burnt Umber

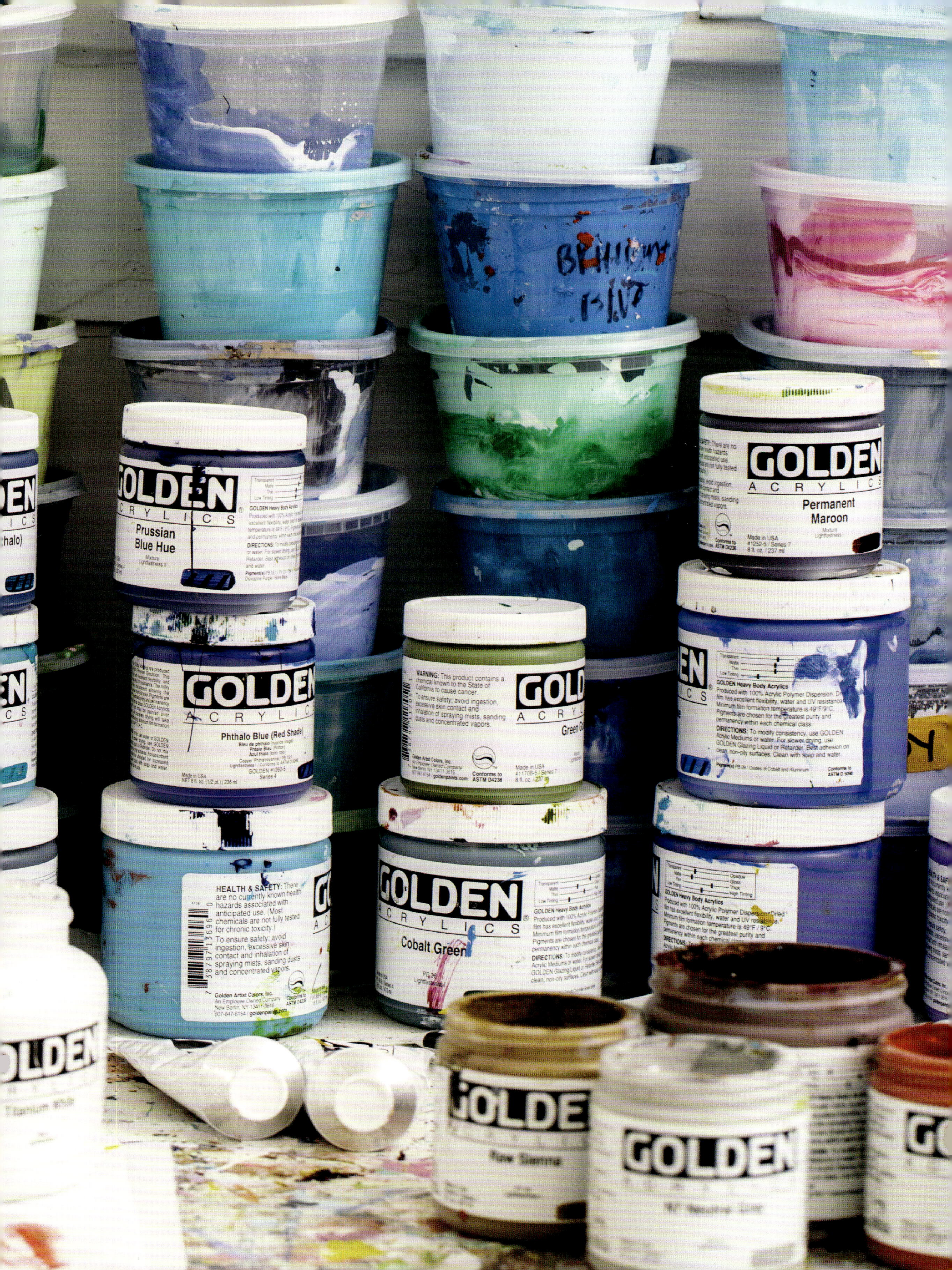

GOLDEN
ACRYLICS
Prussian Blue Hue
GOLDEN
ACRYLICS
Permanent Maroon
GOLDEN
ACRYLICS
Phthalo Blue (Red Shade)
GOLDEN
ACRYLICS
Cobalt Green
GOLDEN
GOLDEN

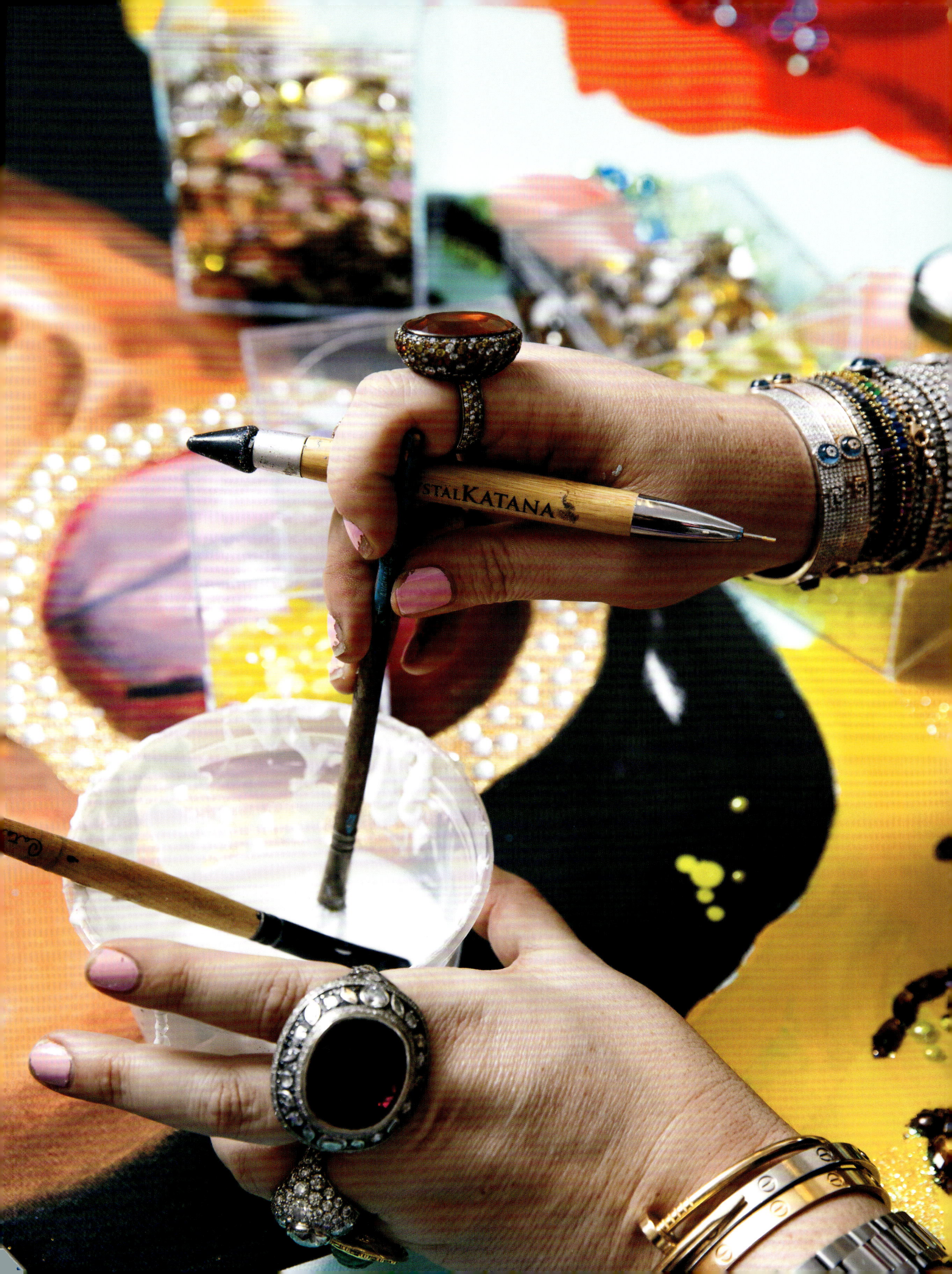
KATANA

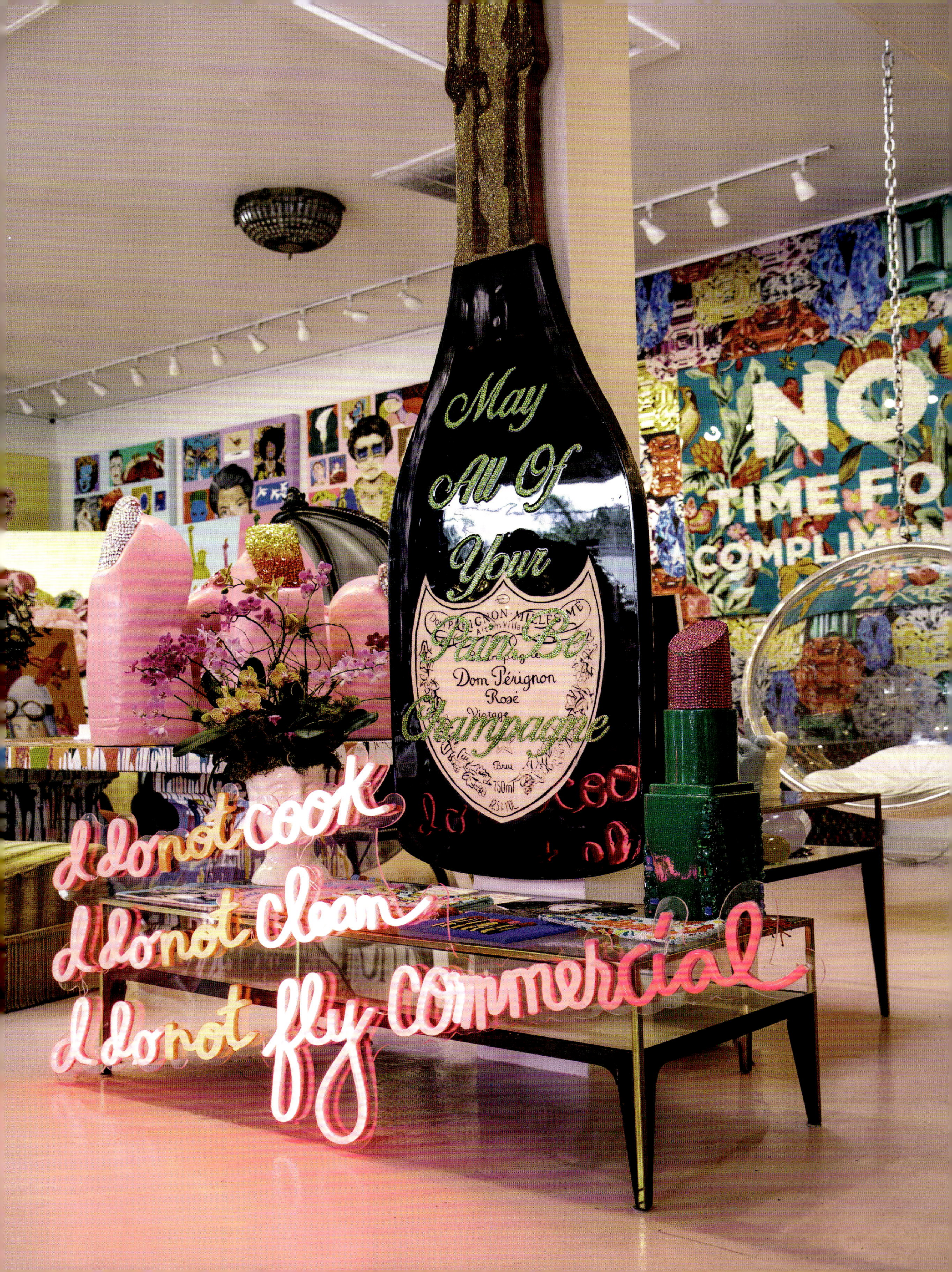
May
All Of
Your
Pain Be
Champagne
Dom Pérignon
Rosé
NO
I do not cook
I do not clean
I do not fly commercial

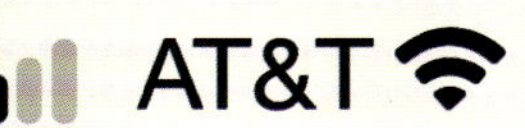

1:22 PM

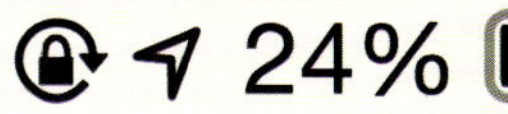

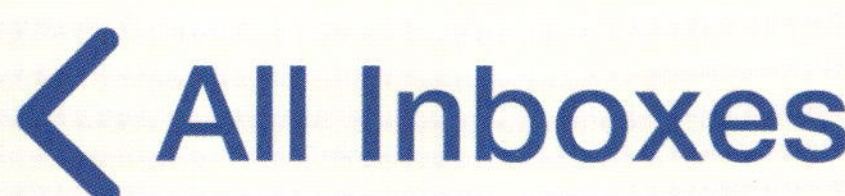

3 Messages

10am

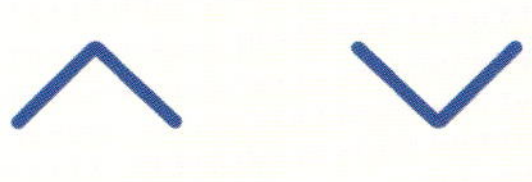

Blake Lively

To: Ashley Longshore

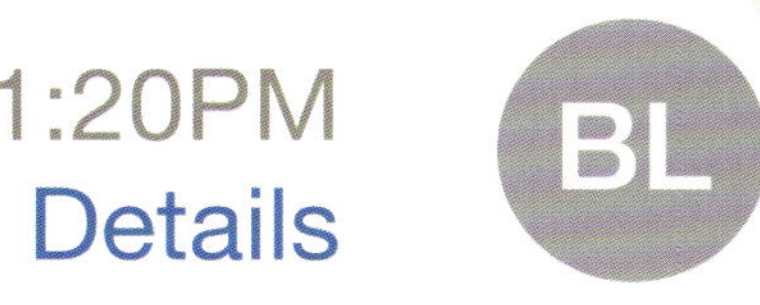

Ashley's work grabs your attention with its celebration of color, life, humor, power, and sparkle. Like her, it stands out in any crowd because of how bold, beautiful, unforgettable, and delightfully intoxicating it is. Her talent is only outmatched by her kindness and humanity. I am a superfan

Sent from my iPhone!

See More from Ashley Longshore

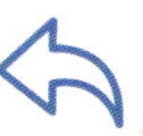

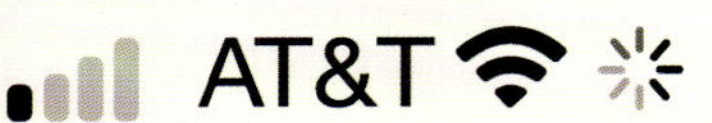

AT&T

6:34 PM

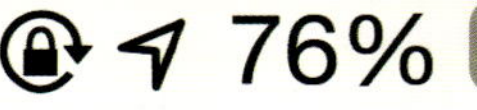

76%

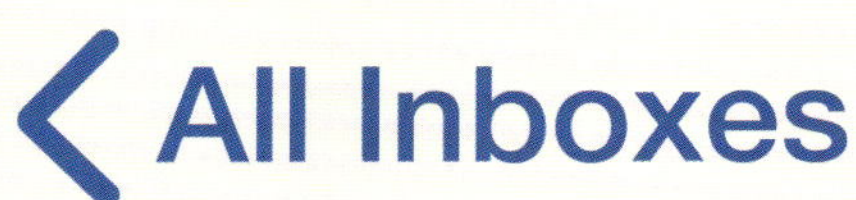

17 Messages

Hey yall!!!

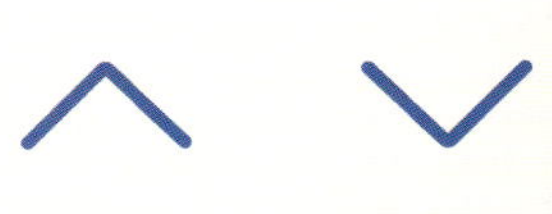

Tommy Hilfiger

To: Ashley Longshore

6:29PM

Details

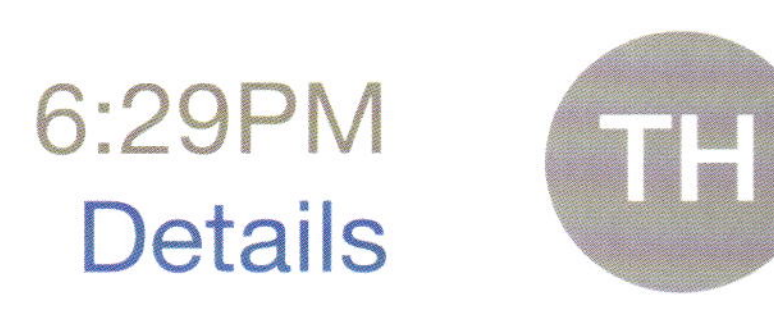

Ashley Longshore is a multi-talented enigma. She is not only an amazing artist but a true entrepreneur with a wicked sense of humor! A pop-culture mover-and-shaker with a bold and brave vision, making history every day! I'm so glad my wife Dee introduced us because I kept hearing about the genius things she was doing, but couldn't really comprehend any of it until I had the amazing opportunity to meet her and see the whole show with my own eyes!

Sent from my iPhone

See More from Ashley Longshore

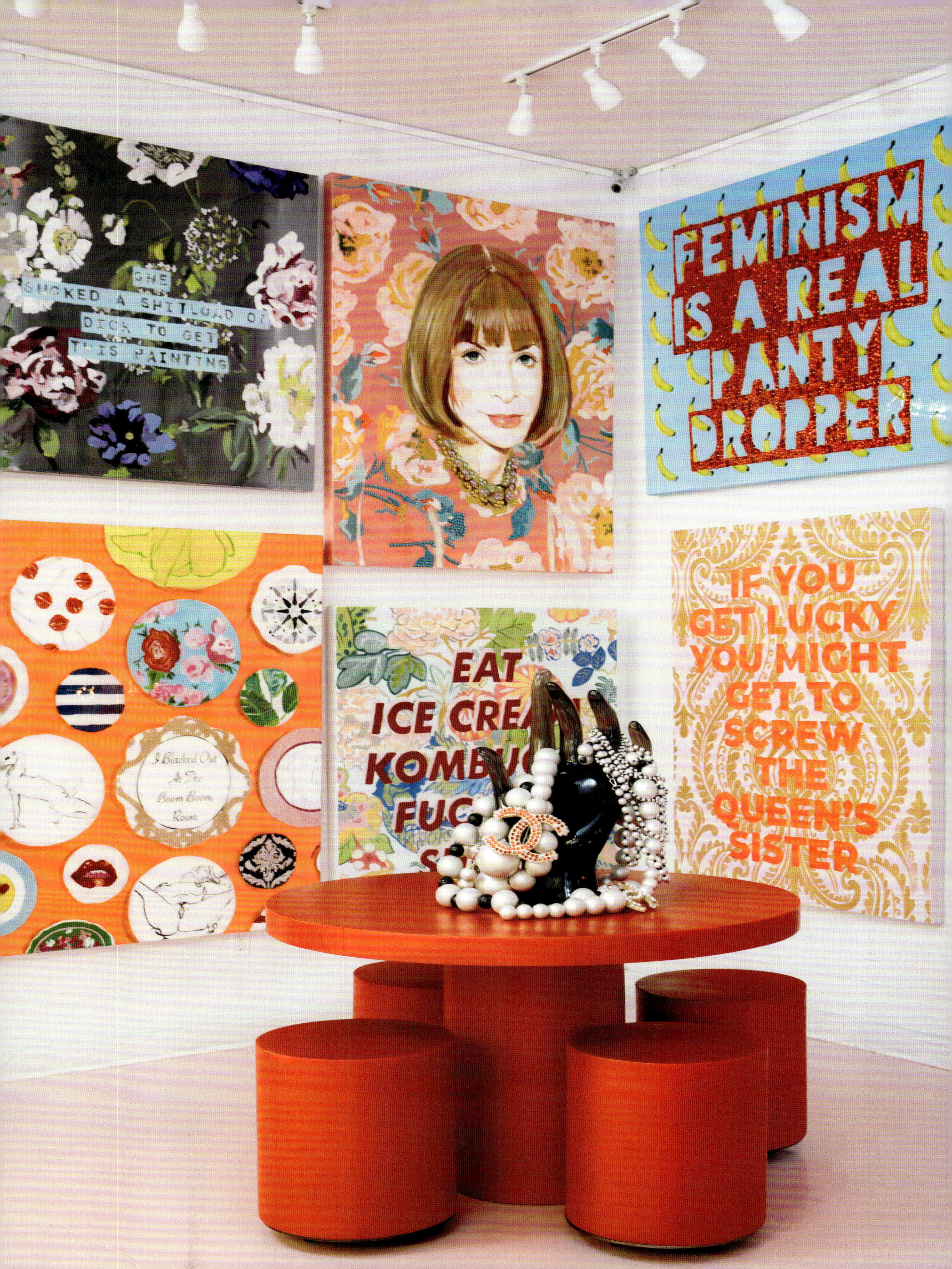
SHE
SUCKED A SHITLOAD OF
DICK TO GET
THIS PAINTING
FEMINISM
IS A REAL
PANTY
DROPPER
I Blacked Out
At The
Boom Boom
Room
EAT
ICE CREA
KOMB
FUC
IF YOU
GET LUCKY
YOU MIGHT
GET TO
SCREW
THE
QUEEN'S
SISTER

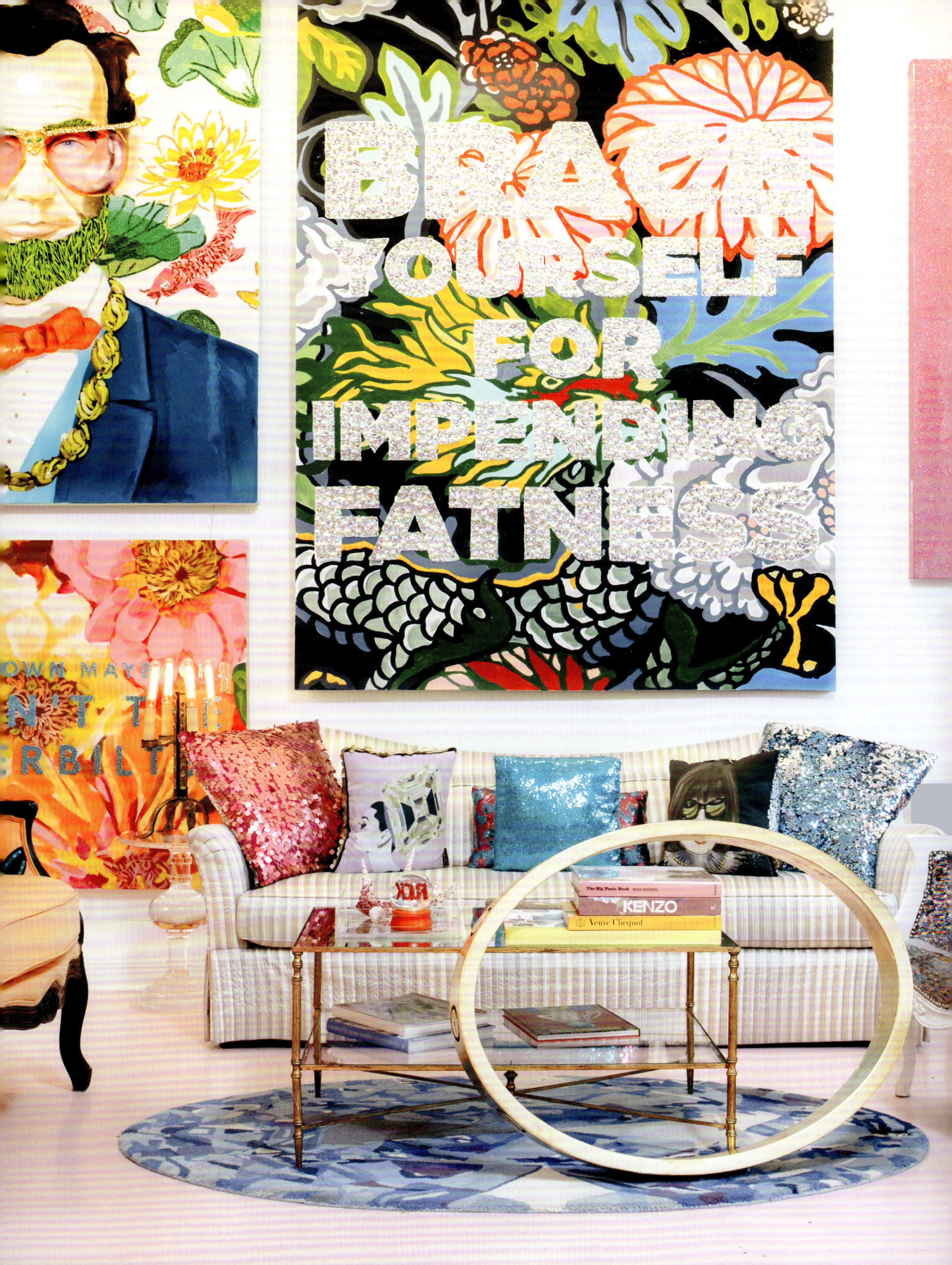
BRACE
YOURSELF
FOR
IMPENDING
FATNESS
KENZO
Veuve Clicquot

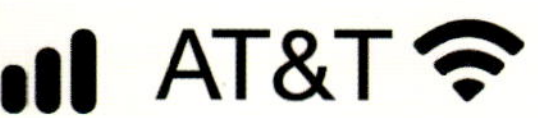
AT&T
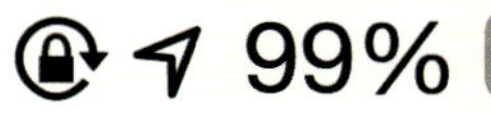
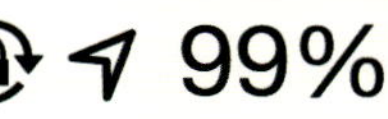

10:04 PM

99%

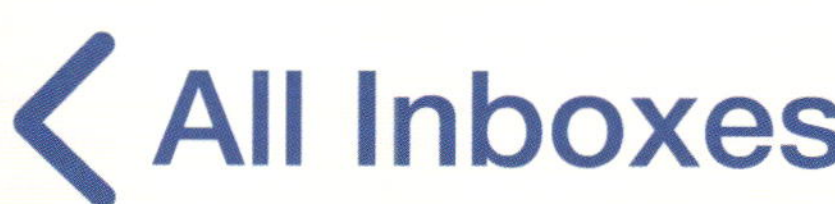

All Inboxes

3 Messages

My Rizzoli Book

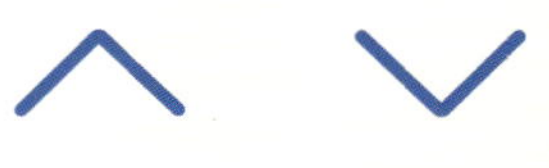

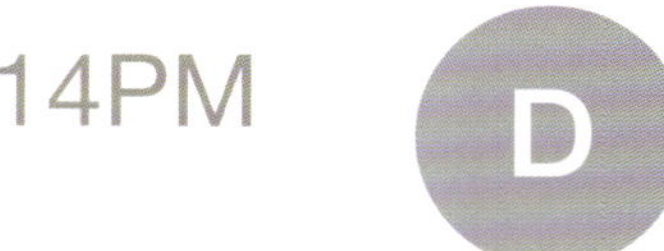

Diane von Furstenberg 9:14PM

To: Ashley Longshore

D

Ashley Longshore came into the world of art and fashion as a tornado and her impact has only started! Ashley is sensitive to the characters of the people she paints; it's not just about colors, it's about emotions! She is a contemporary painter who has captured the zeitgeist of the moment.

Sent from my iPhone

See More from Ashley Longshore

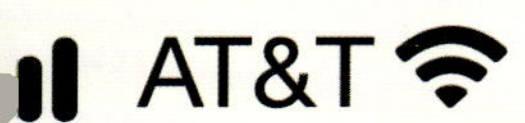
8:24 PM
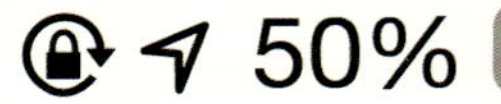

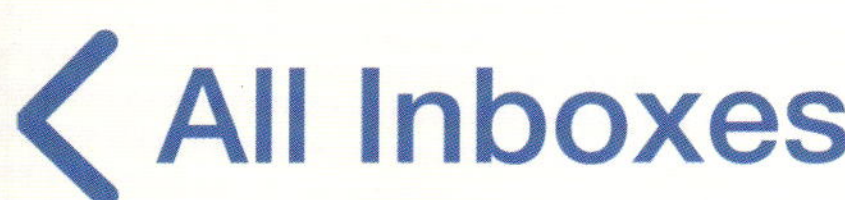

6 Messages

Latest Date

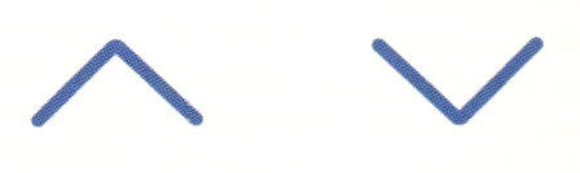

Linda Fargo

To: Ashley Longshore

7:11PM

Details

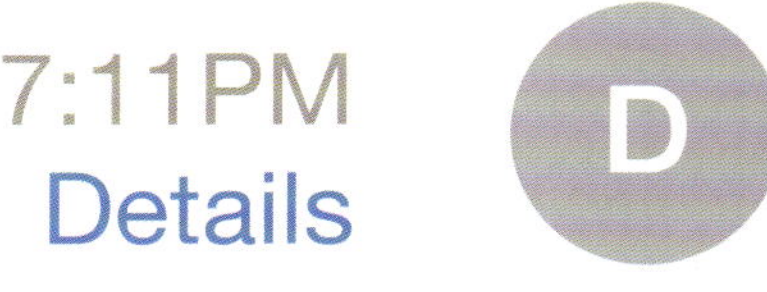

I'll give you ten reasons why Ashley Longshore is on my shortlist of "Most Admired People":

1. Because SHE'S FREE!
2. She gives herself permission!
3. She is her own creation and she doesn't apologize!
4. She has something to say, and she doesn't hold back!
5. Because sometimes she scares me!
6. Because she knows how to live, and that work can be play!
7. Because there's no one like her!
8. Because she's outrageous and kind and sincere and responsible and smart all at the same time!
9. Because she inspires me to fight imprisoning conventions!
10. Because she's a damn good artist!

Sent from my iPhone

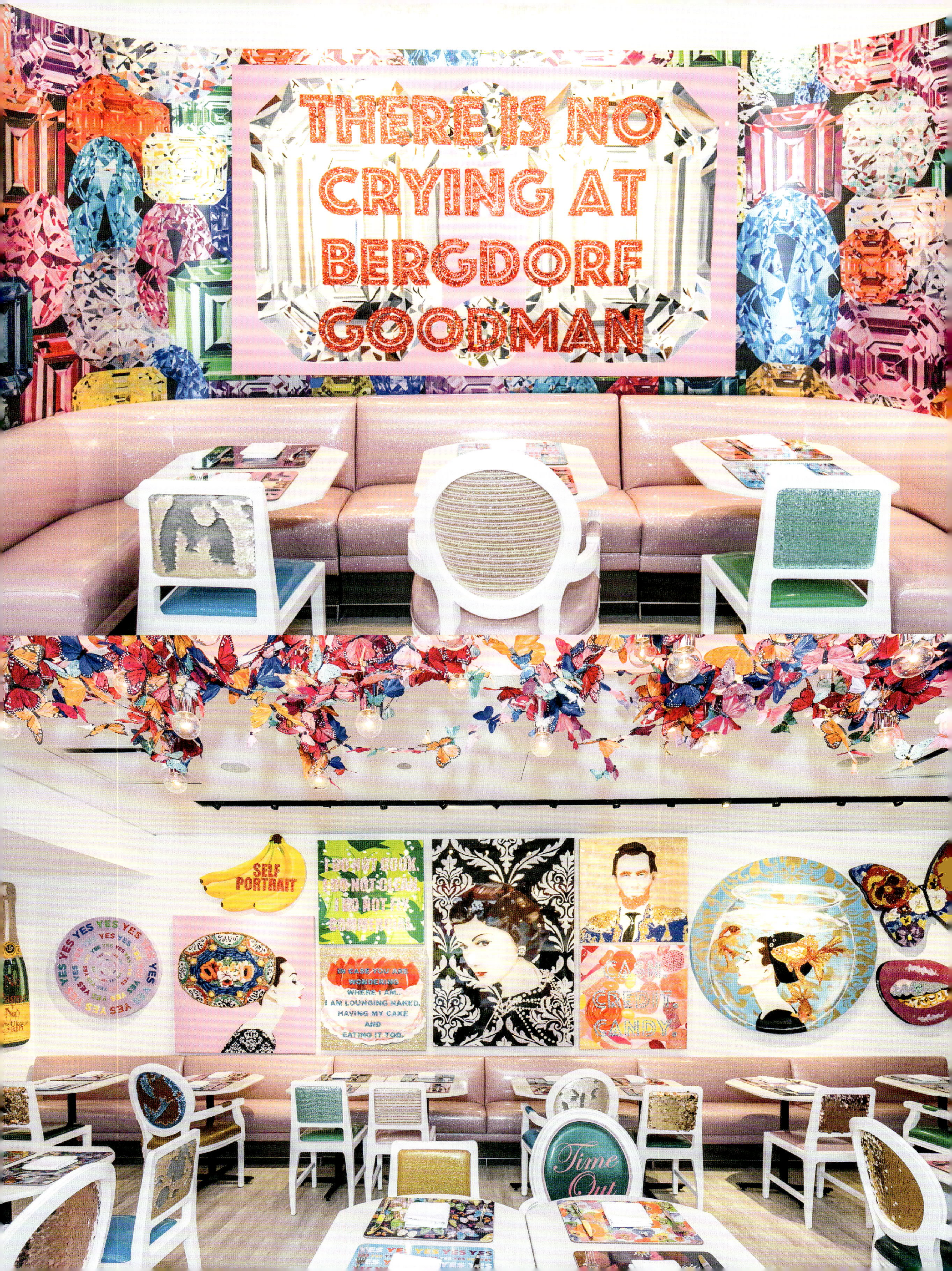
THERE IS NO CRYING AT BERGDORF GOODMAN
SELF PORTRAIT
IN CASE YOU ARE WONDERING WHERE I AM.. I AM LOUNGING NAKED, HAVING MY CAKE AND EATING IT TOO.
Time Out

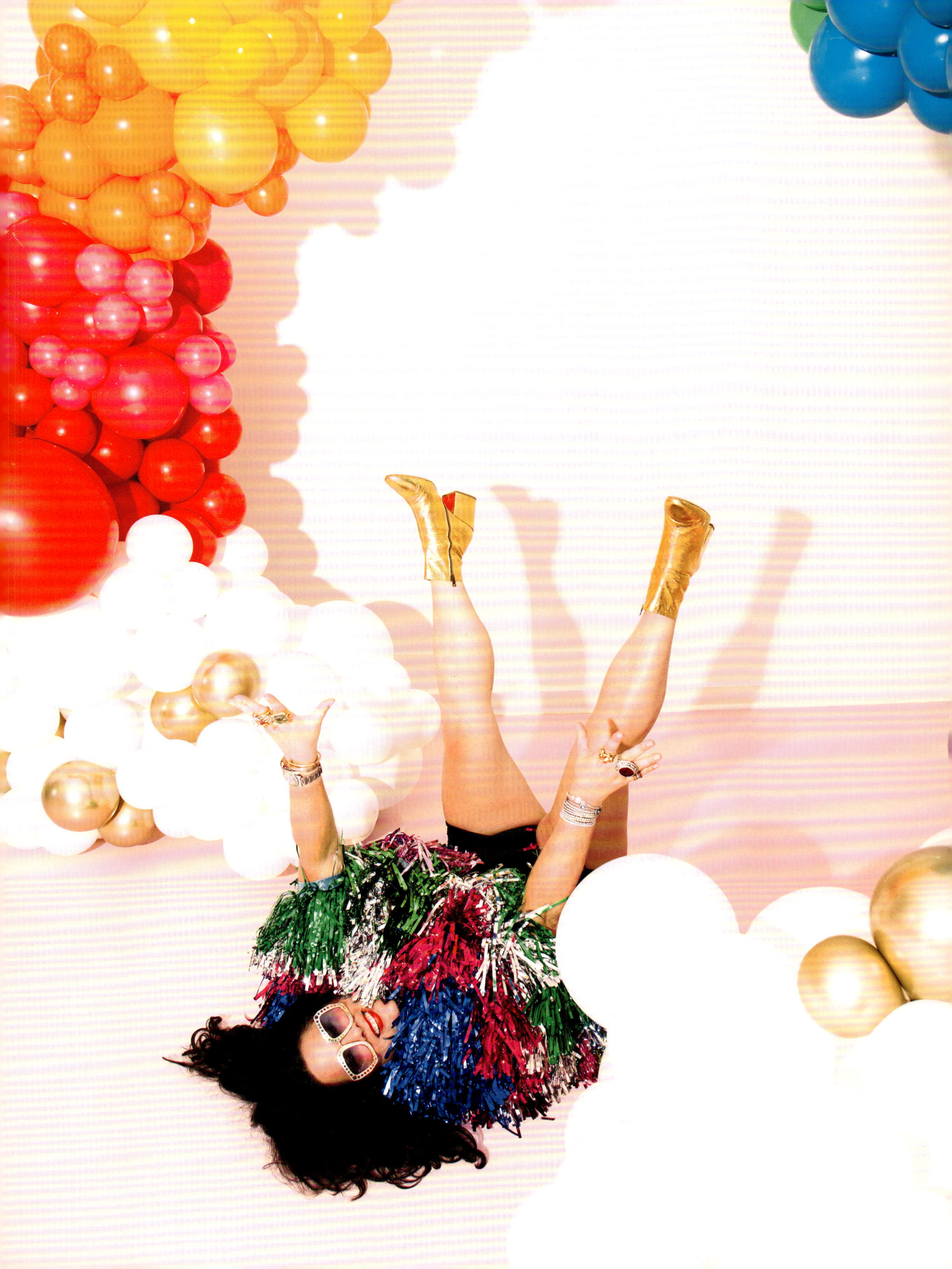

BOTTLE FED

When you finish a
bottle of bubbles...
Tip it over and
pour it....
until it drips...
then look at
everyone and
Hollar....
MAKE IT CRY.

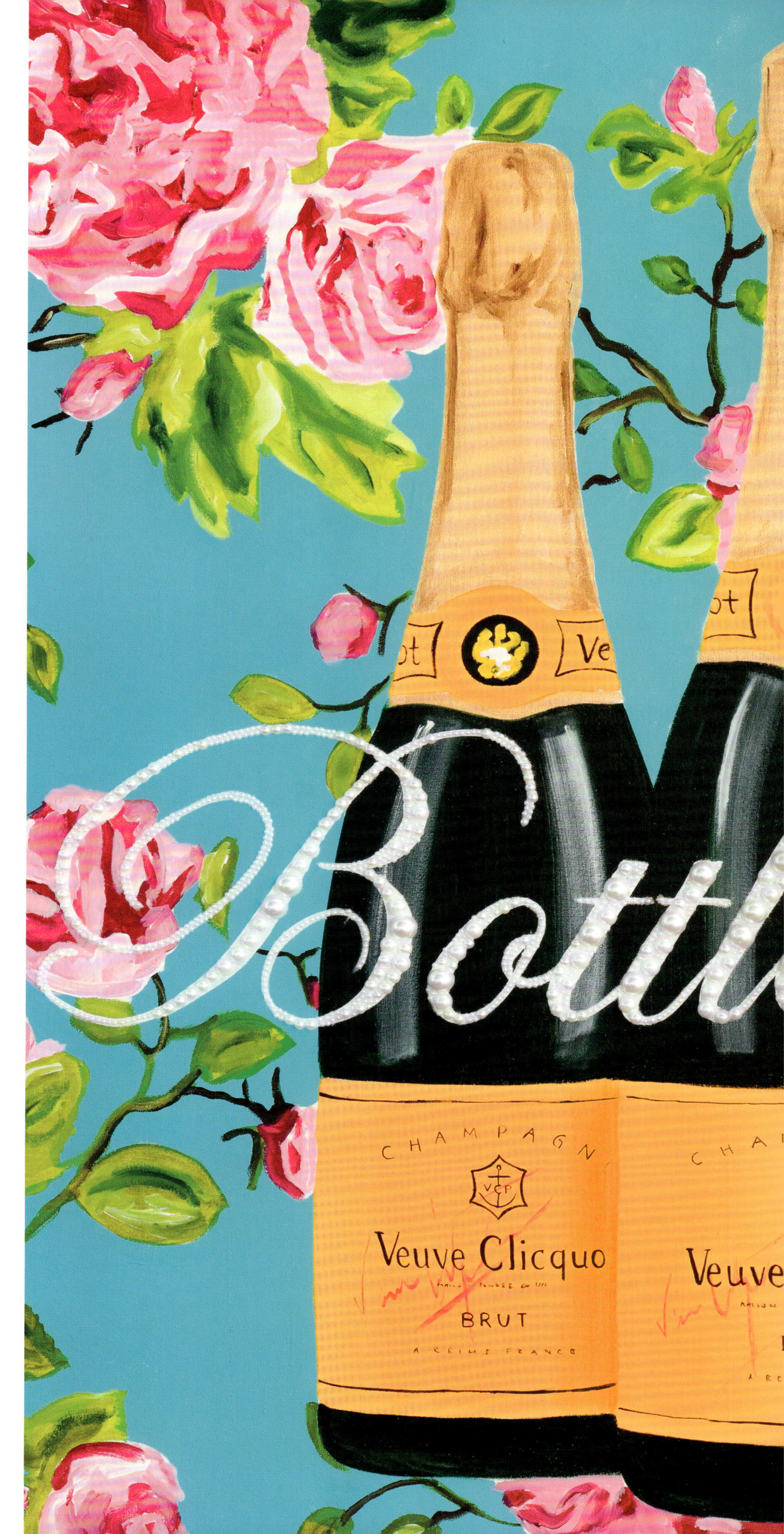
Bottl
Ve
CHAMPAGN
Veuve Clicquo
BRUT
A REIMS FRANCE
CHAM
Veuve

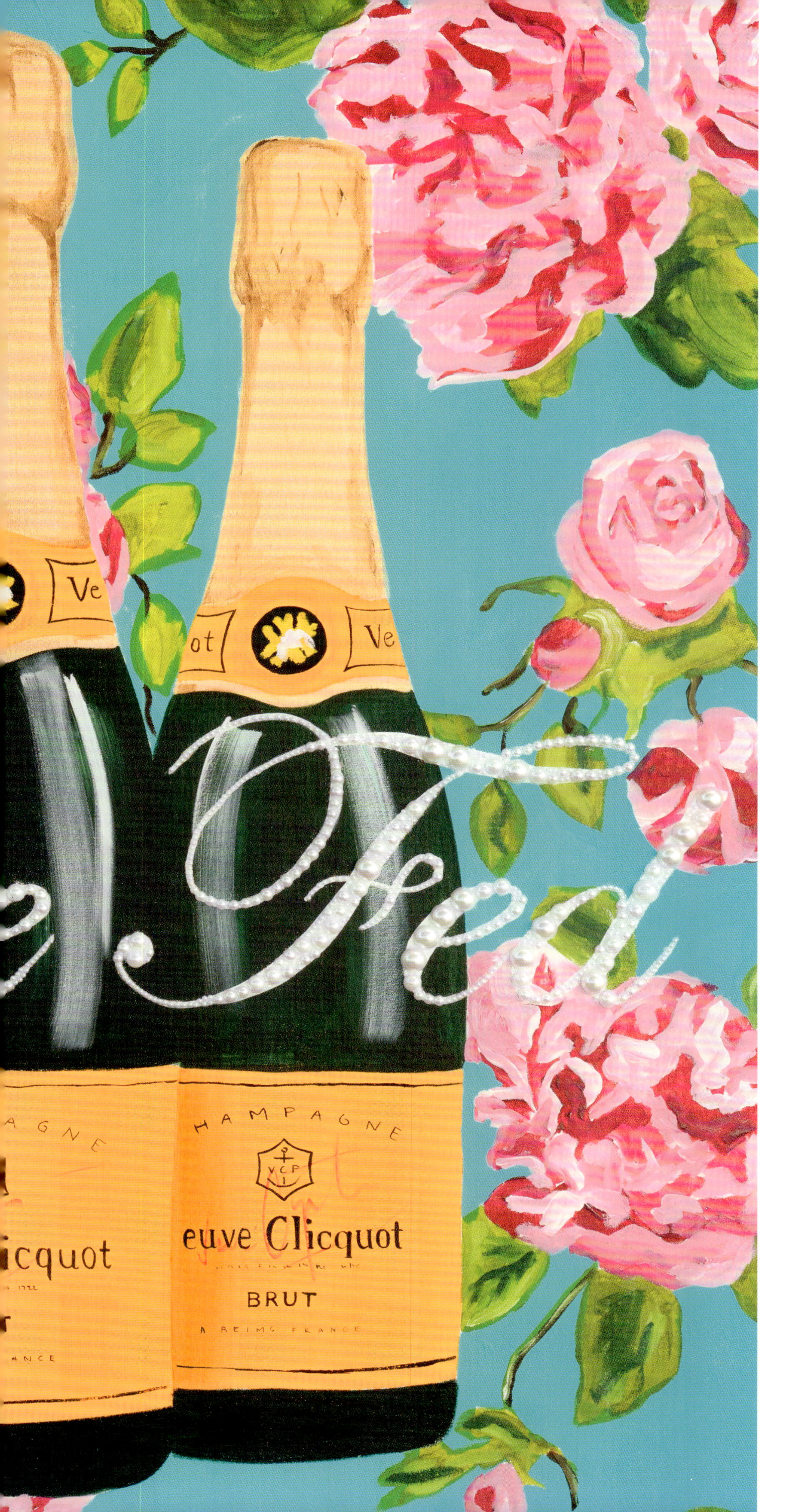

HAMPAGNE
euve Clicquot
BRUT
icquot

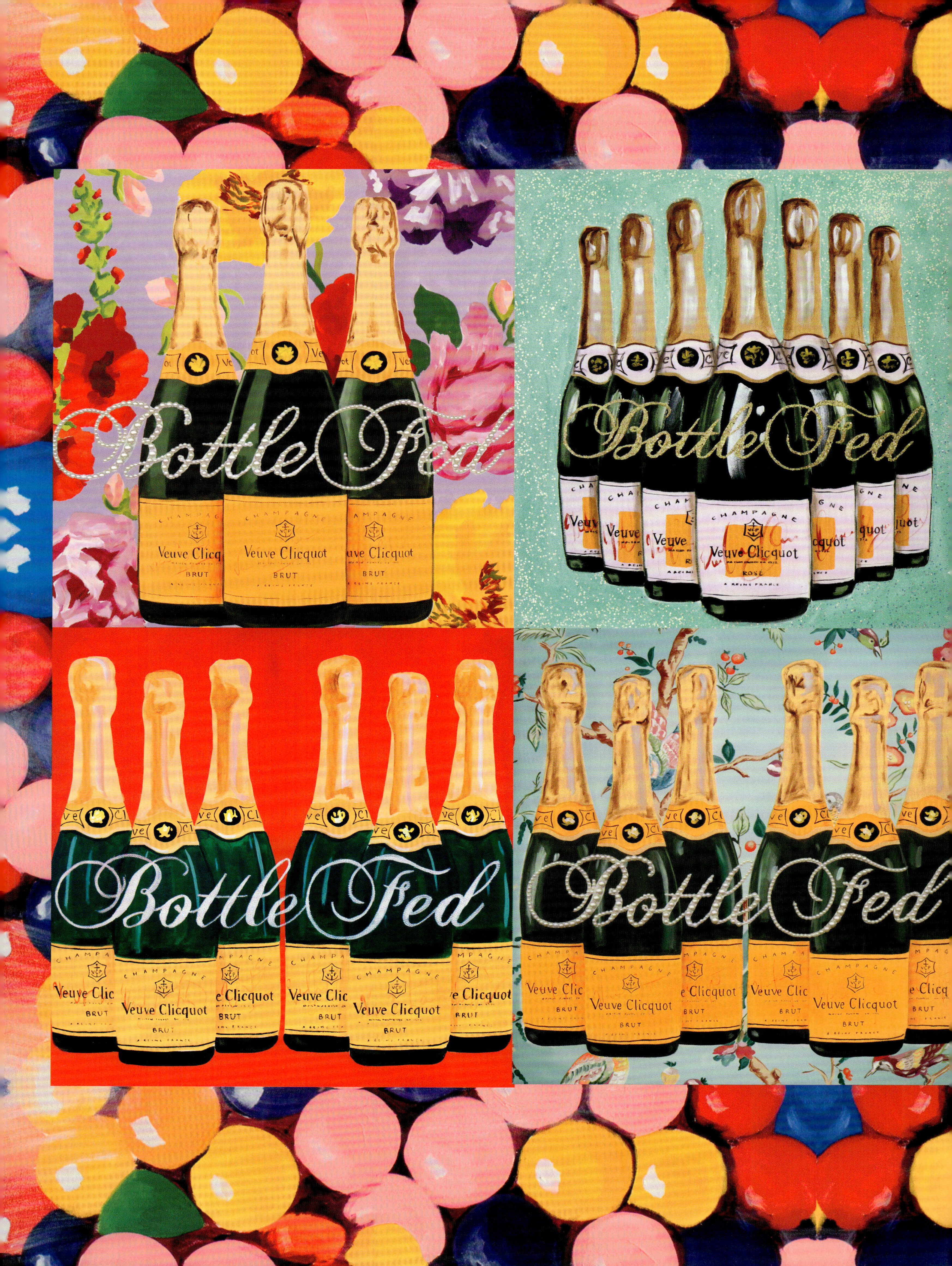
Bottle Fed
CHAMPAGNE
Veuve Clicquot
BRUT
Bottle Fed
CHAMPAGNE
Veuve Clicquot
ROSÉ
Bottle Fed
CHAMPAGNE
Veuve Clicquot
BRUT
Bottle Fed
CHAMPAGNE
Veuve Clicquot
BRUT

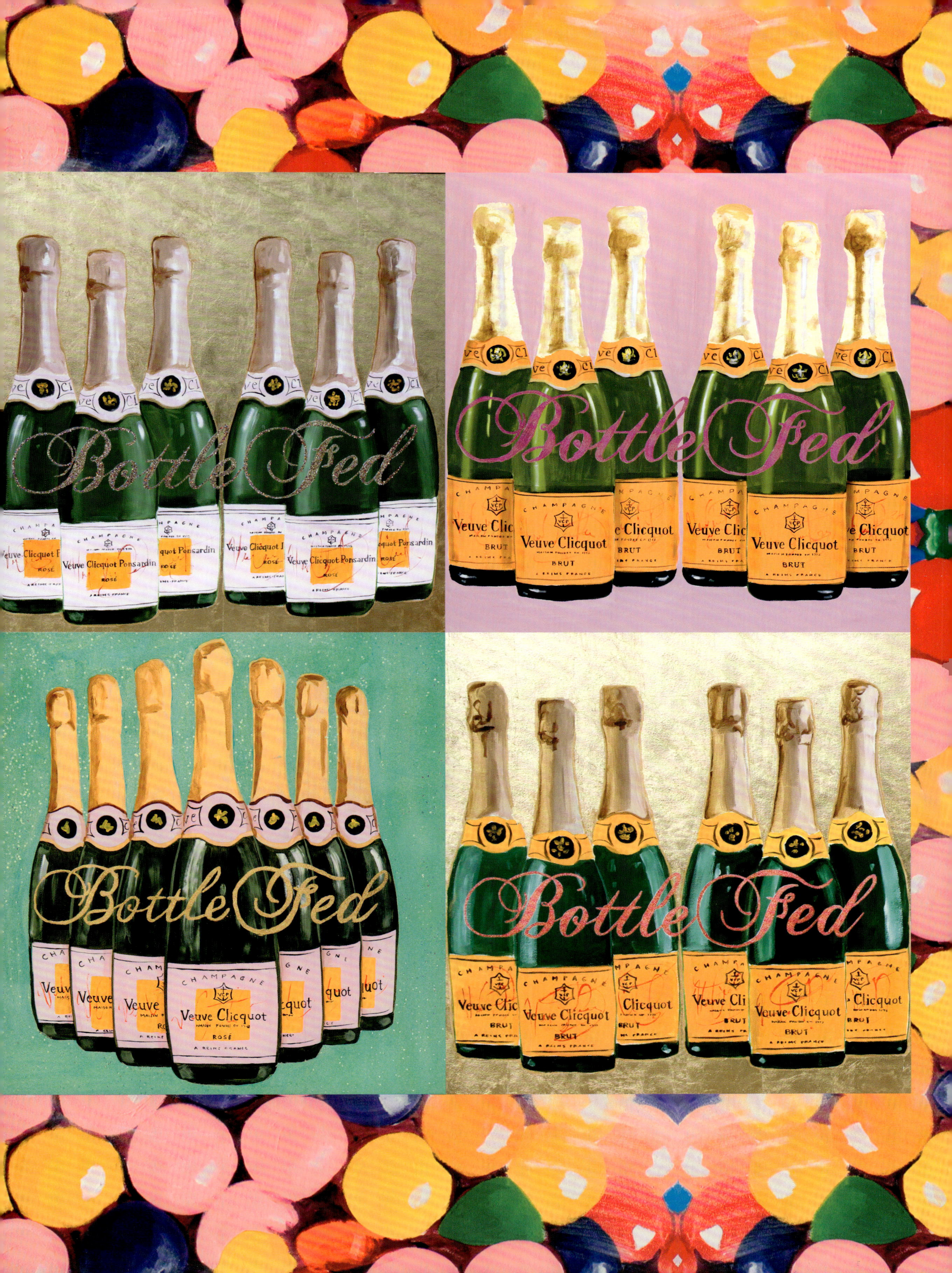
Bottle Fed
Veuve Clicquot Ponsardin
ROSÉ
Bottle Fed
CHAMPAGNE
Veuve Clicquot
BRUT
Bottle Fed
CHAMPAGNE
Veuve Clicquot
ROSÉ
Bottle Fed
Veuve Clicquot
BRUT

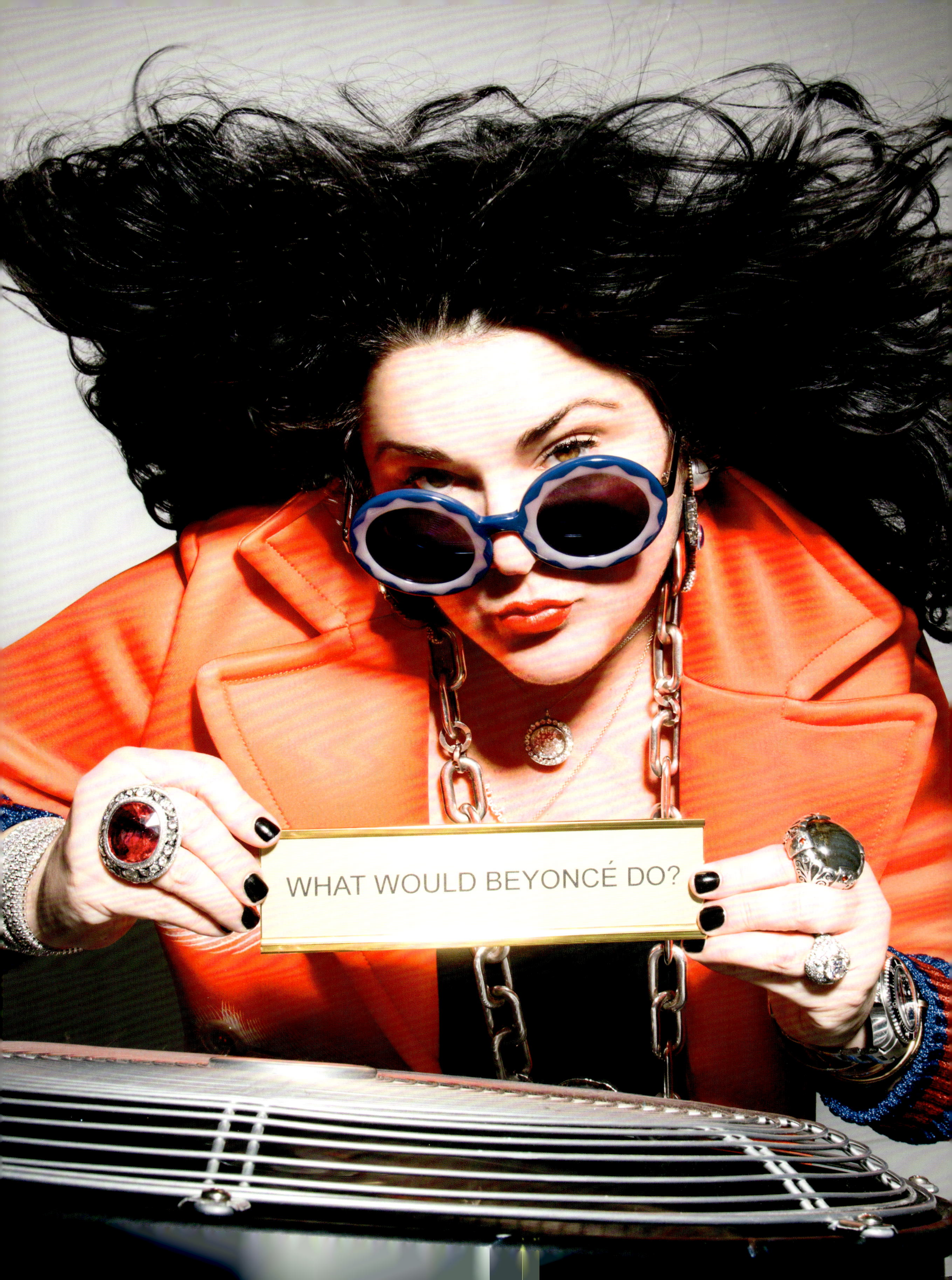
WHAT WOULD BEYONCÉ DO?

FASHION ICONS

Judging you...

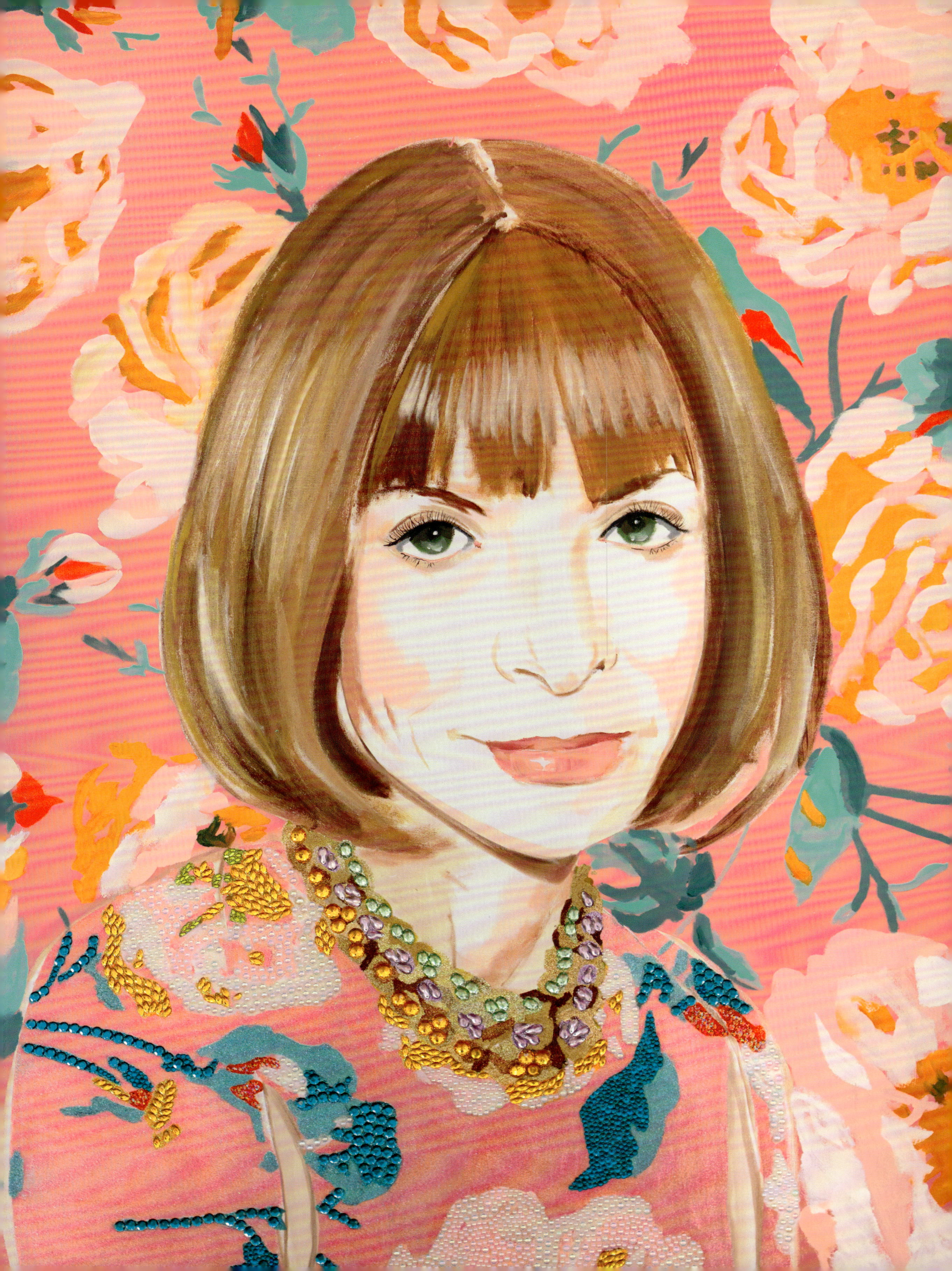

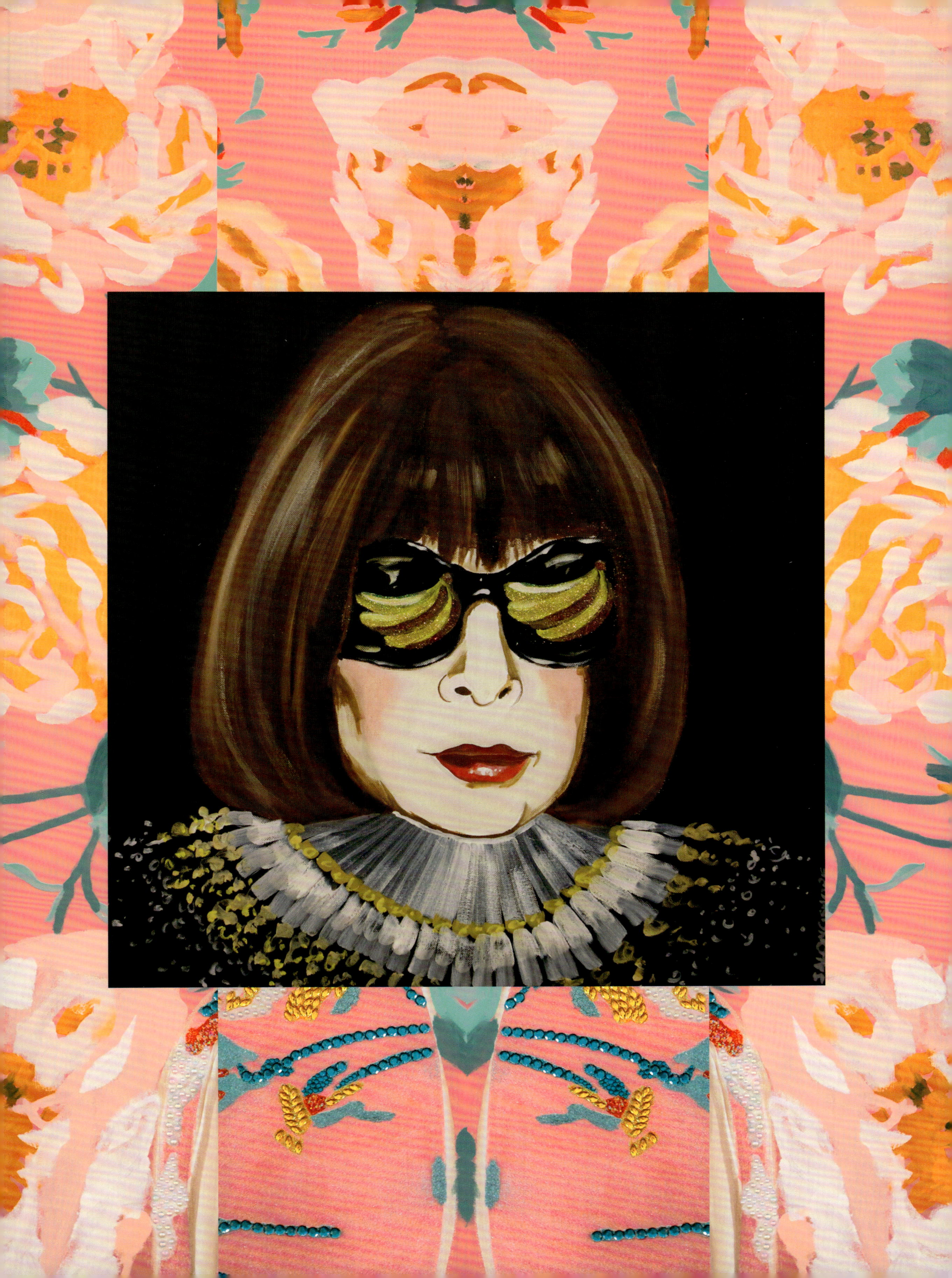

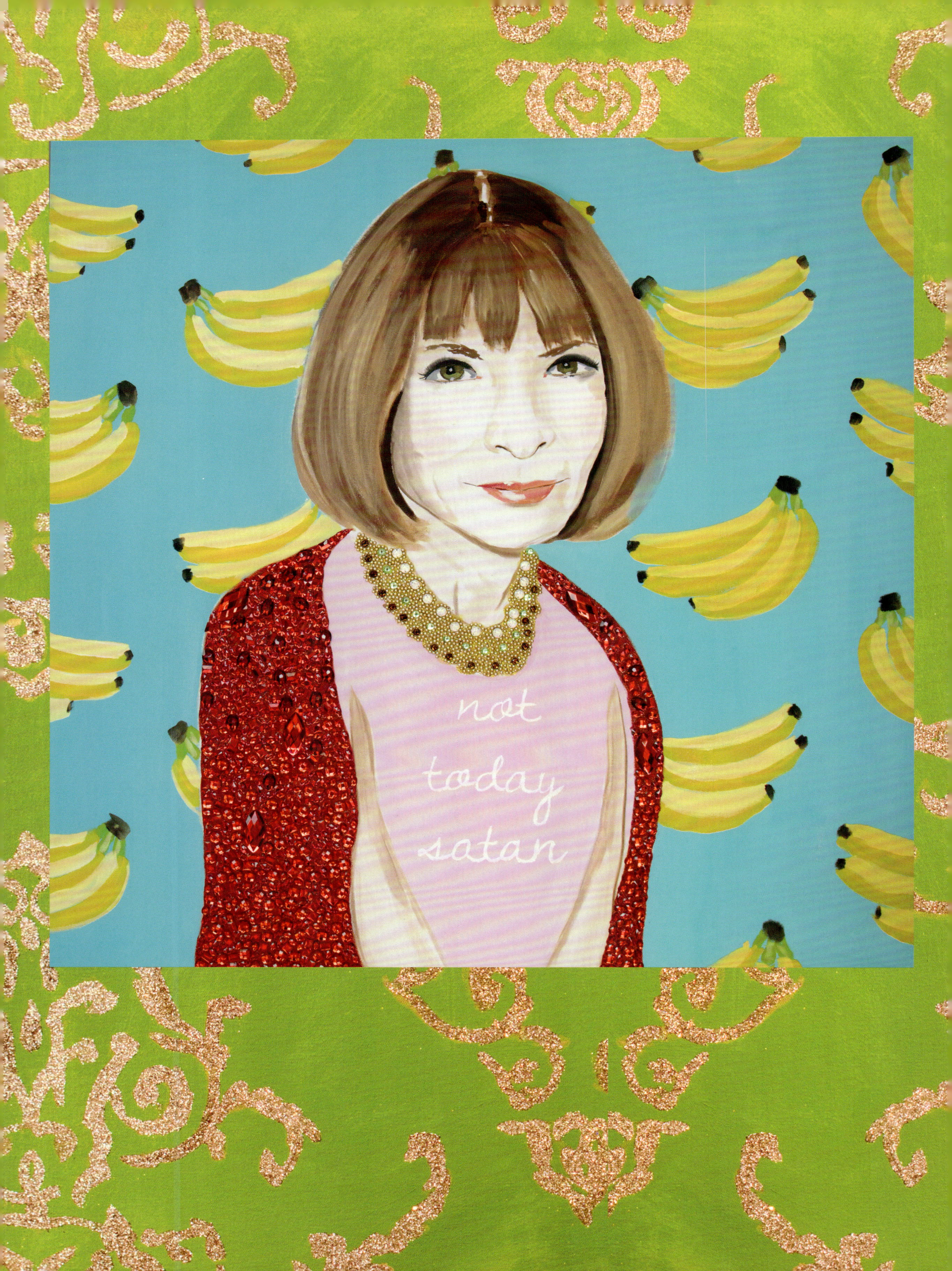
not
today
satan

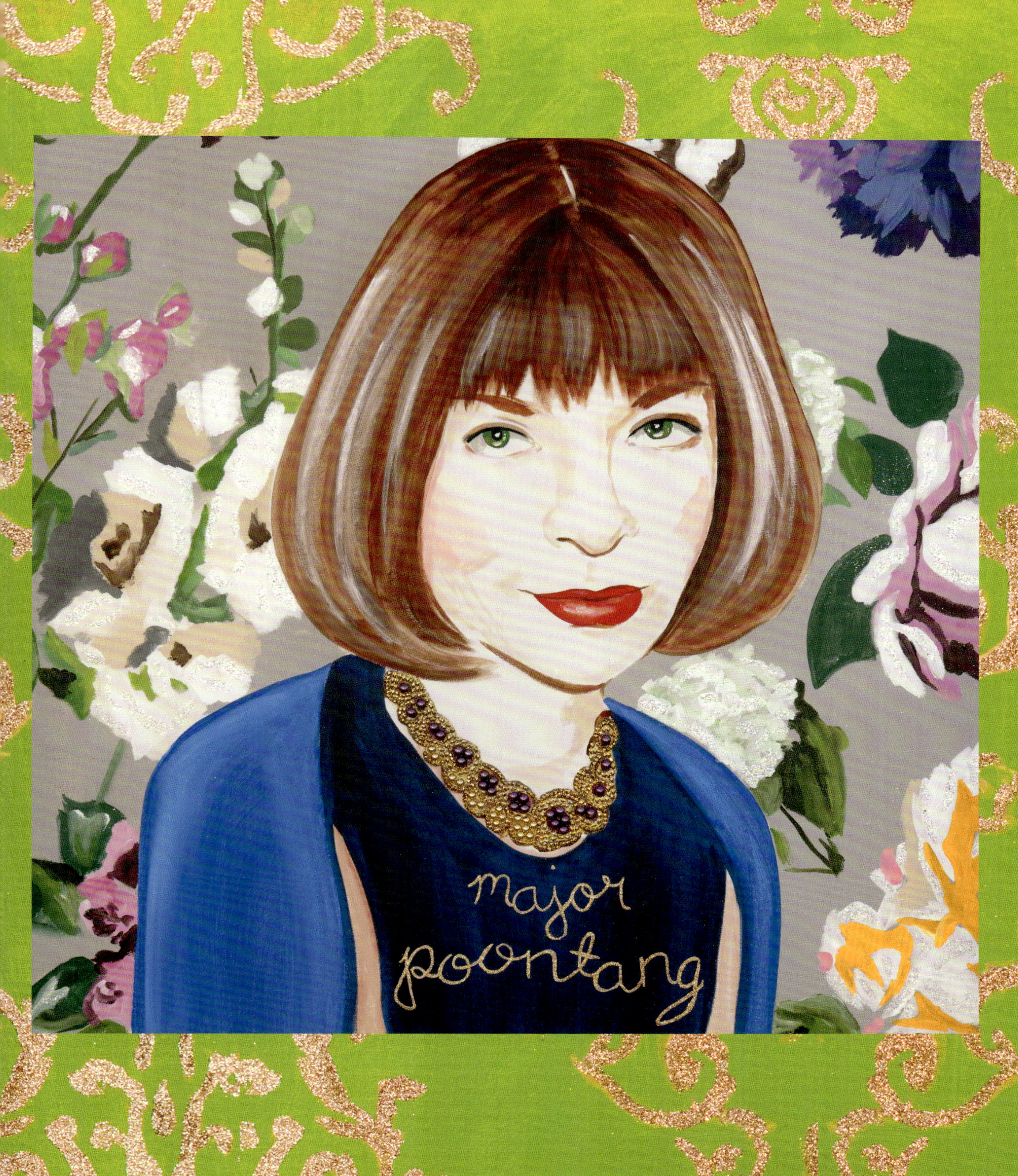
major
poontang

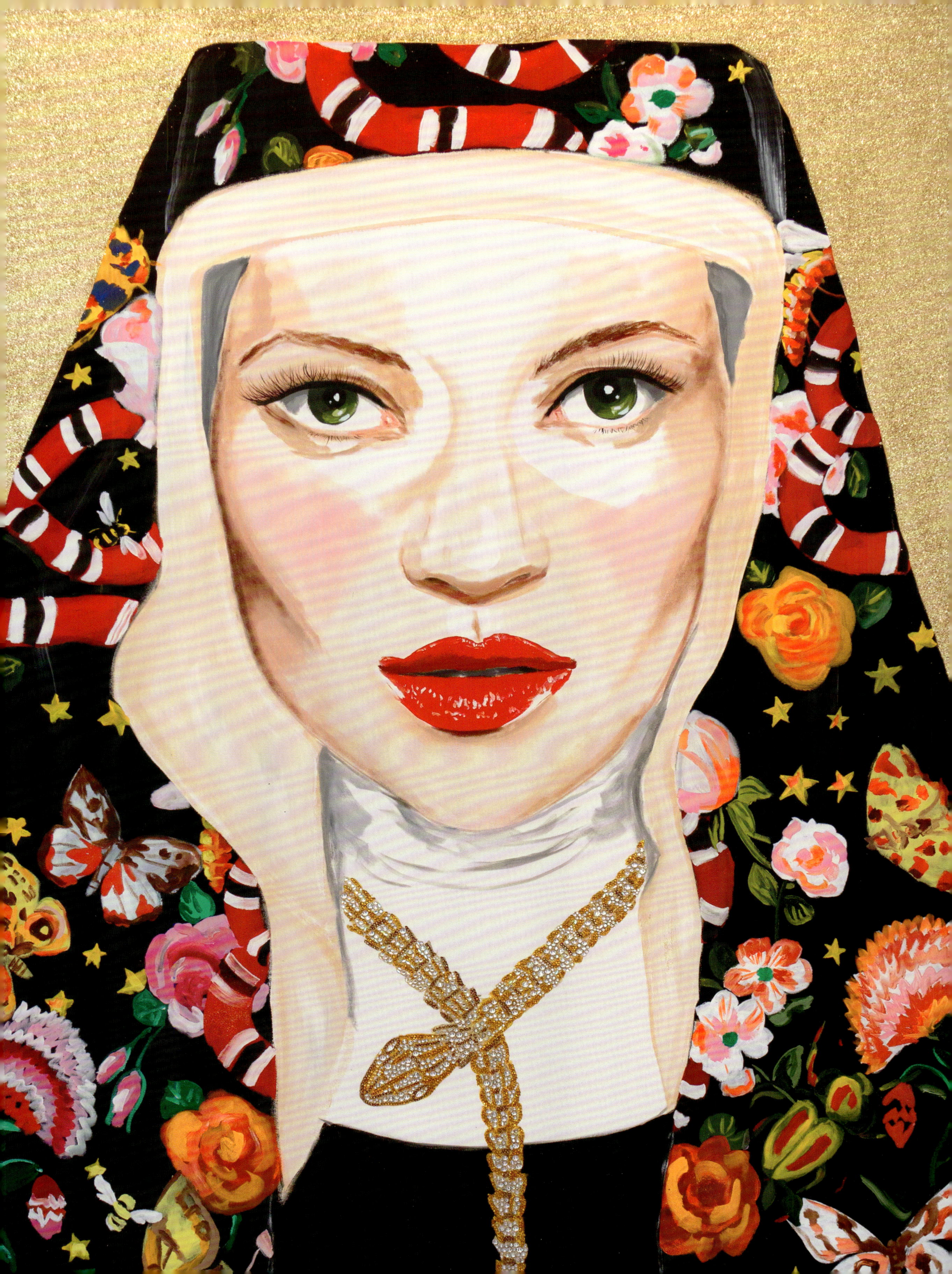

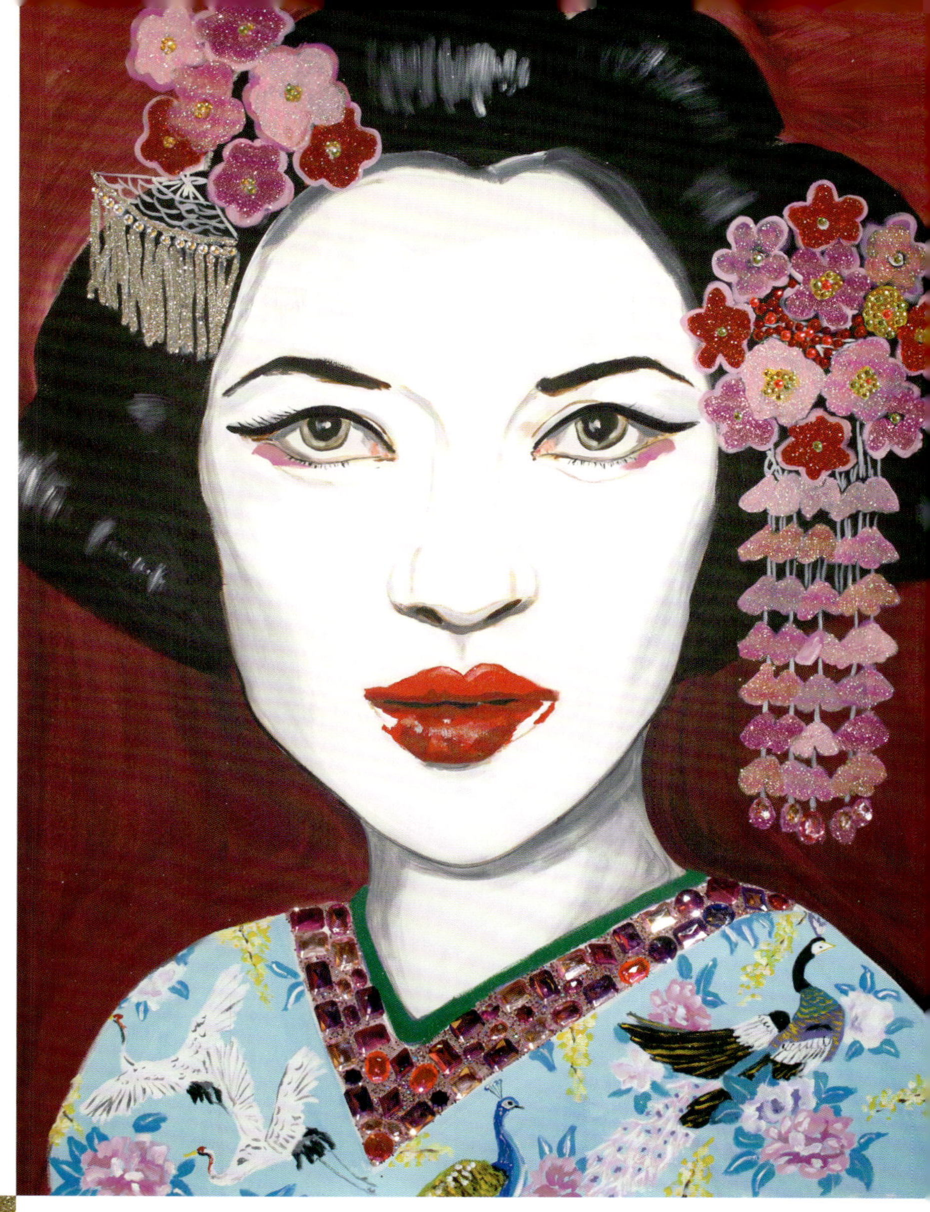

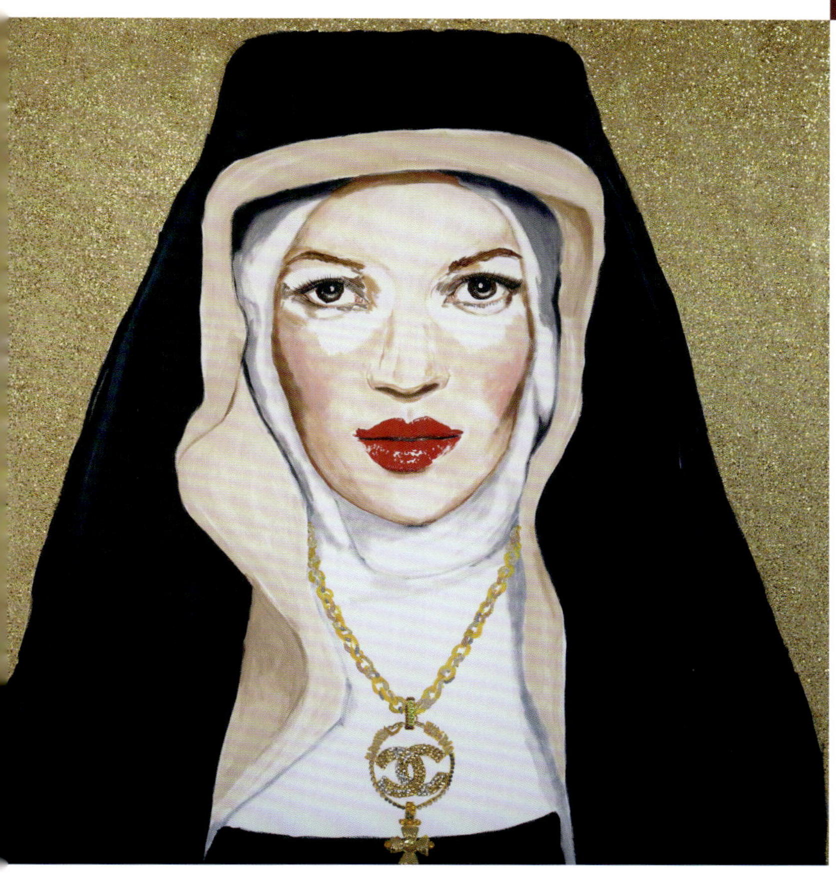

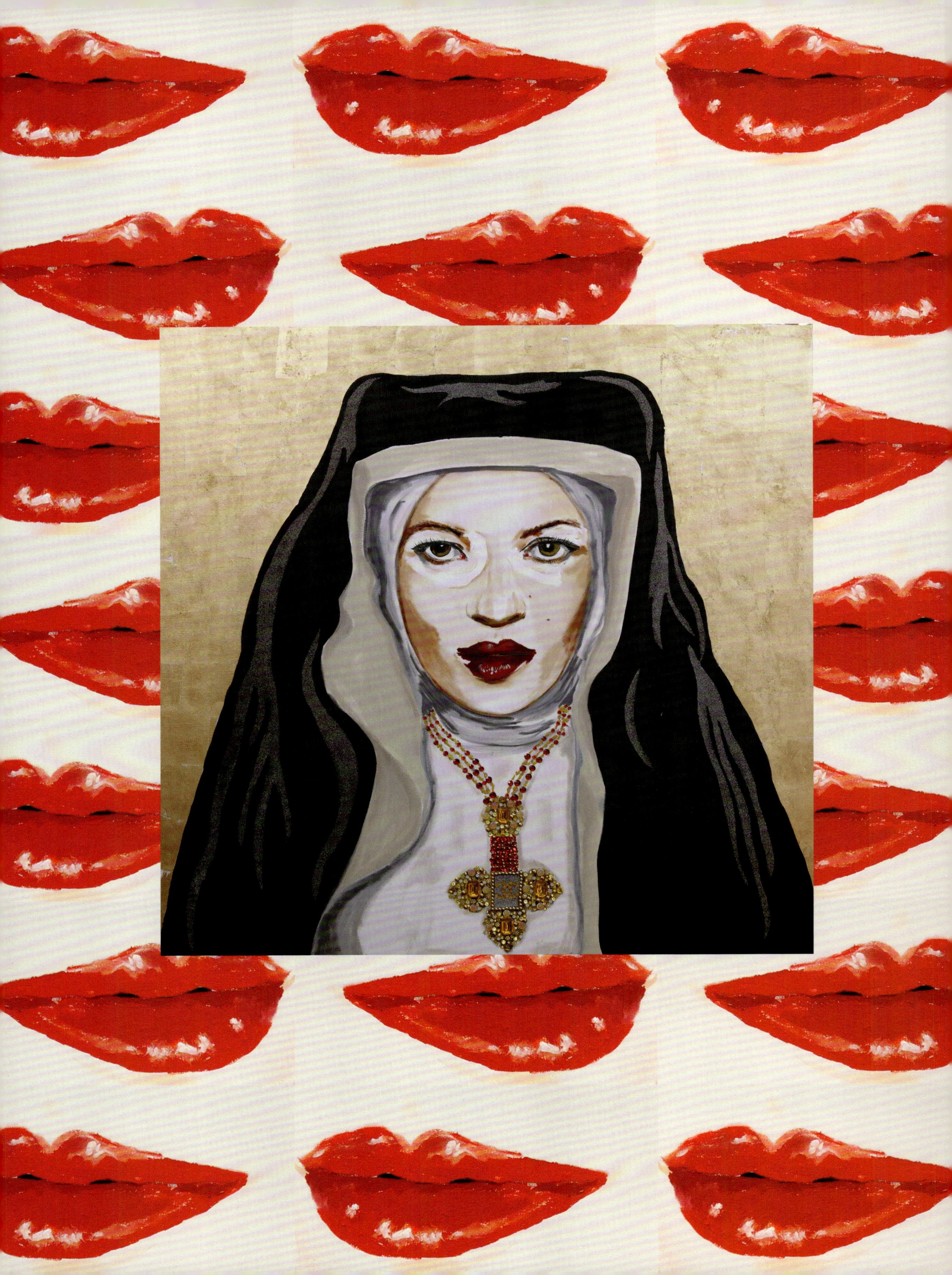

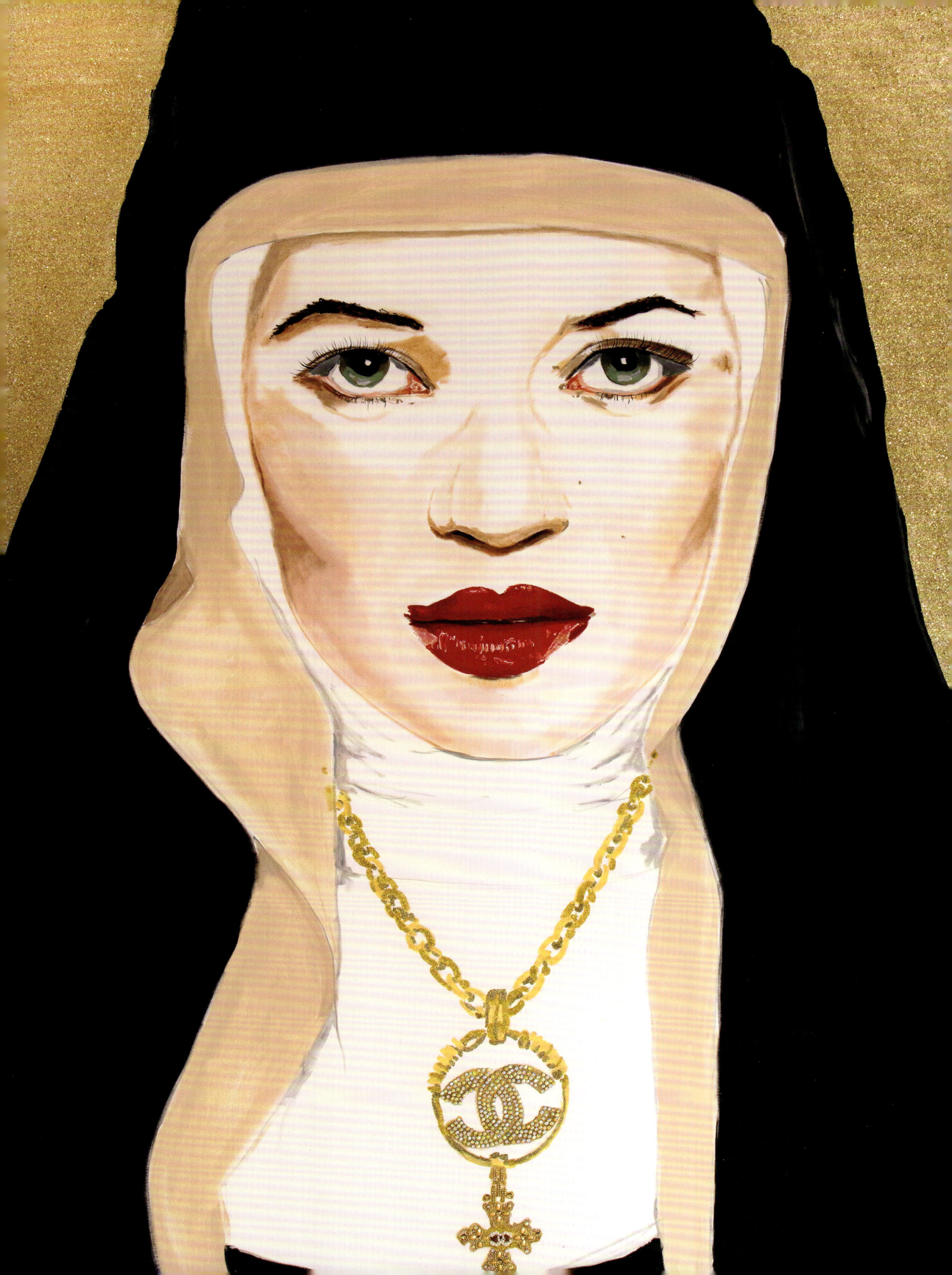

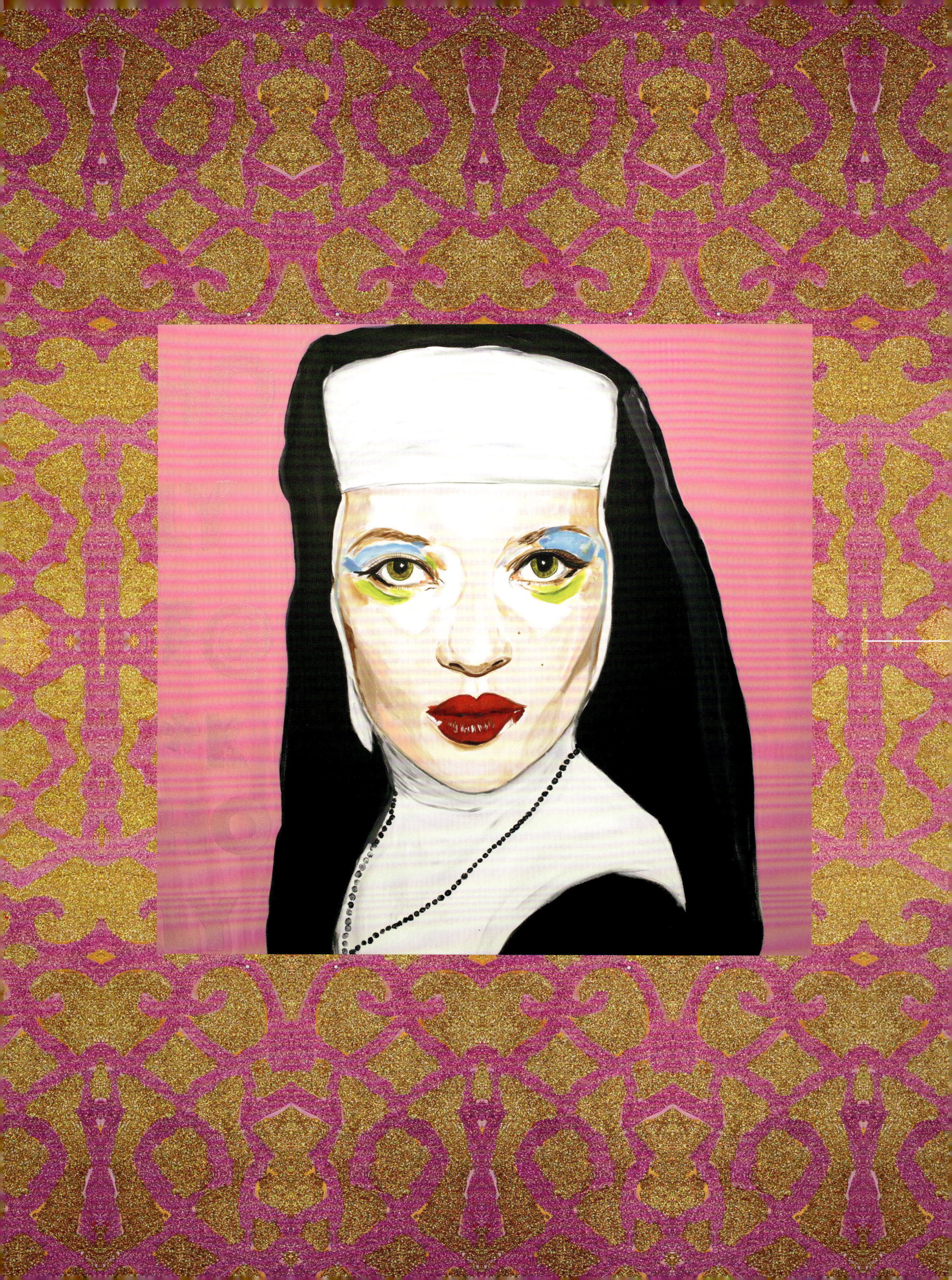

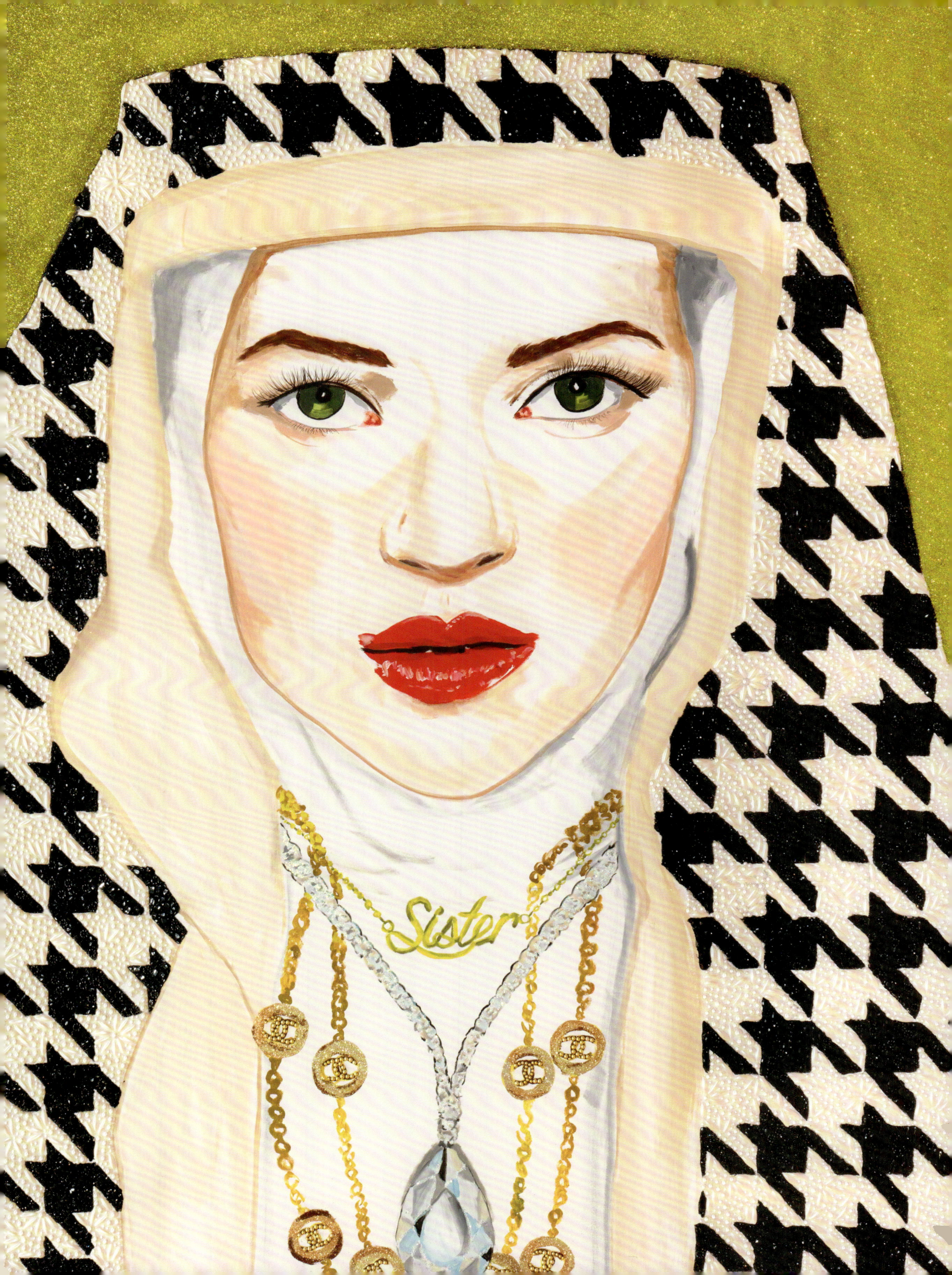
Sister

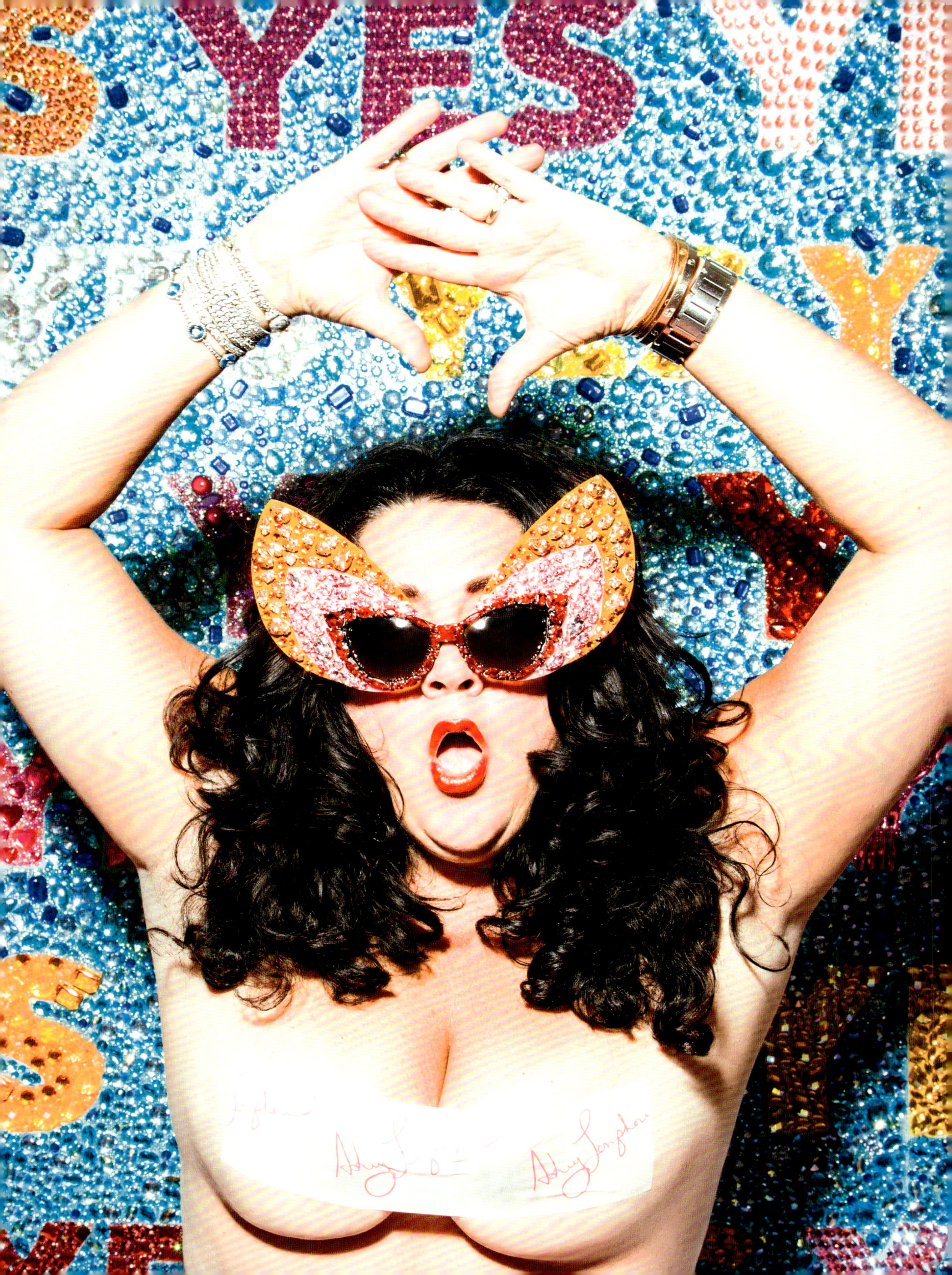
YES

LABELED

I am a Self proclaimed Label Whore... But I make my own money so I ain't sorry. I've never sucked a dick For Fashion....

God's Honest...

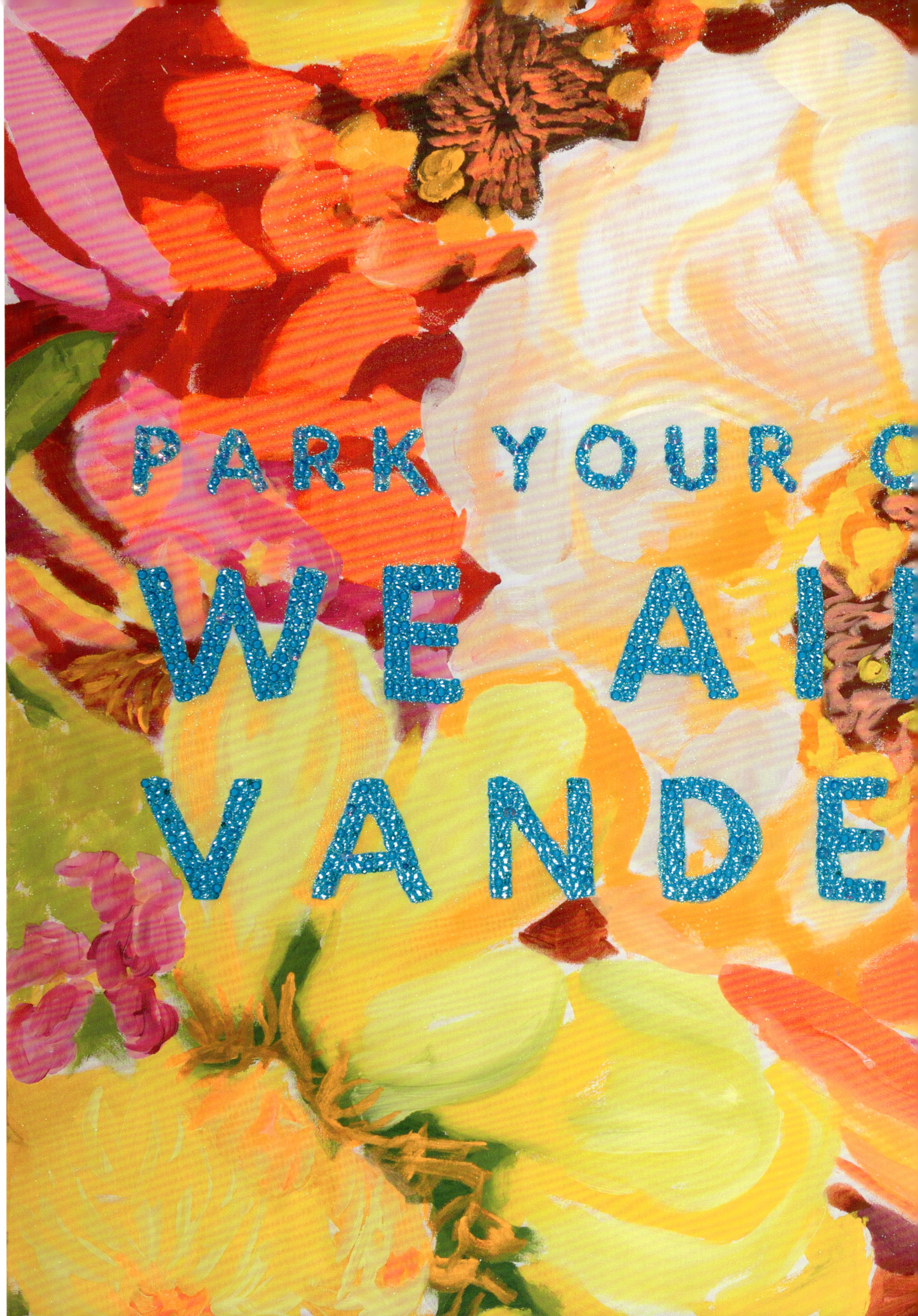
PARK YOUR
WE A
VANDE

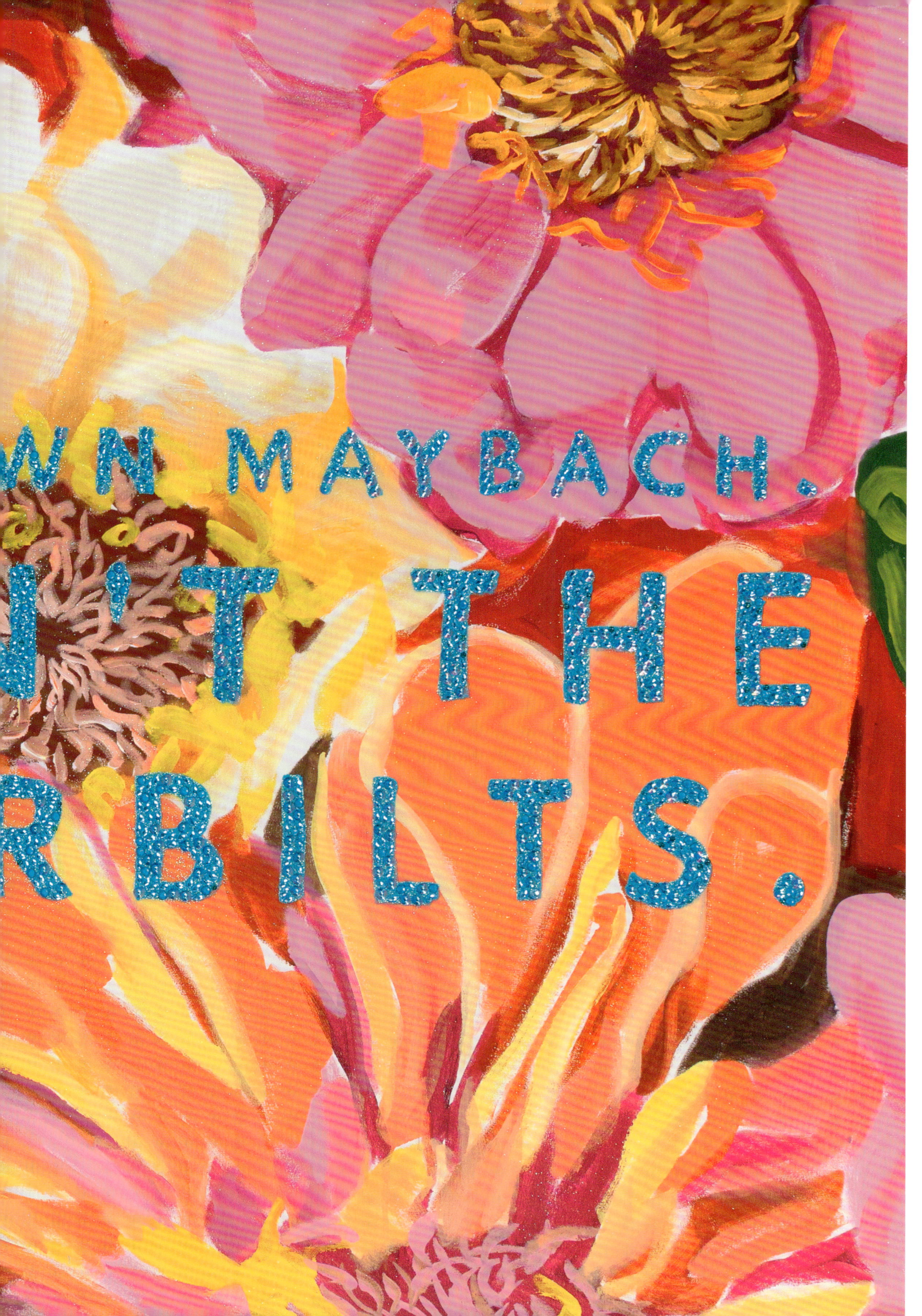
WN MAYBACH.
'T THE
R'BILTS.

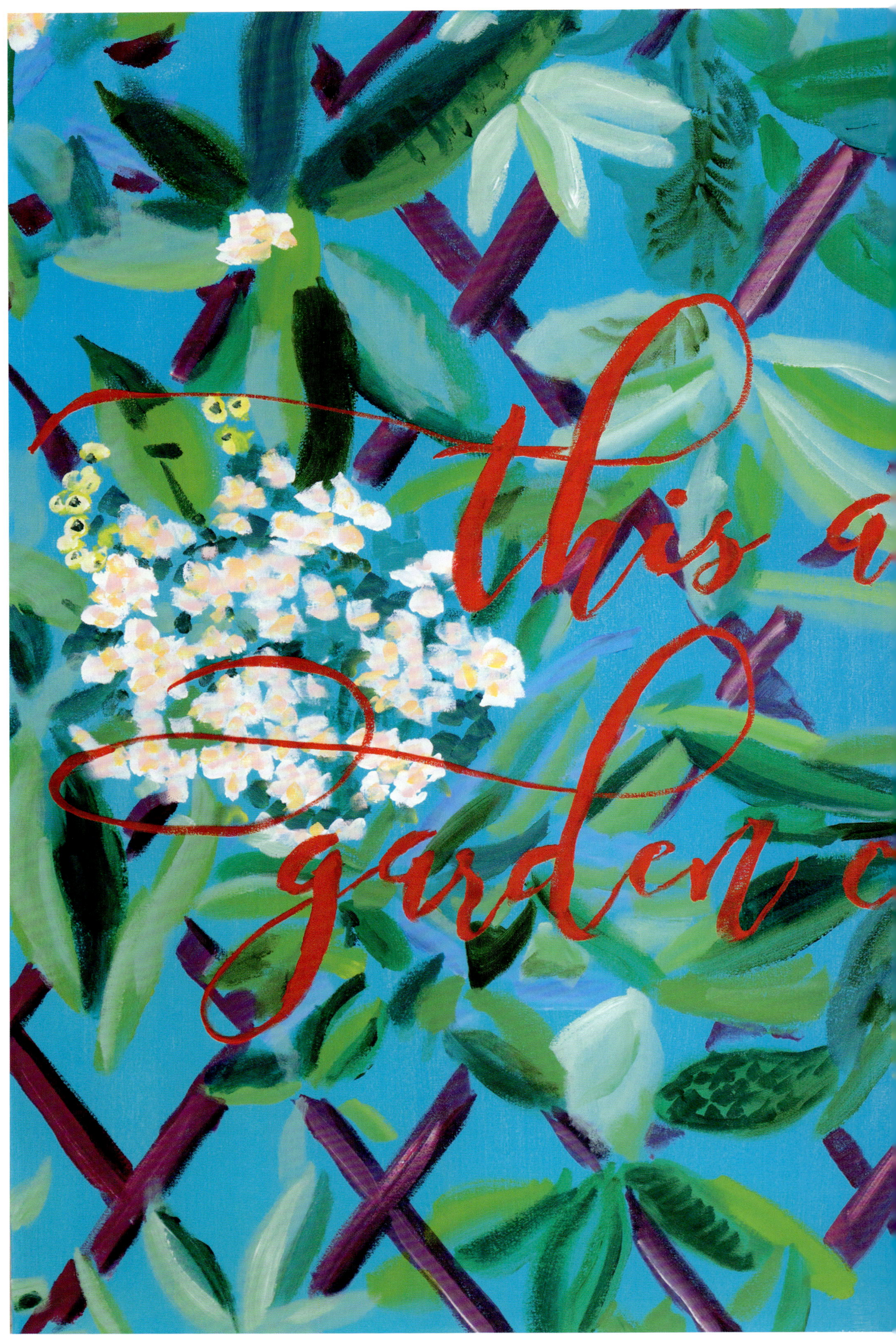
this a
garden o

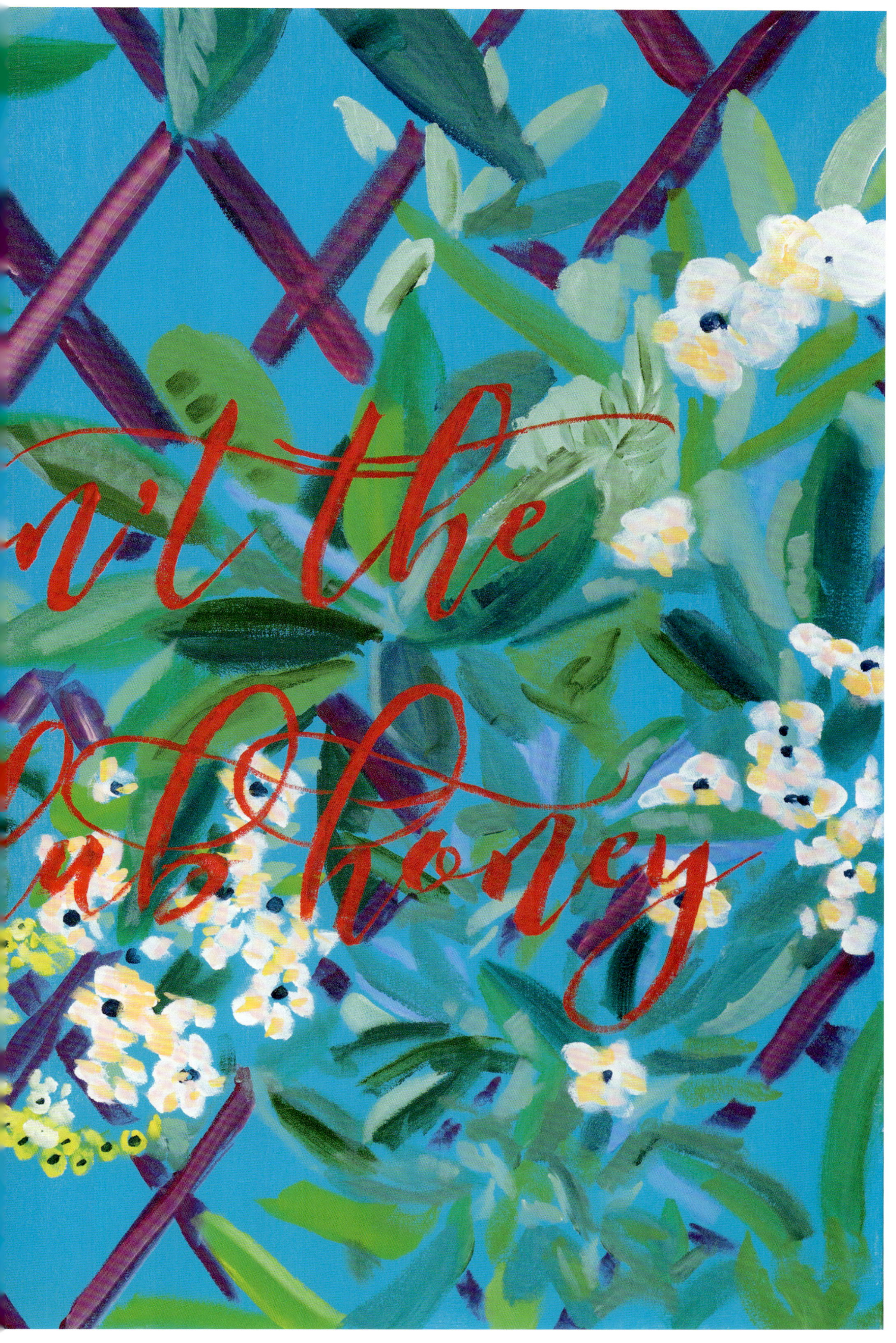
n't the
ub honey

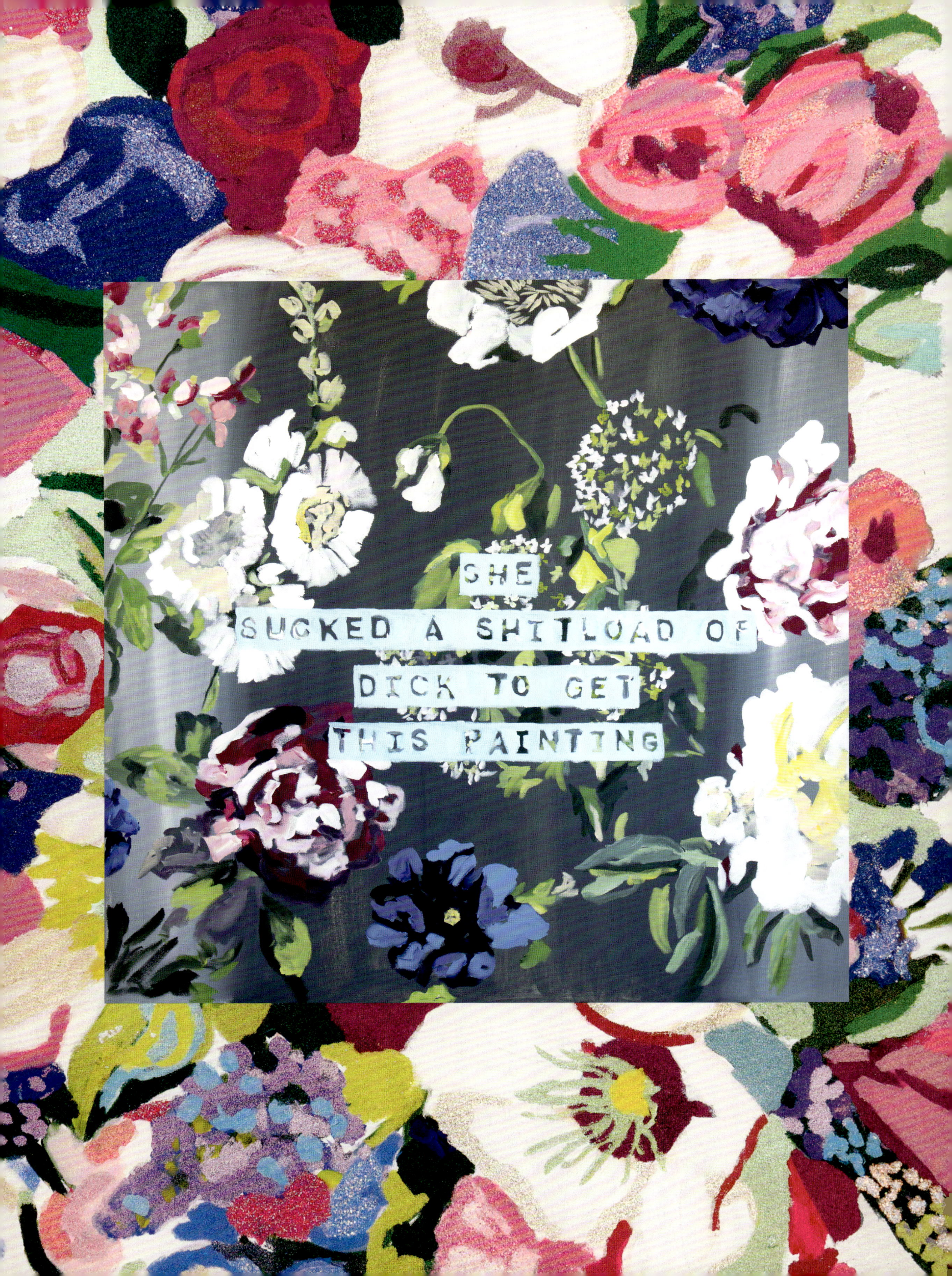
SHE
SUCKED A SHITLOAD OF
DICK TO GET
THIS PAINTING

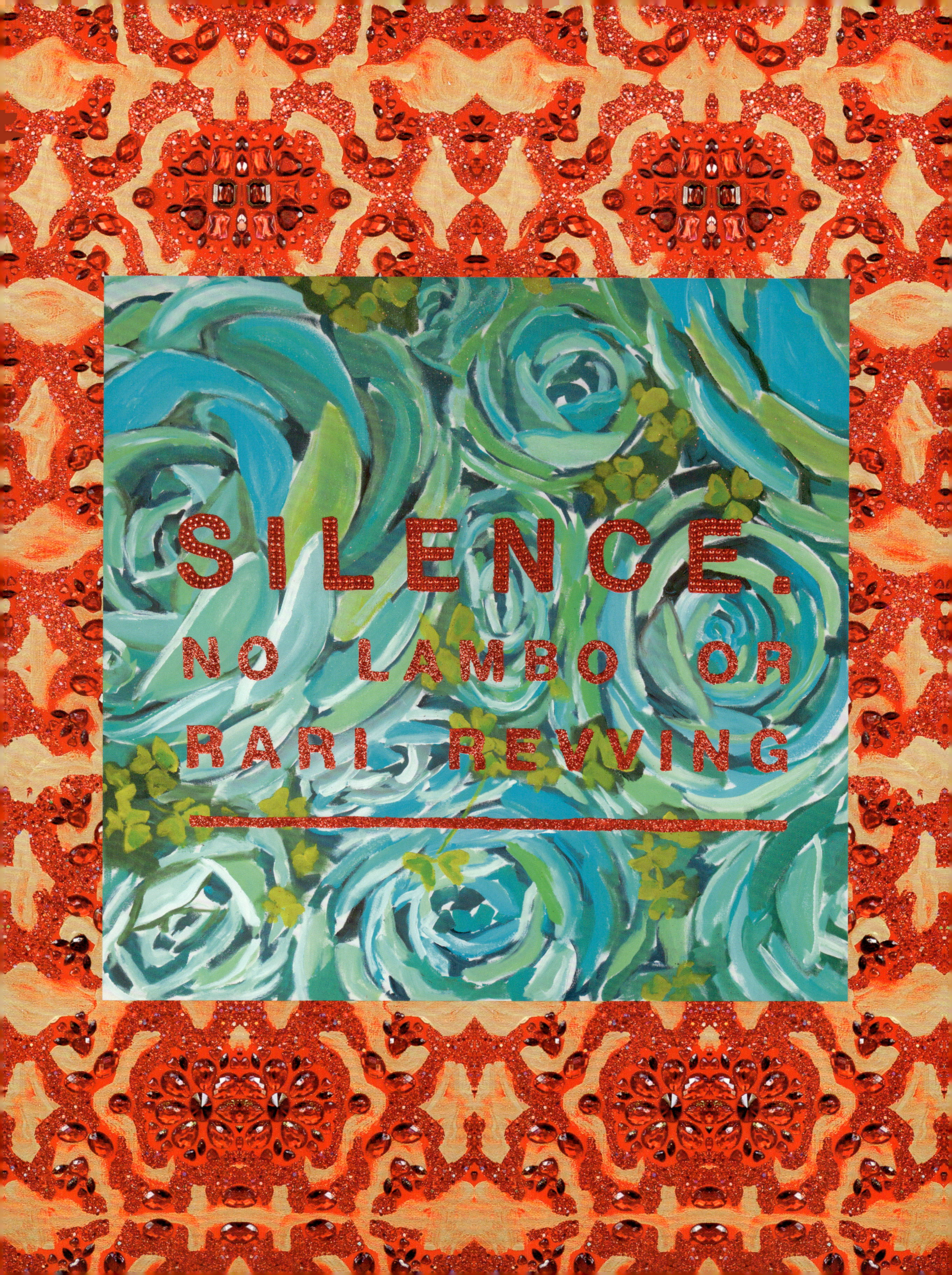
SILENCE.
NO LAMBO OR
RARI REVVING

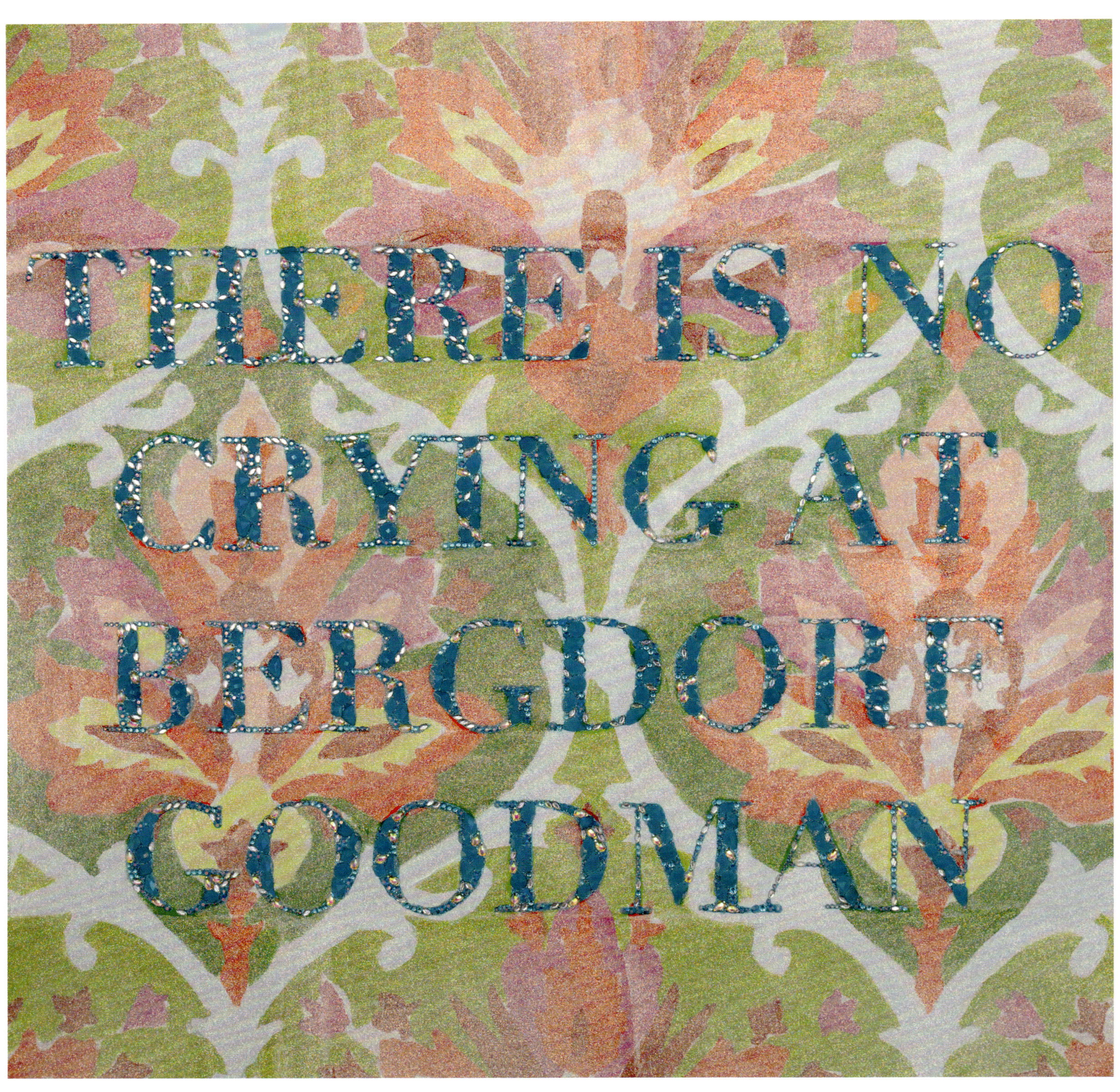
THERE IS NO
CRYING AT
BERGDORF
GOODMAN

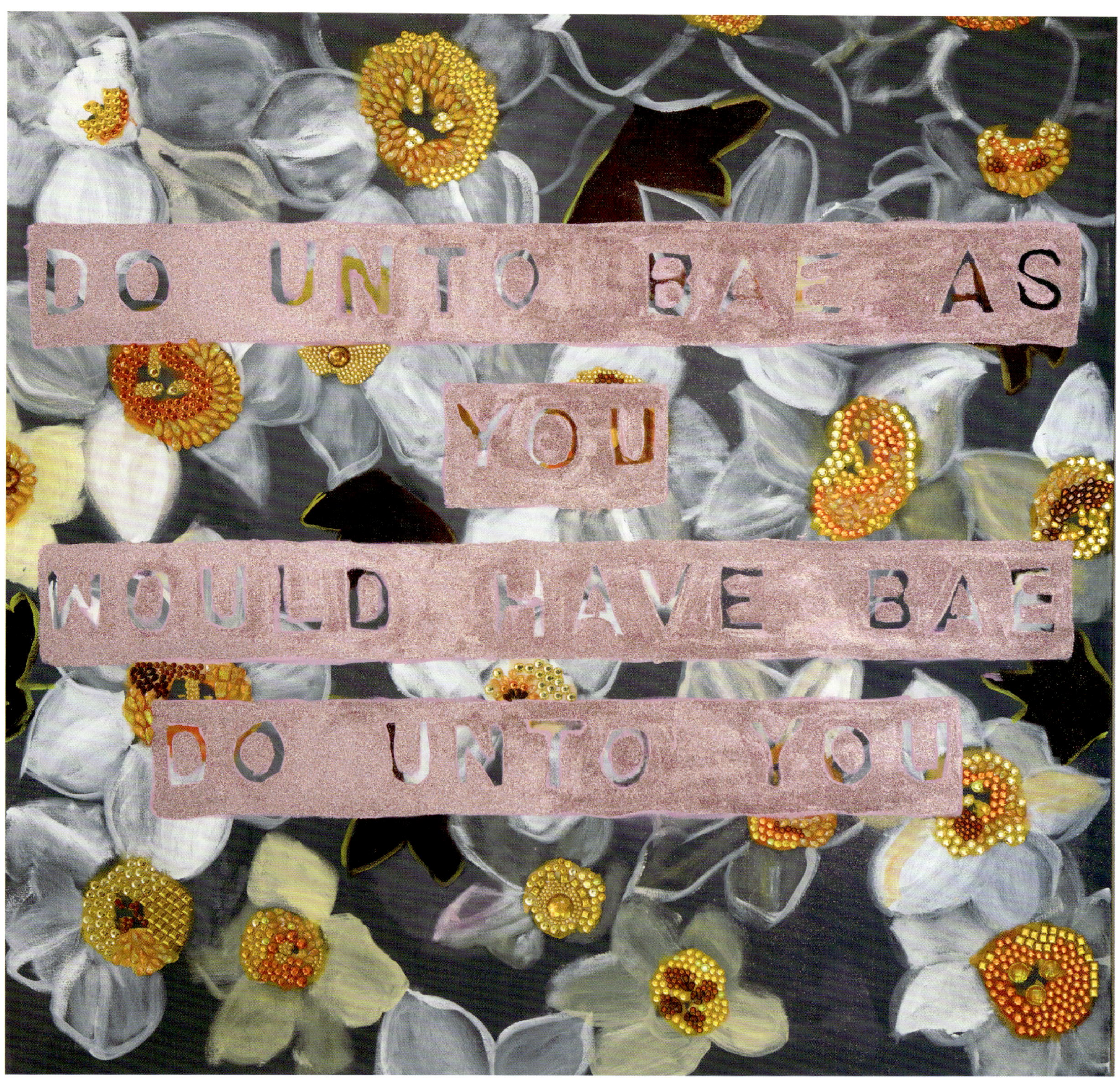
DO UNTO BAE AS
YOU
WOULD HAVE BAE
DO UNTO YOU

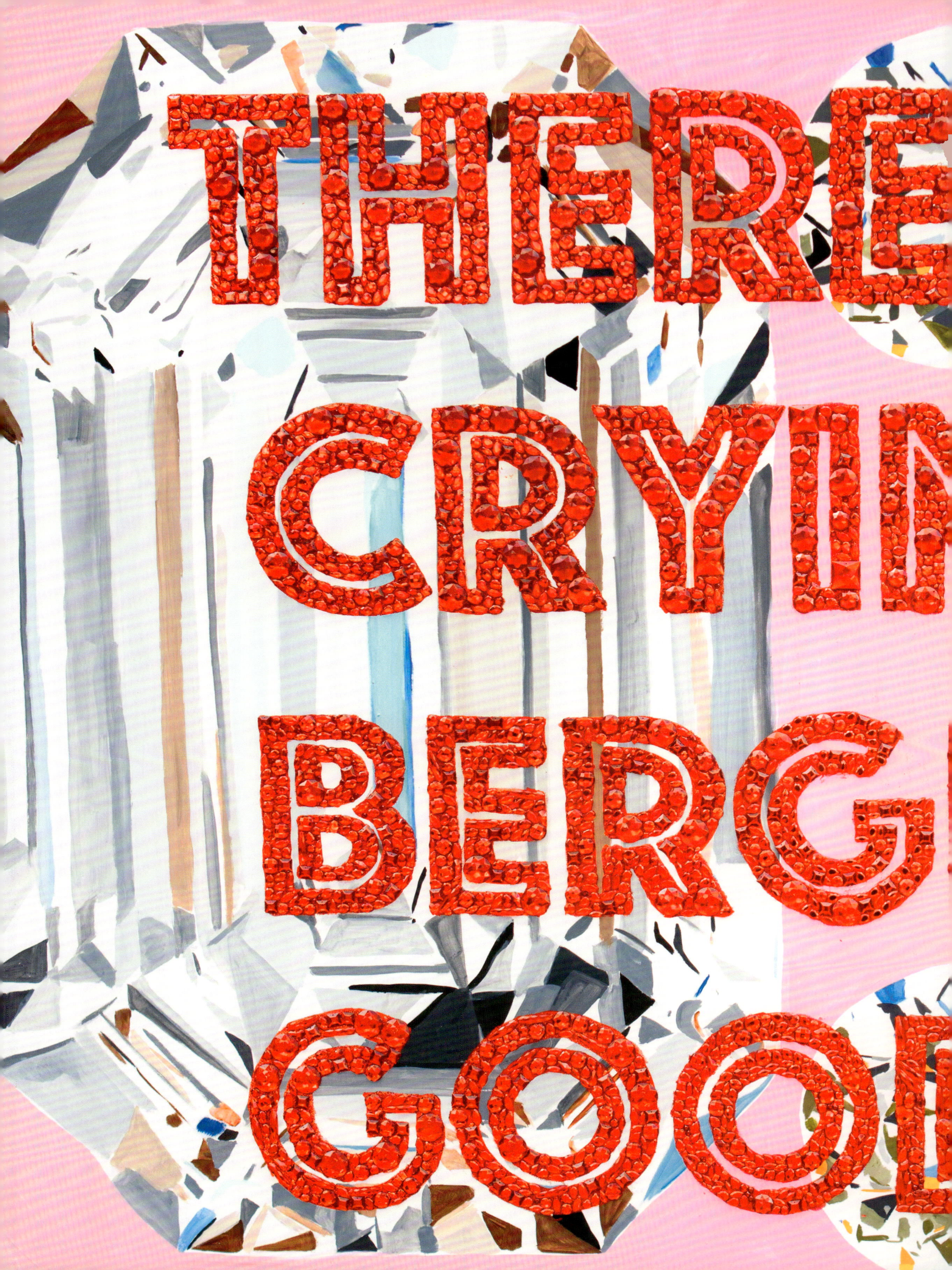
THERE
CRYIN
BERG
GOOI

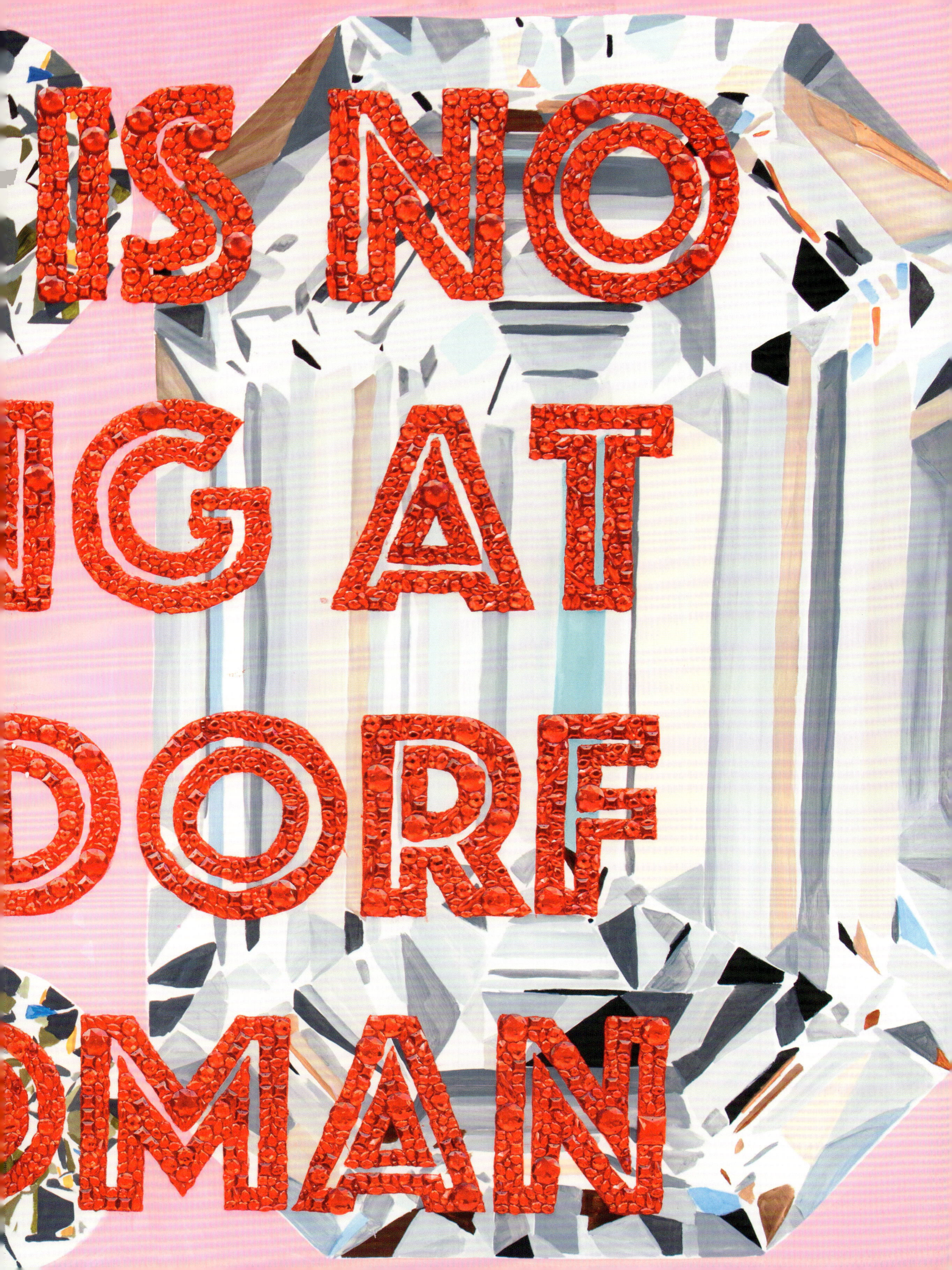
IS NO
IG AT
DORF
MAN

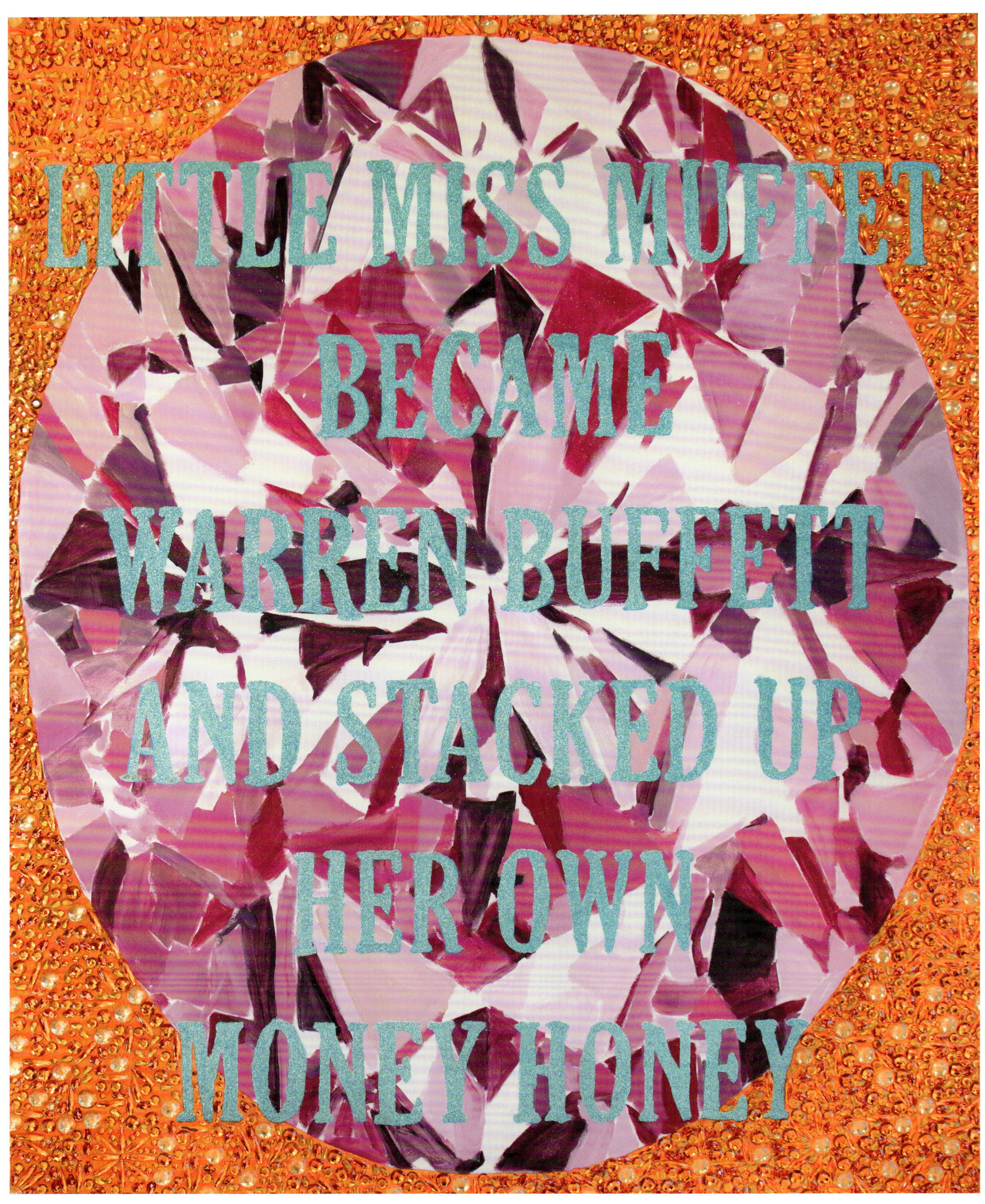
LITTLE MISS MUFFET
BECAME
WARREN BUFFETT
AND STACKED UP
HER OWN
MONEY HONEY

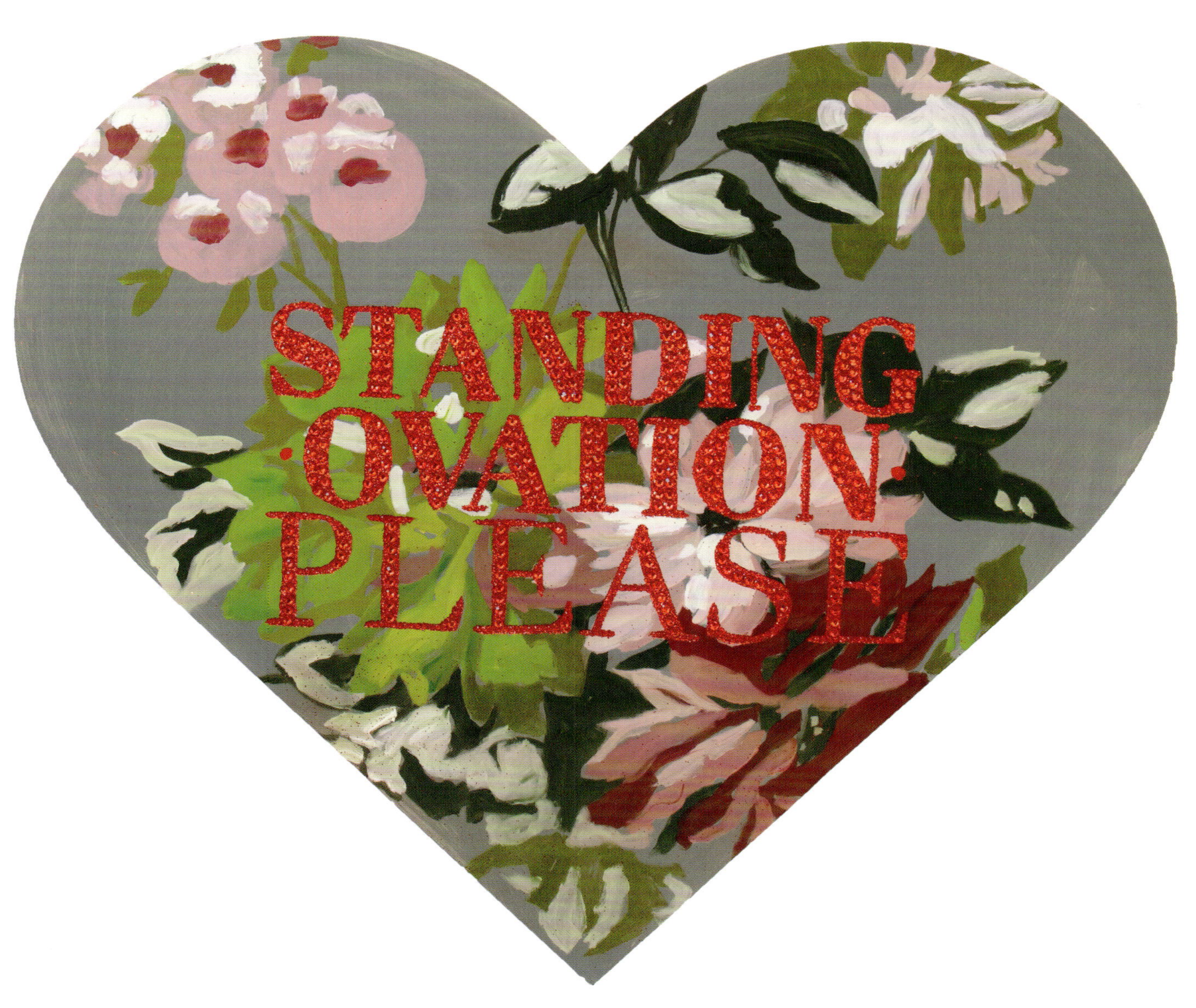
STANDING
OVATION
PLEASE

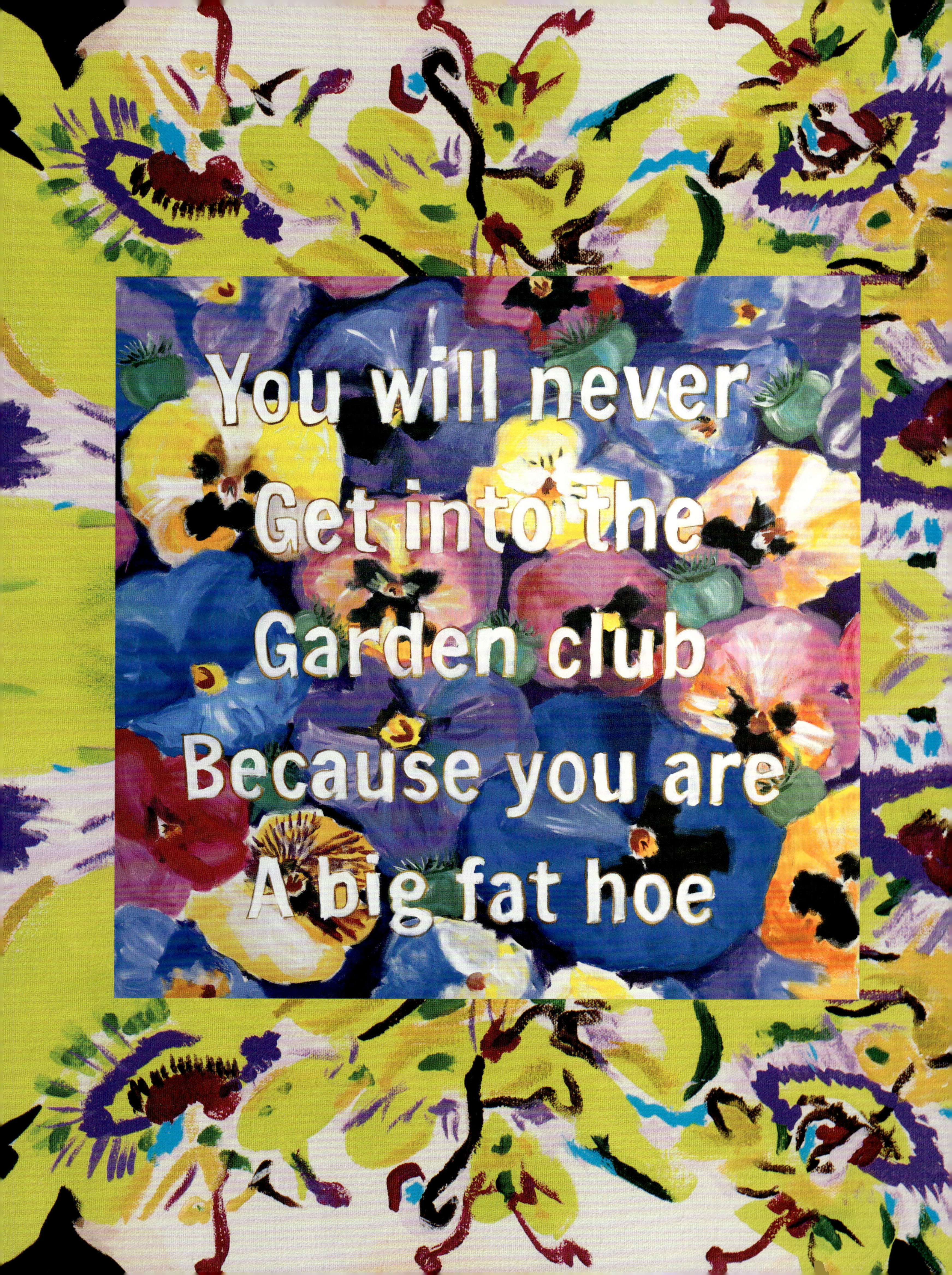
You will never
Get into the
Garden club
Because you are
A big fat hoe

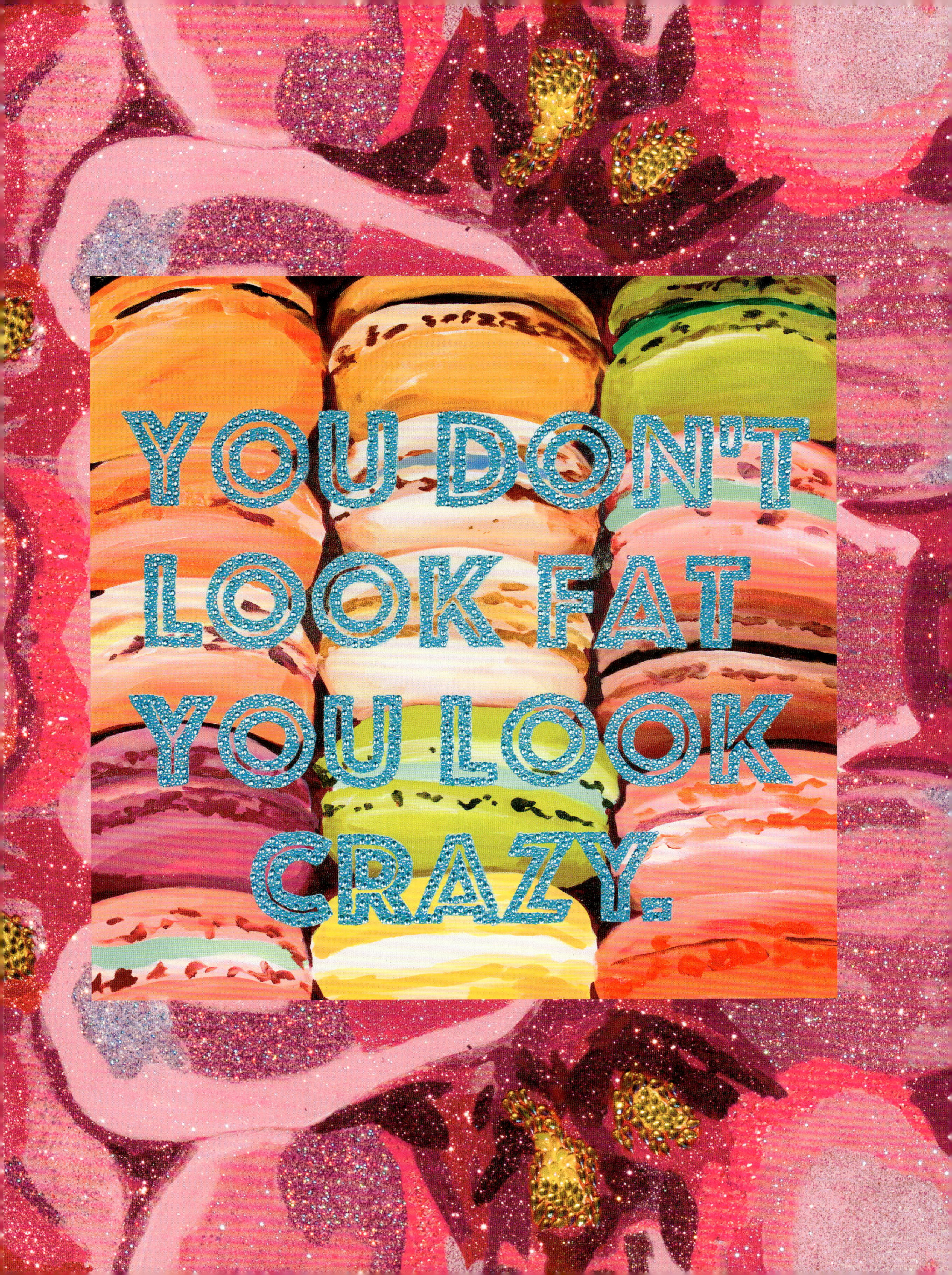
YOU DON'T
LOOK FAT
YOU LOOK
CRAZY.

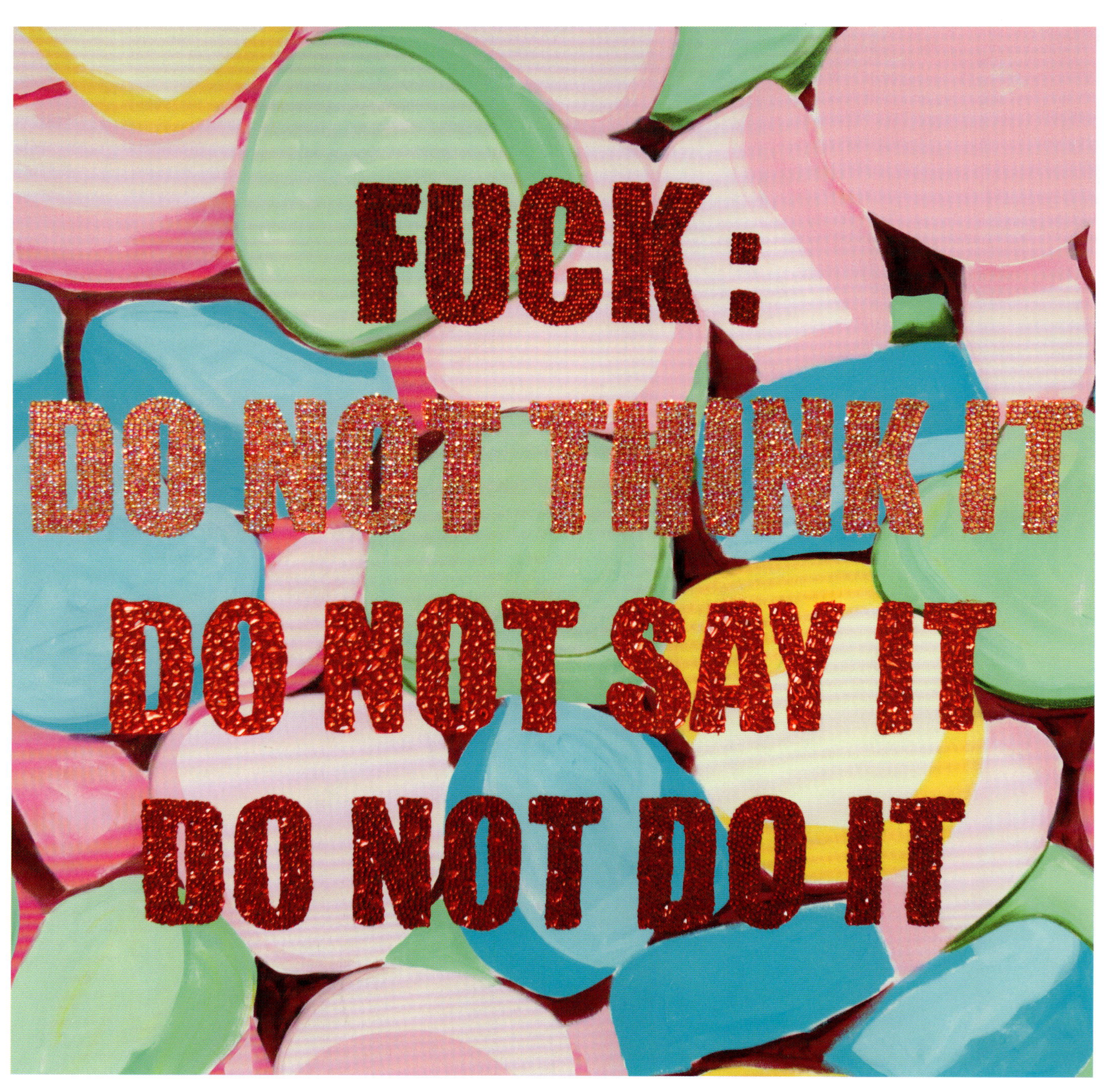
FUCK:
DO NOT THINK IT
DO NOT SAY IT
DO NOT DO IT

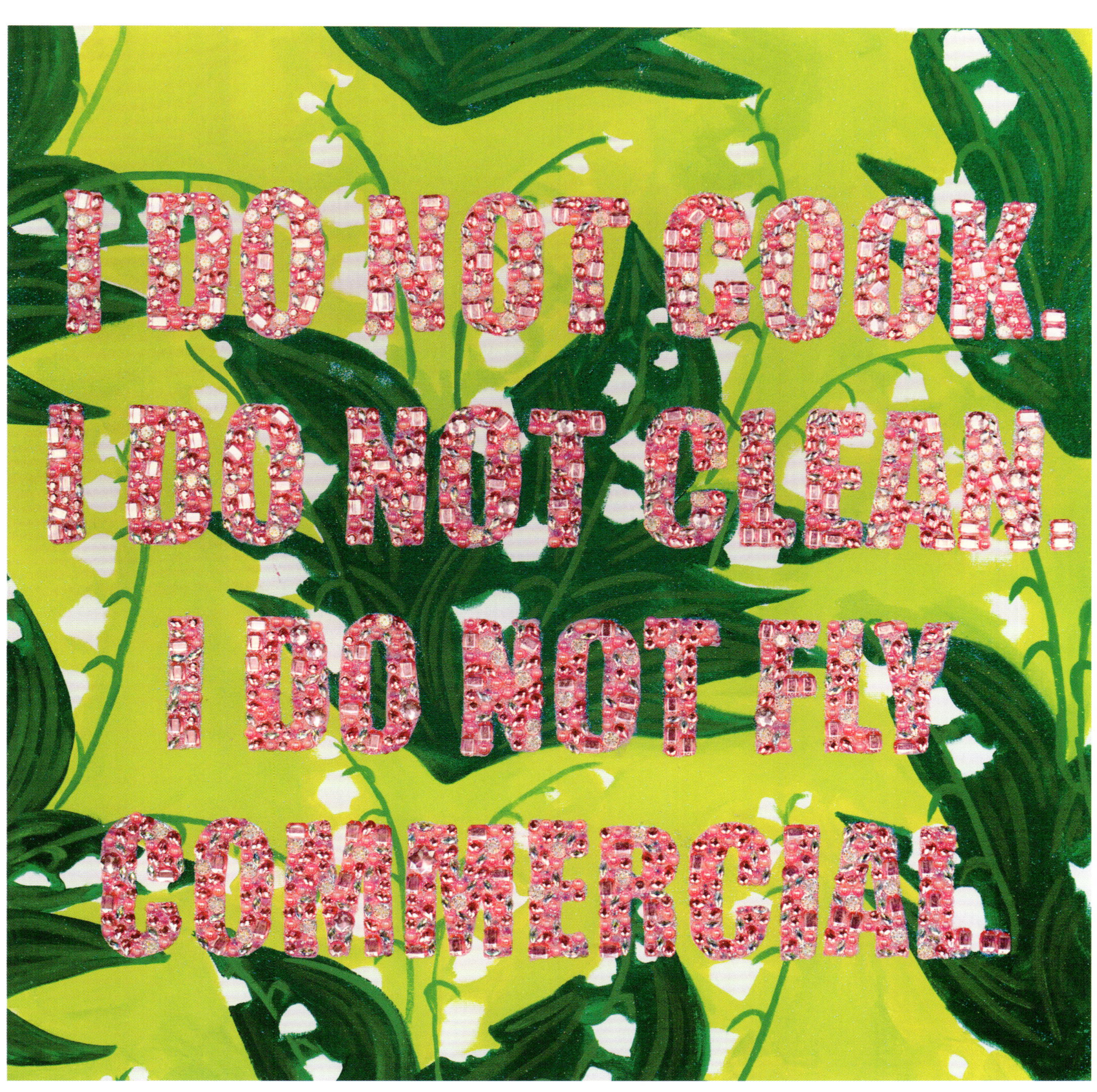
I DO NOT COOK.
I DO NOT CLEAN.
I DO NOT FLY
COMMERCIAL.

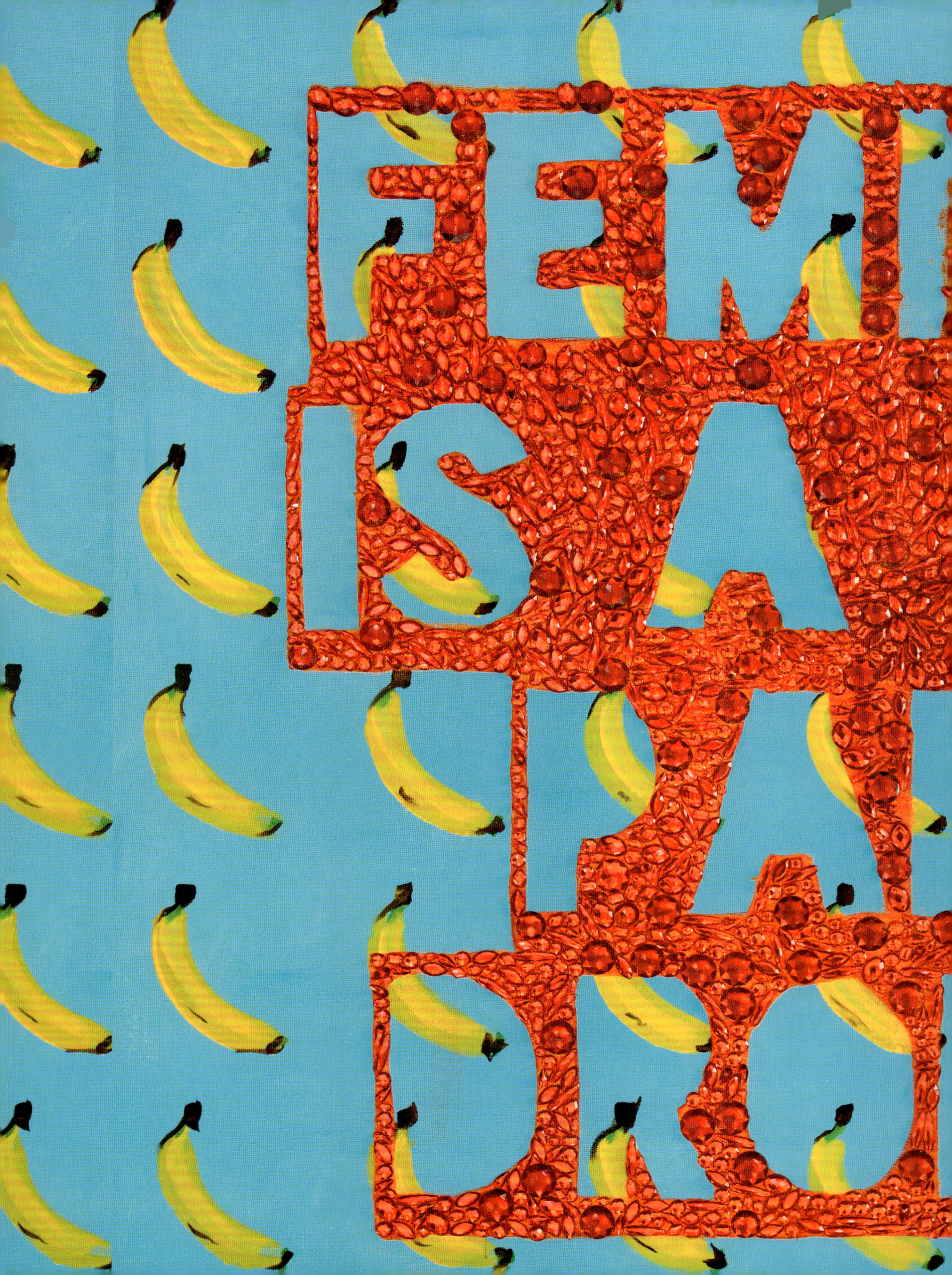

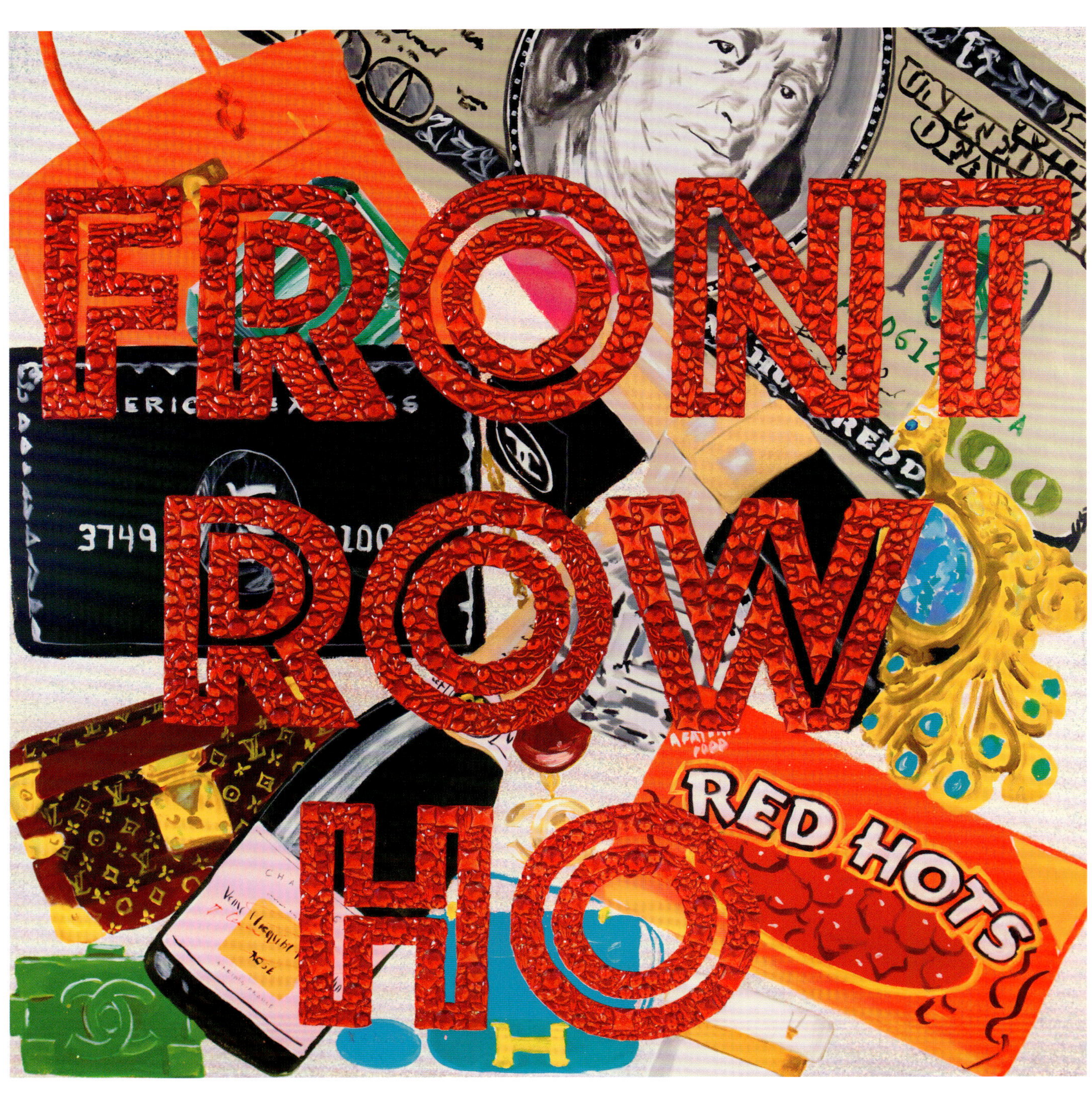
FRONT
ROW
HO
RED HOTS
3749

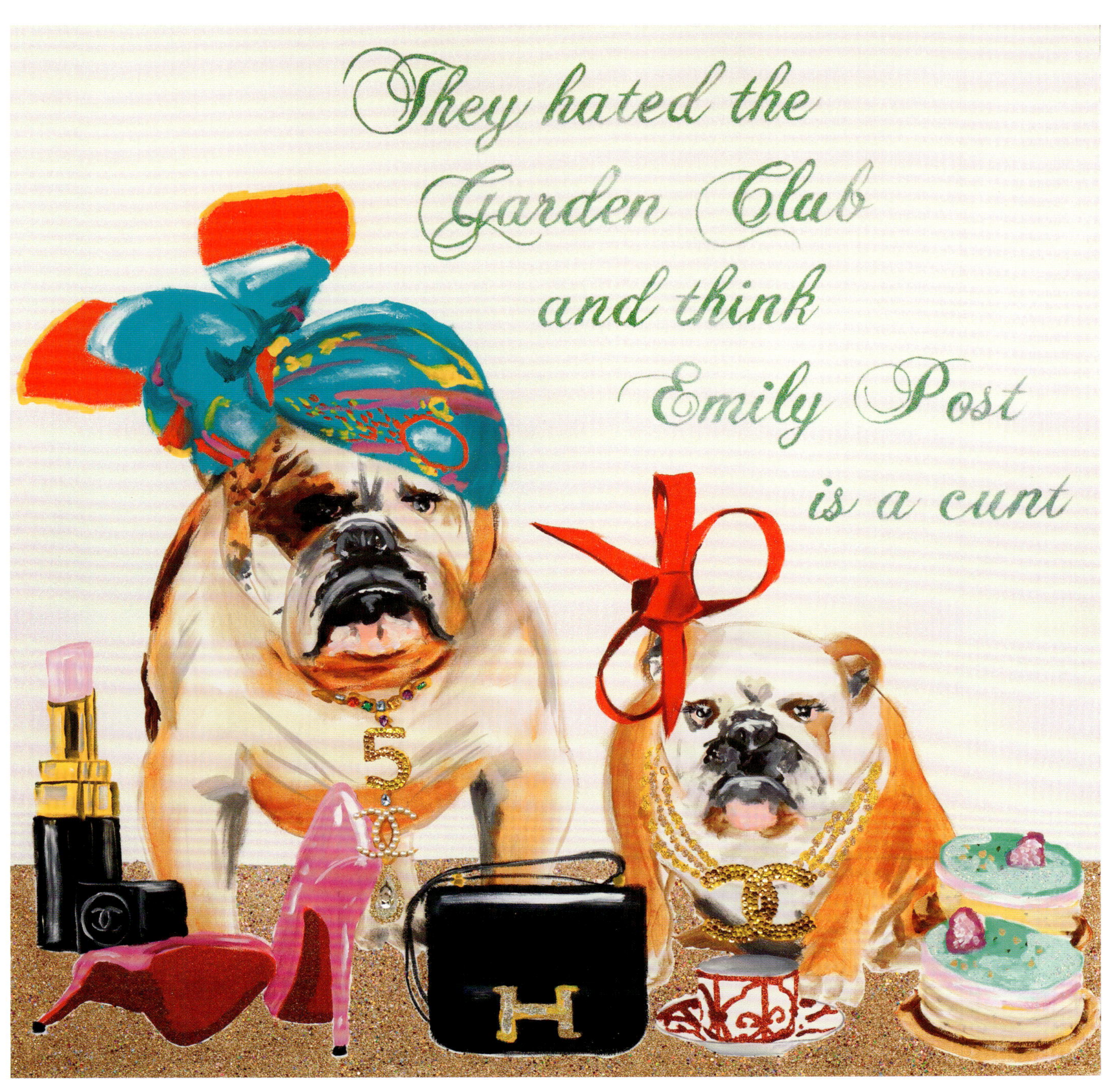
They hated the
Garden Club
and think
Emily Post
is a cunt

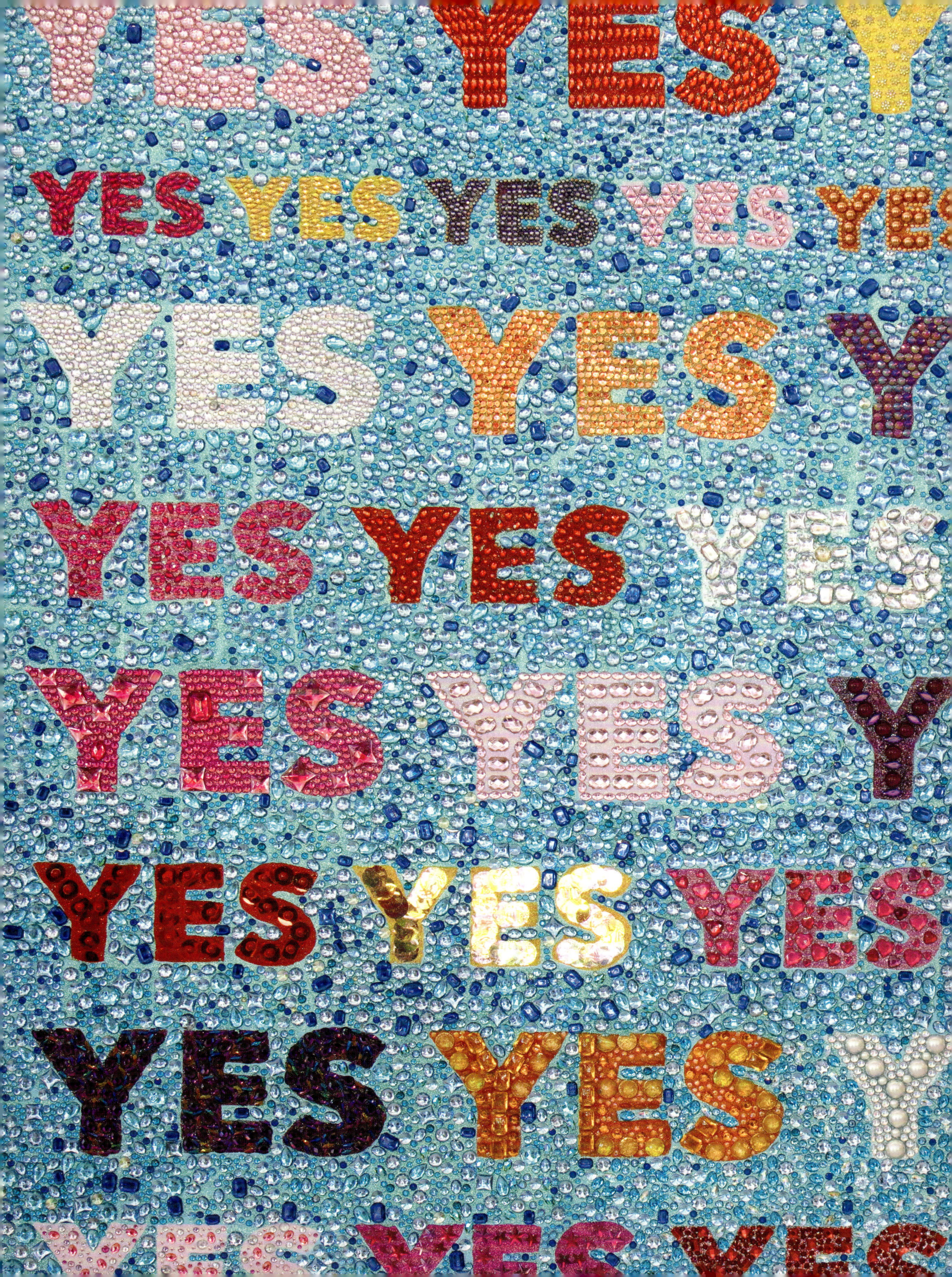

YES YES
YES YES YES YES YES
YES YES
YES YES YES
YES YES
YES YES YES
YES YES

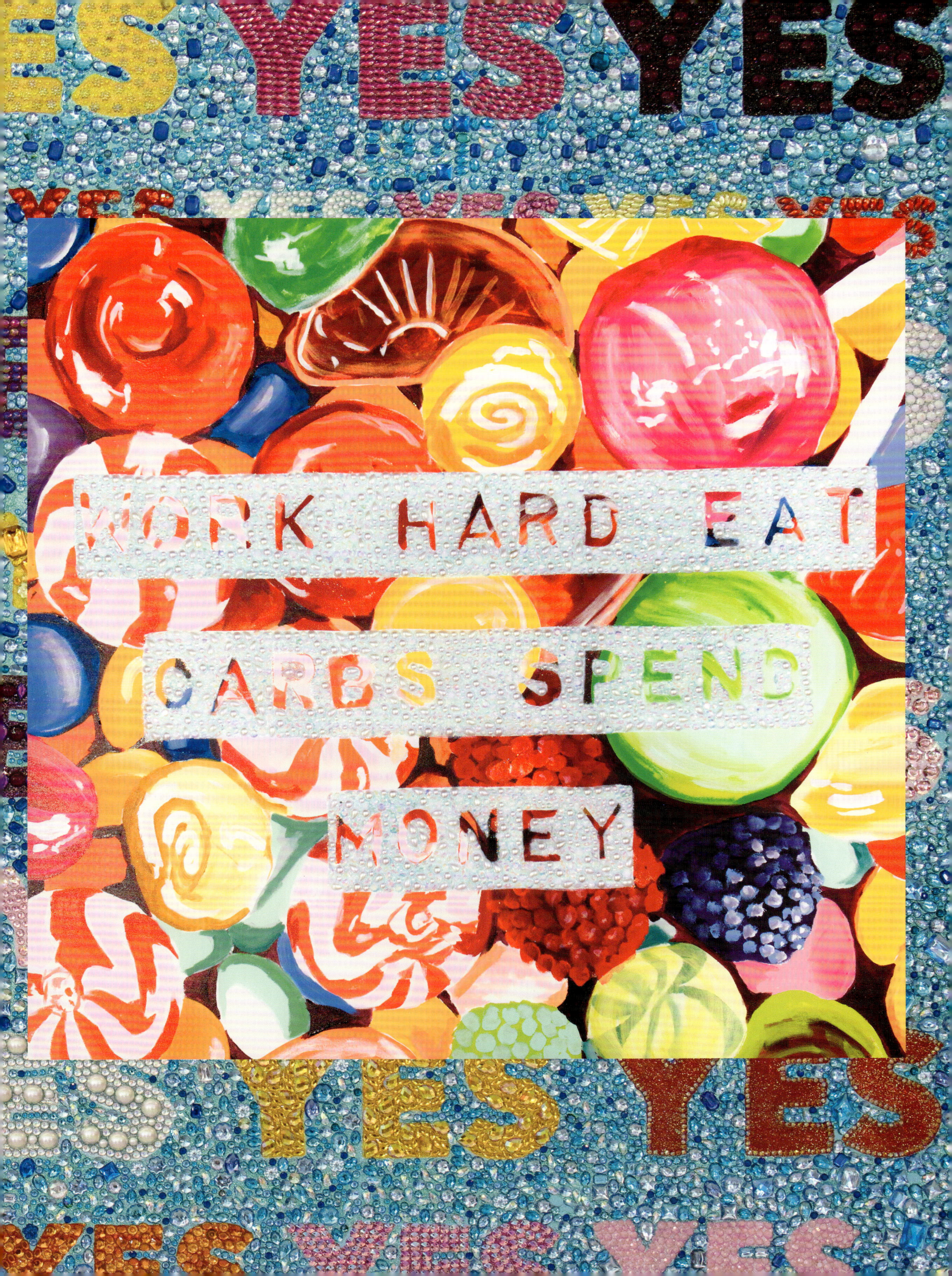
YES YES YES
WORK HARD EAT
CARBS SPEND
MONEY
YES YES

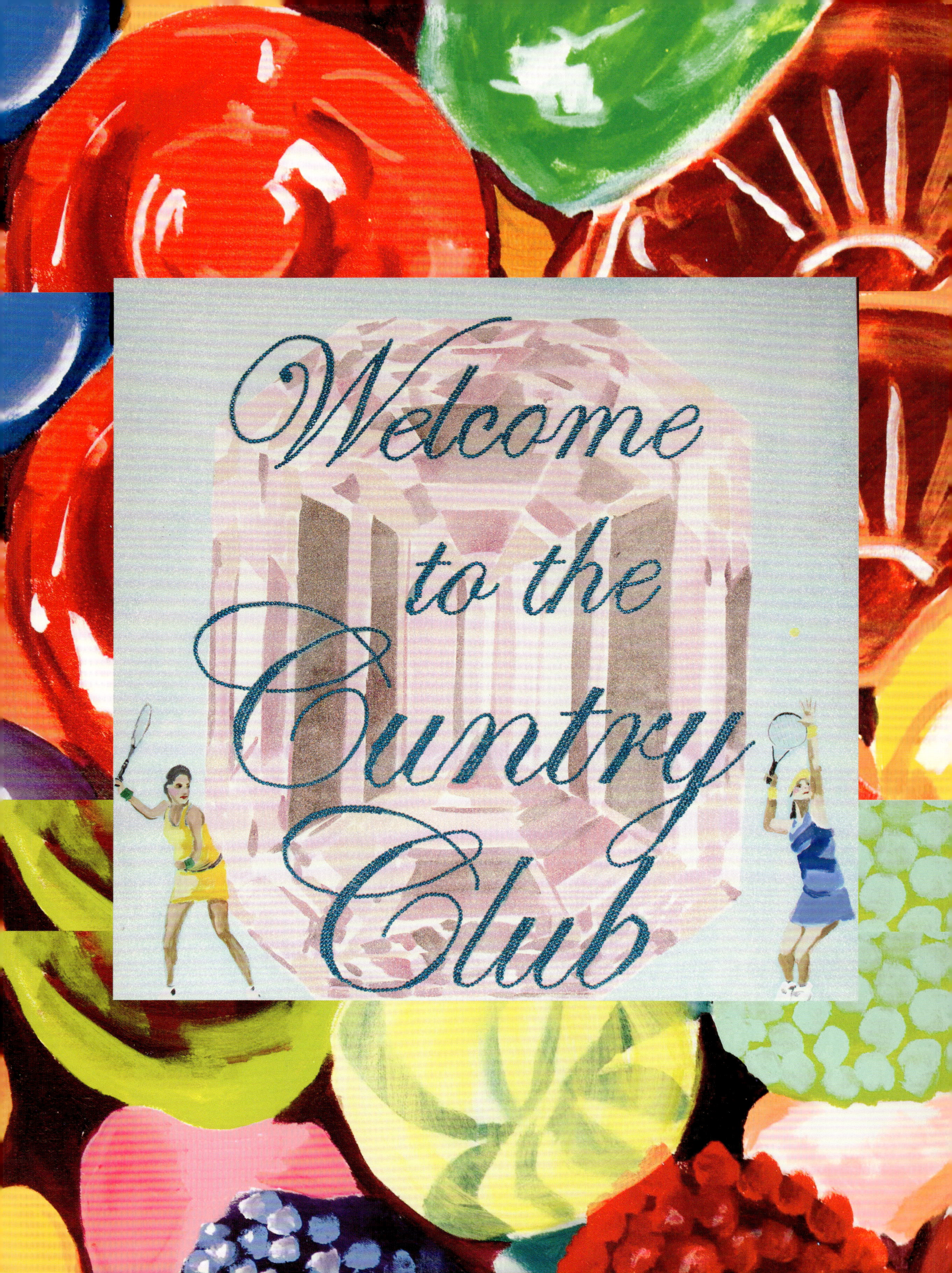
Welcome
to the
Cuntry
Club

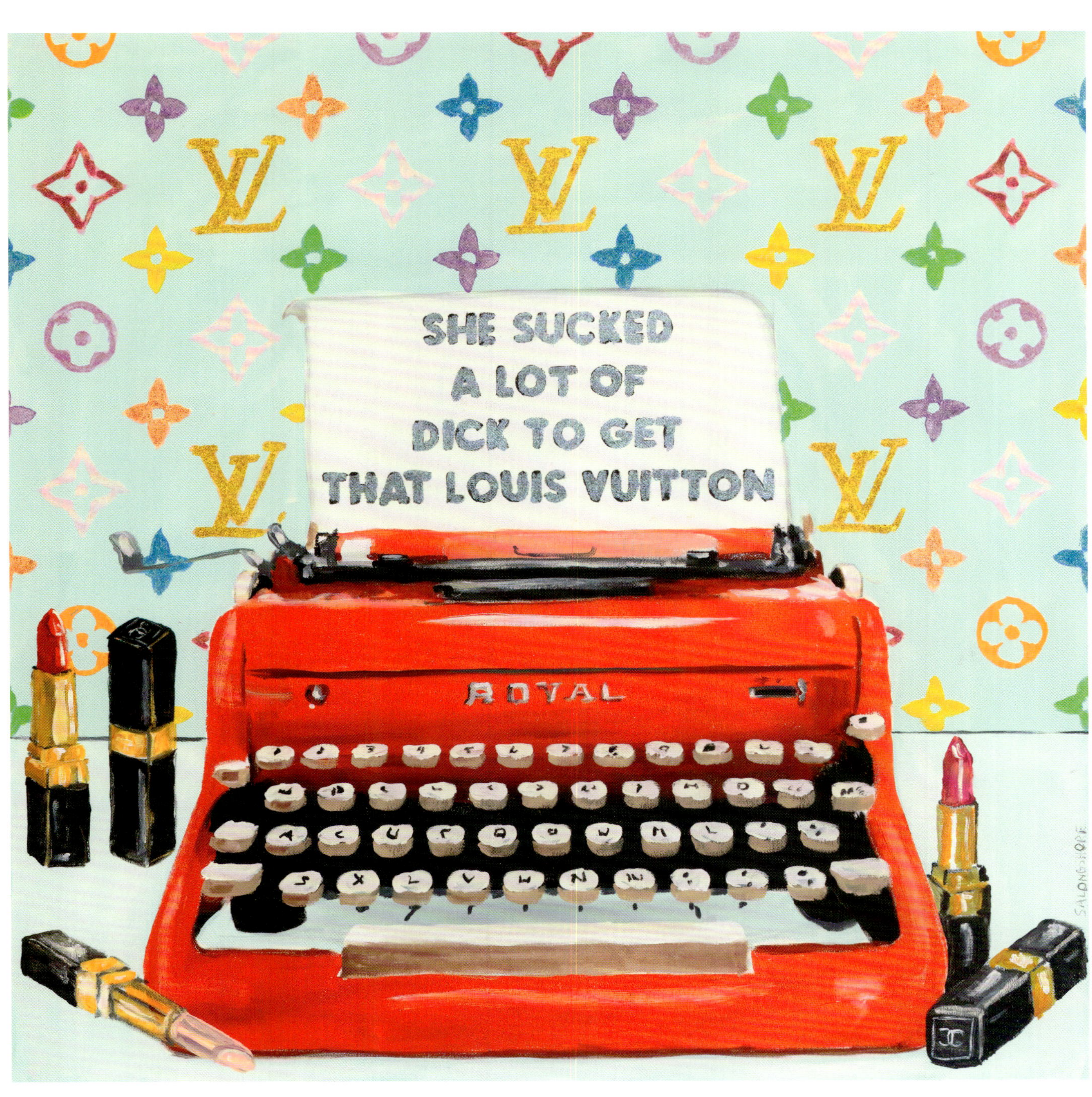
SHE SUCKED
A LOT OF
DICK TO GET
THAT LOUIS VUITTON
ROYAL

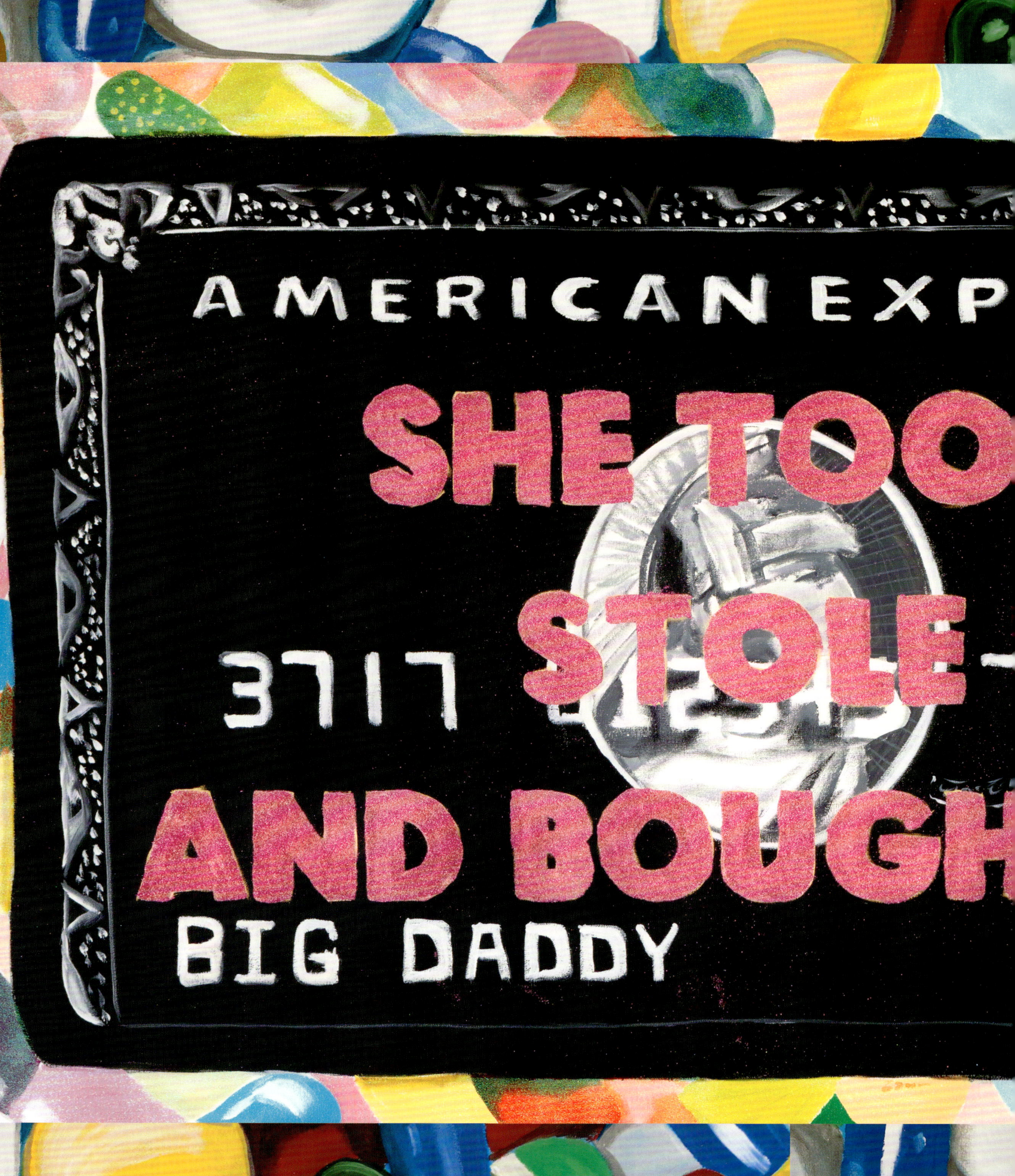
AMERICAN EXP
SHE TOO
STOLE
3717
AND BOUGH
BIG DADDY

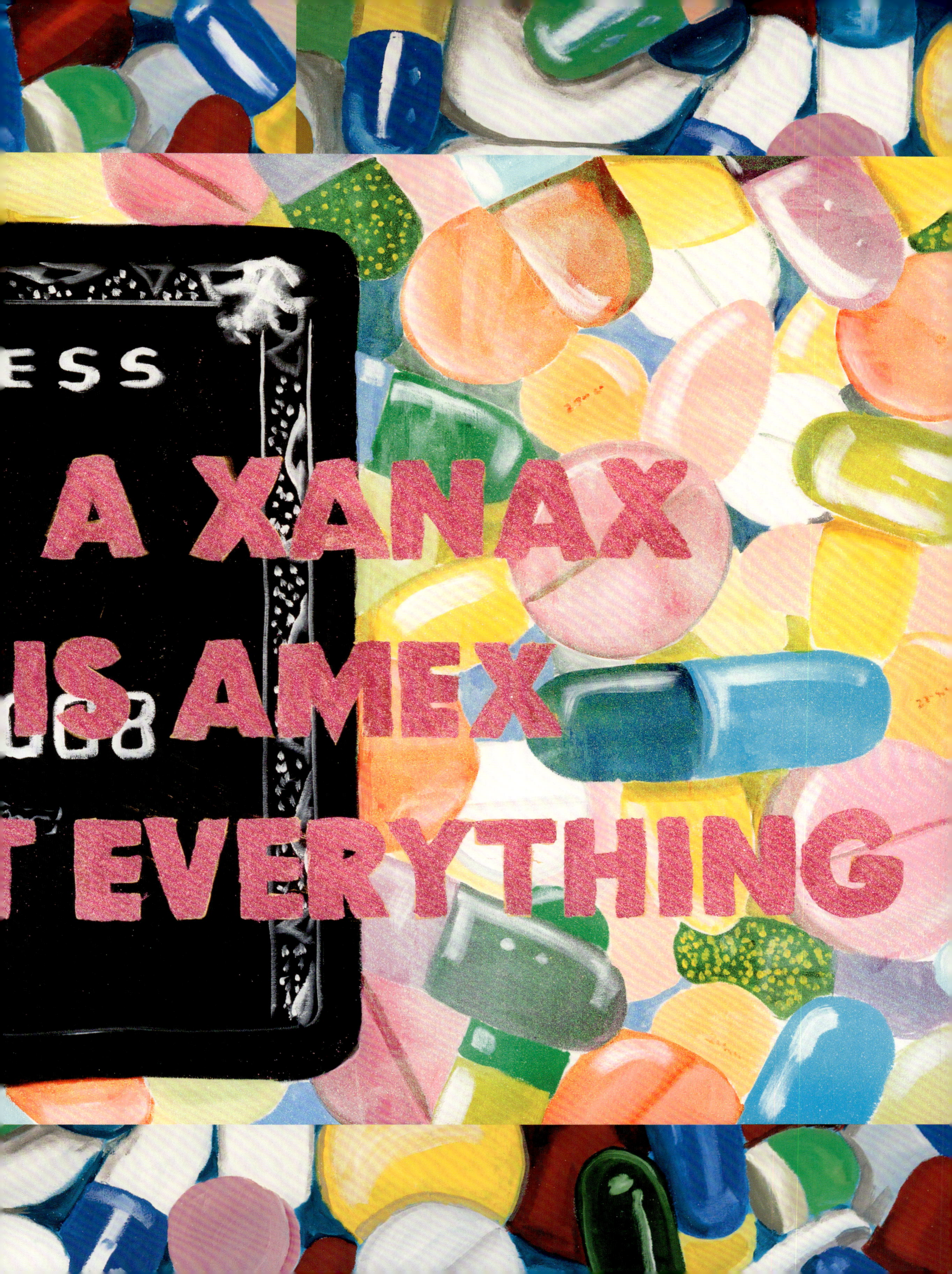
ESS
A XANAX
IS AMEX
EVERYTHING

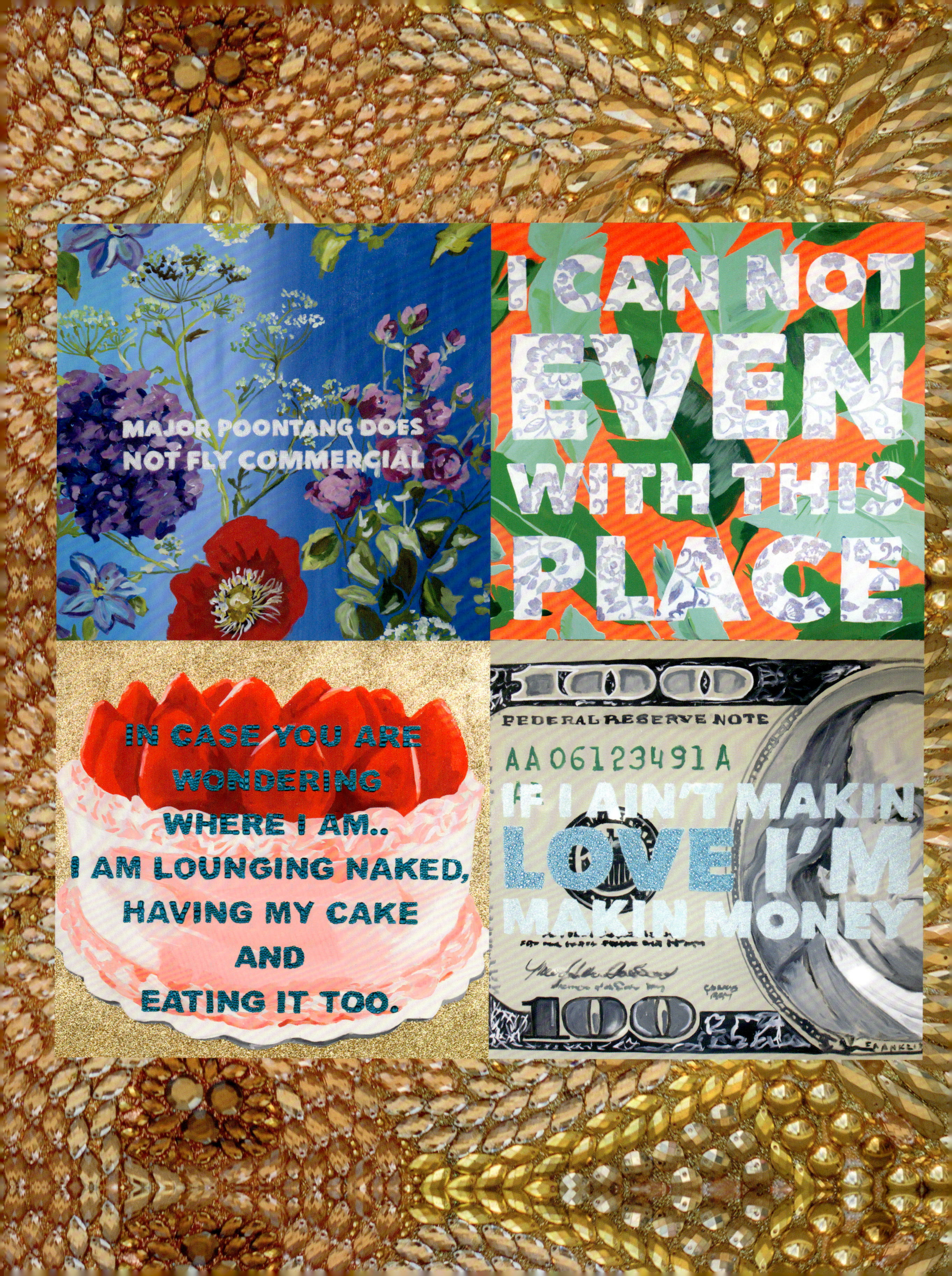
MAJOR POONTANG DOES
NOT FLY COMMERCIAL
I CAN NOT
EVEN
WITH THIS
PLACE
IN CASE YOU ARE
WONDERING
WHERE I AM..
I AM LOUNGING NAKED,
HAVING MY CAKE
AND
EATING IT TOO.
FEDERAL RESERVE NOTE
AA 06123491 A
IF I AIN'T MAKIN
LOVE I'M
MAKIN MONEY
100

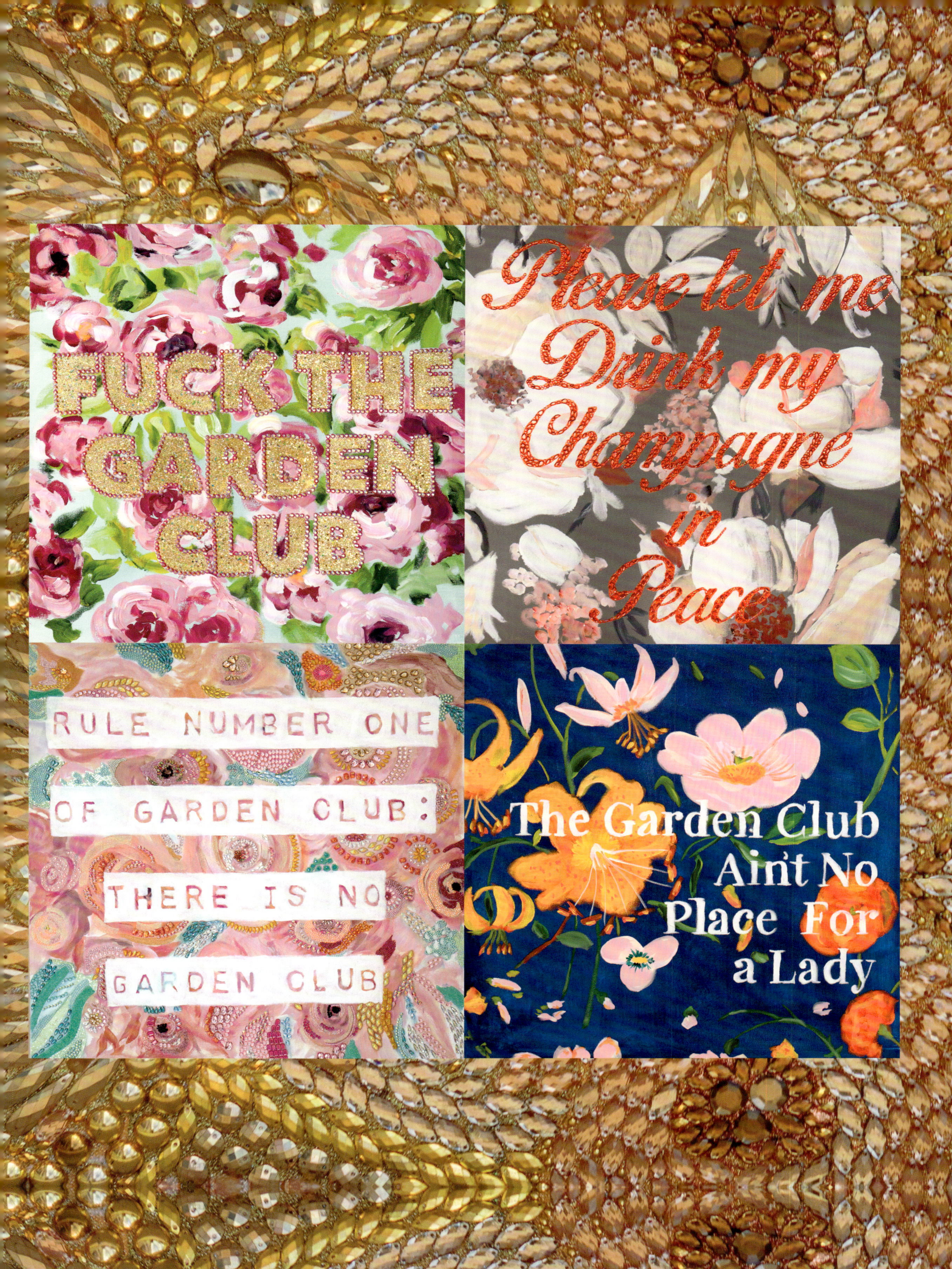
FUCK THE GARDEN CLUB
Please let me Drink my Champagne in Peace
RULE NUMBER ONE
OF GARDEN CLUB:
THERE IS NO
GARDEN CLUB
The Garden Club
Ain't No
Place For
a Lady

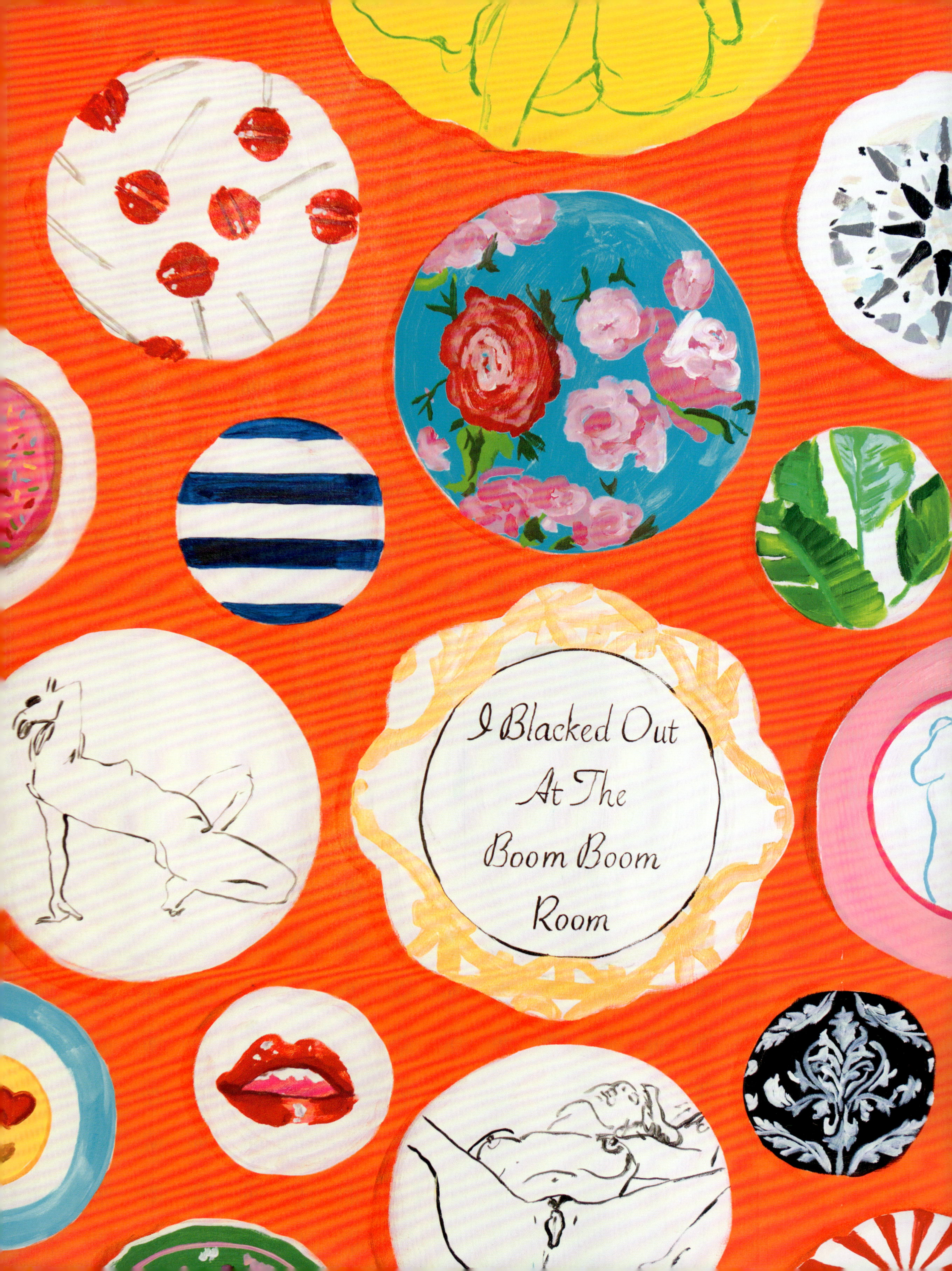
I Blacked Out
At The
Boom Boom
Room

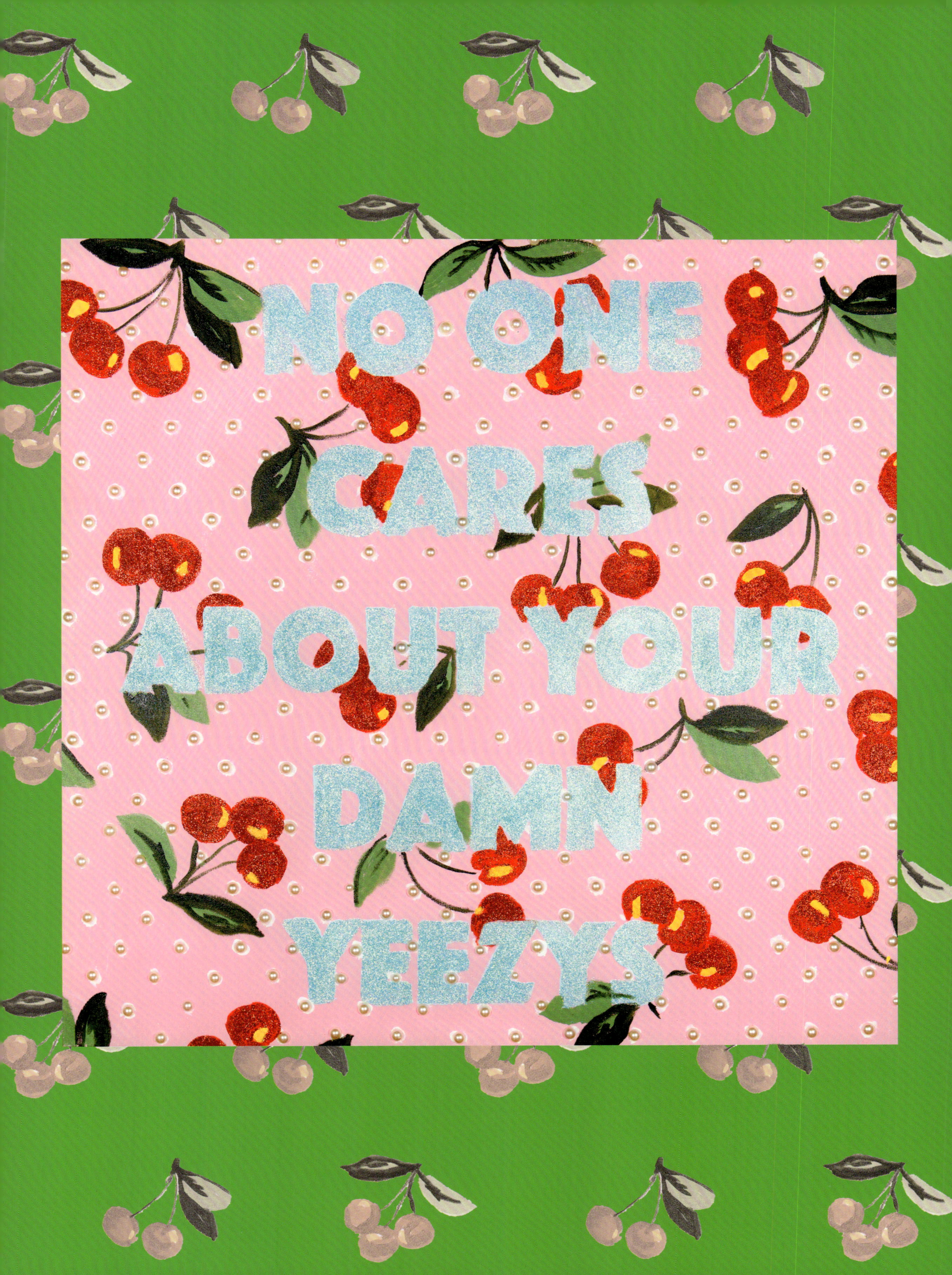
NO ONE
CARES
ABOUT YOUR
DAMN
YEEZYS

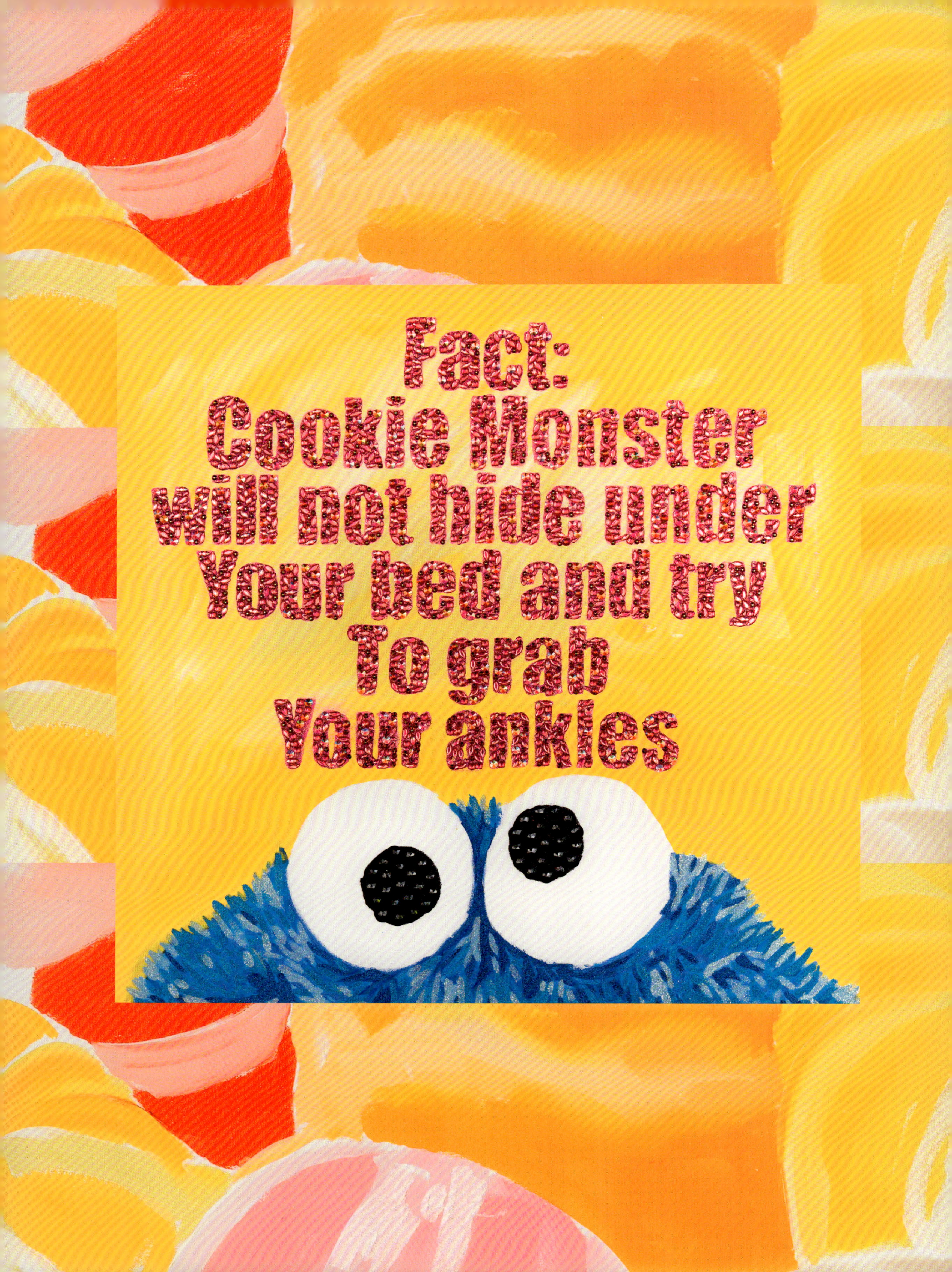
Fact:
Cookie Monster
will not hide under
Your bed and try
To grab
Your ankles

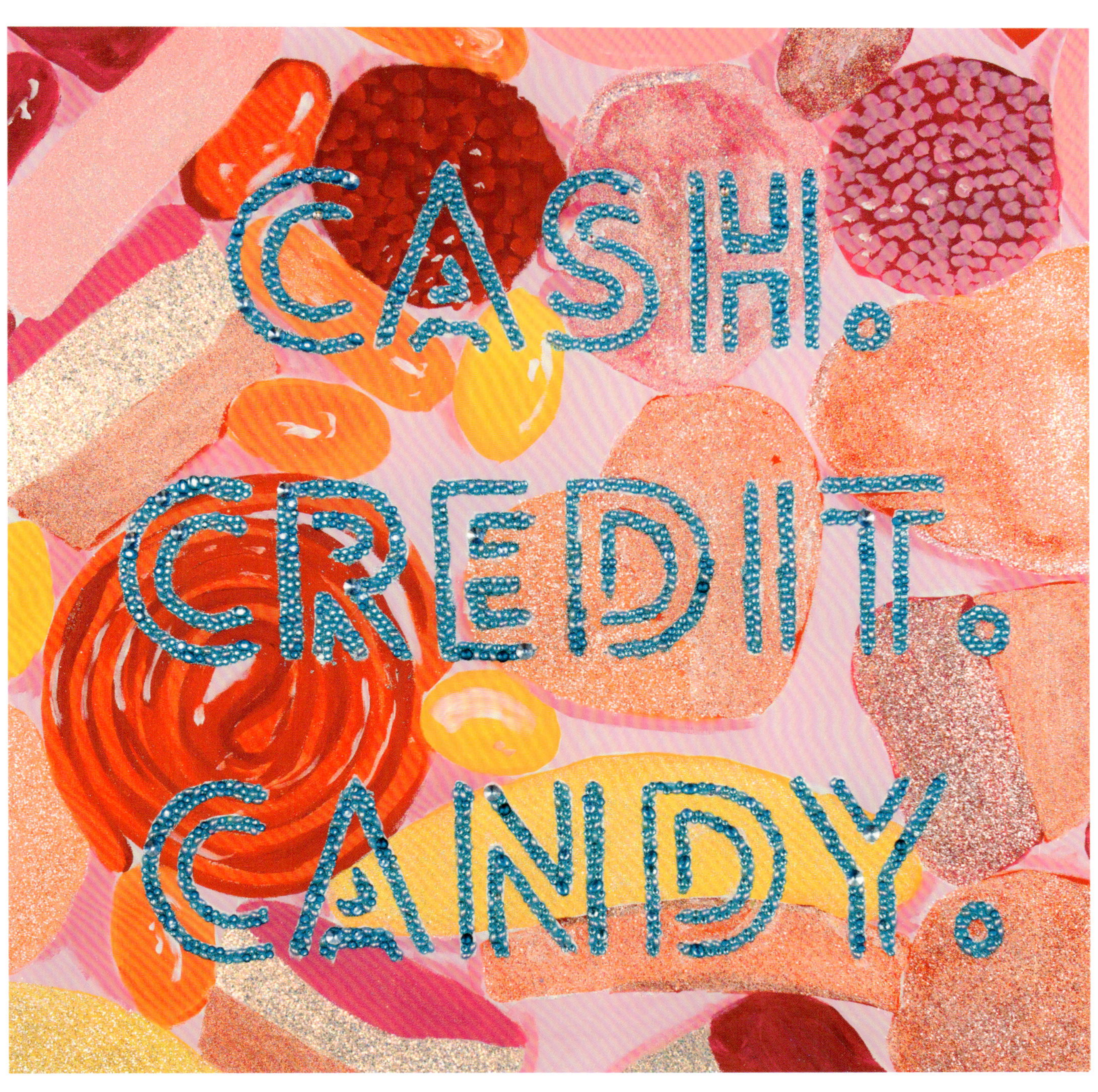
CASH.
CREDIT.
CANDY.

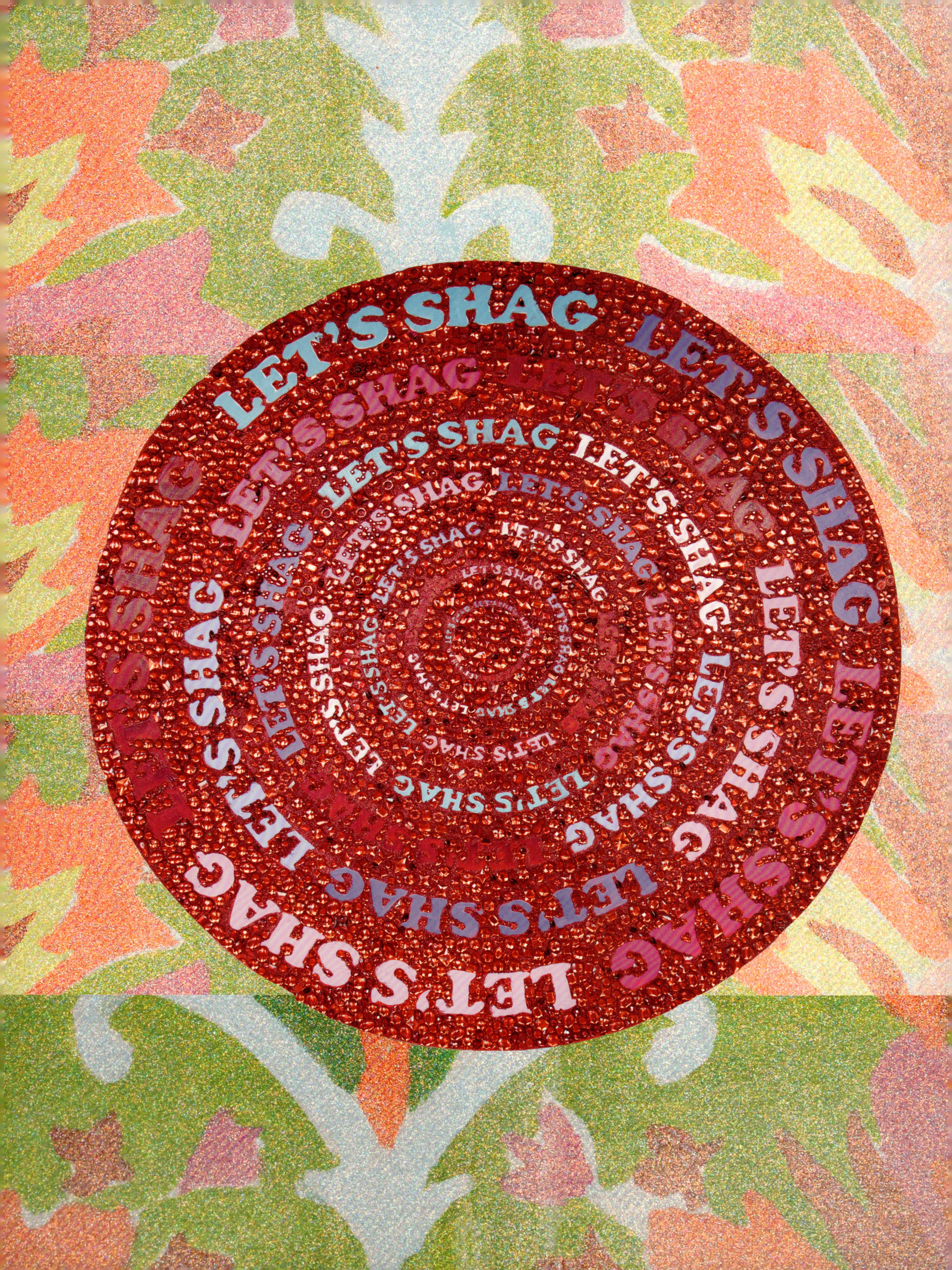
LET'S SHAG LET'S SHAG LET'S SHAG LET'S SHAG LET'S SHAG
LET'S SHAG LET'S SHAG LET'S SHAG LET'S SHAG
LET'S SHAG LET'S SHAG LET'S SHAG LET'S SHAG
LET'S SHAG LET'S SHAG LET'S SHAG

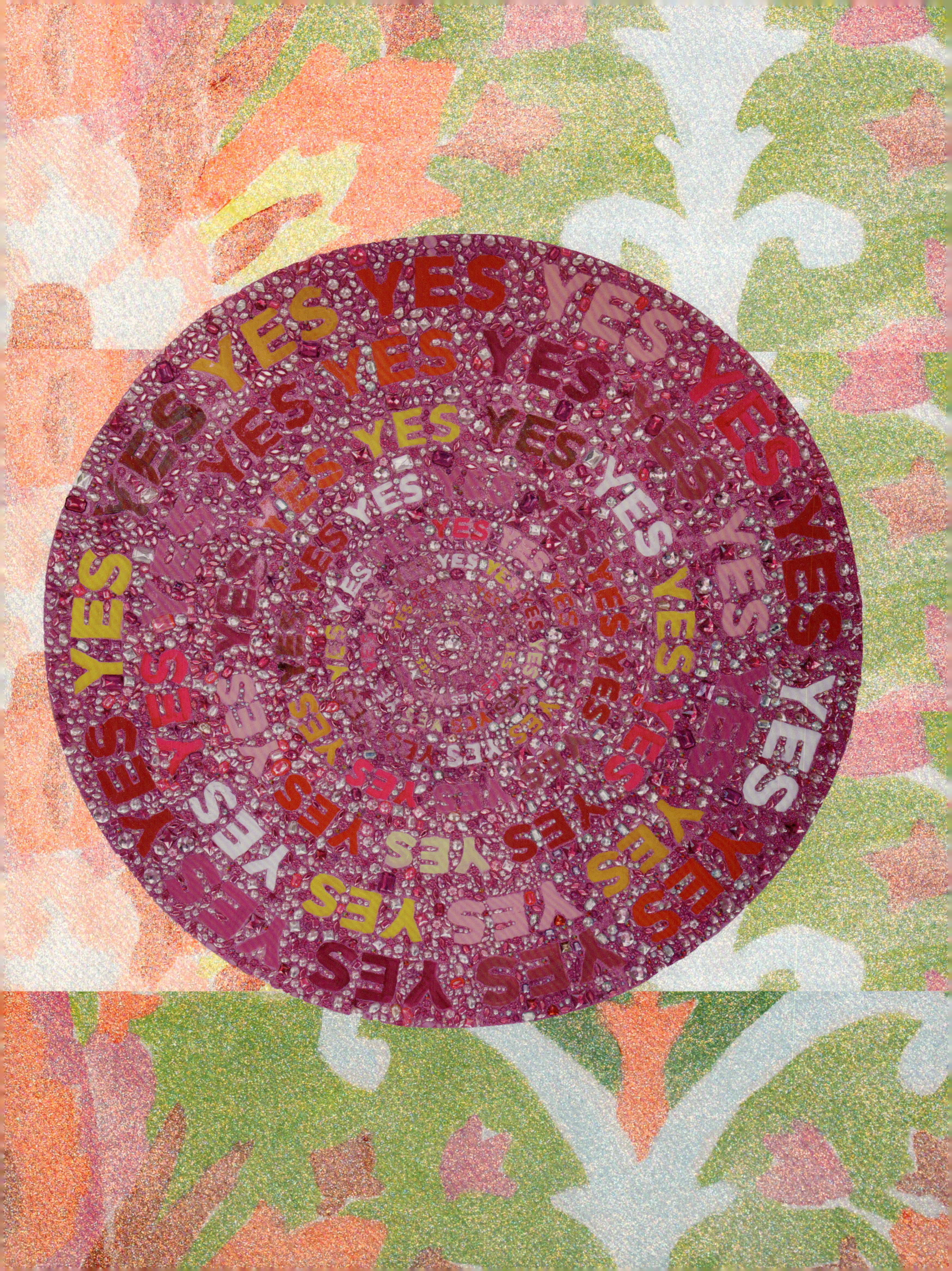
YES

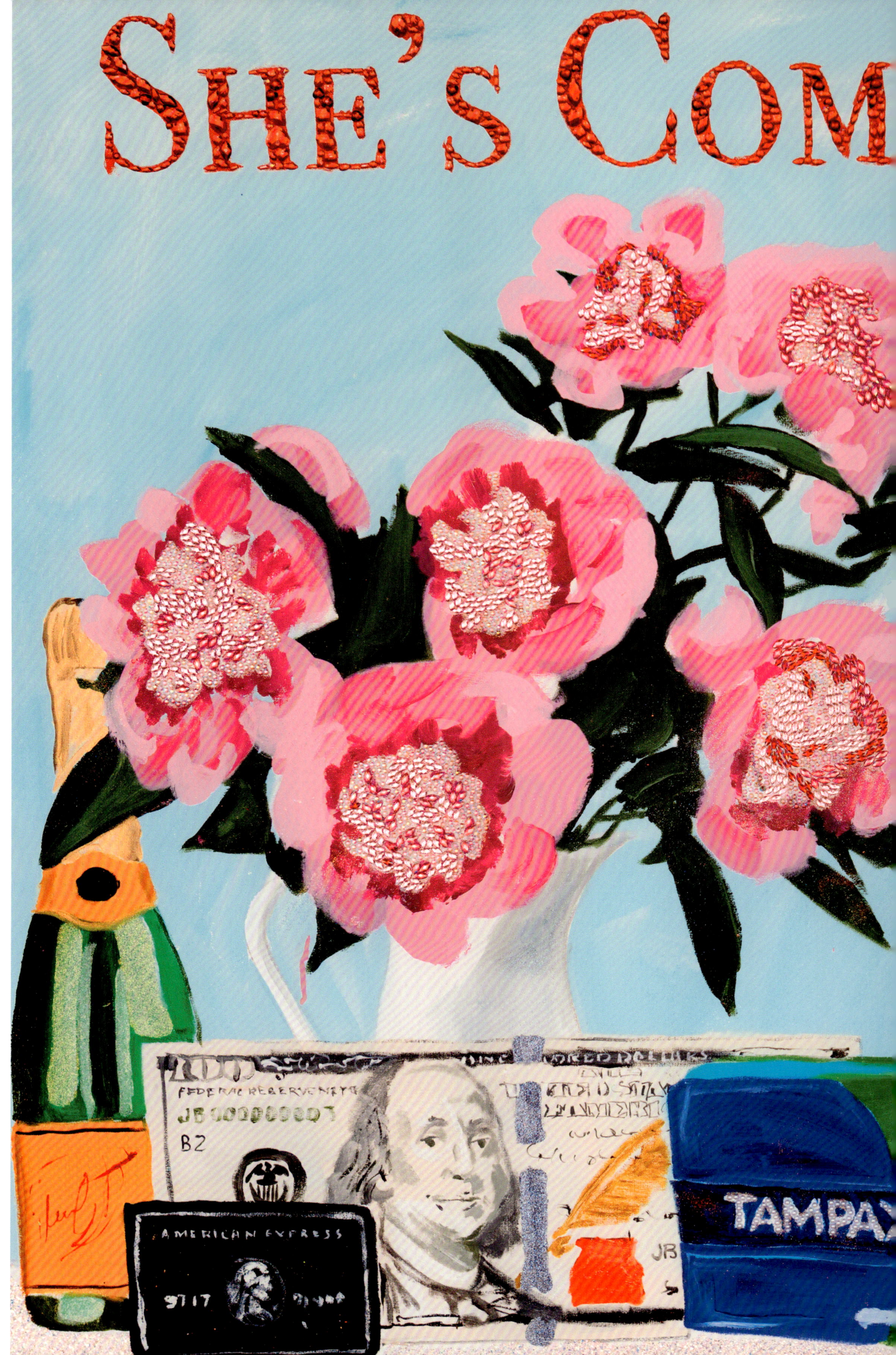
SHE'S COM
AMERICAN EXPRESS
TAMPA

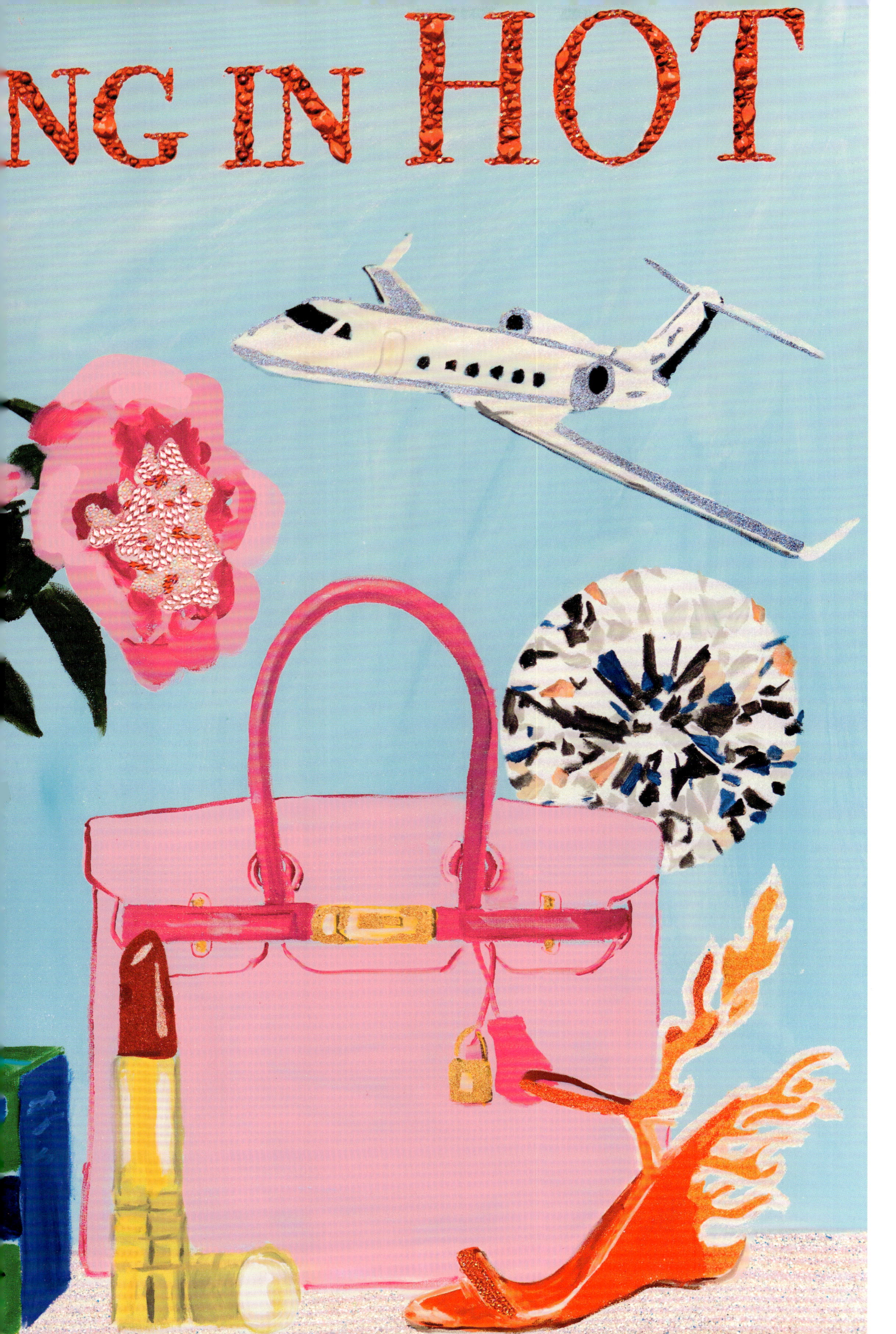
NG IN HOT

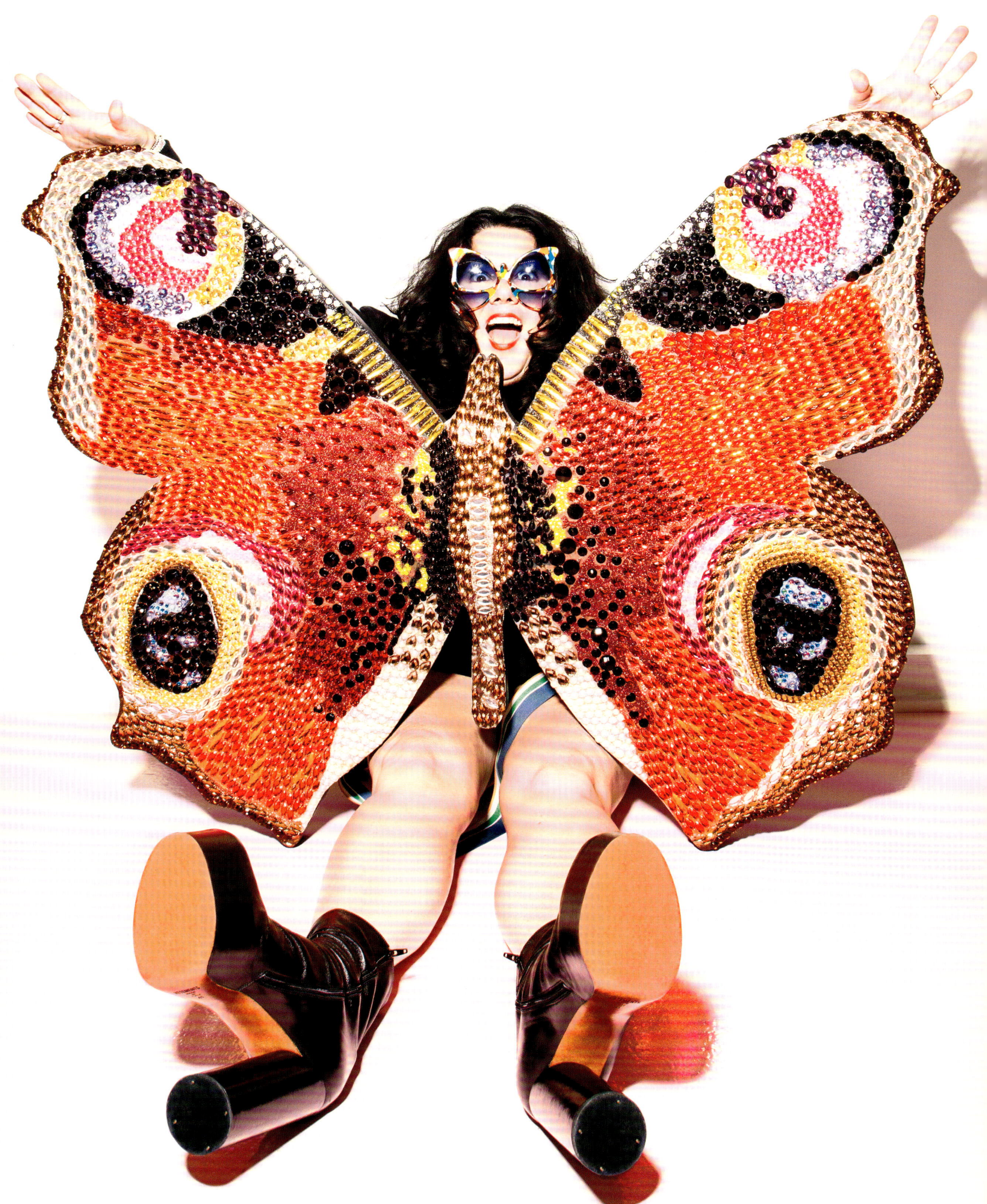

RENOWNED WOMEN

I am in Awe
of women..
especialy
Mothers..
The women before
me make me
wanna be my
VERY BEST!!..

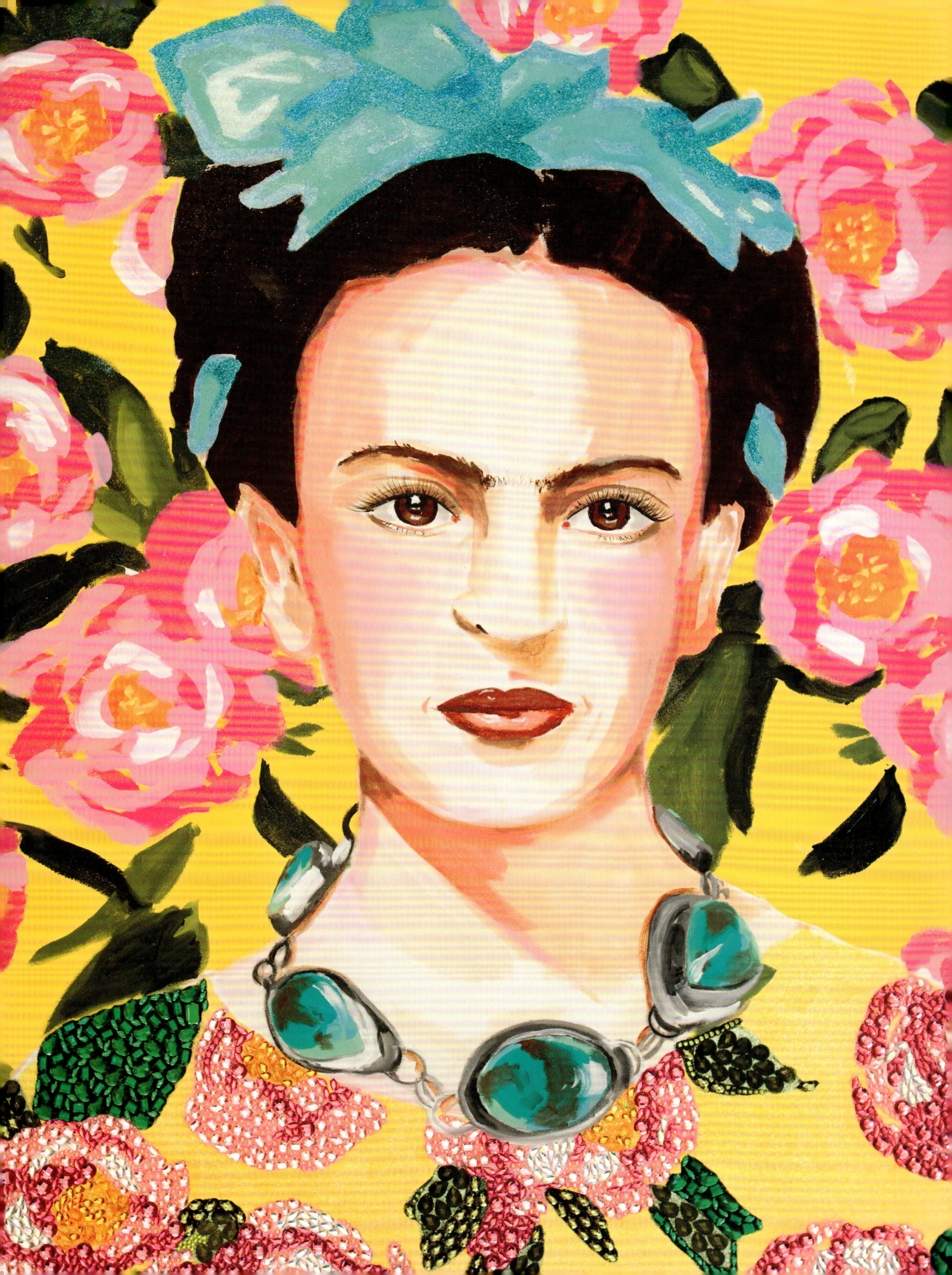

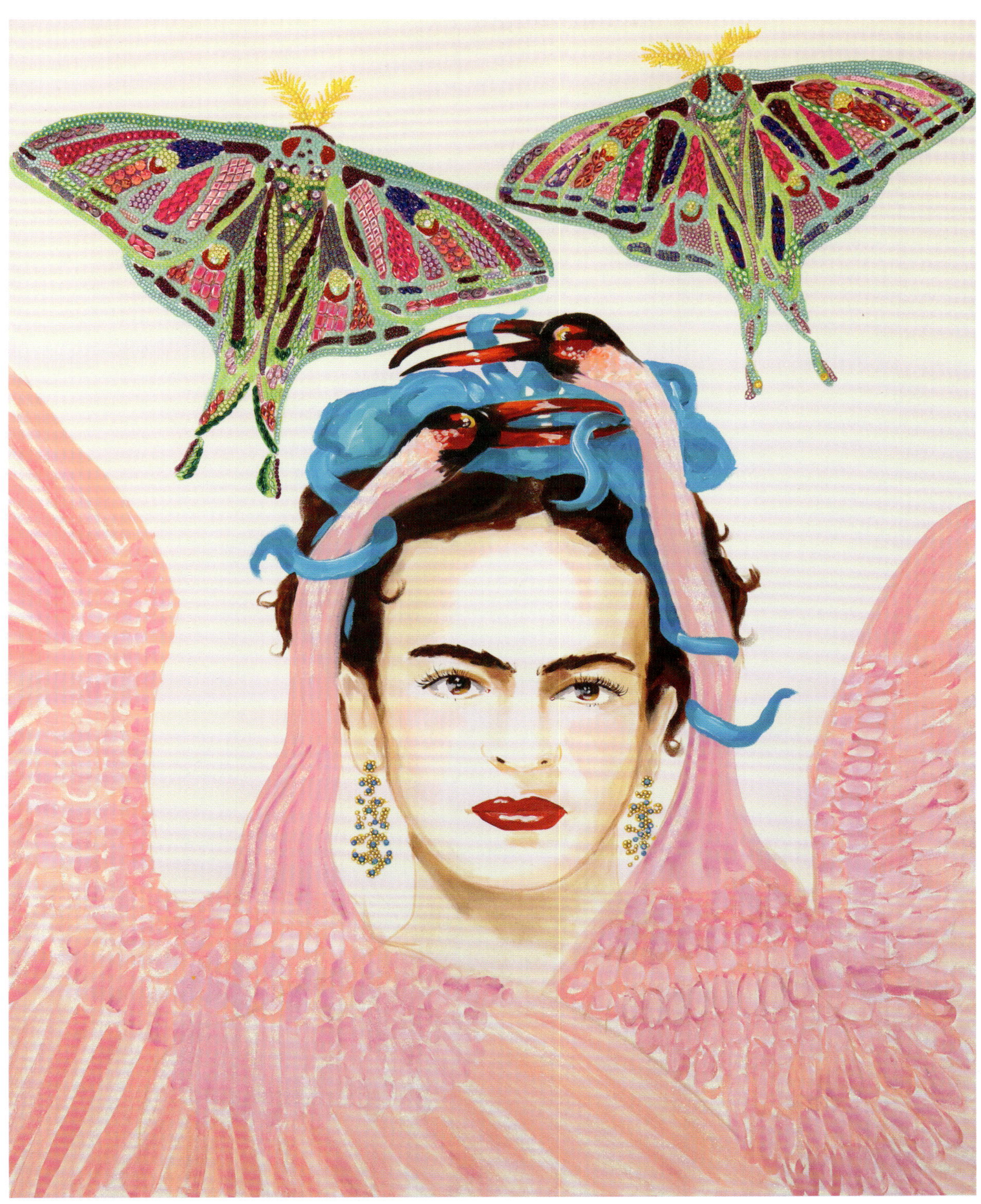

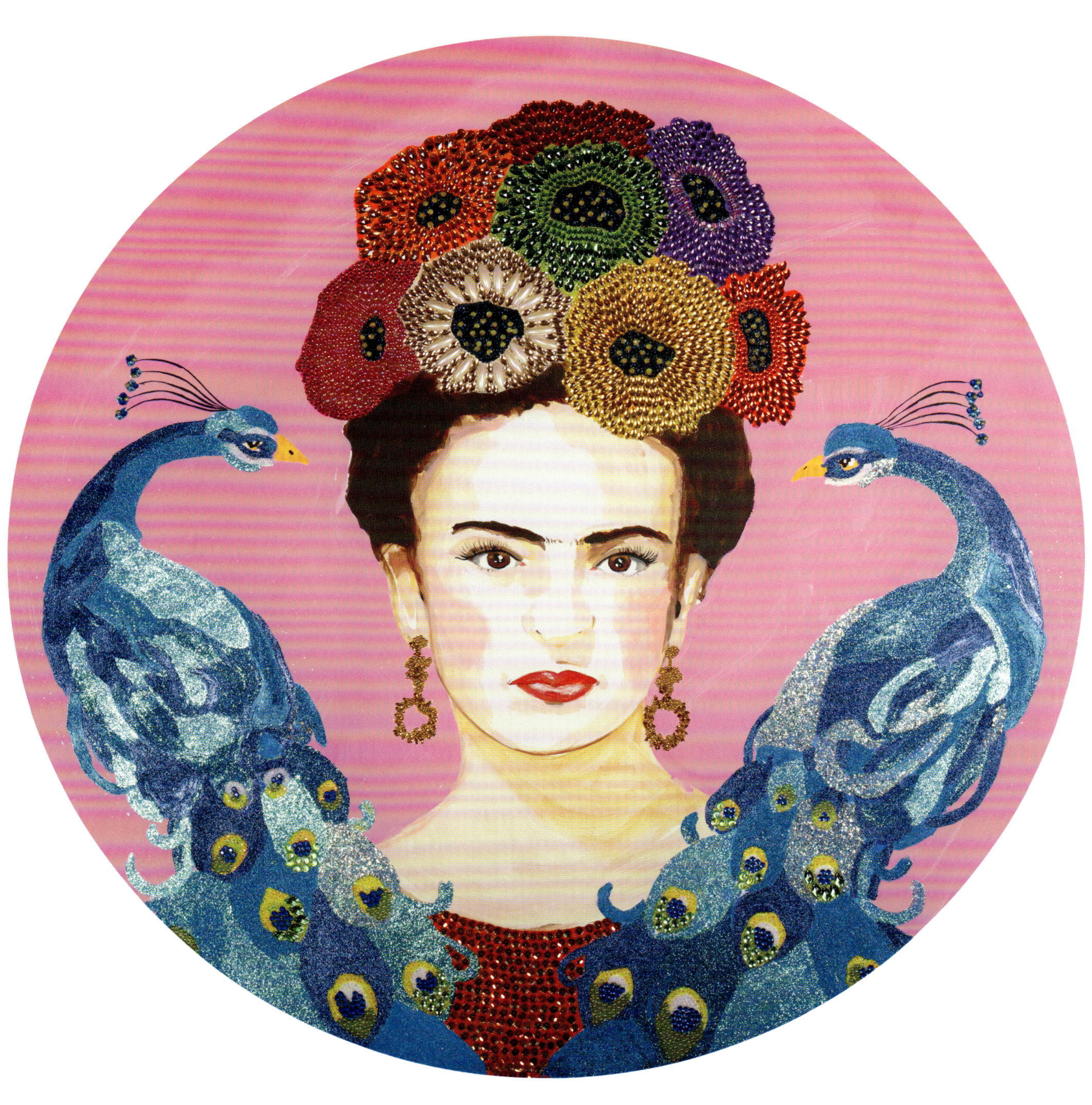

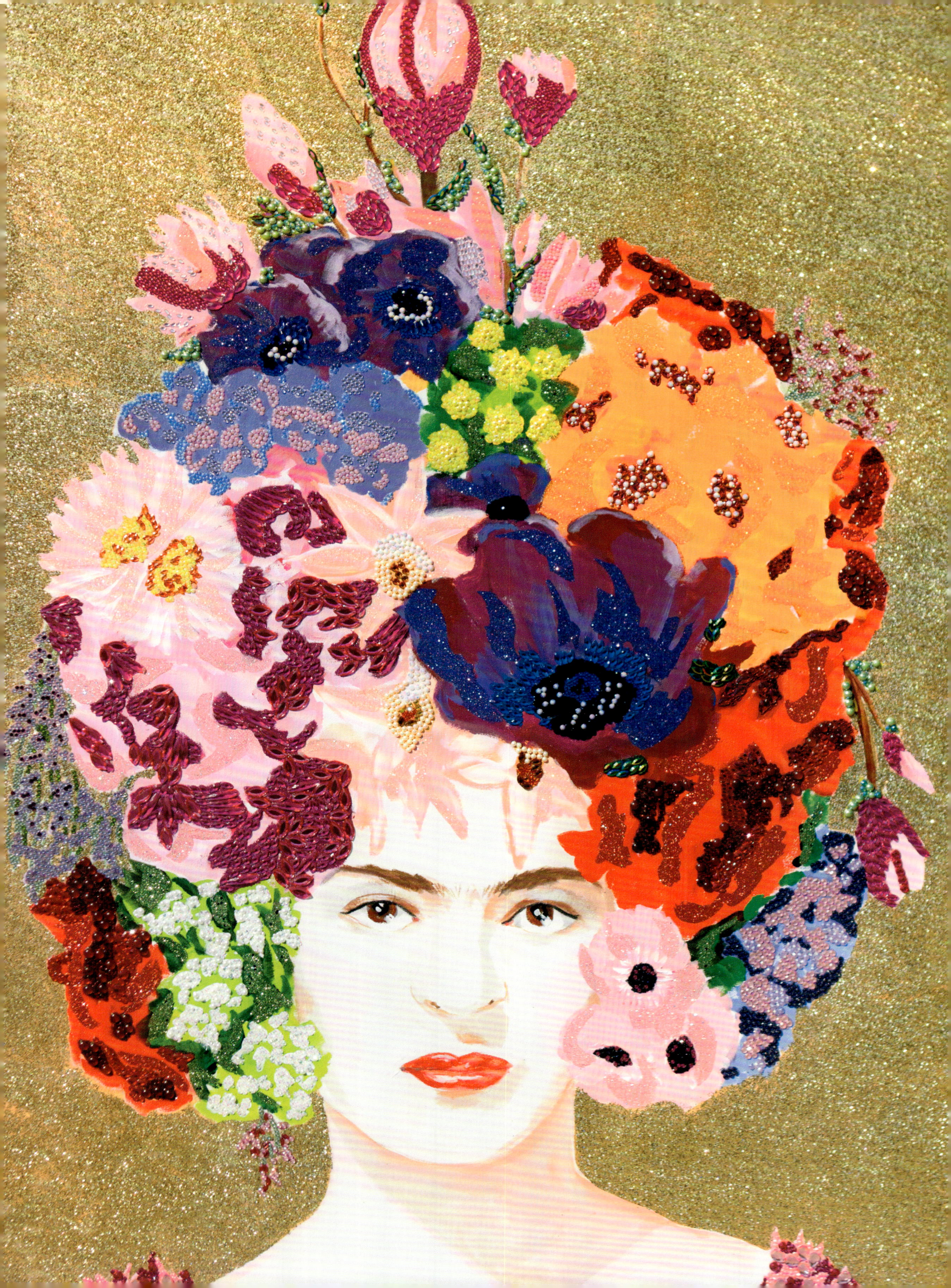

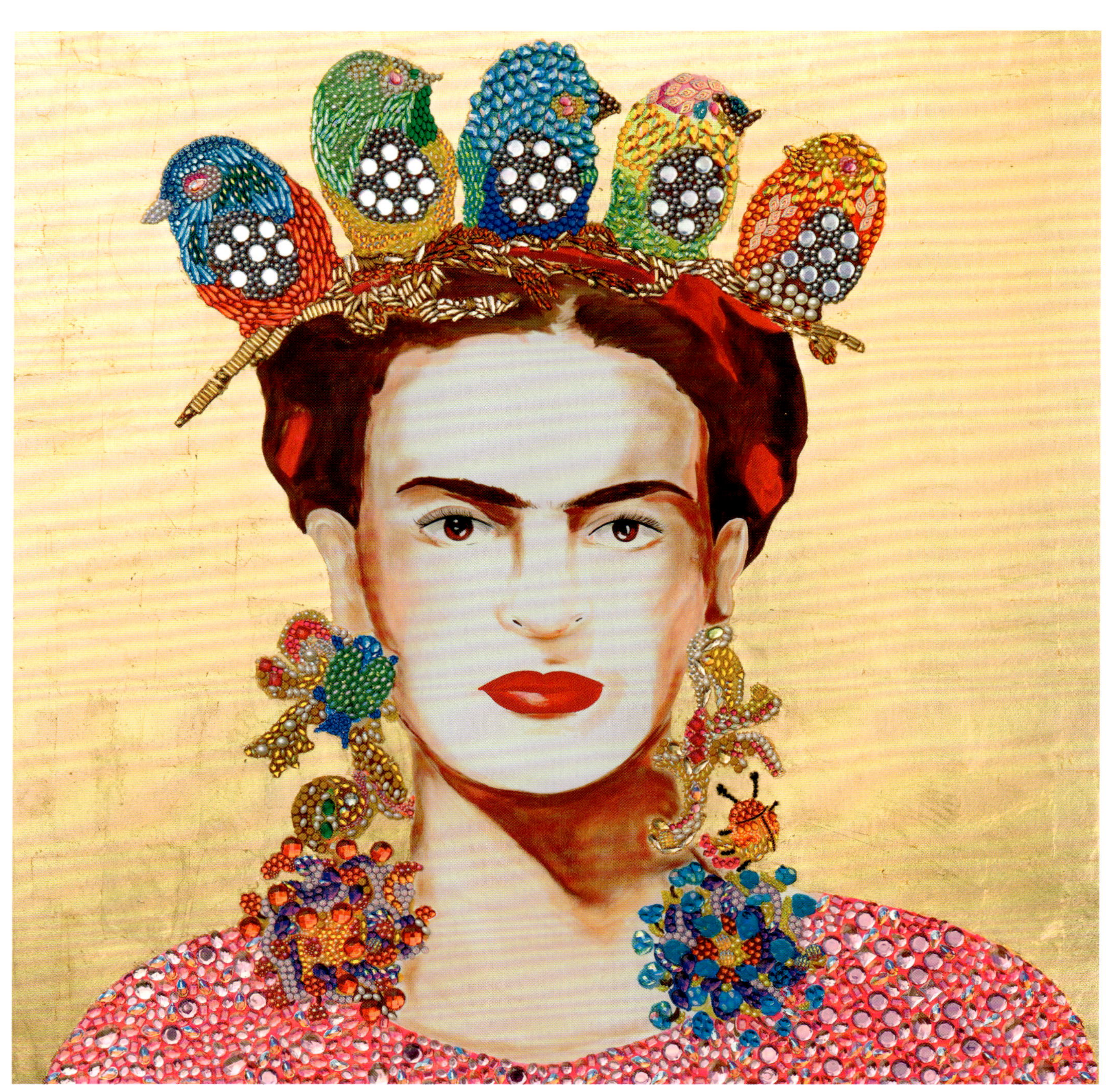

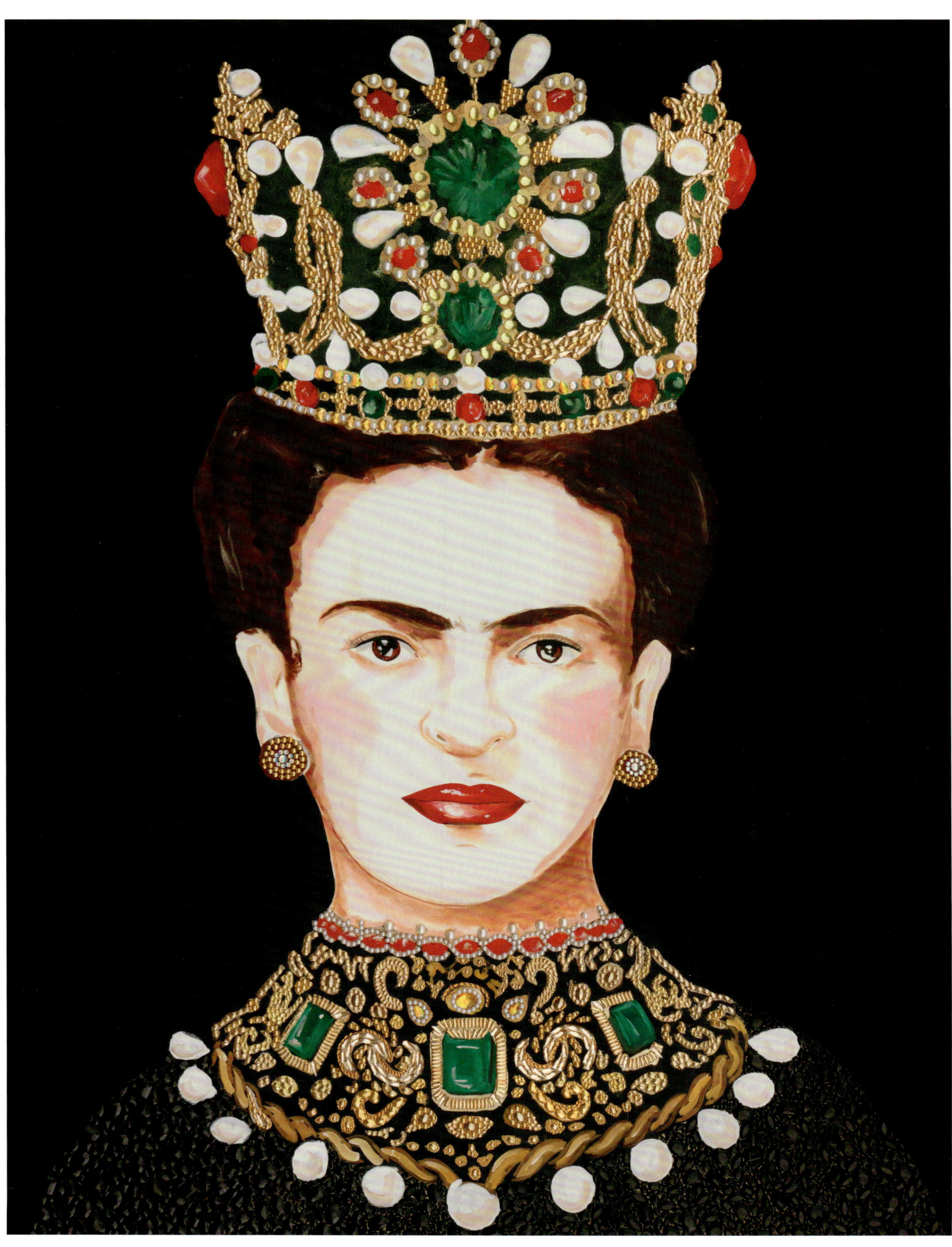

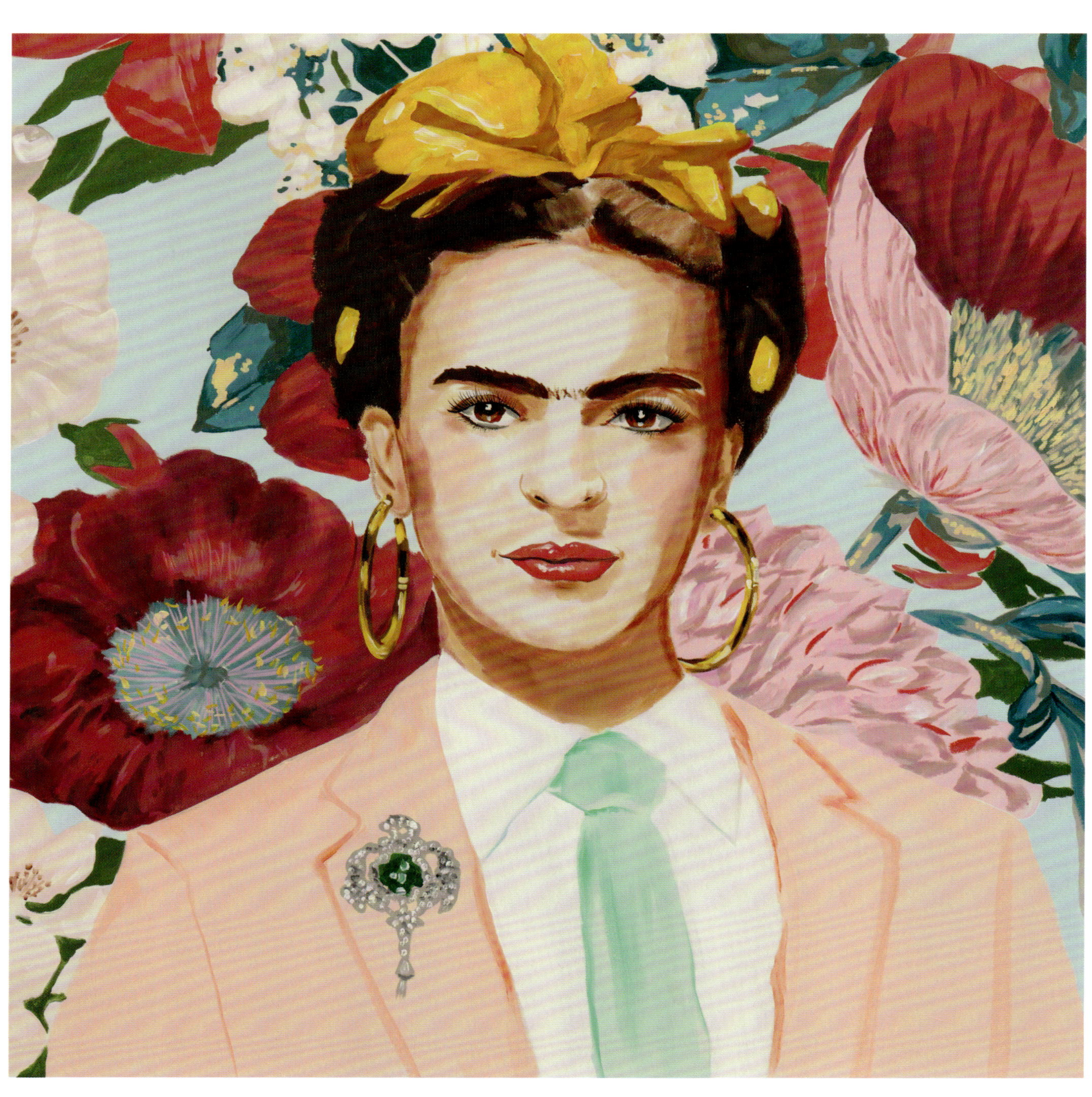

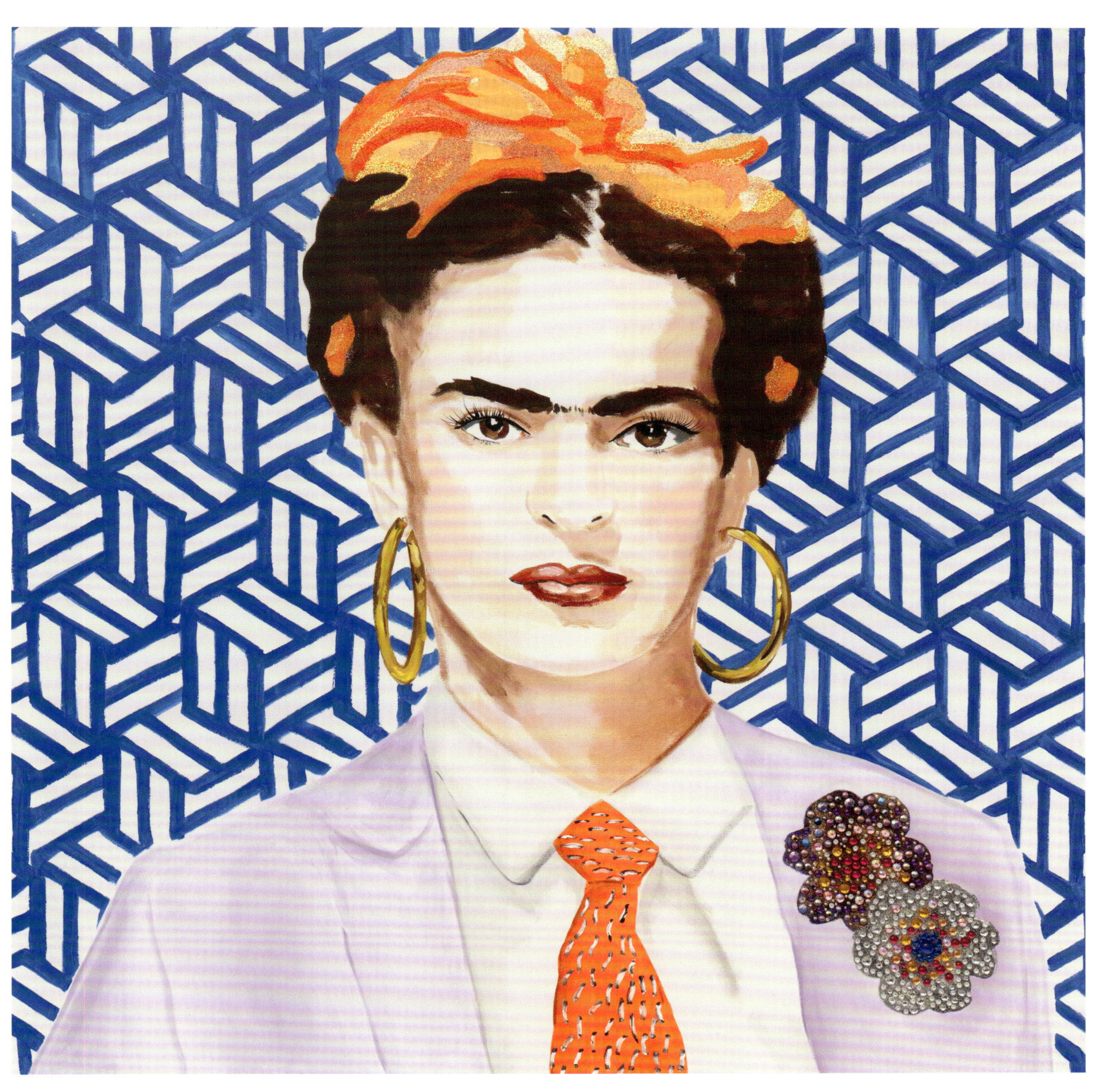

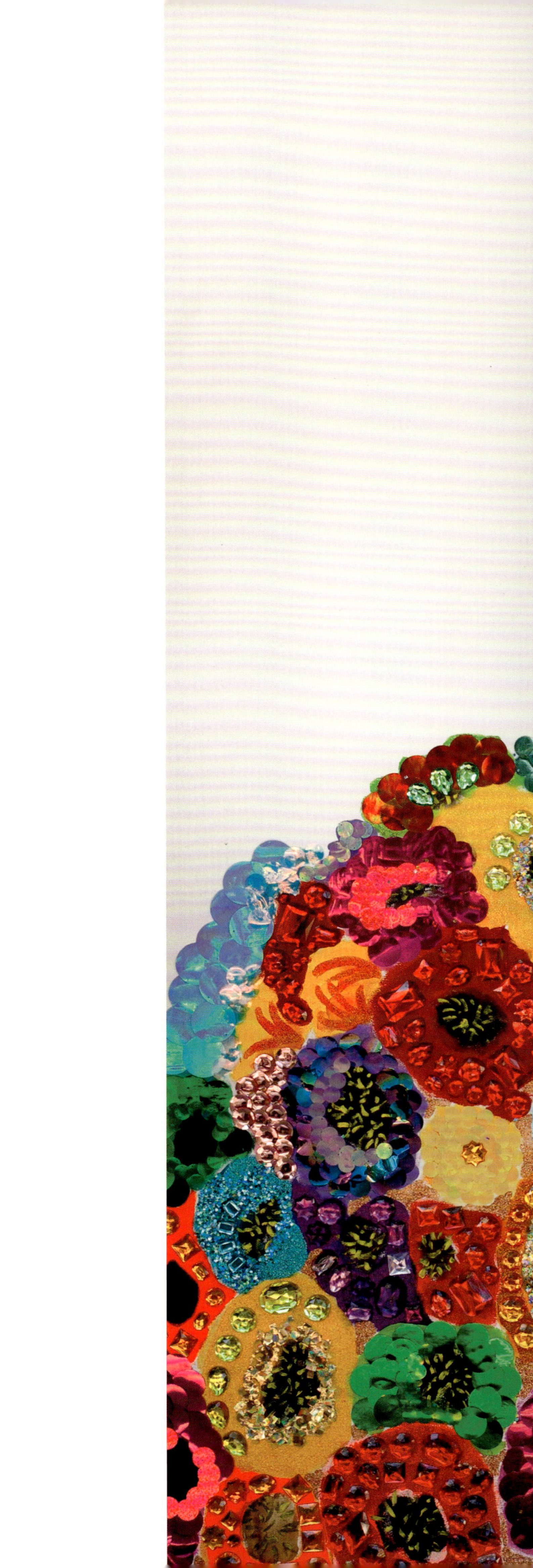

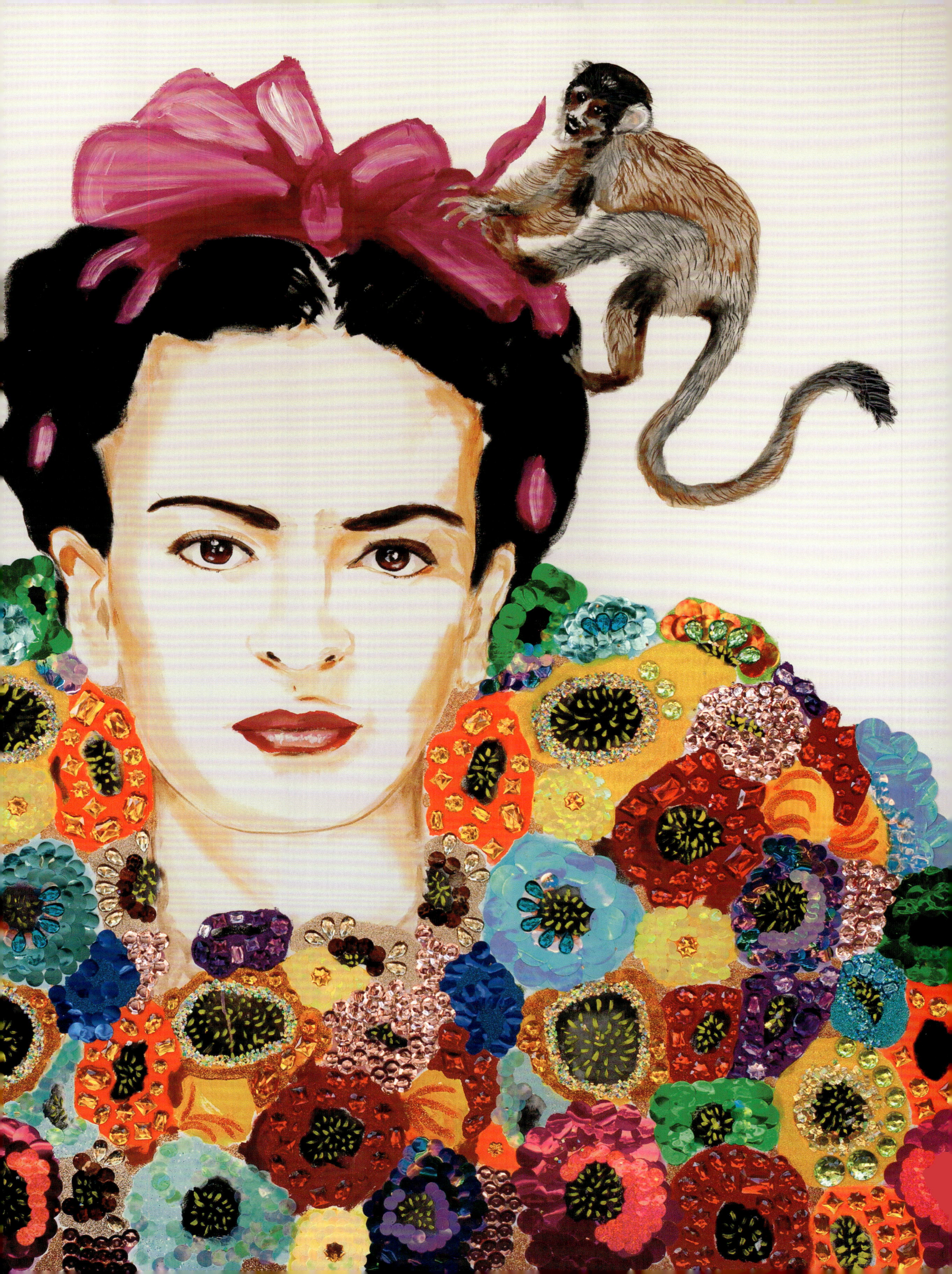

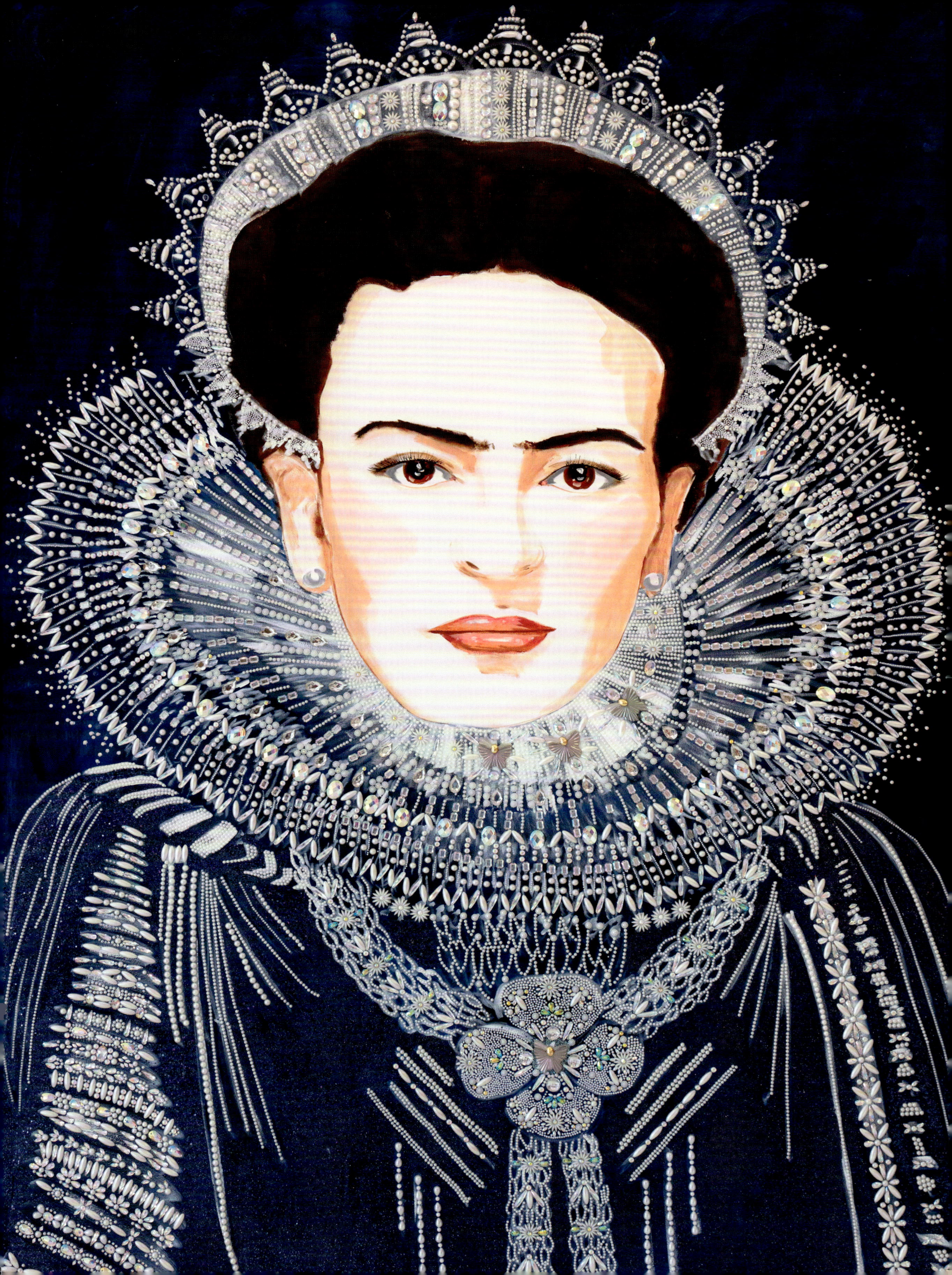

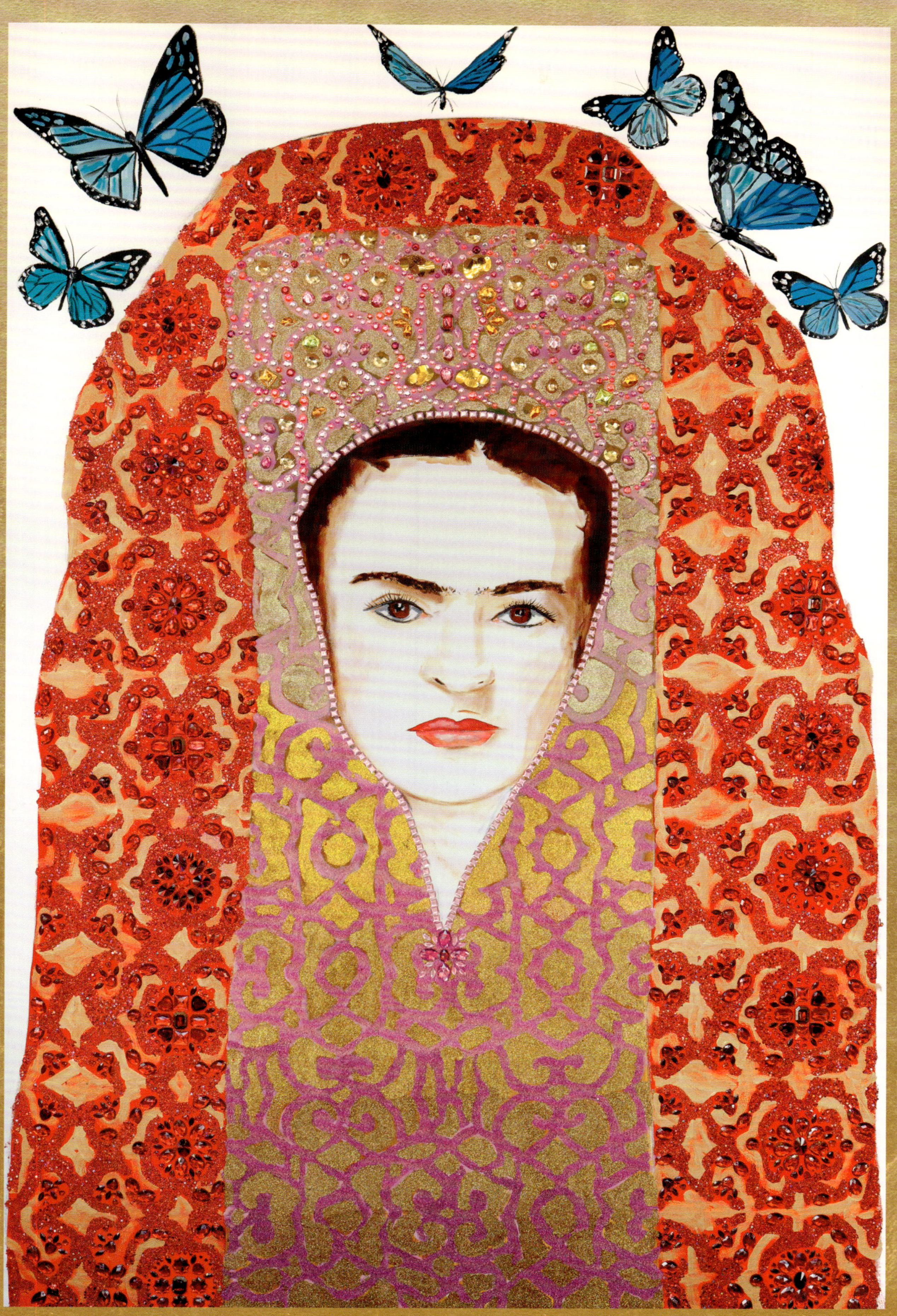

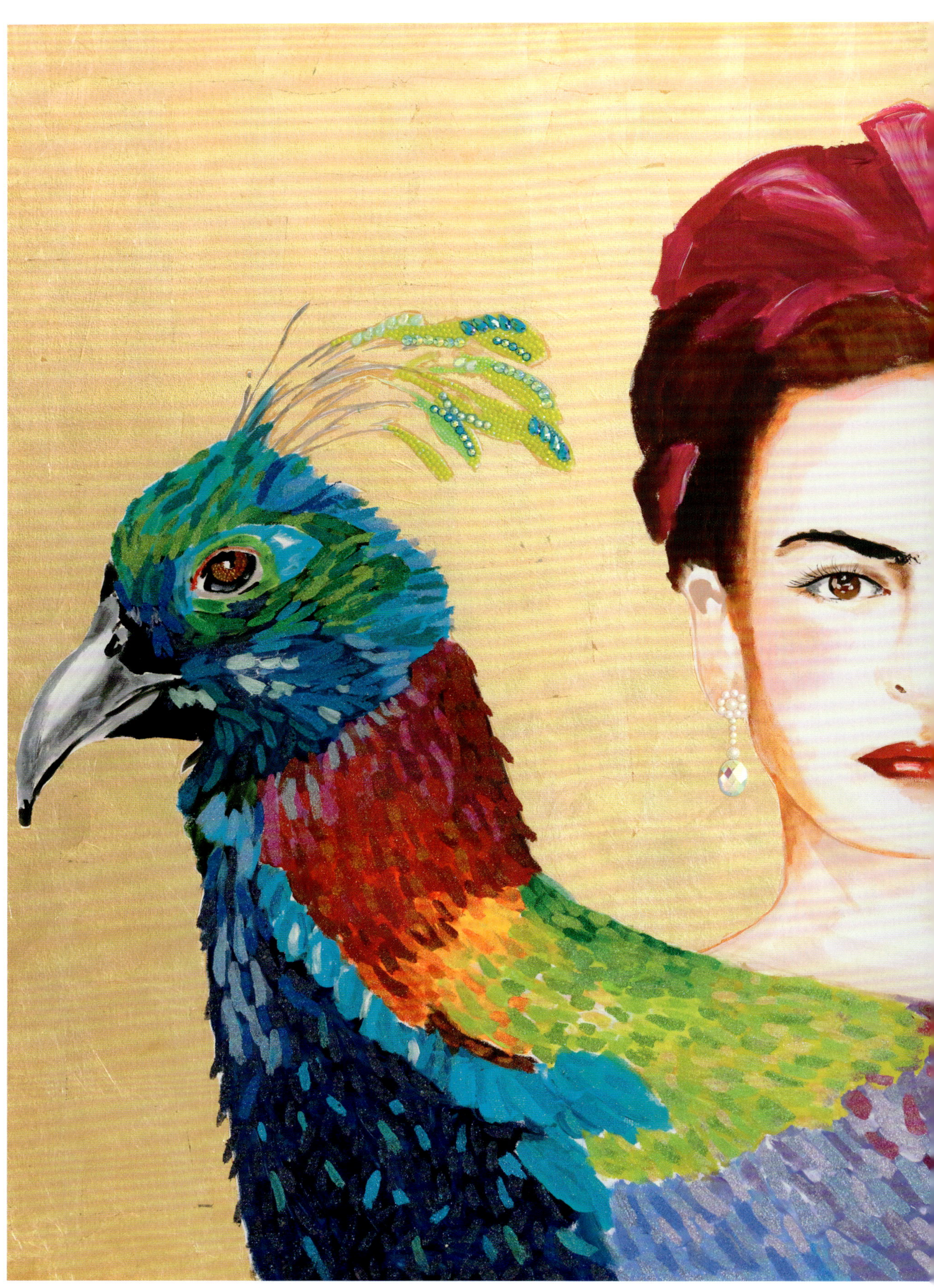

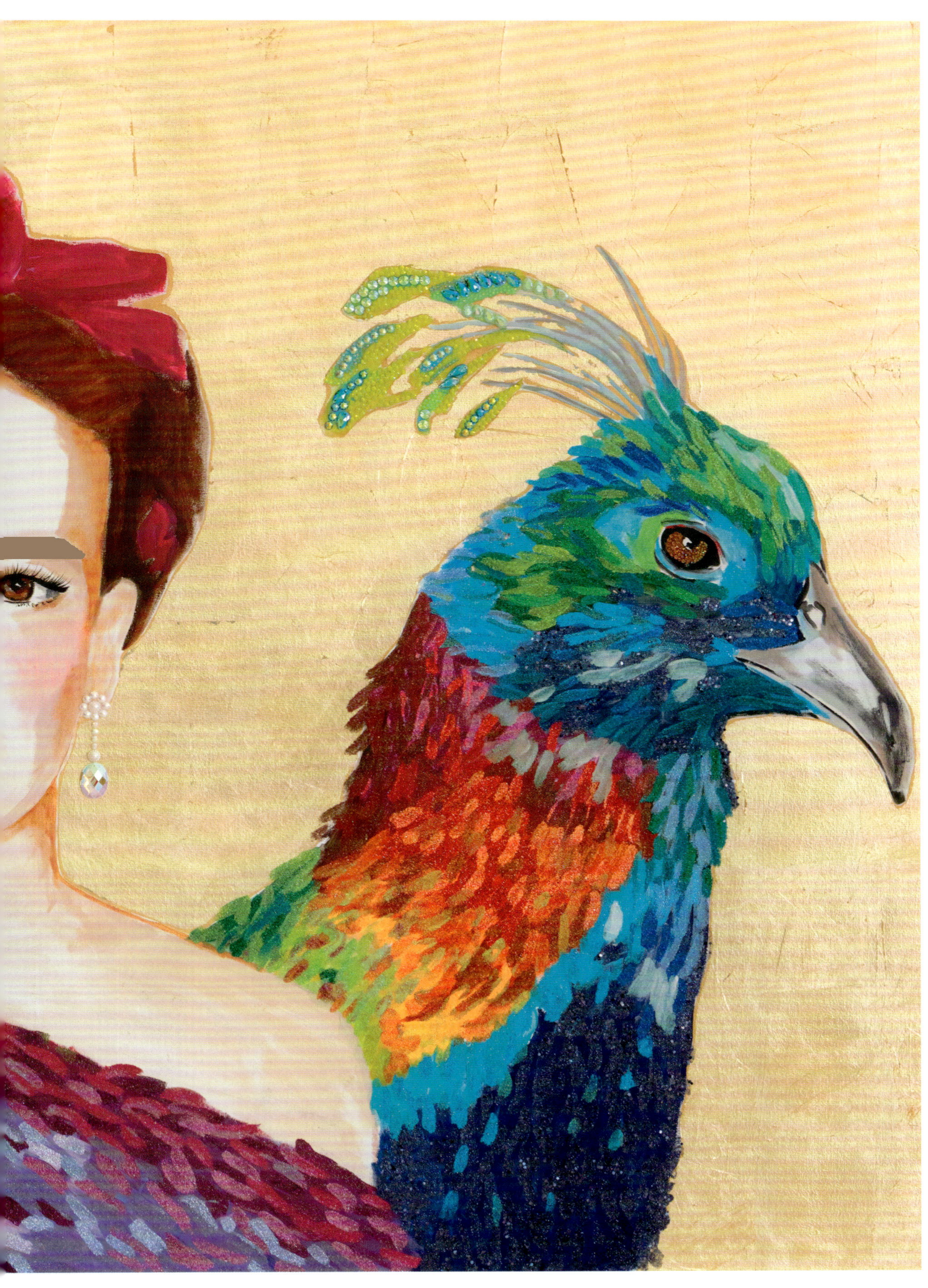

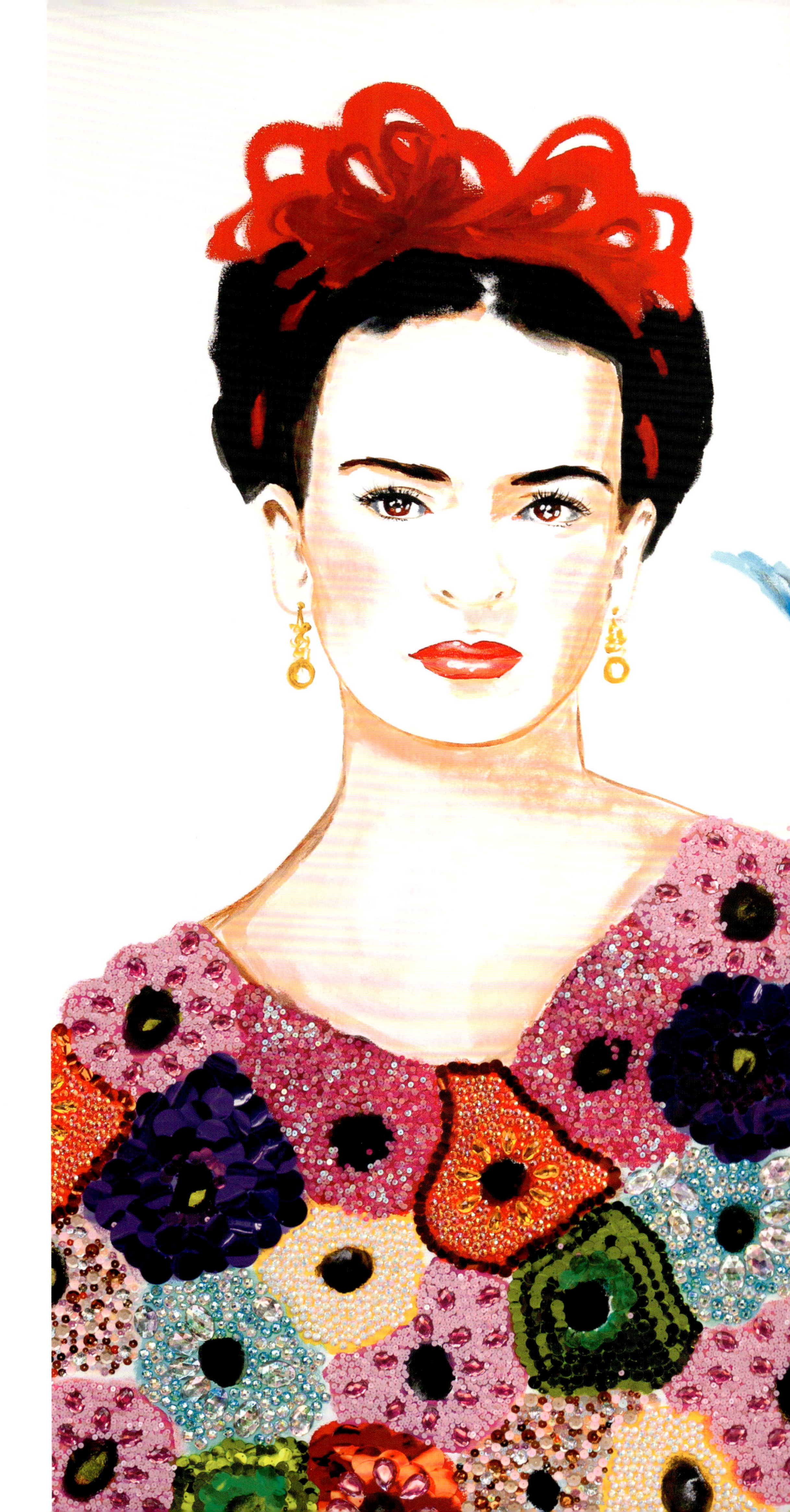

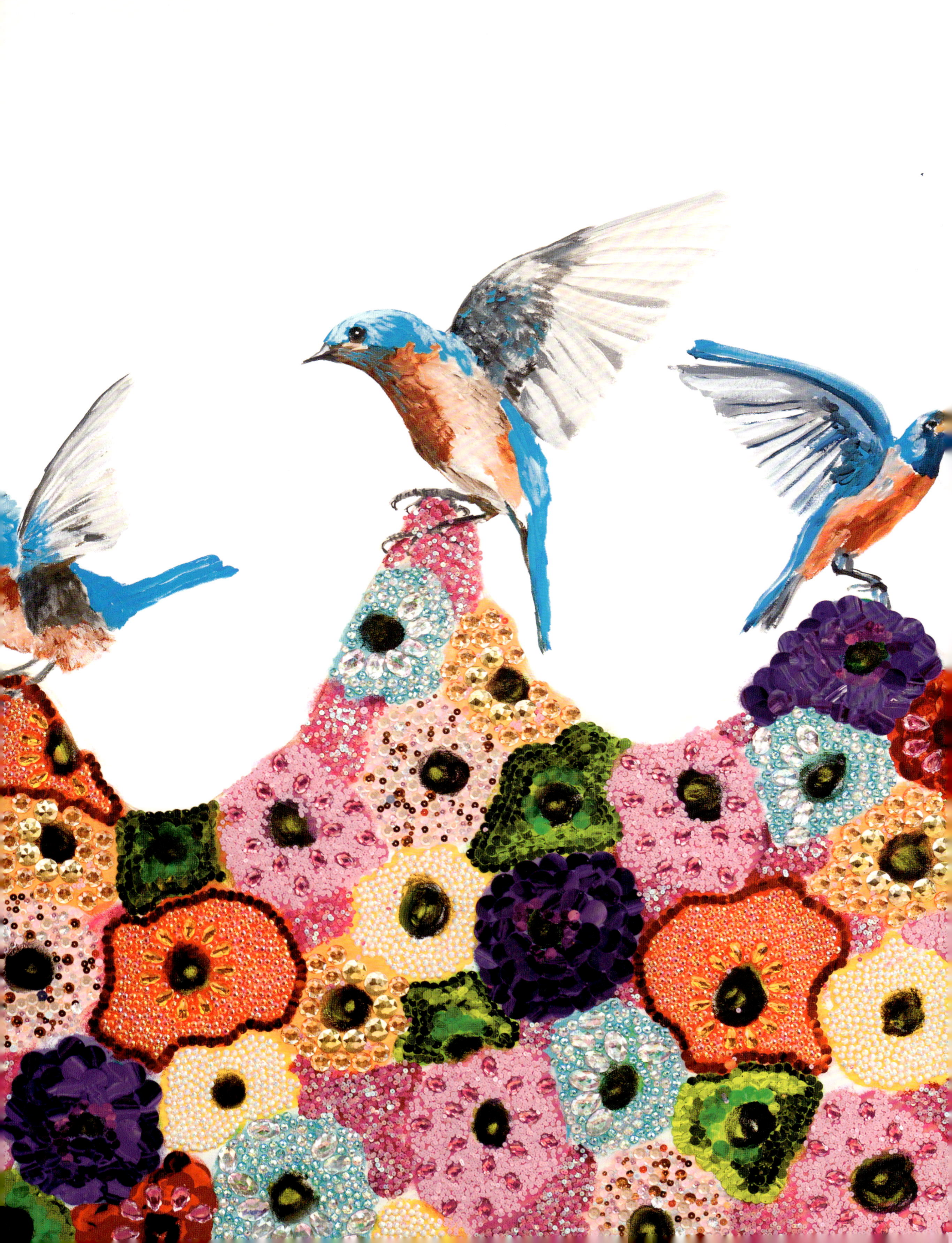

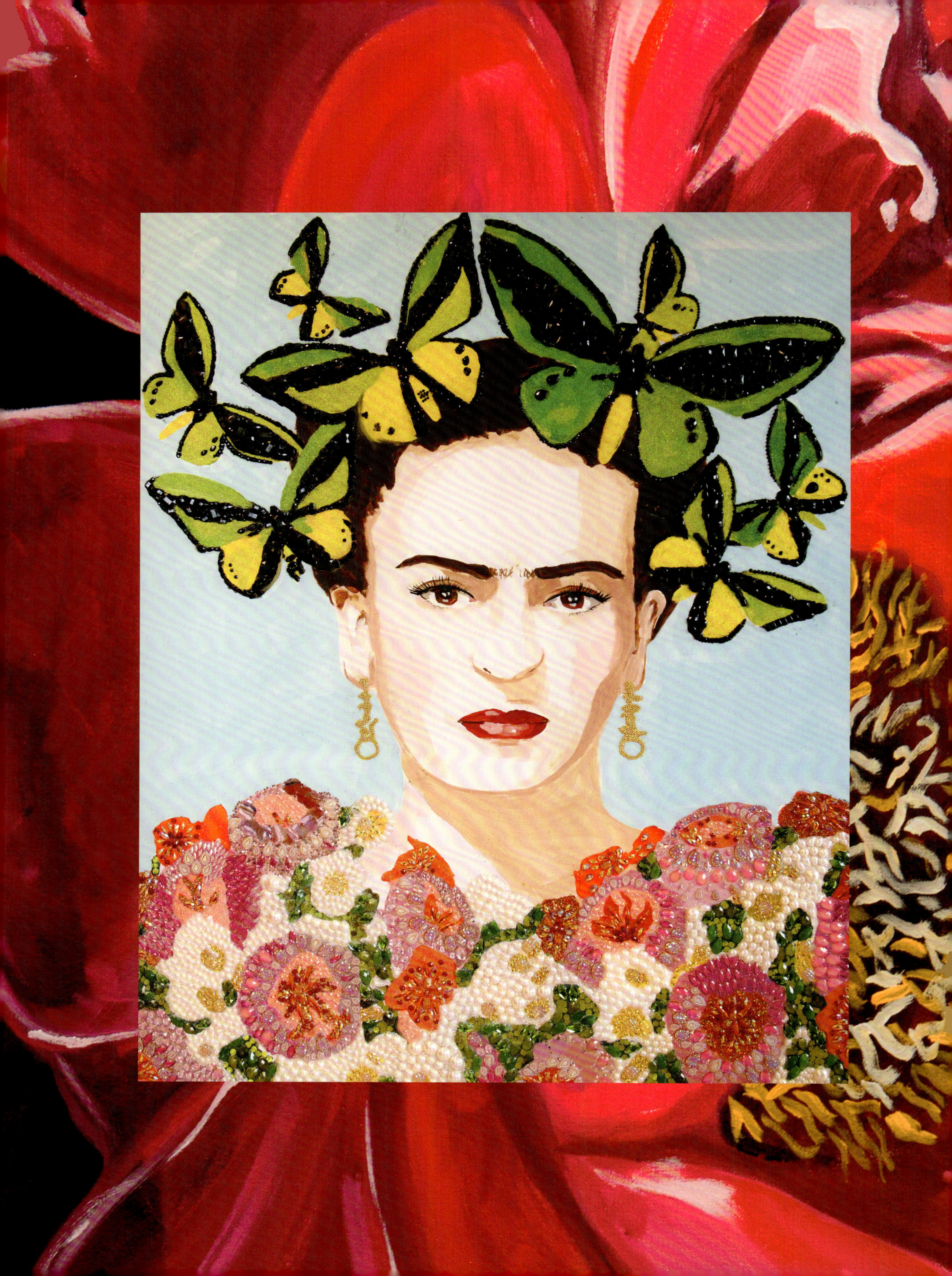

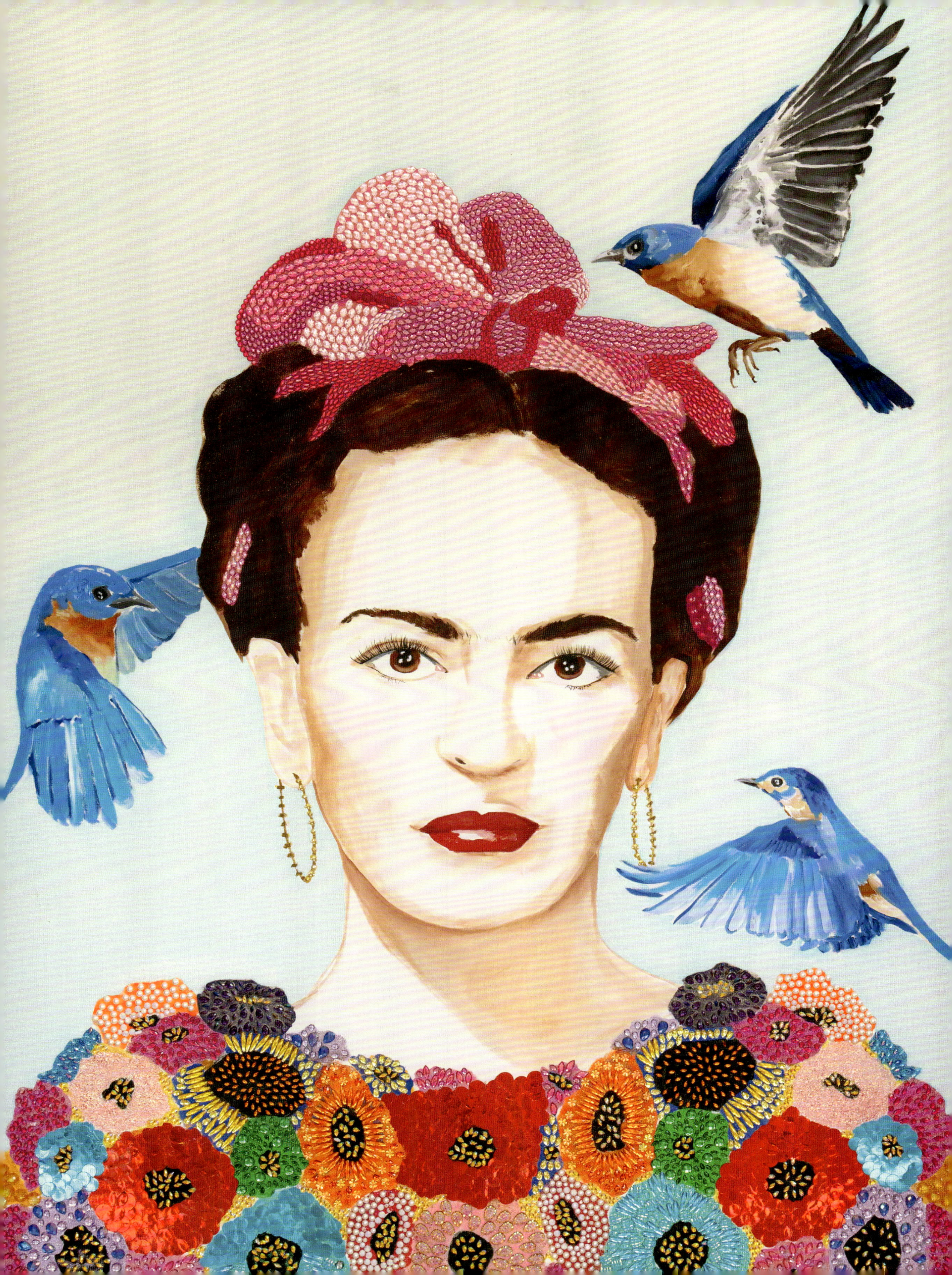

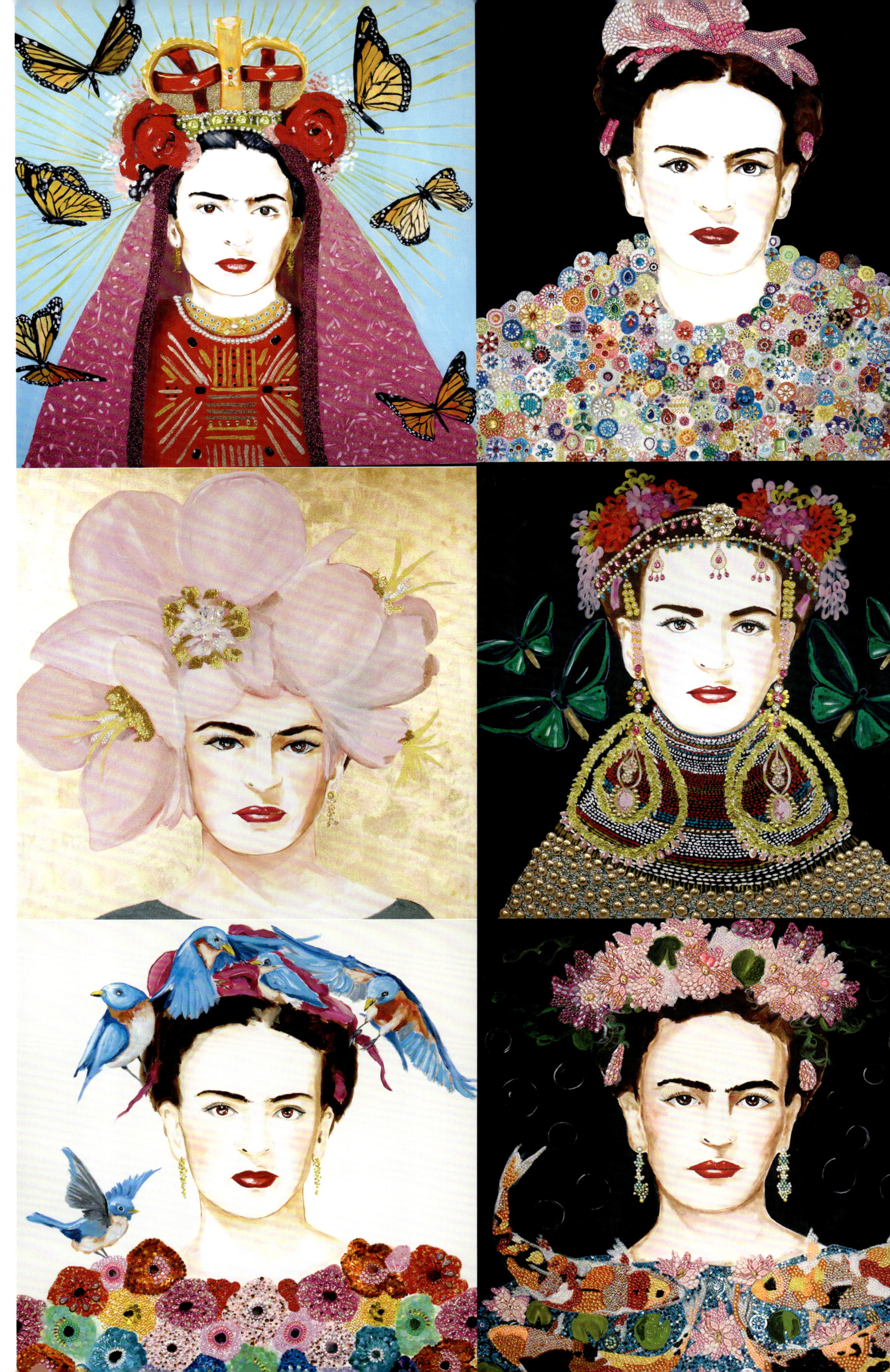

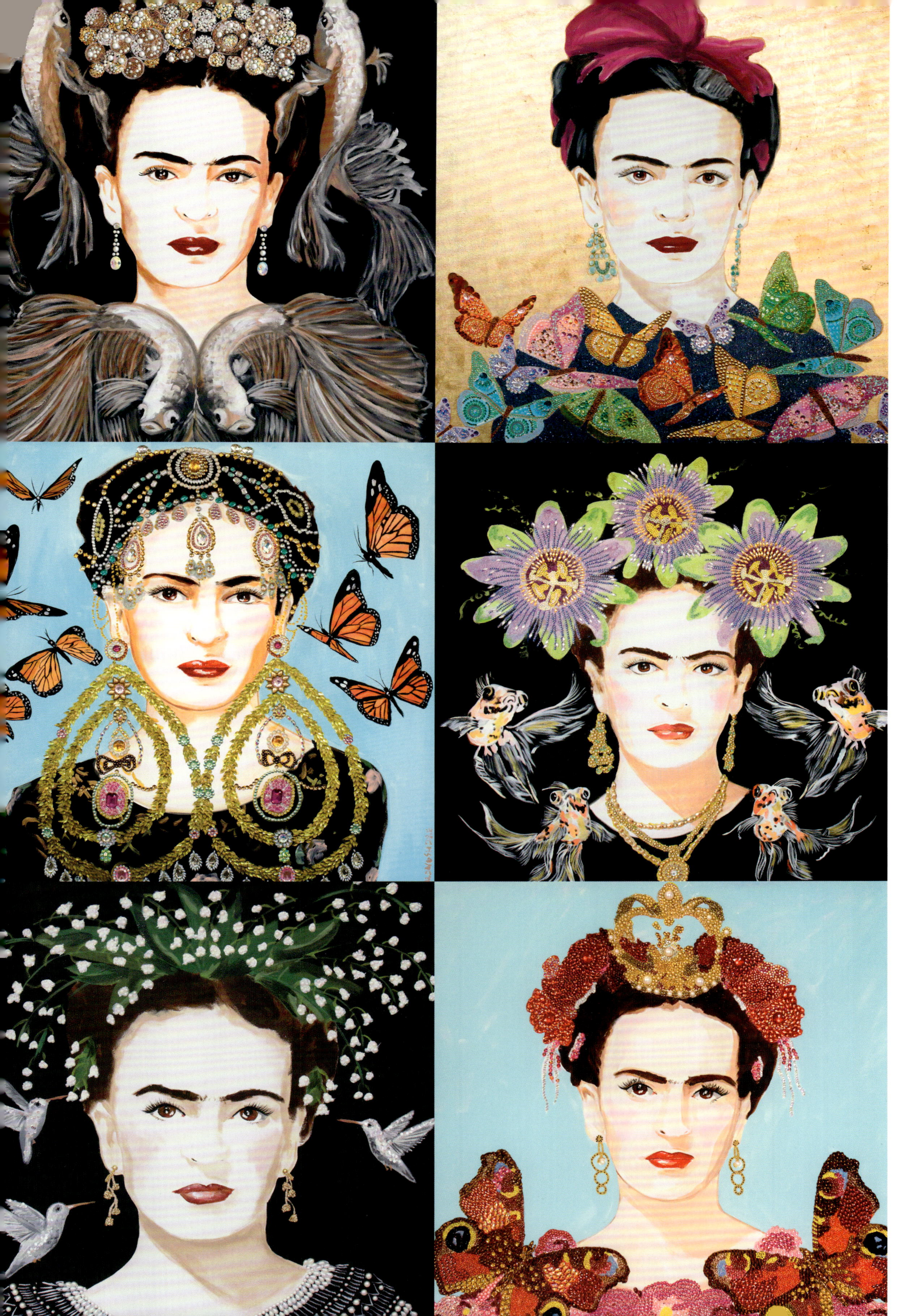

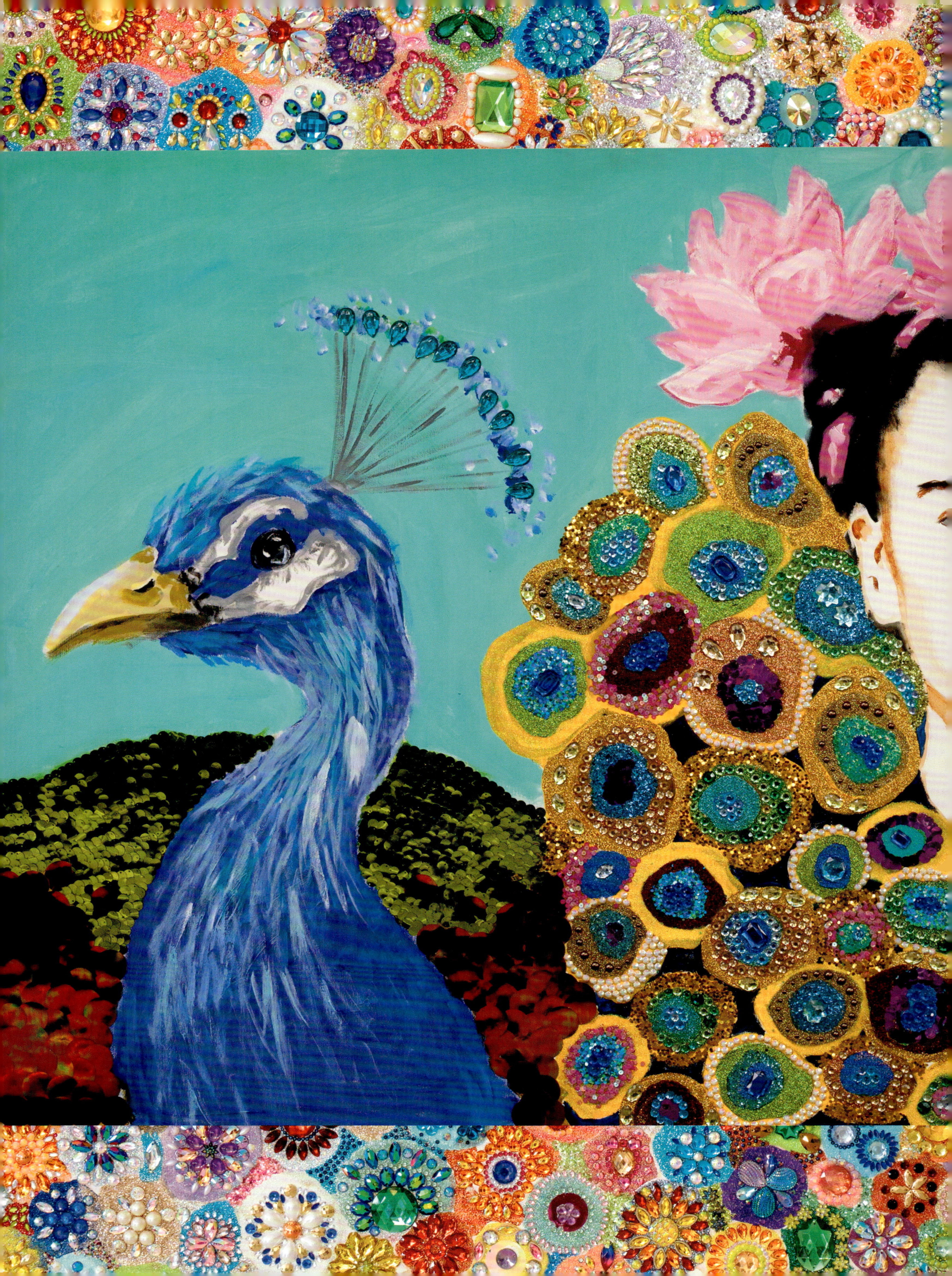

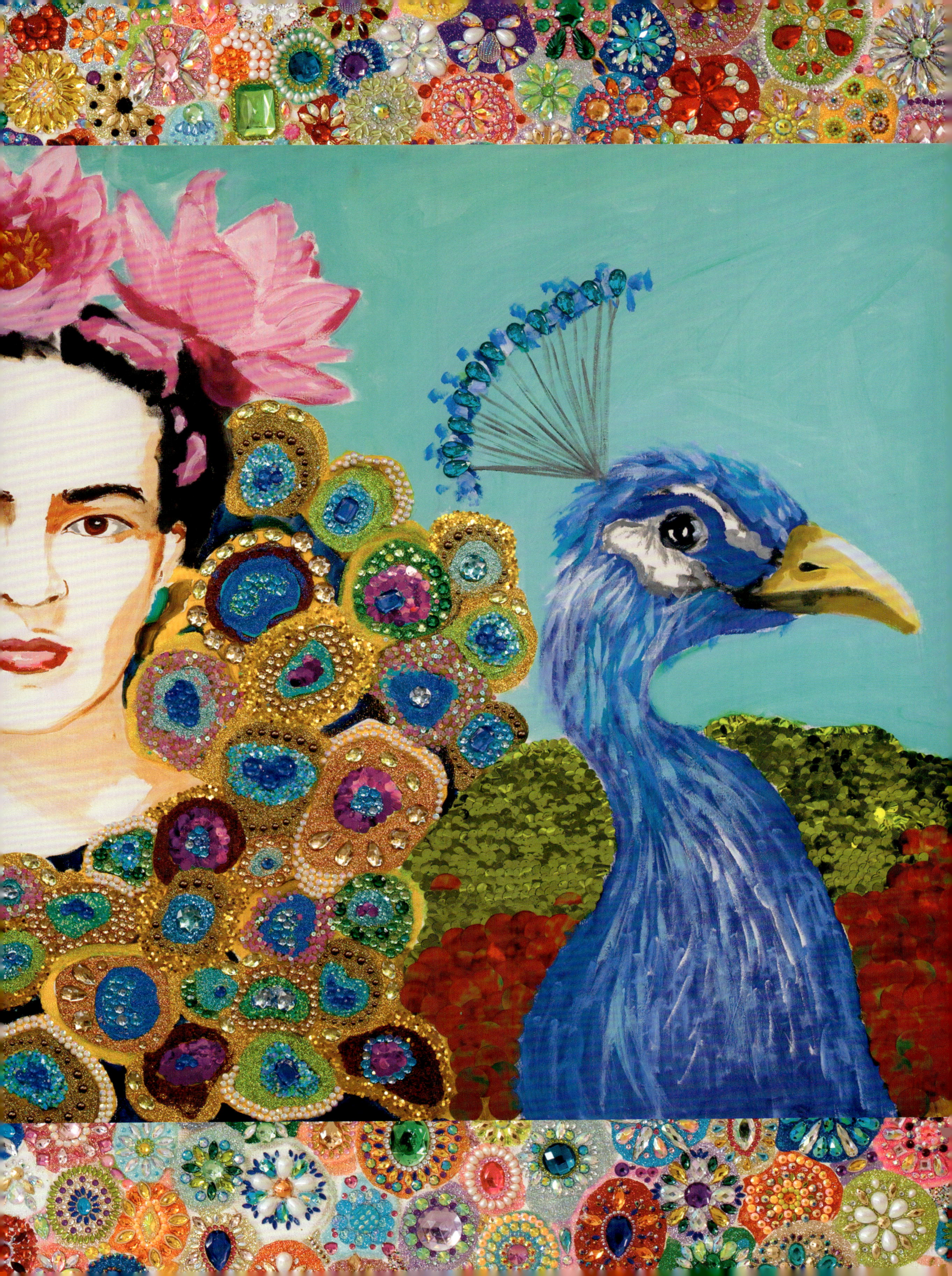

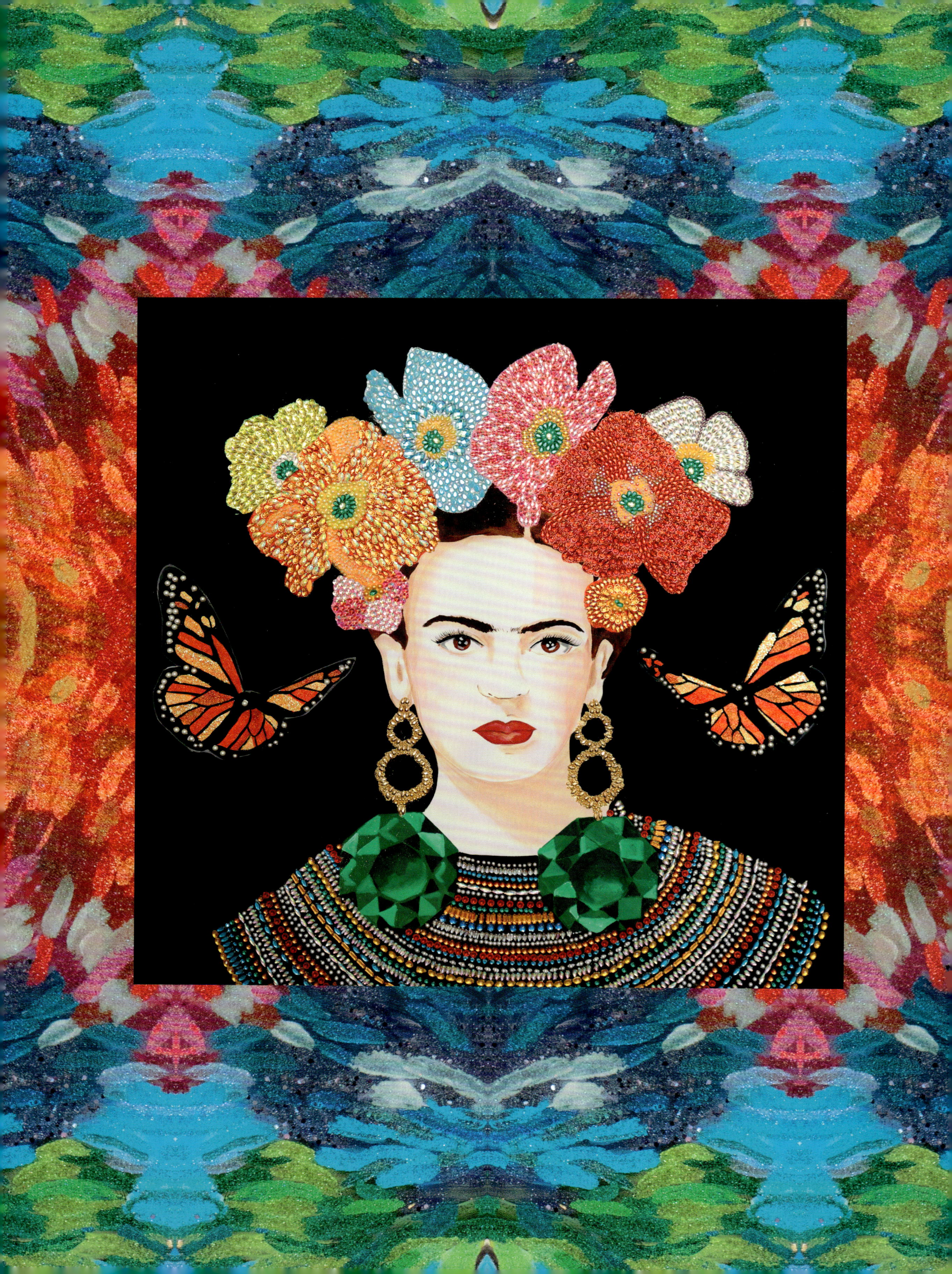

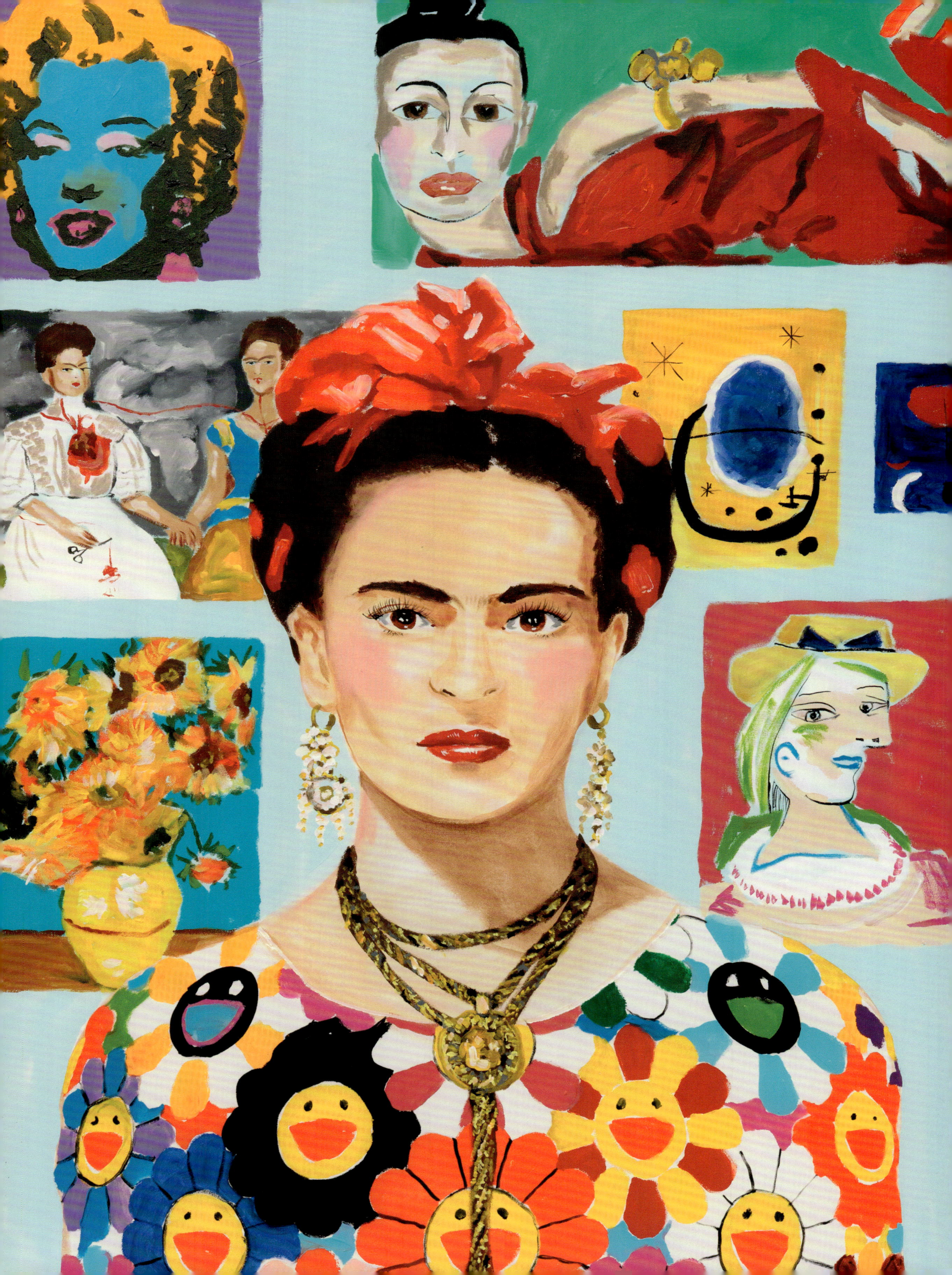

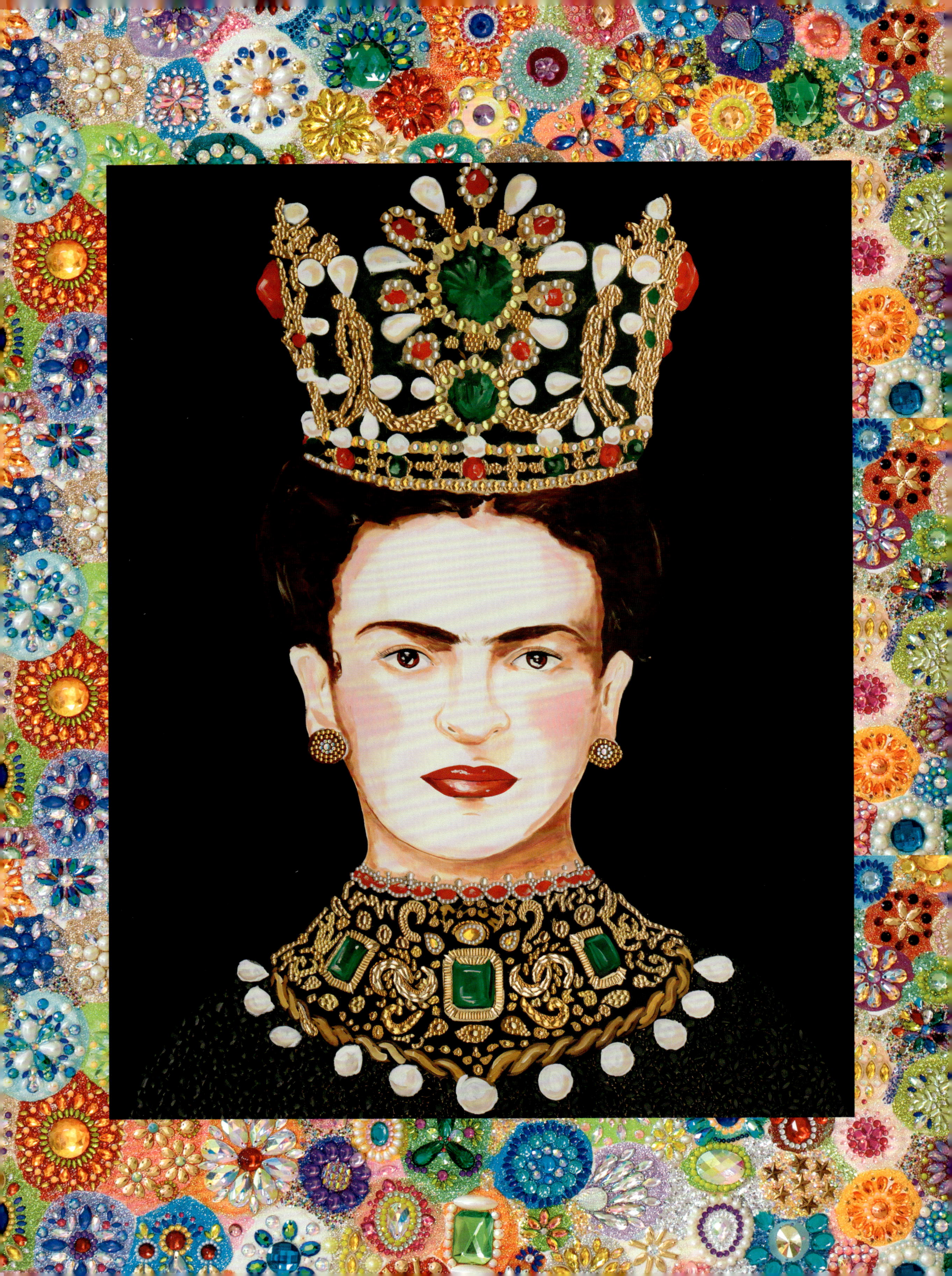

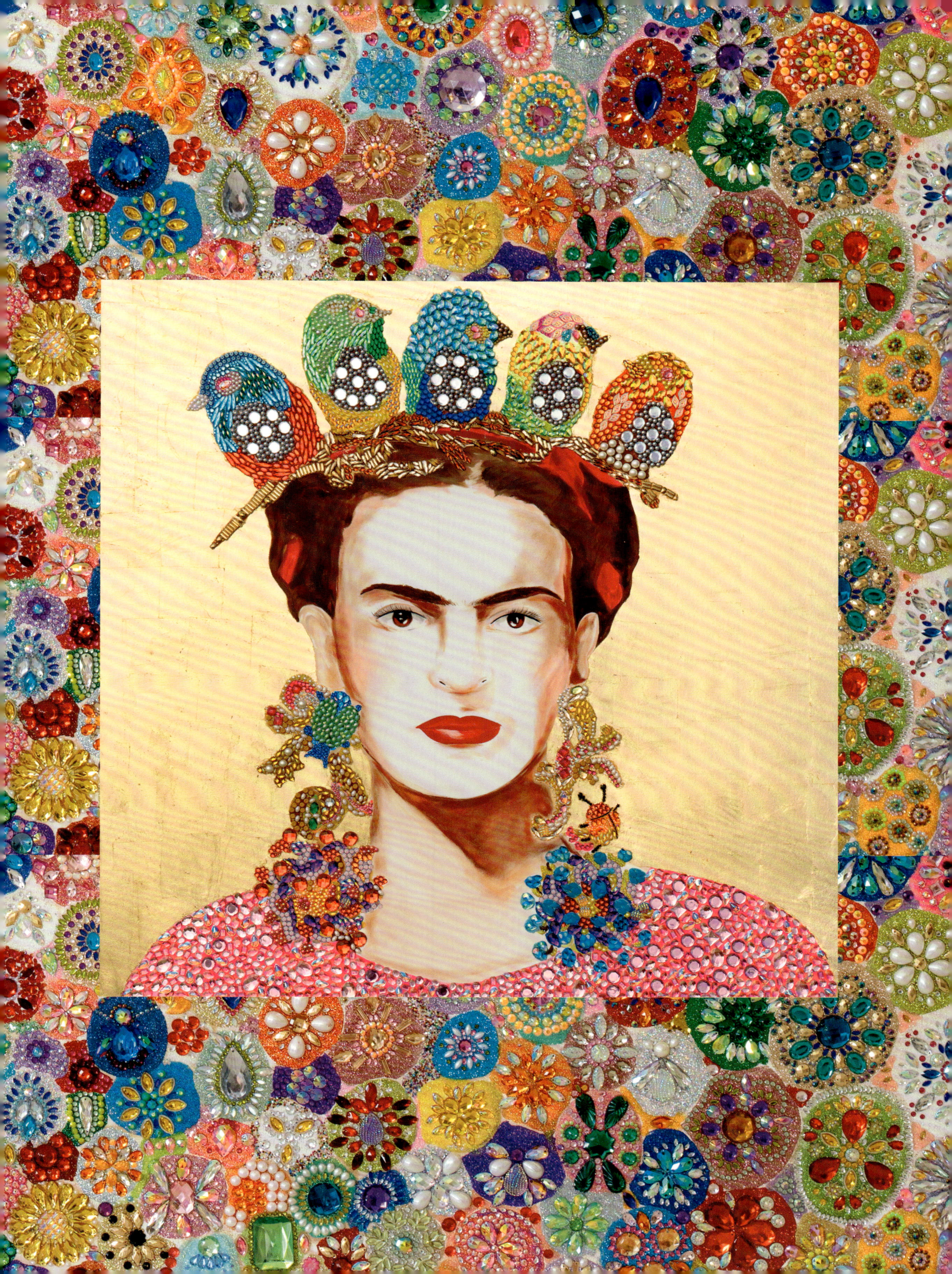

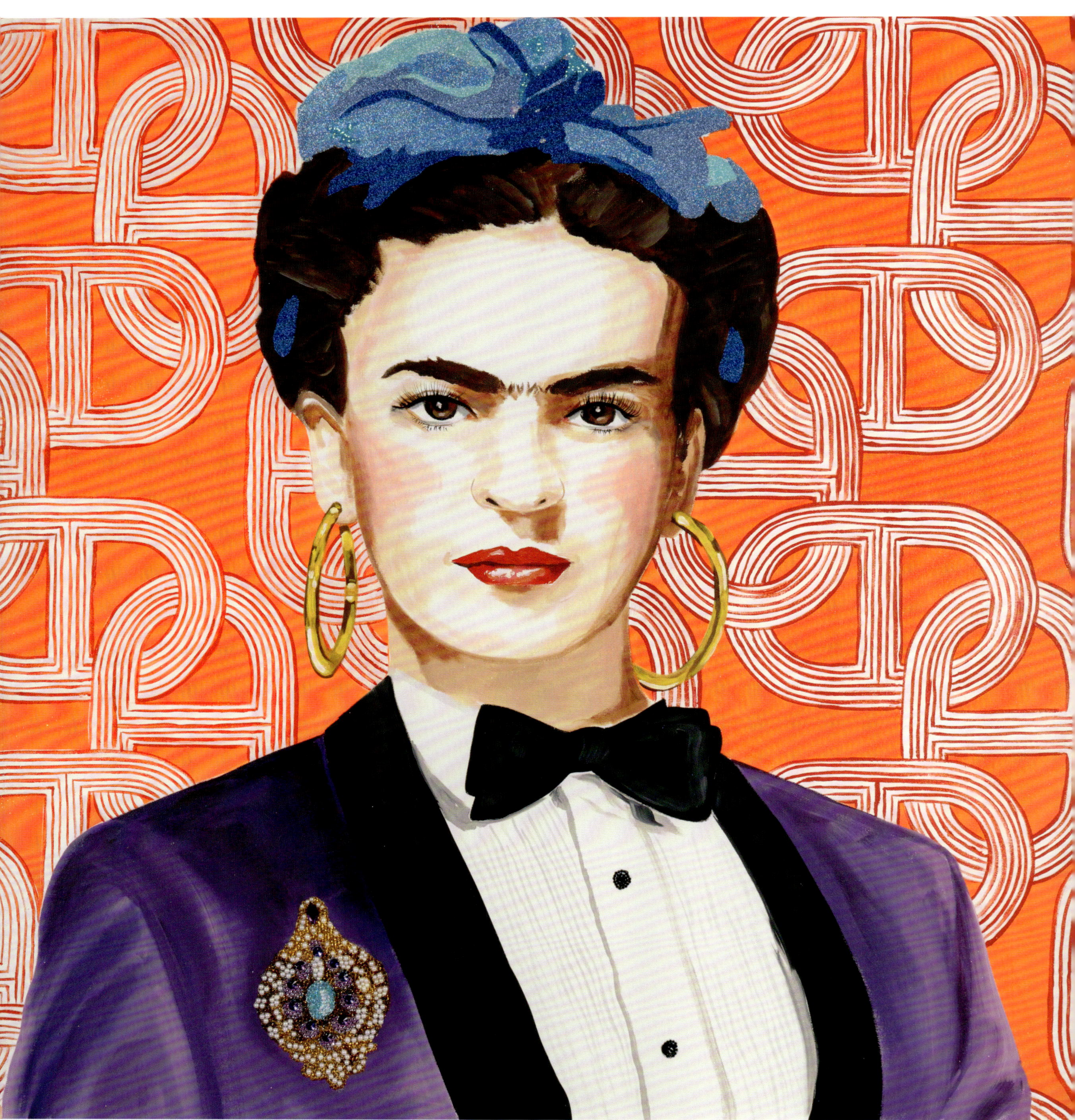

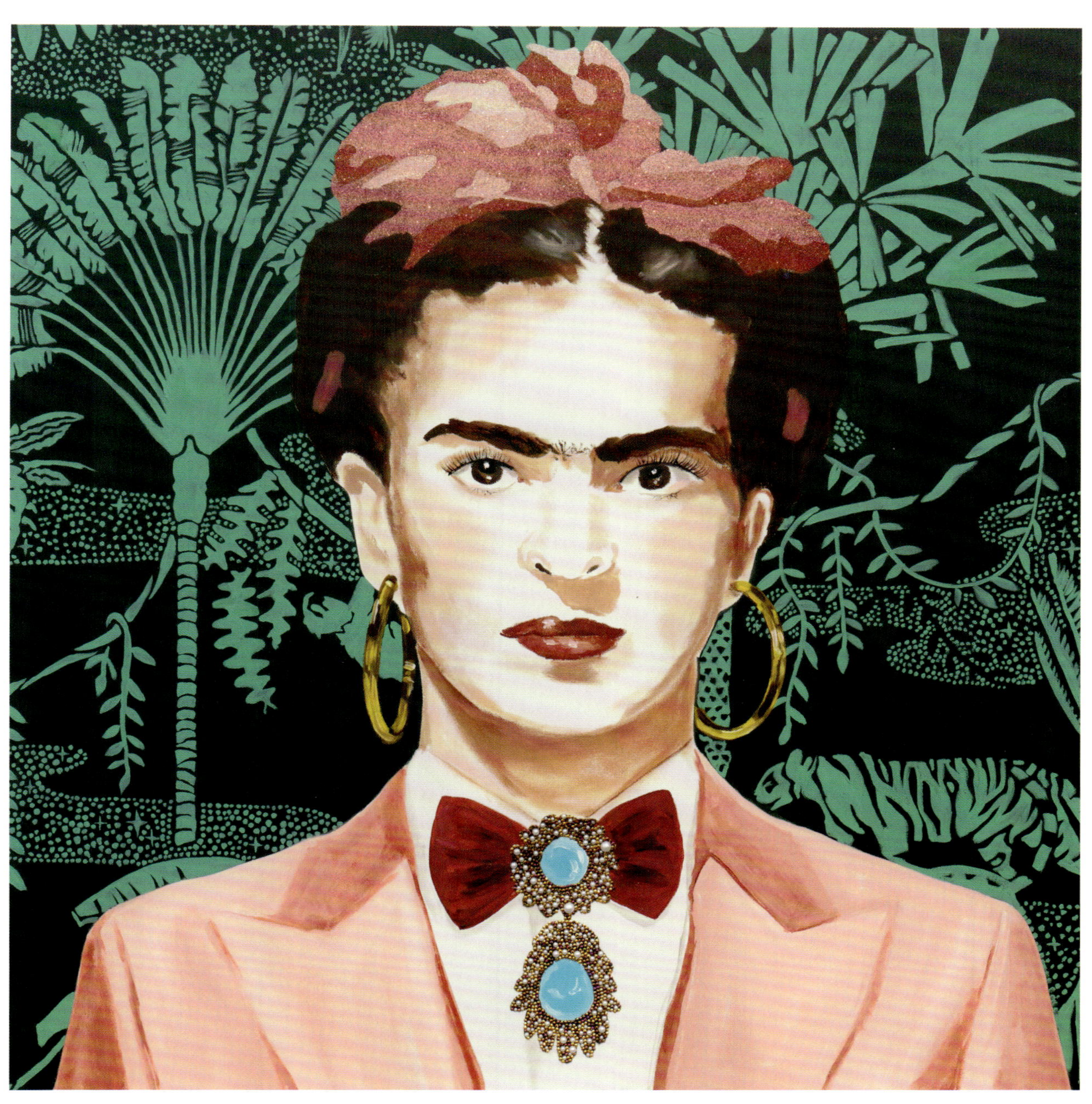

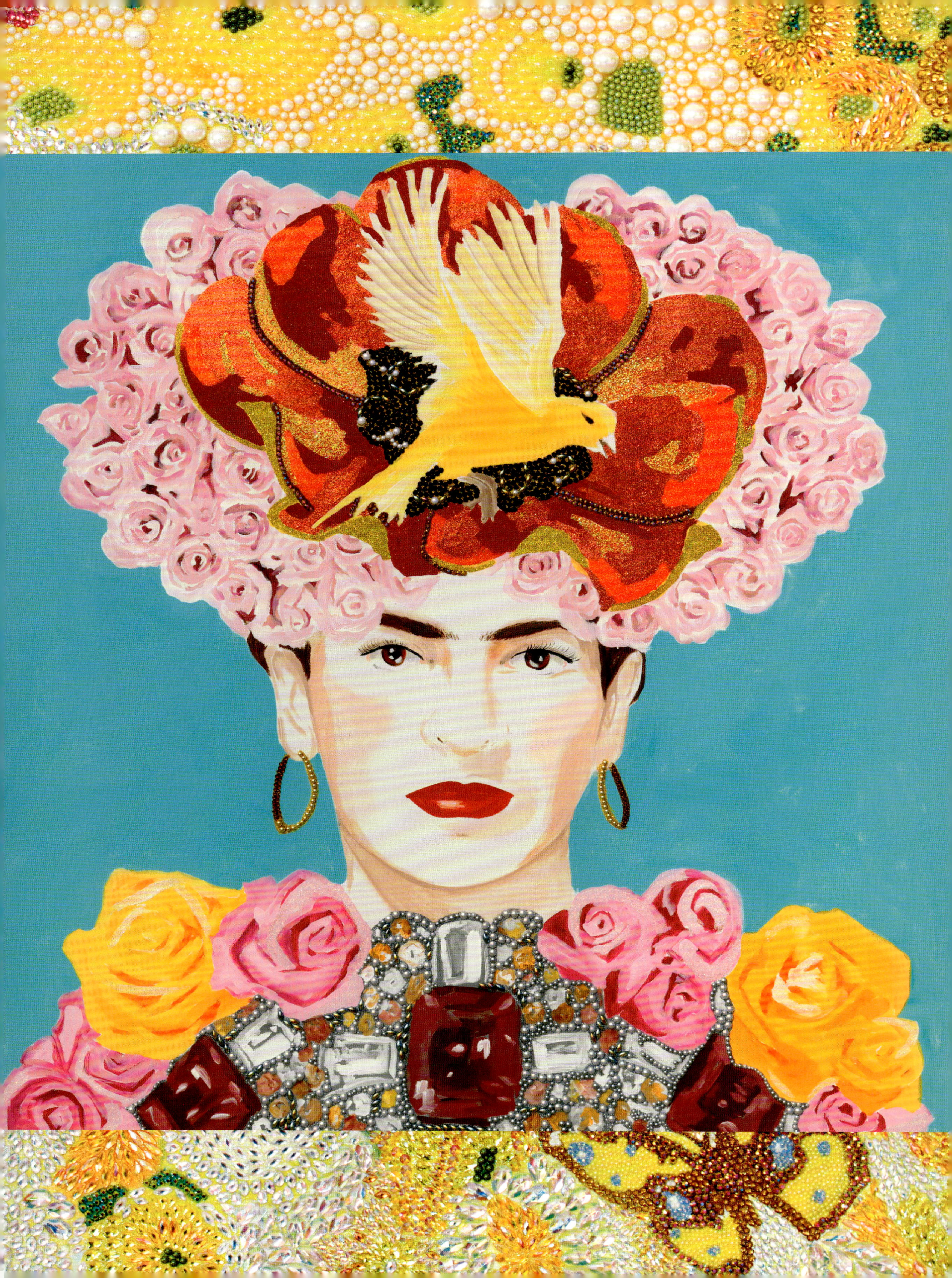

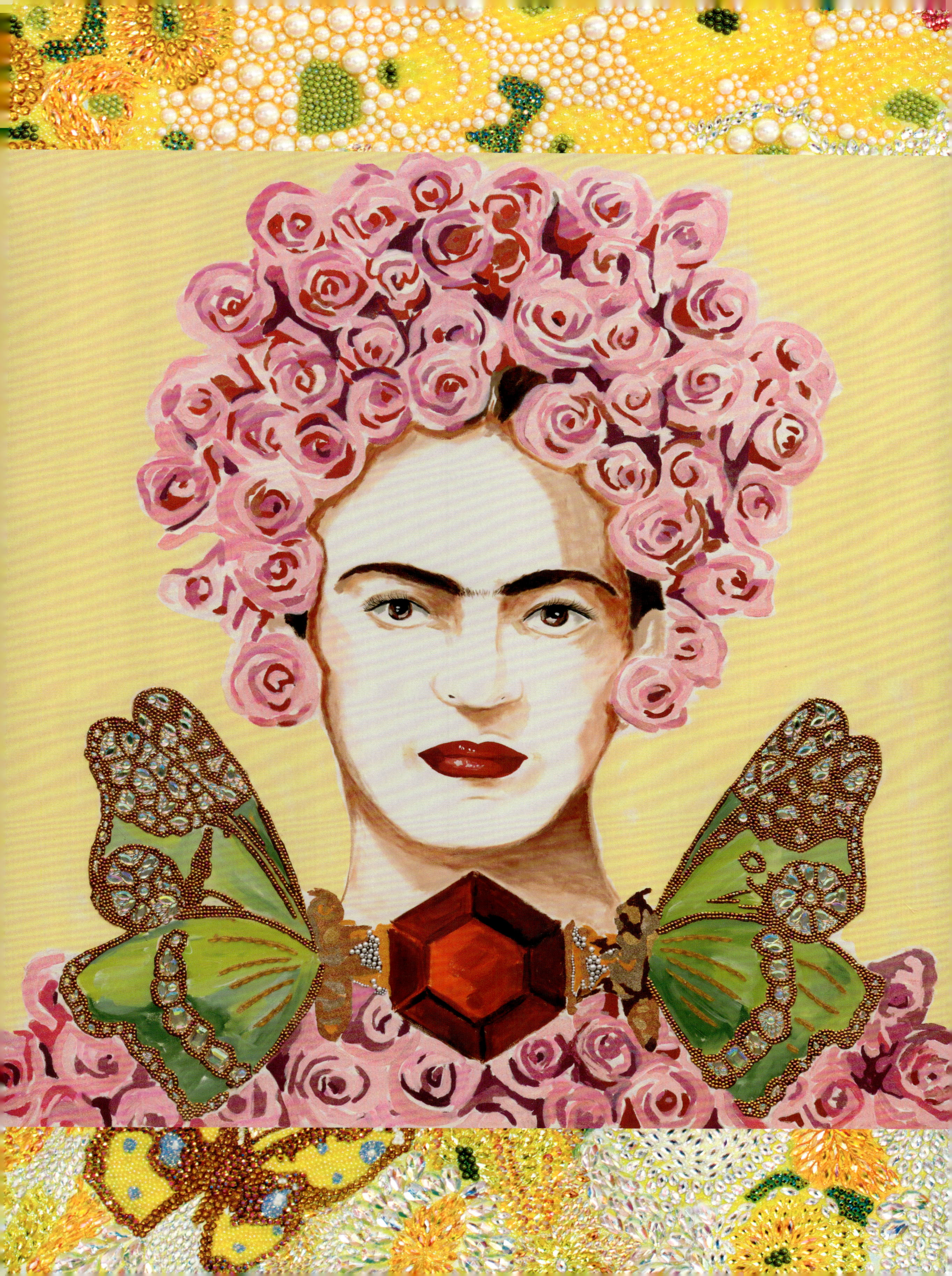

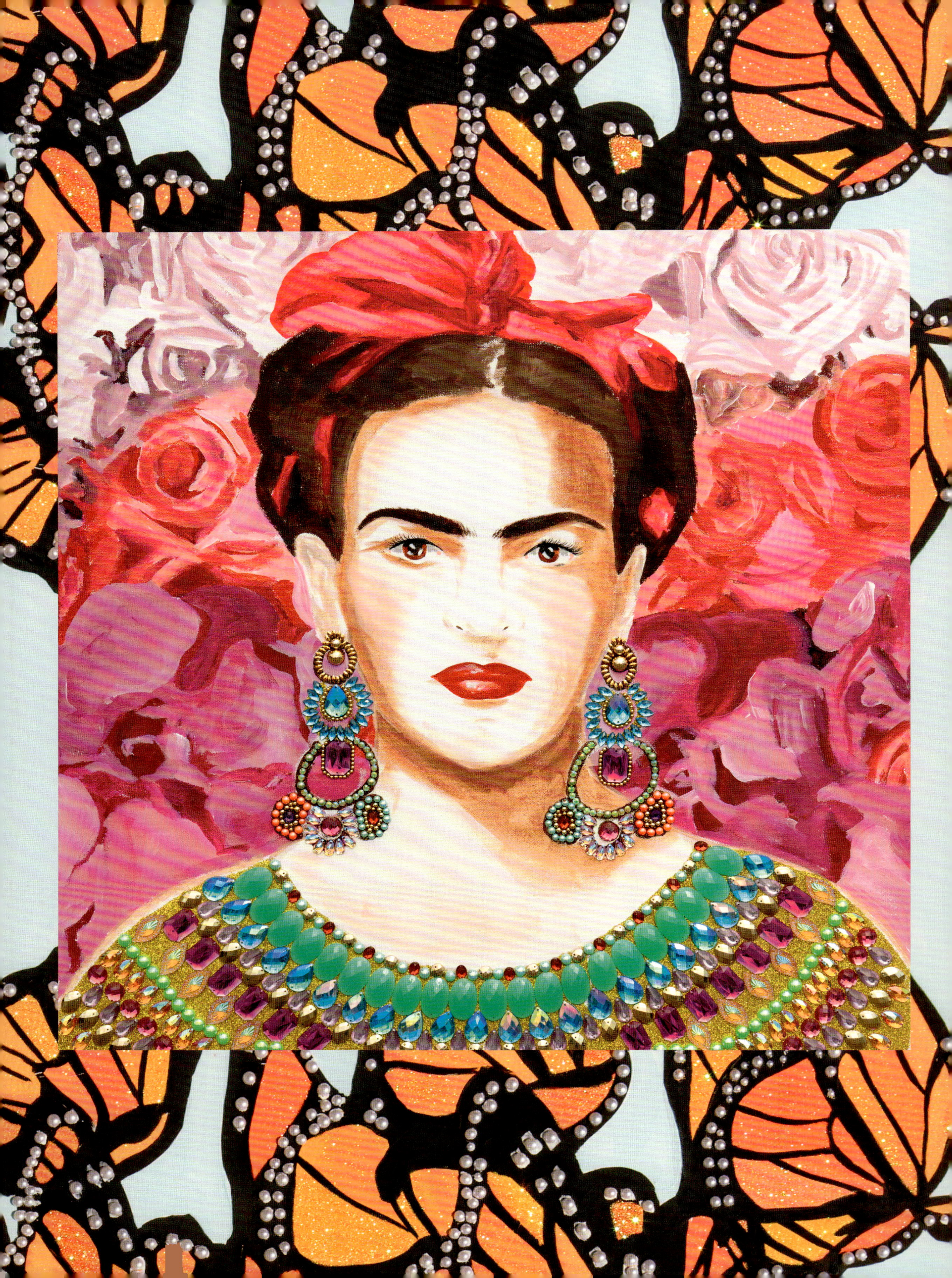

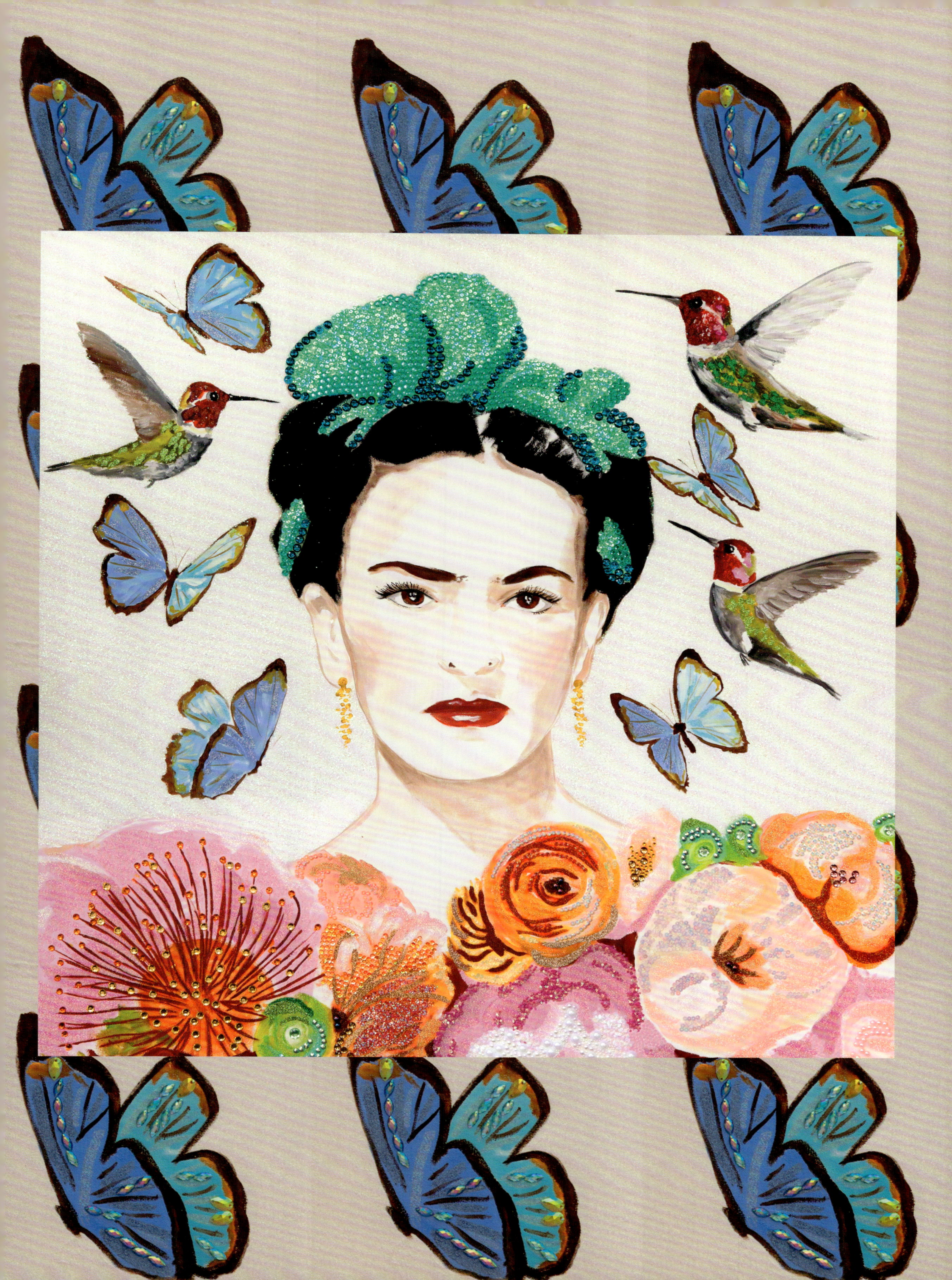

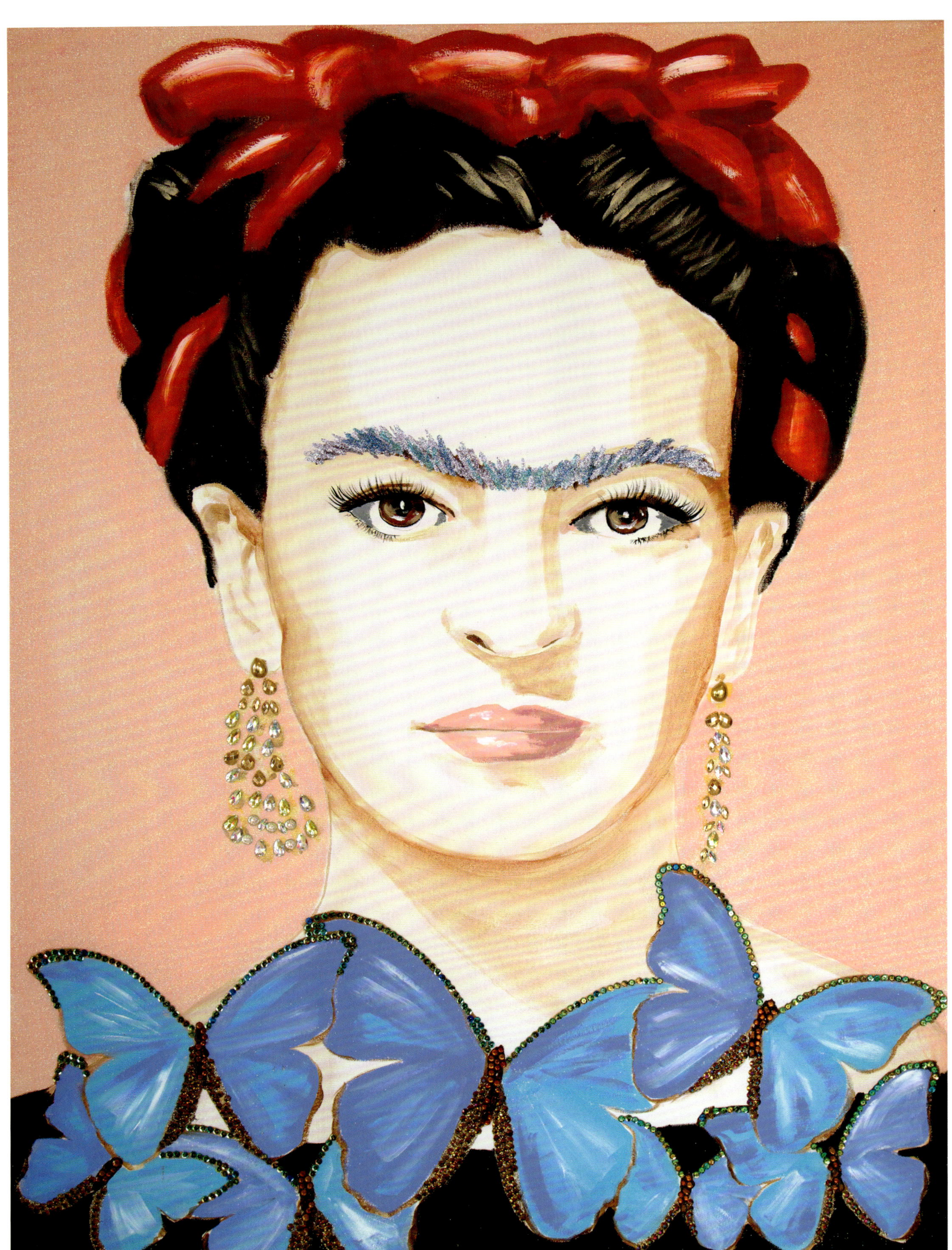

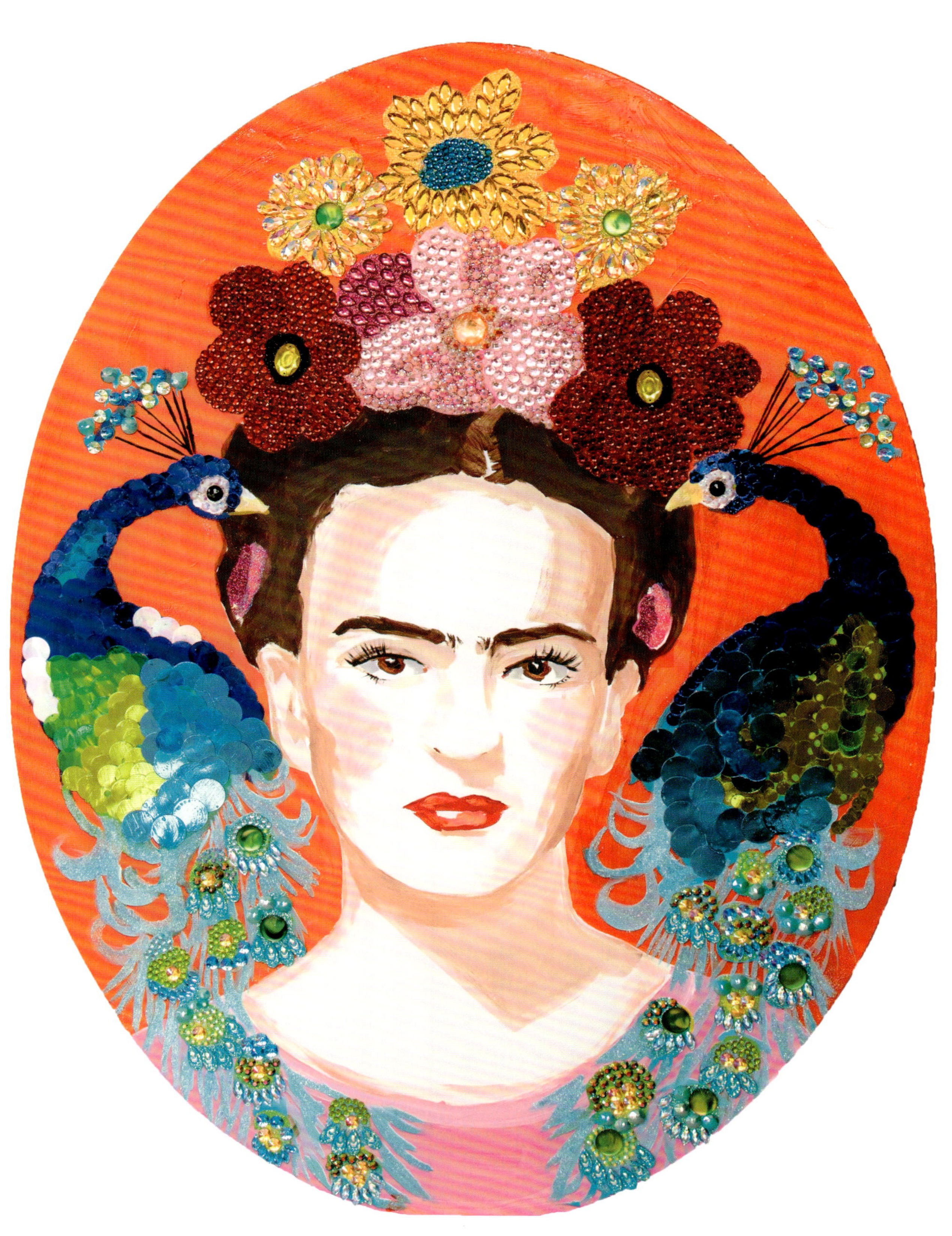

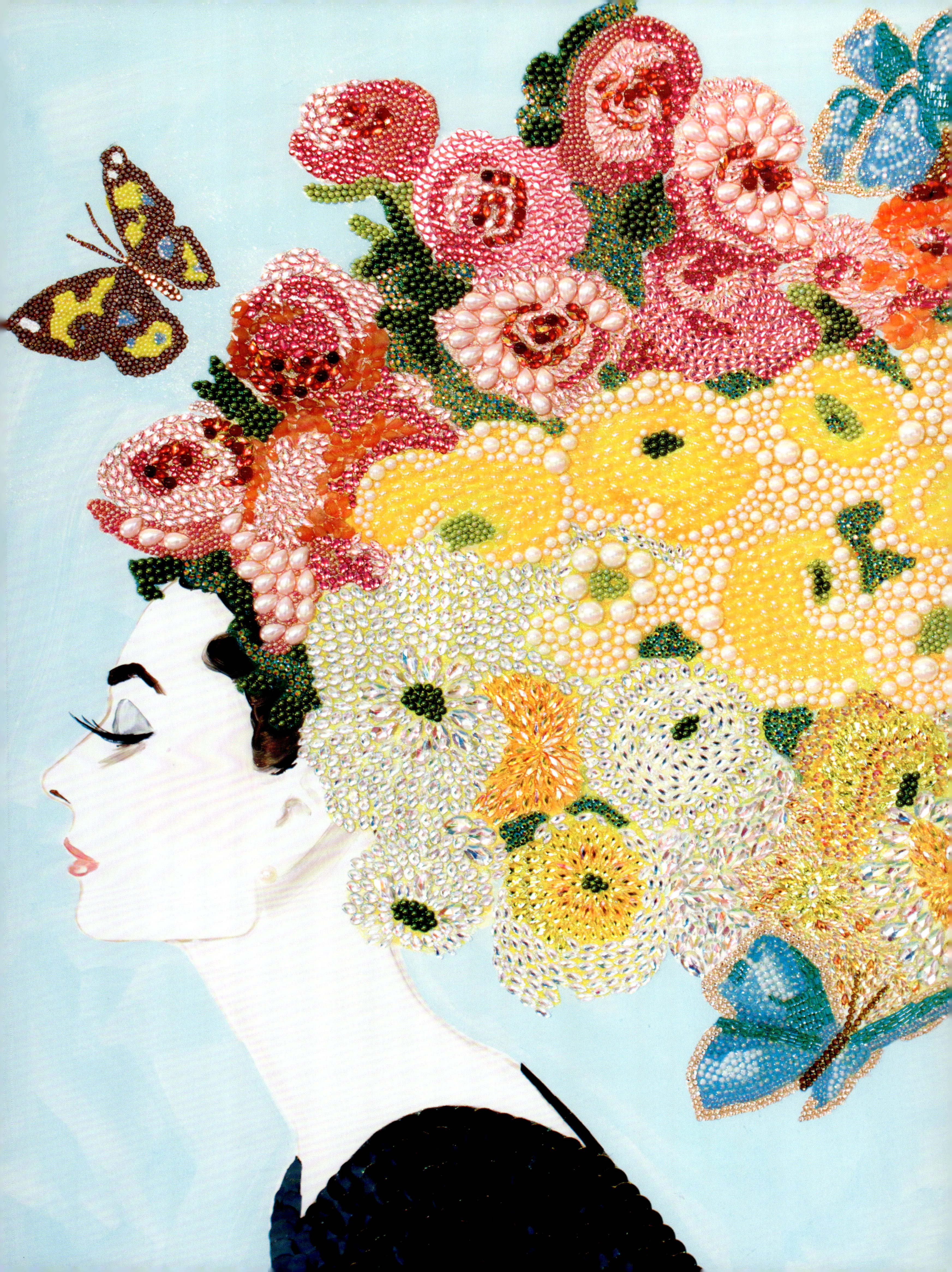

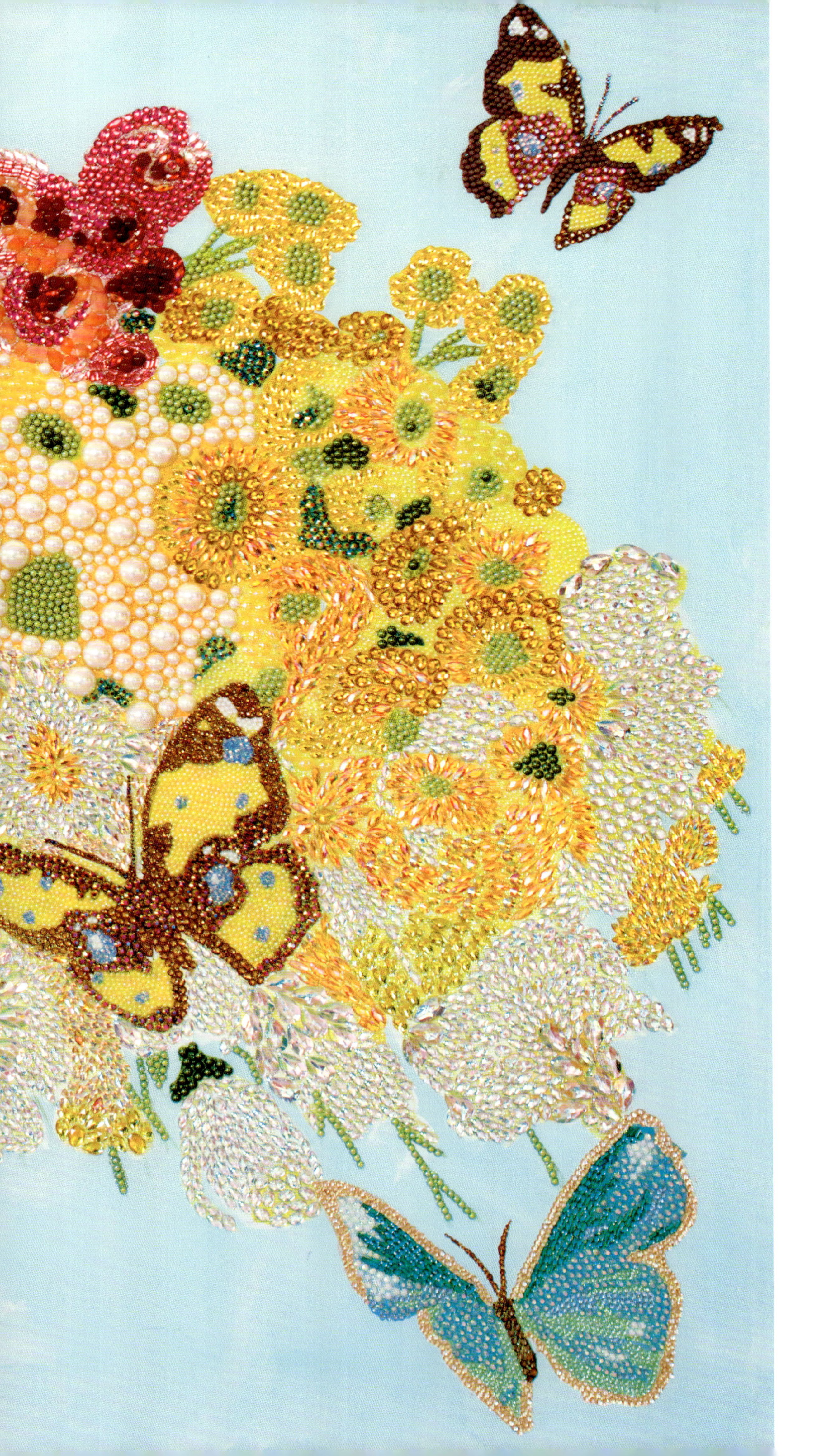

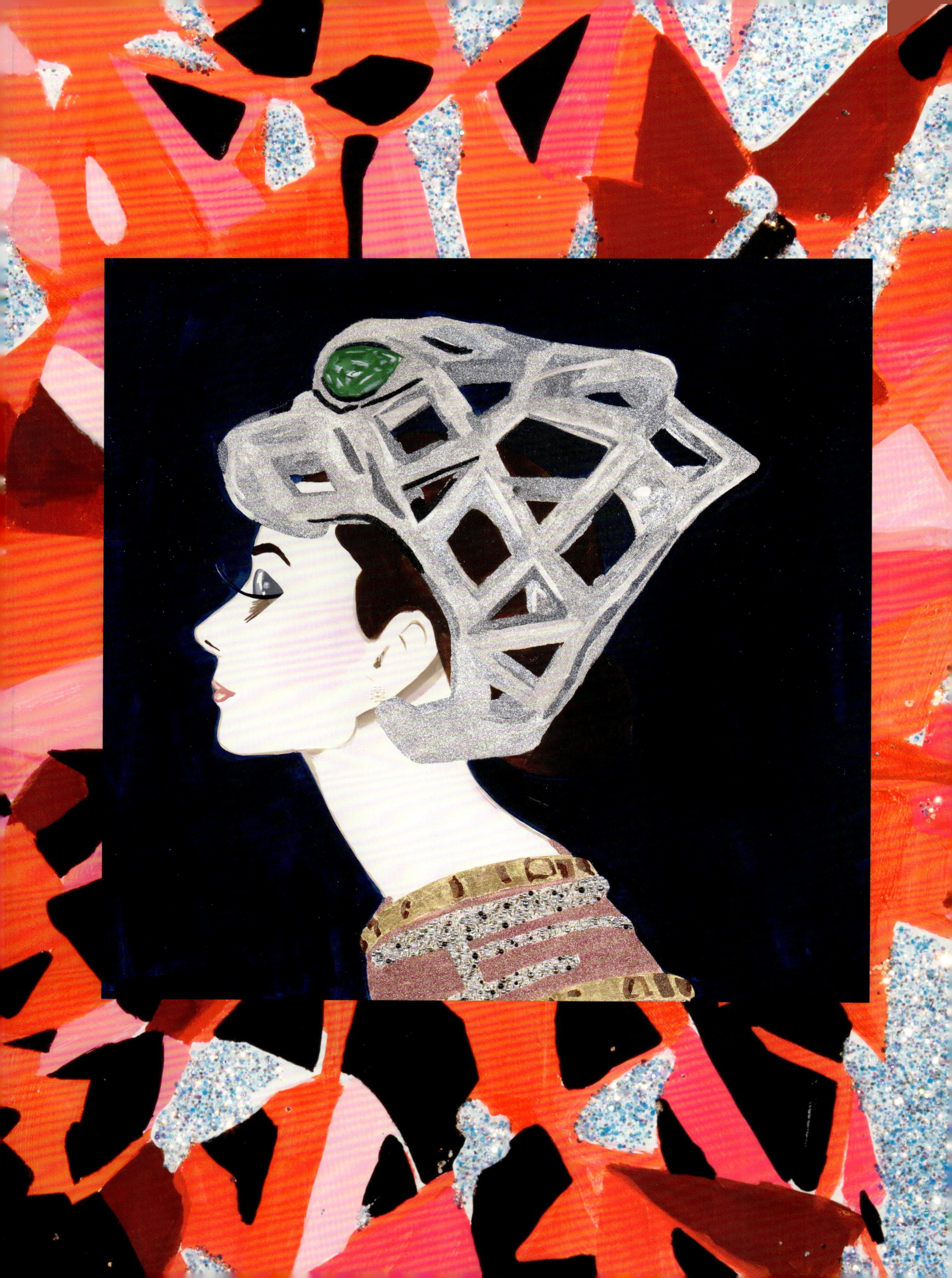

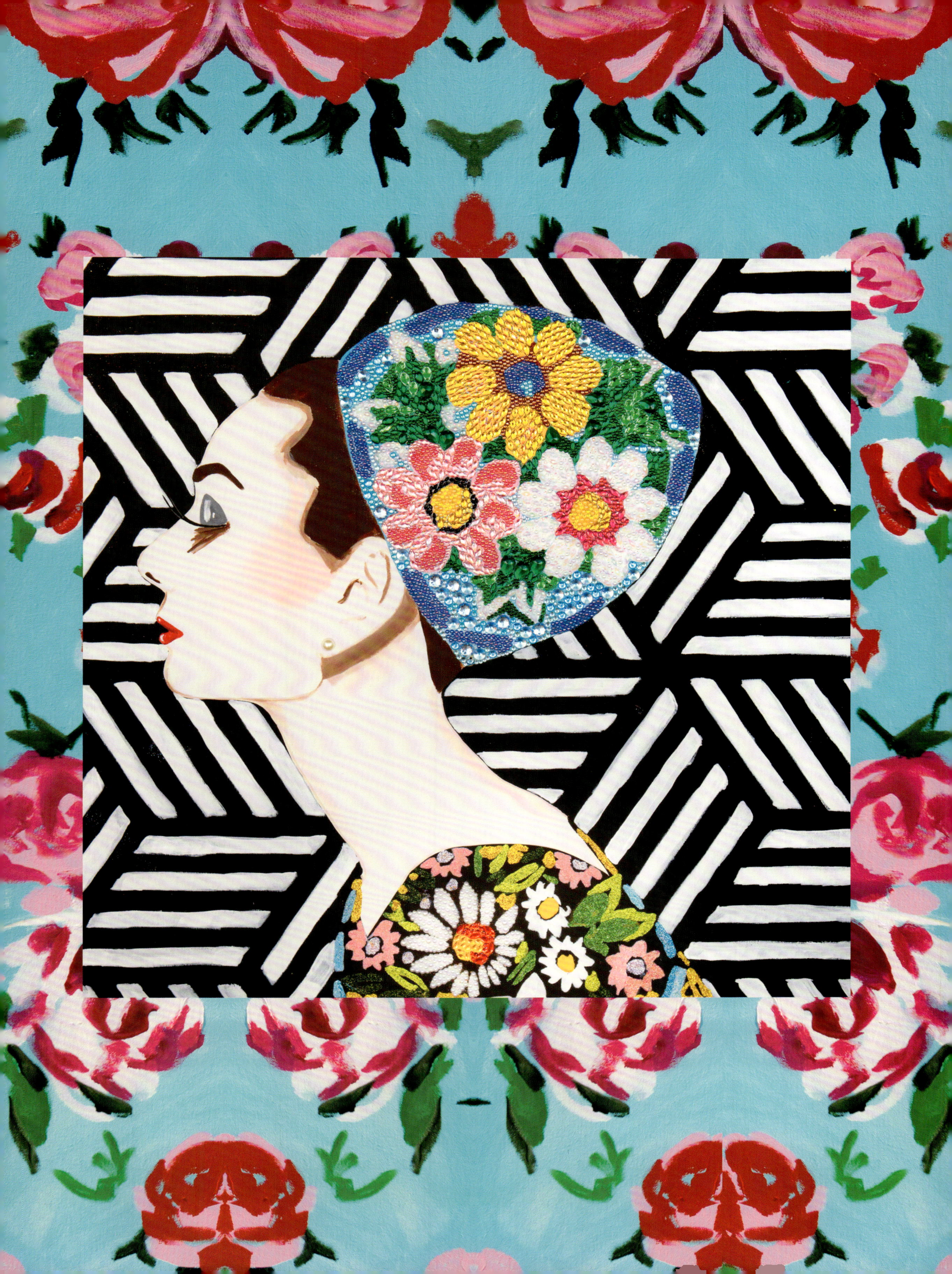

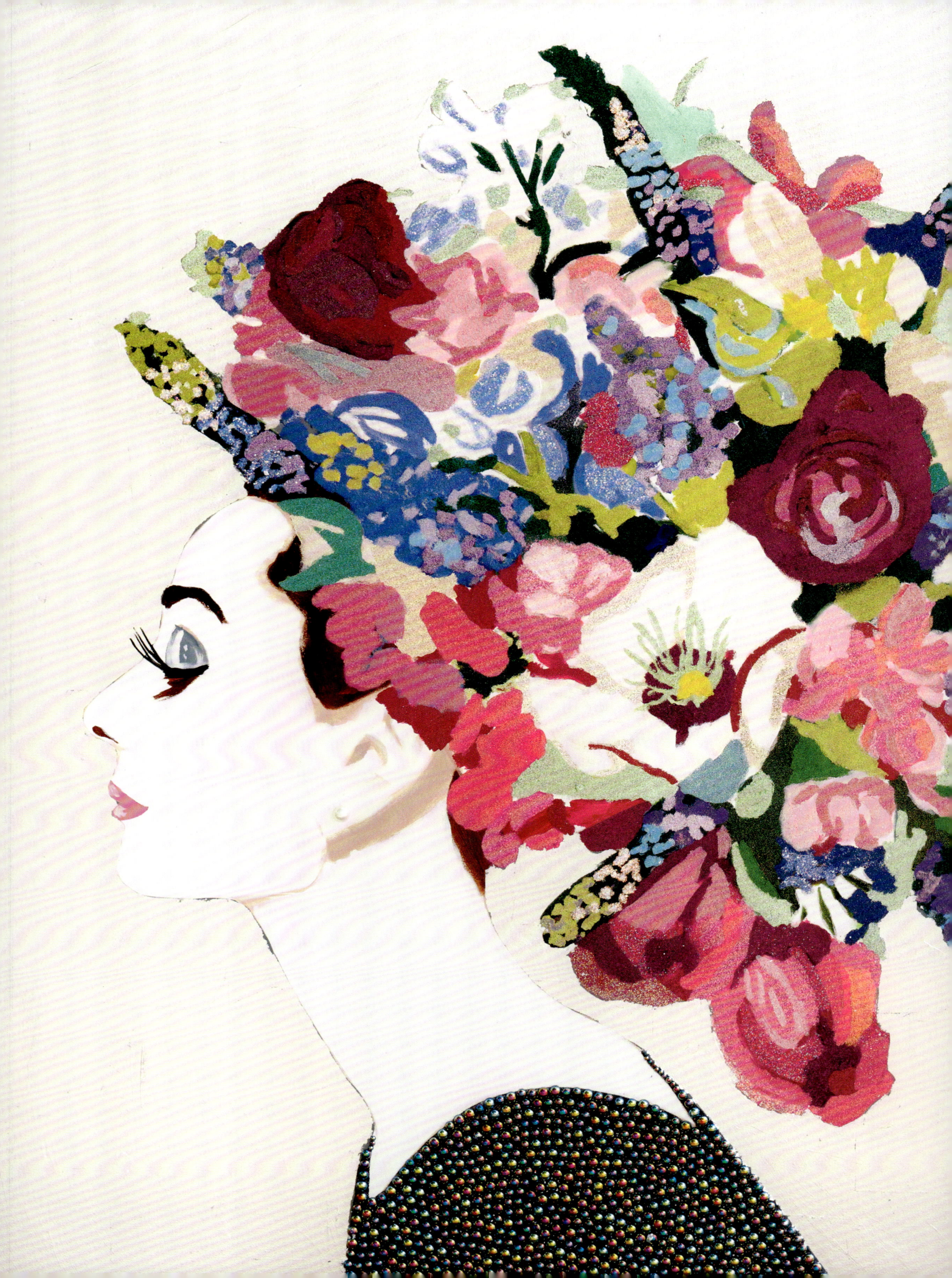

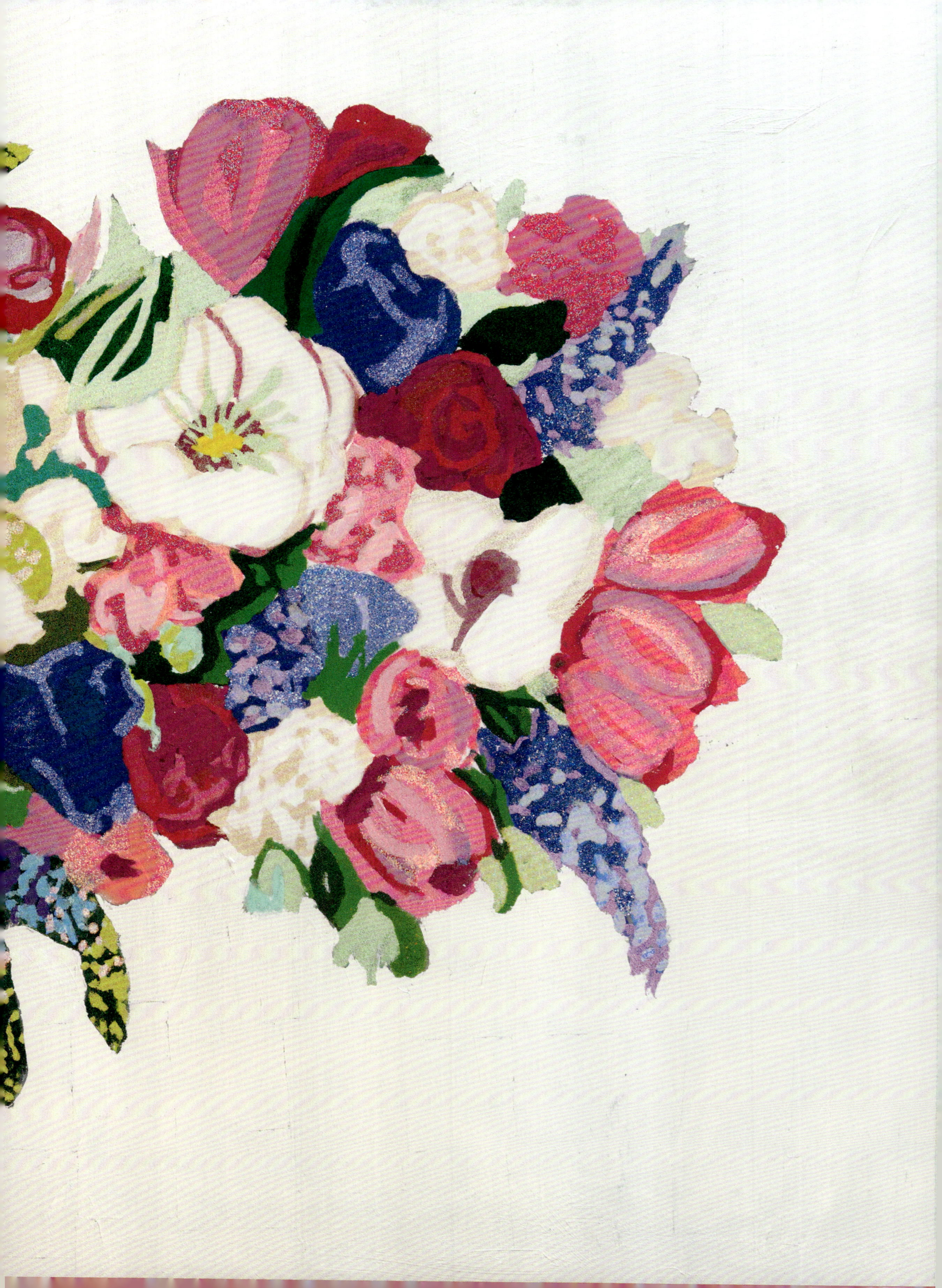

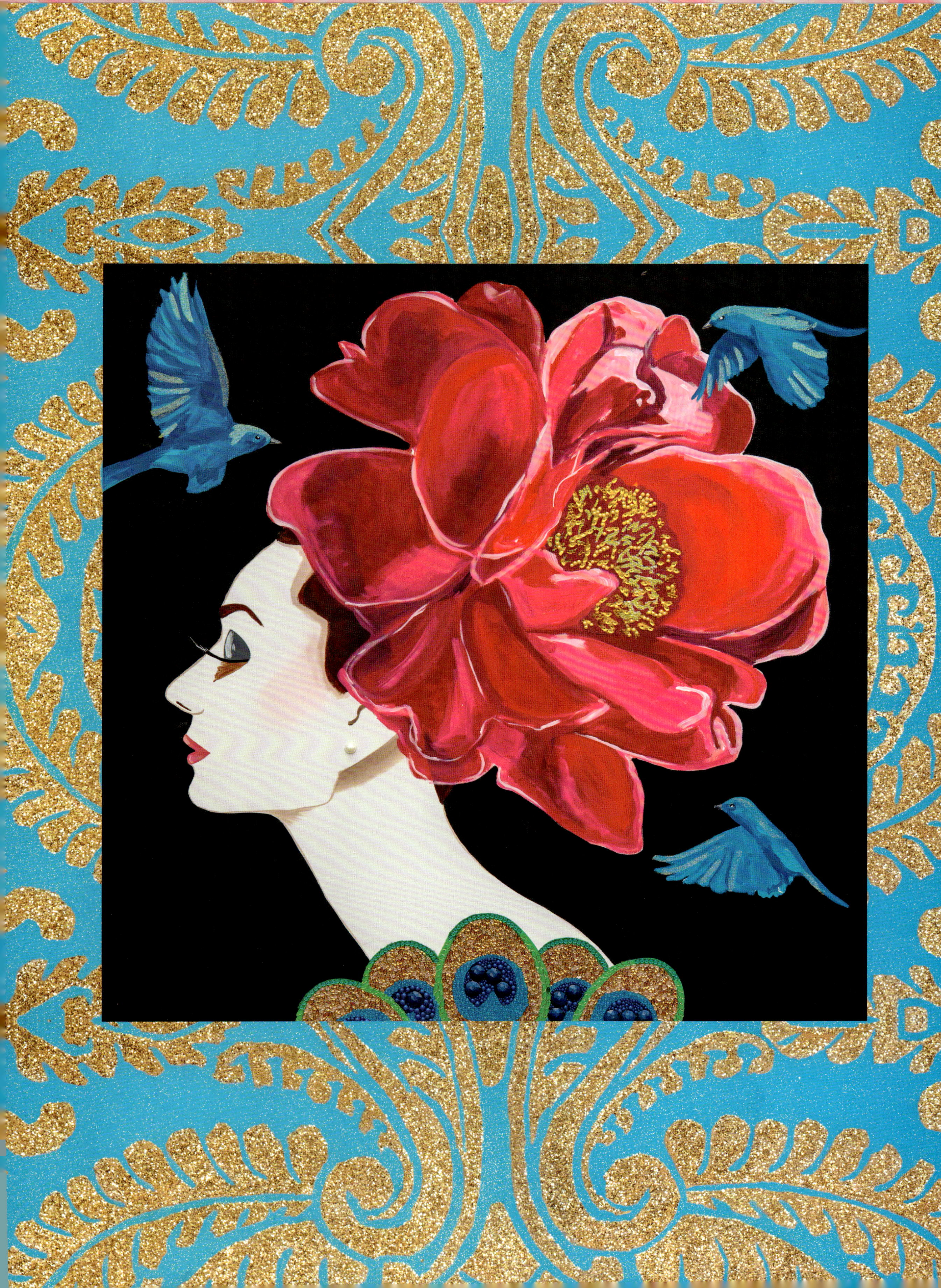

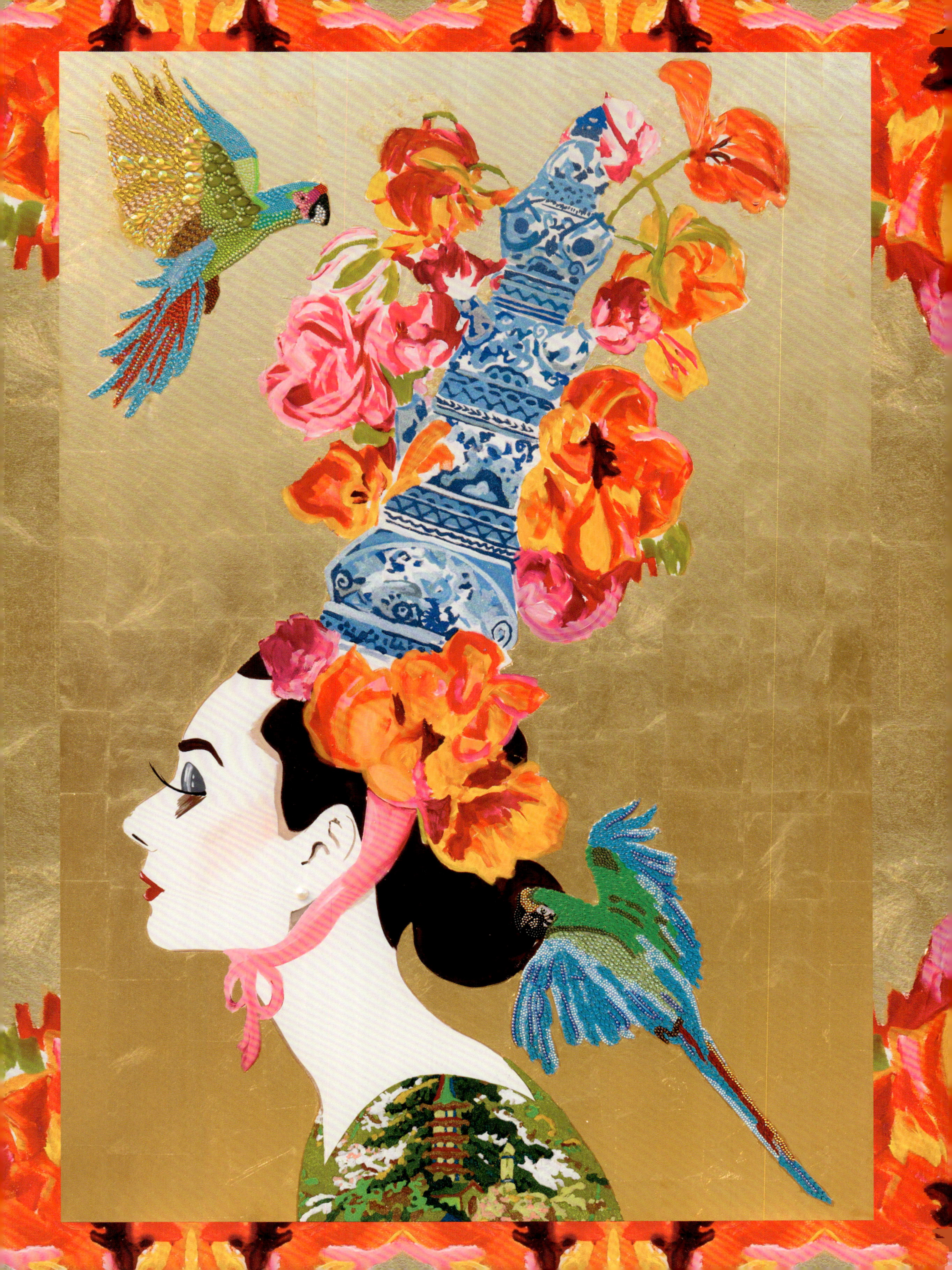

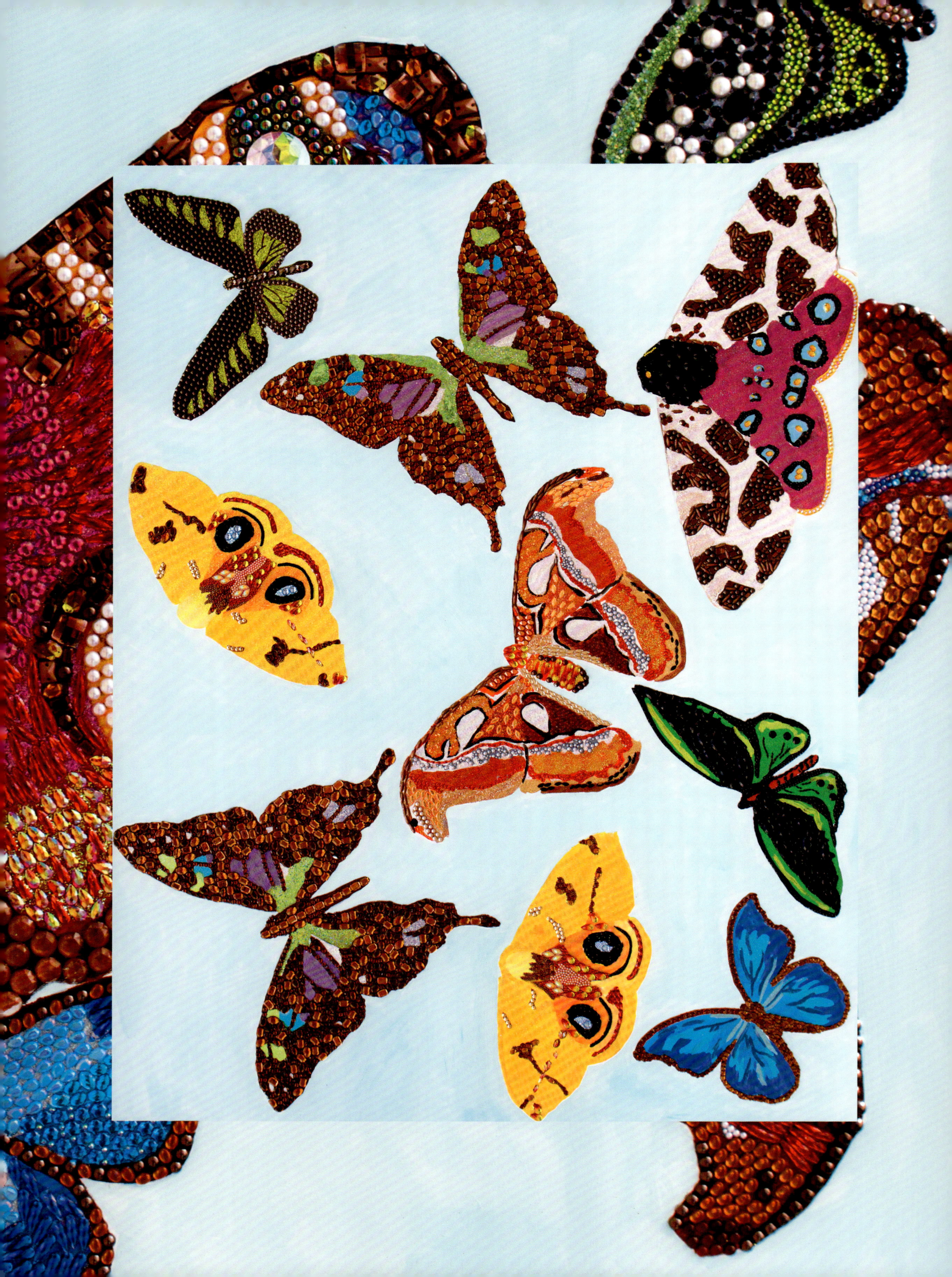

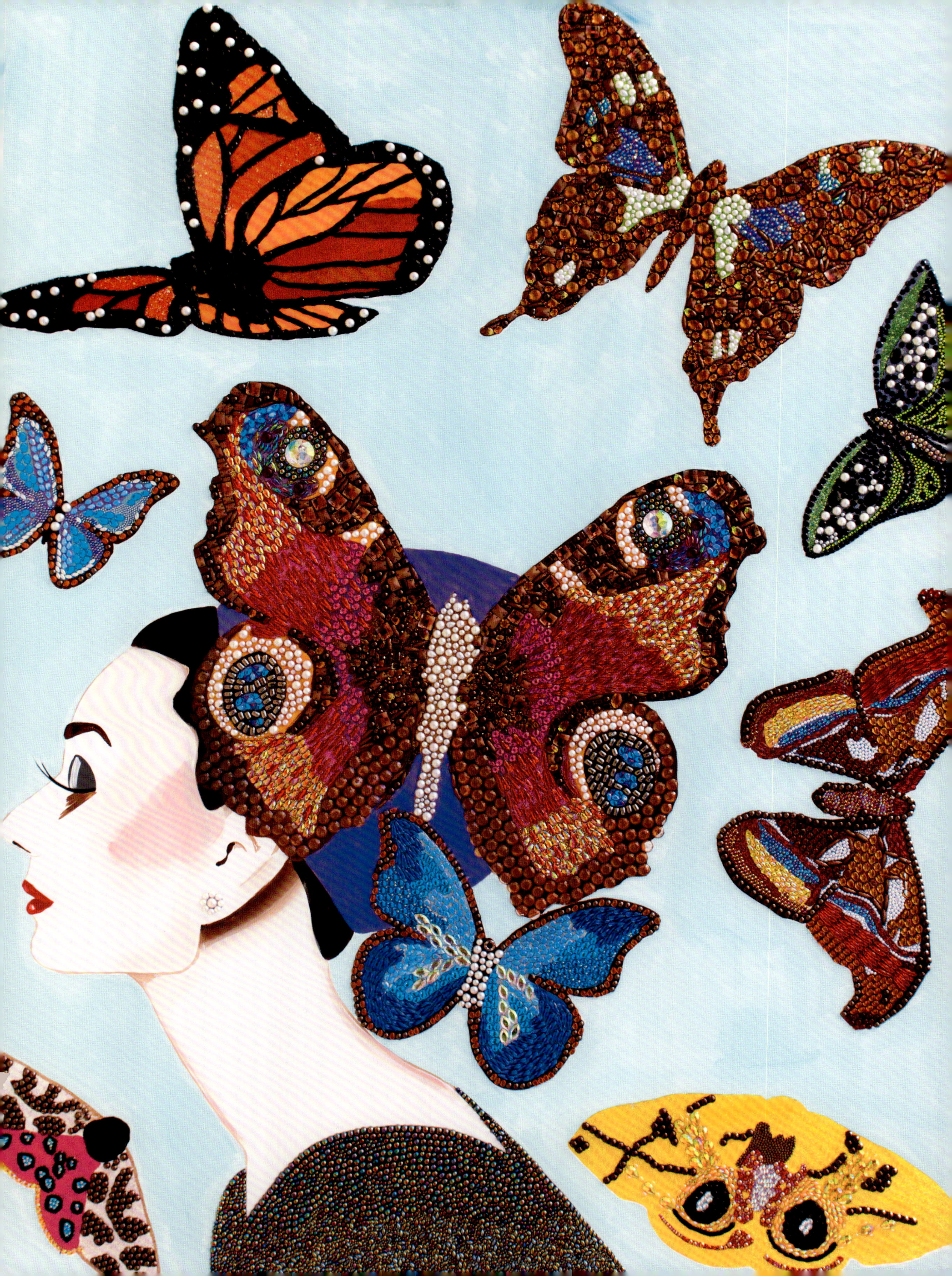

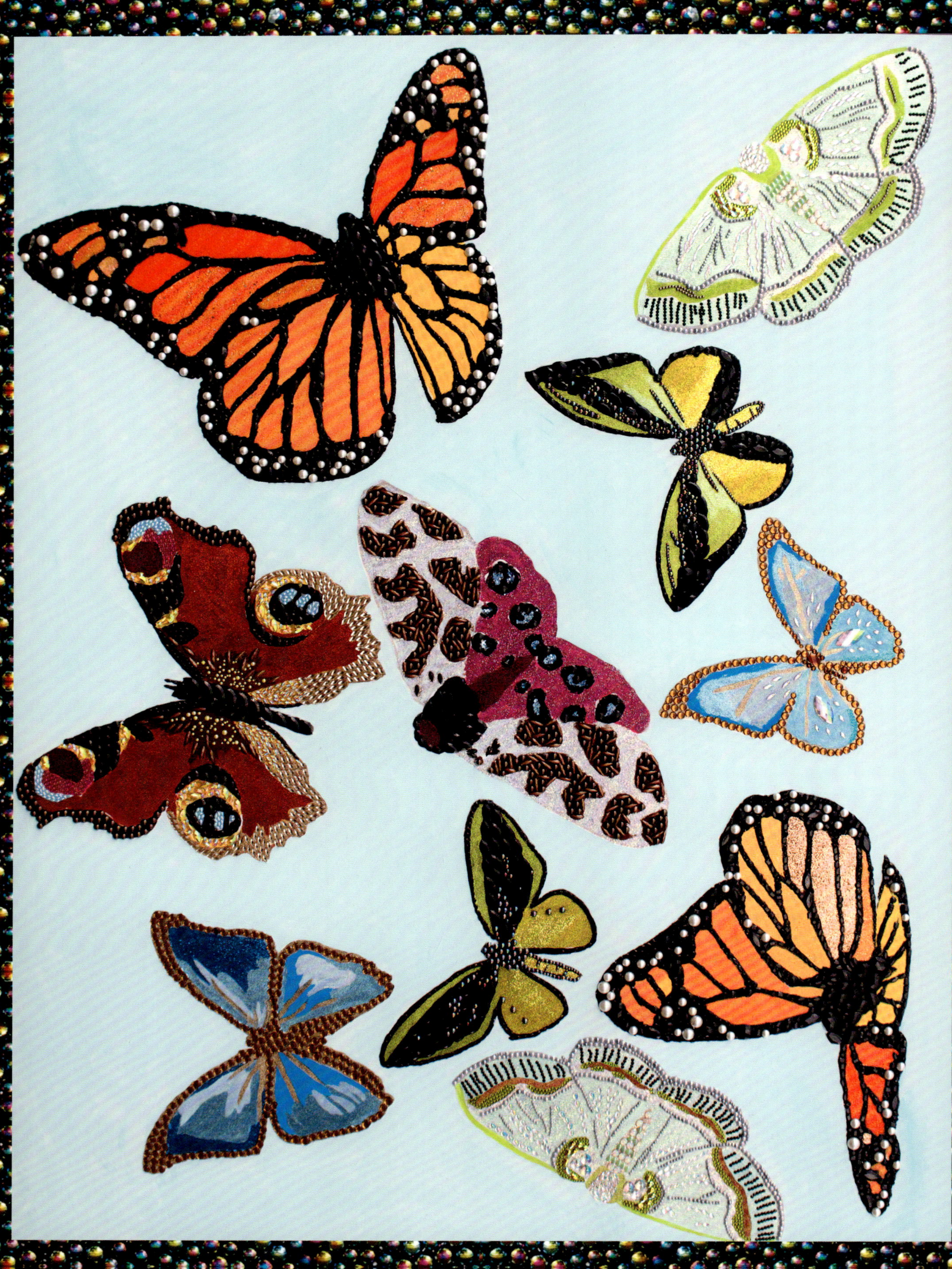

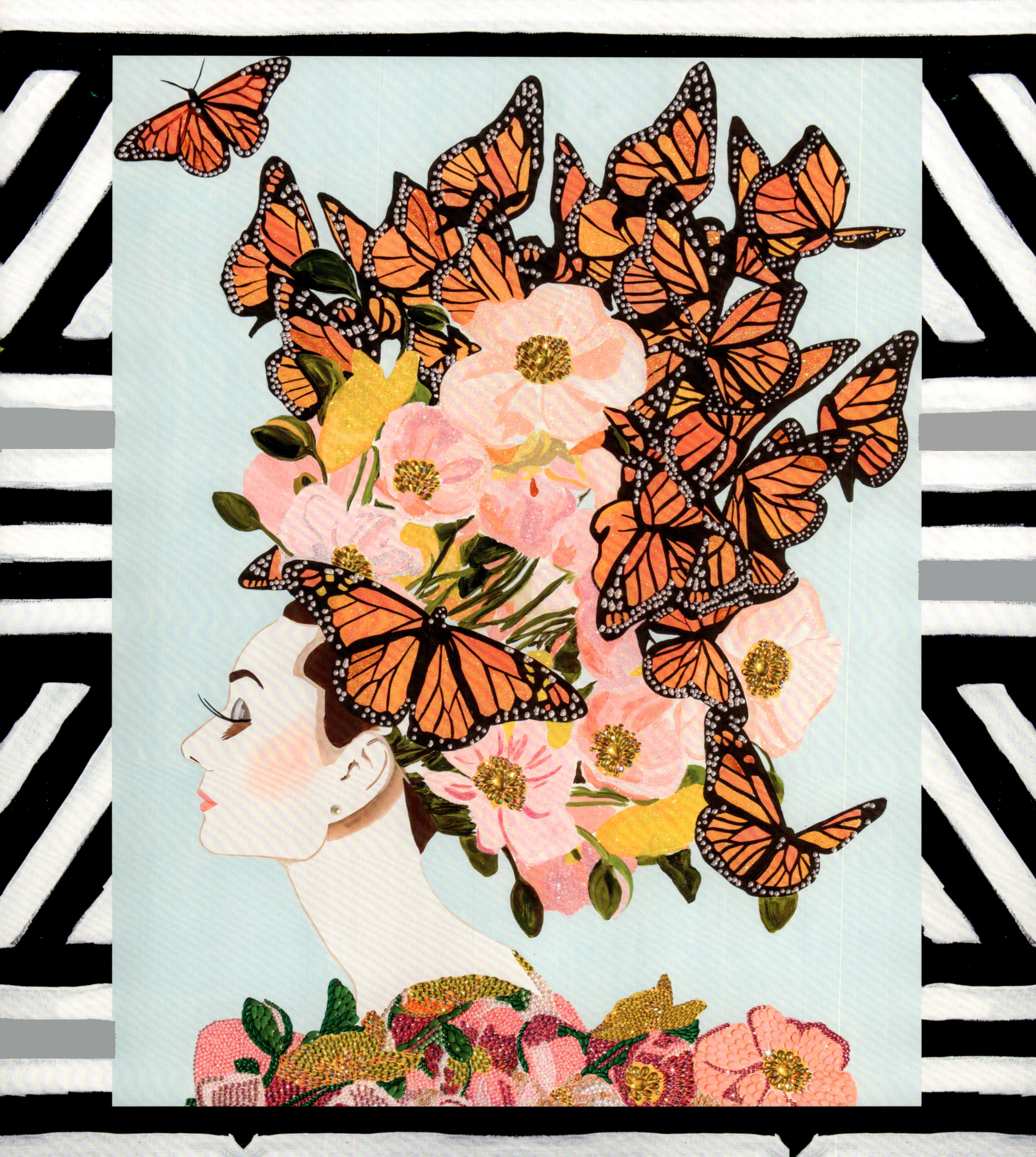

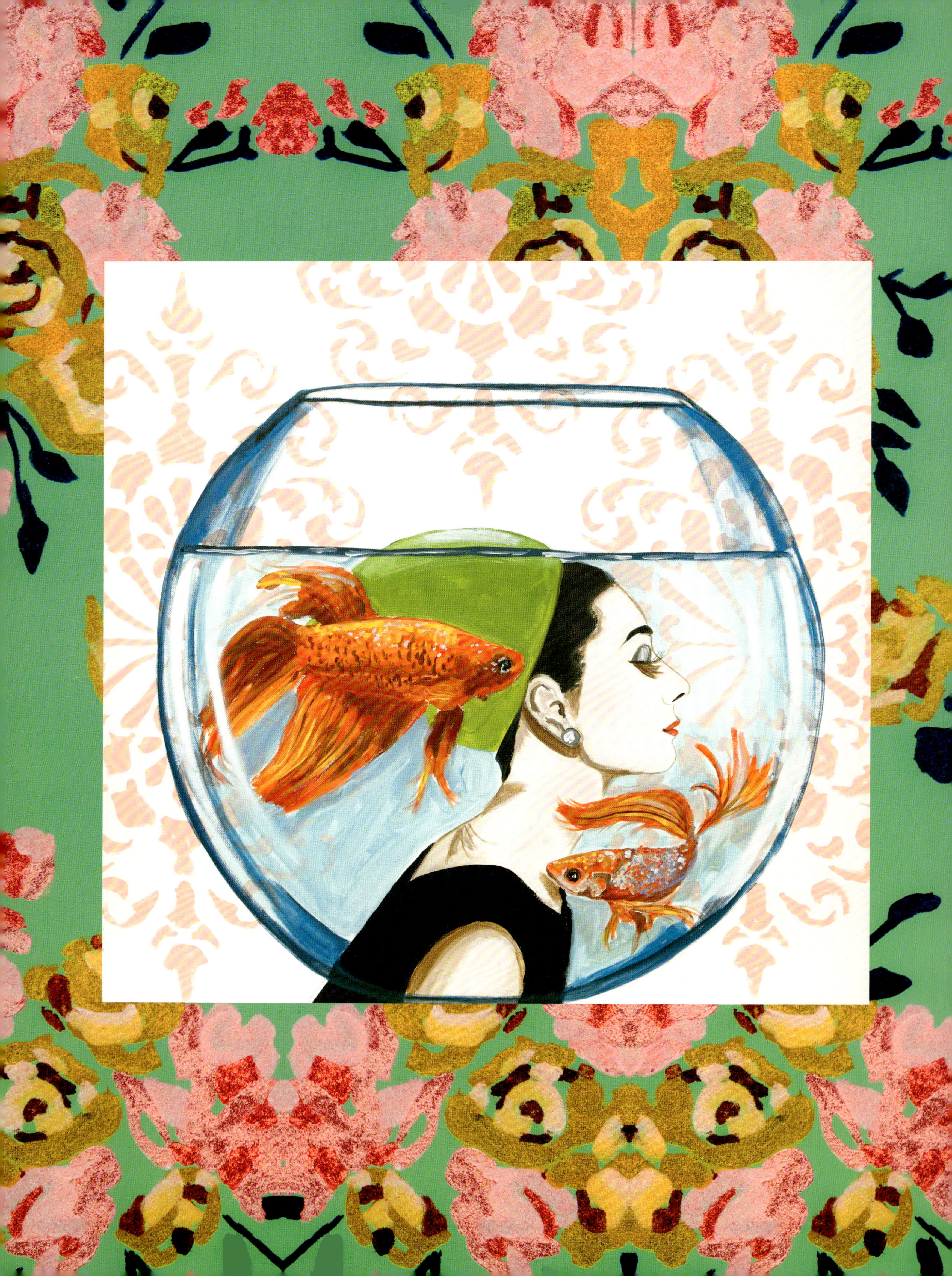

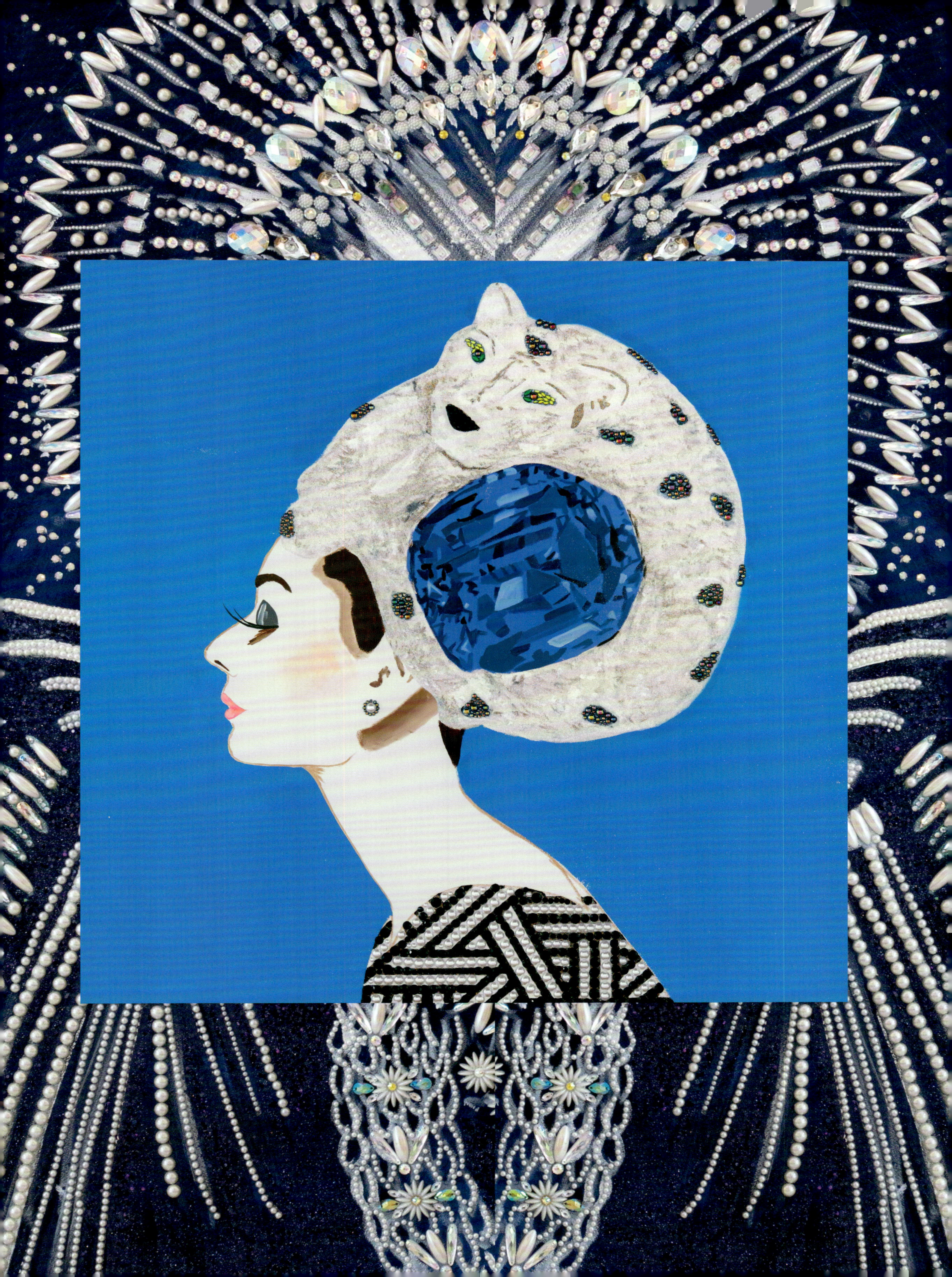

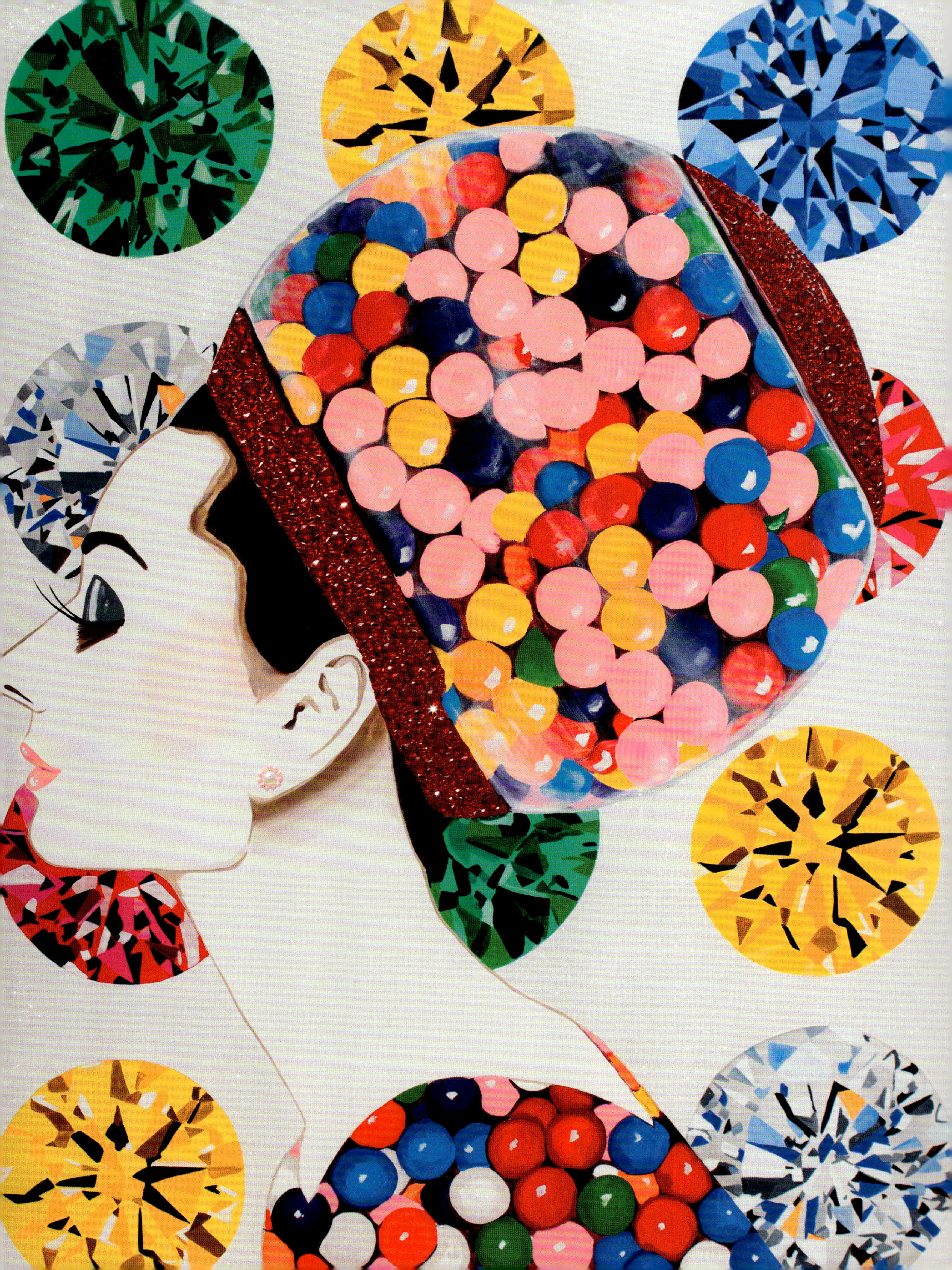

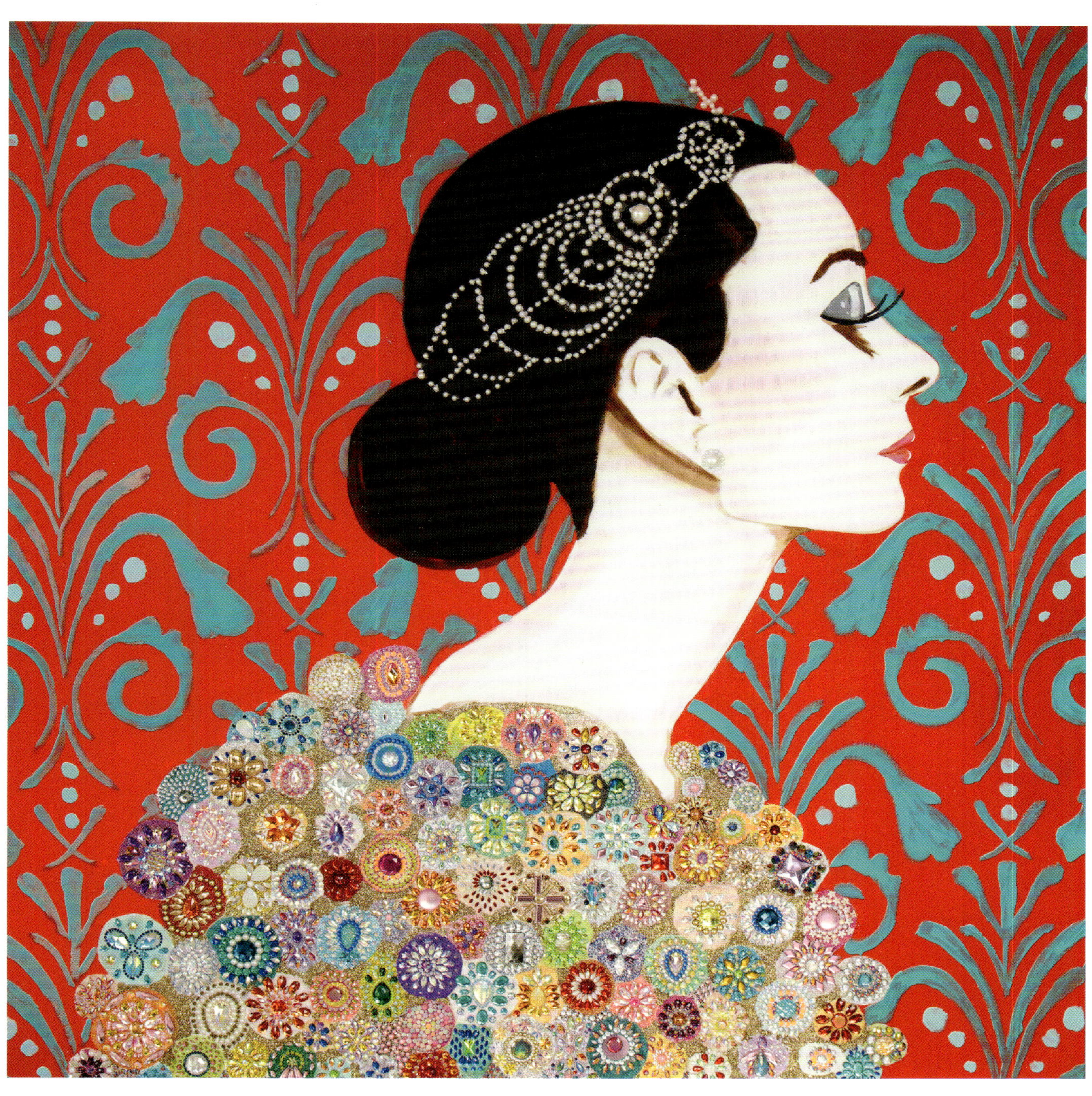

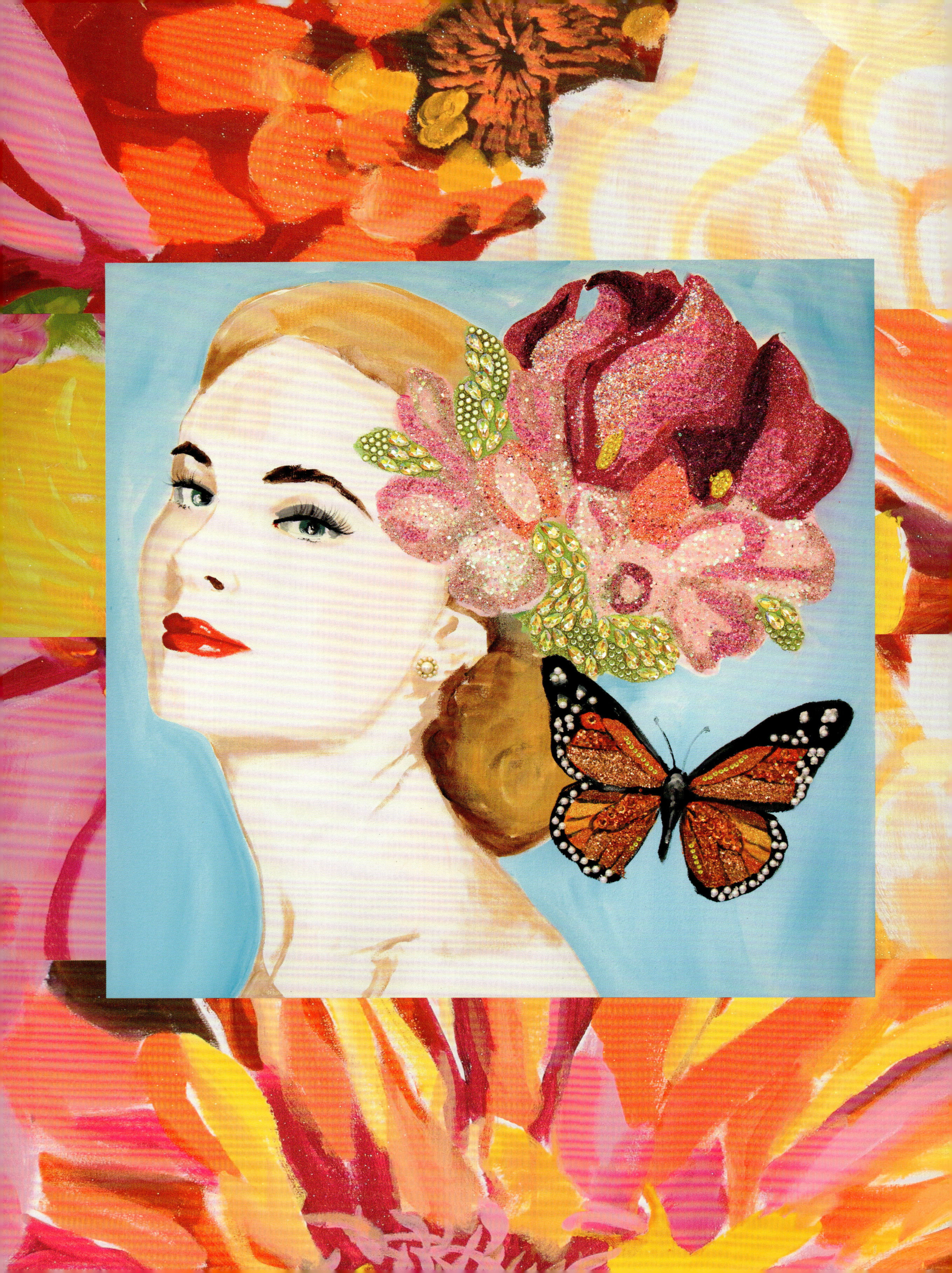

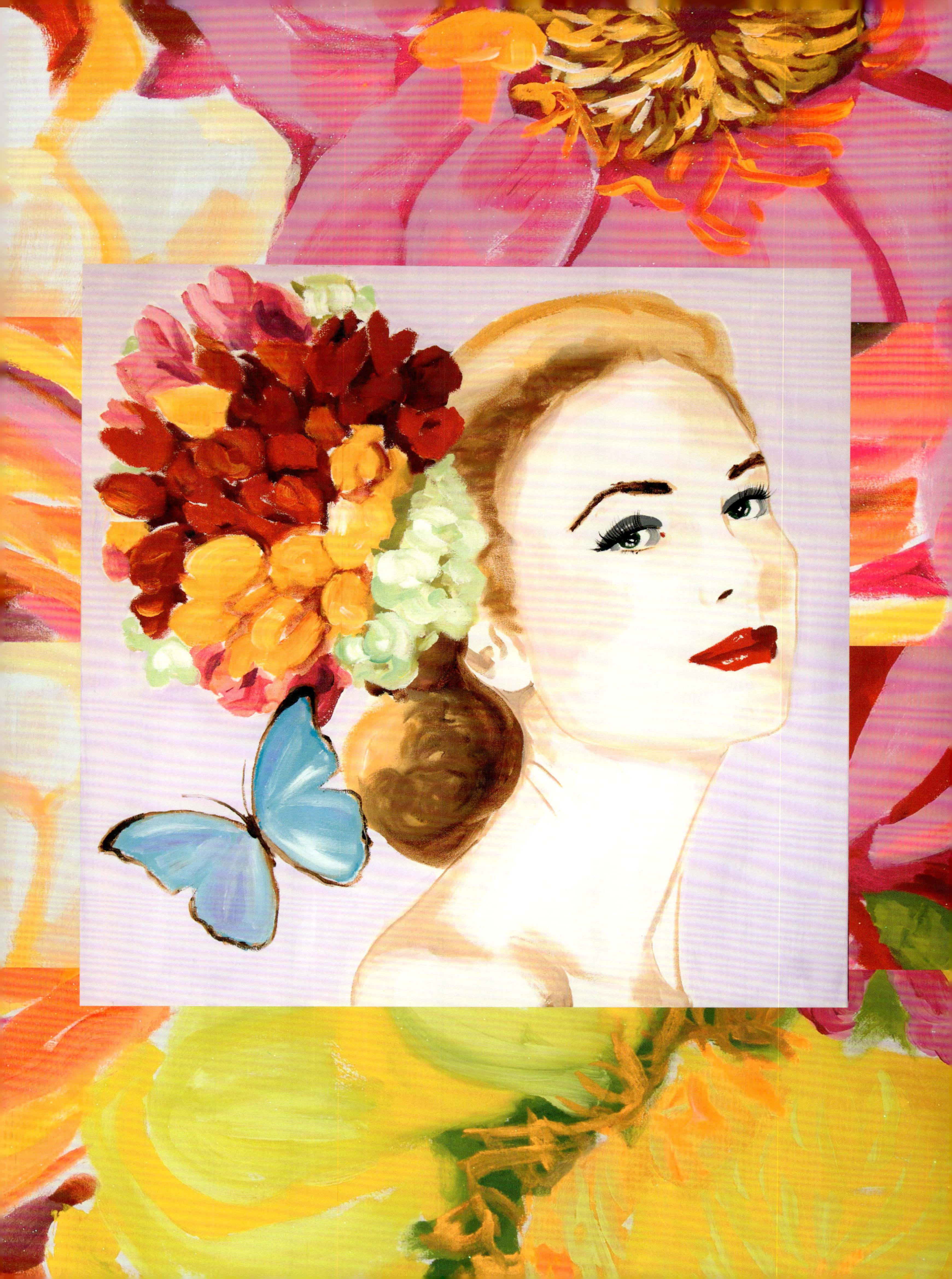

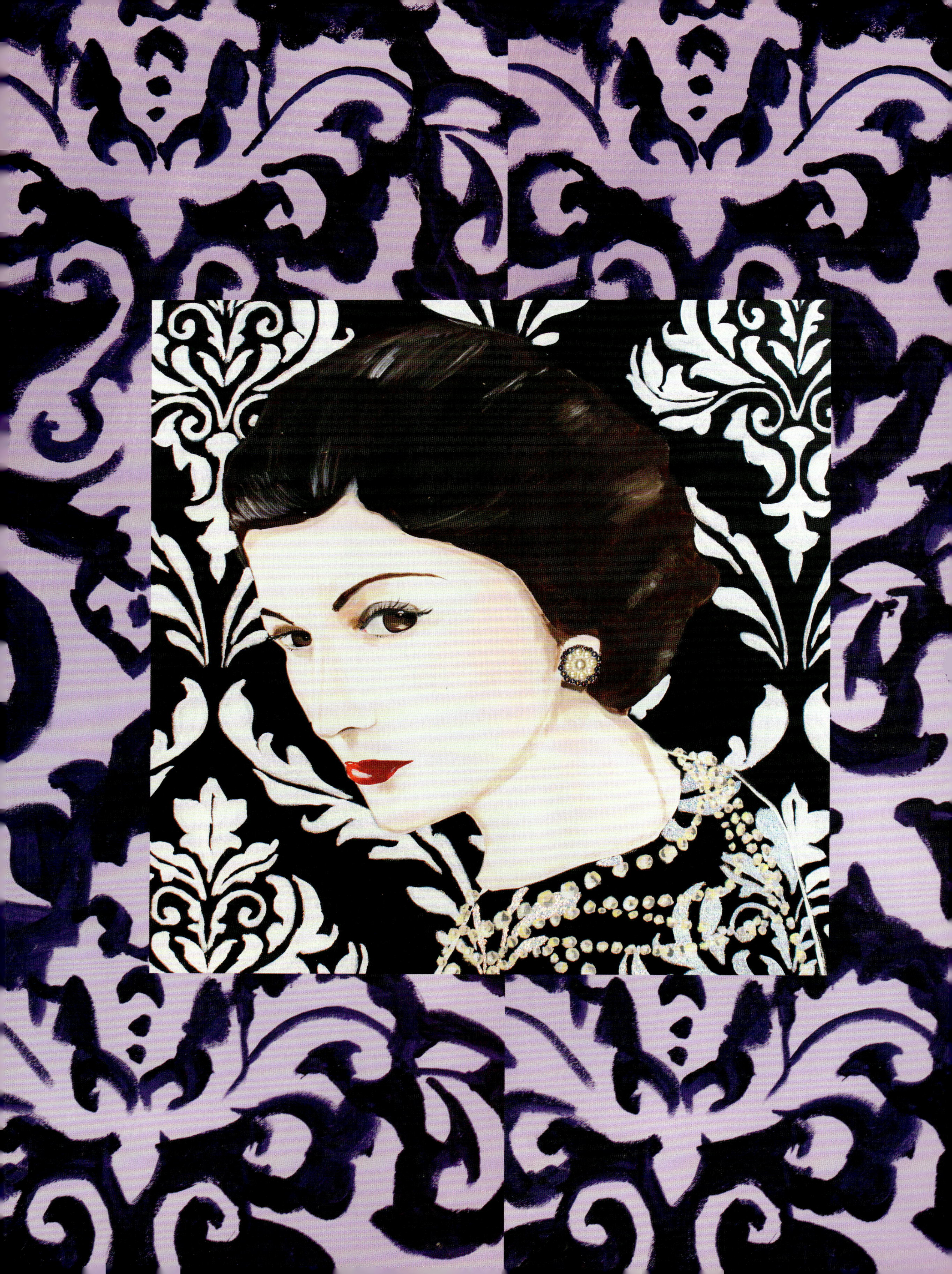

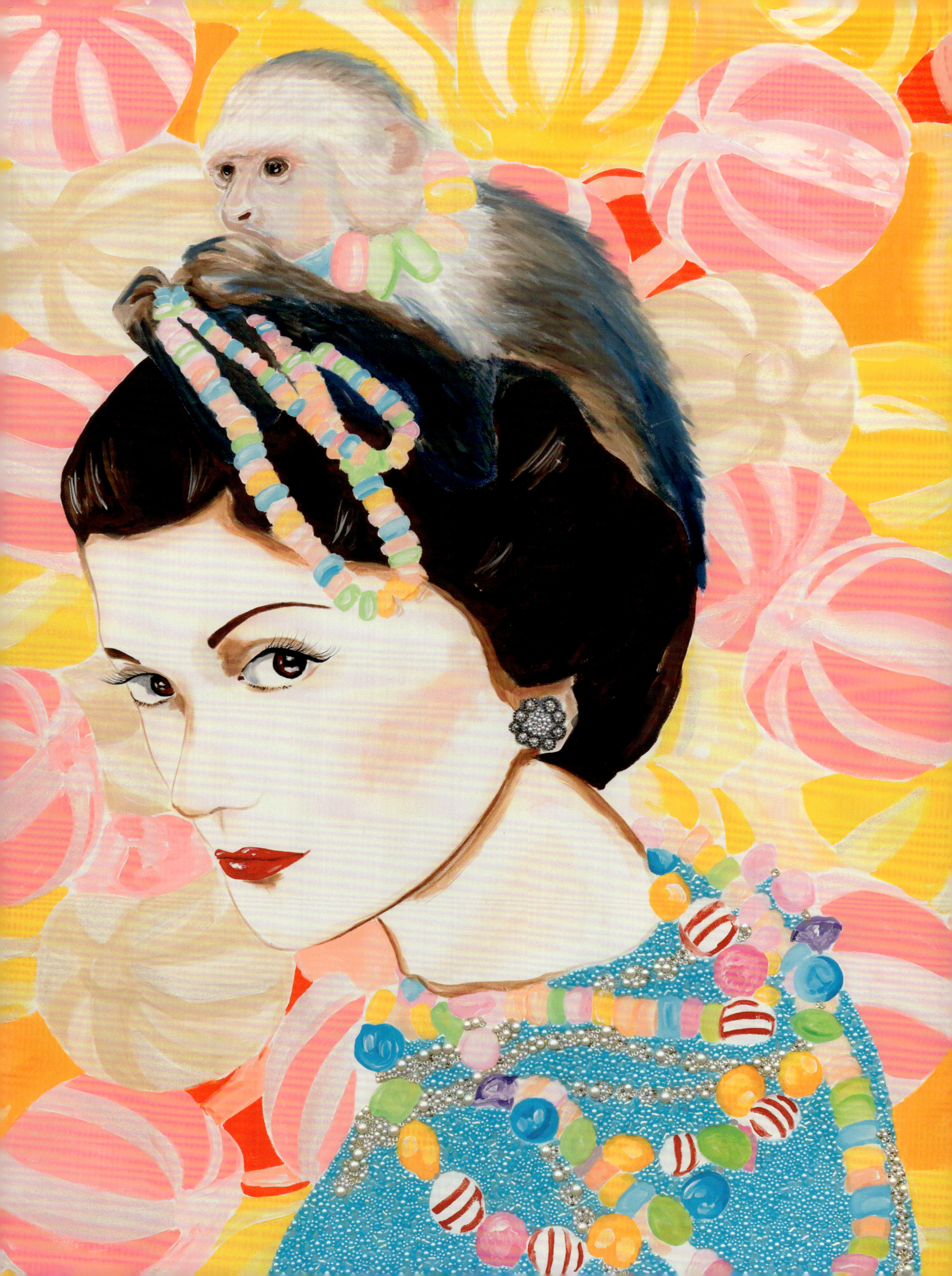

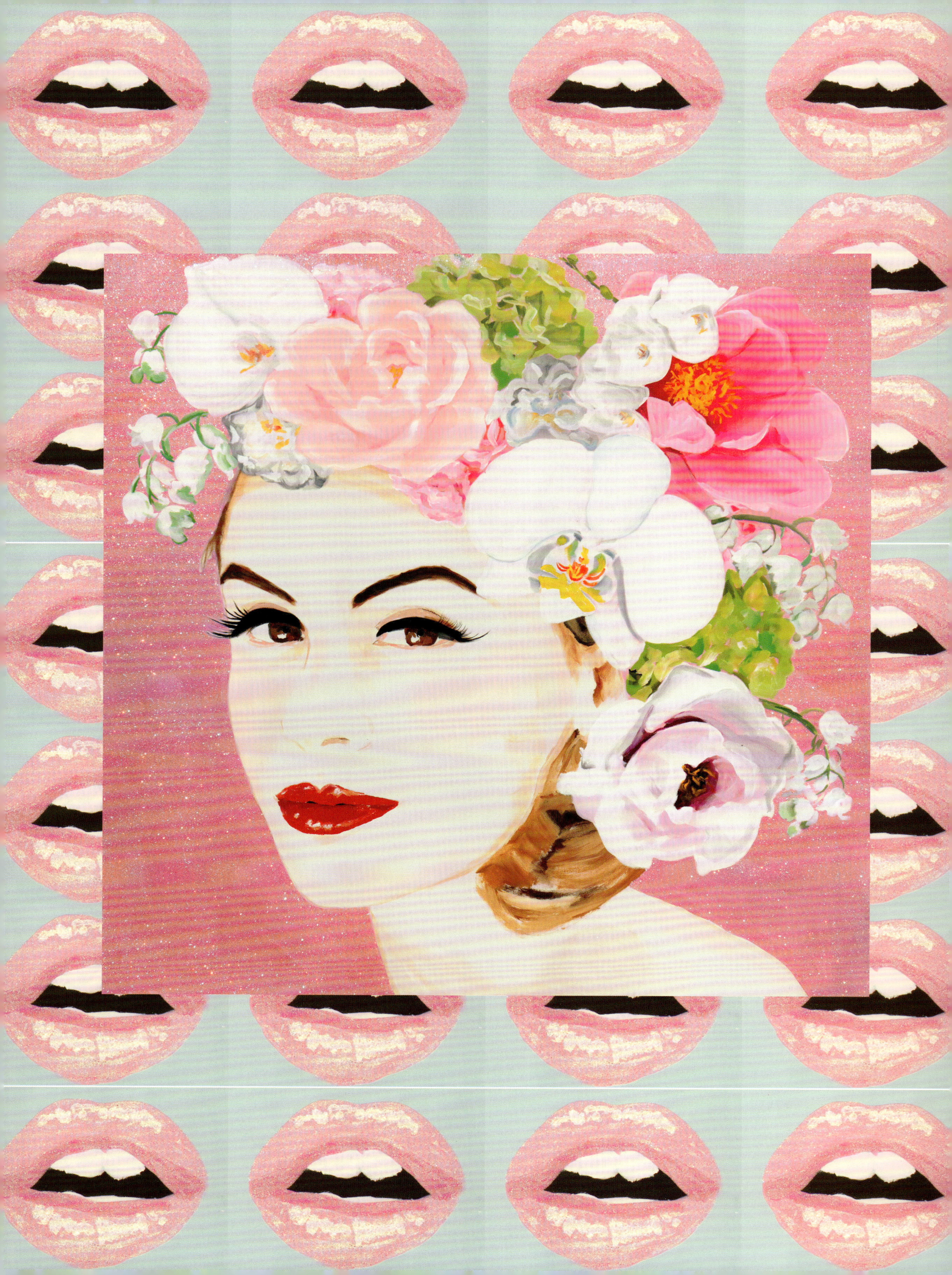

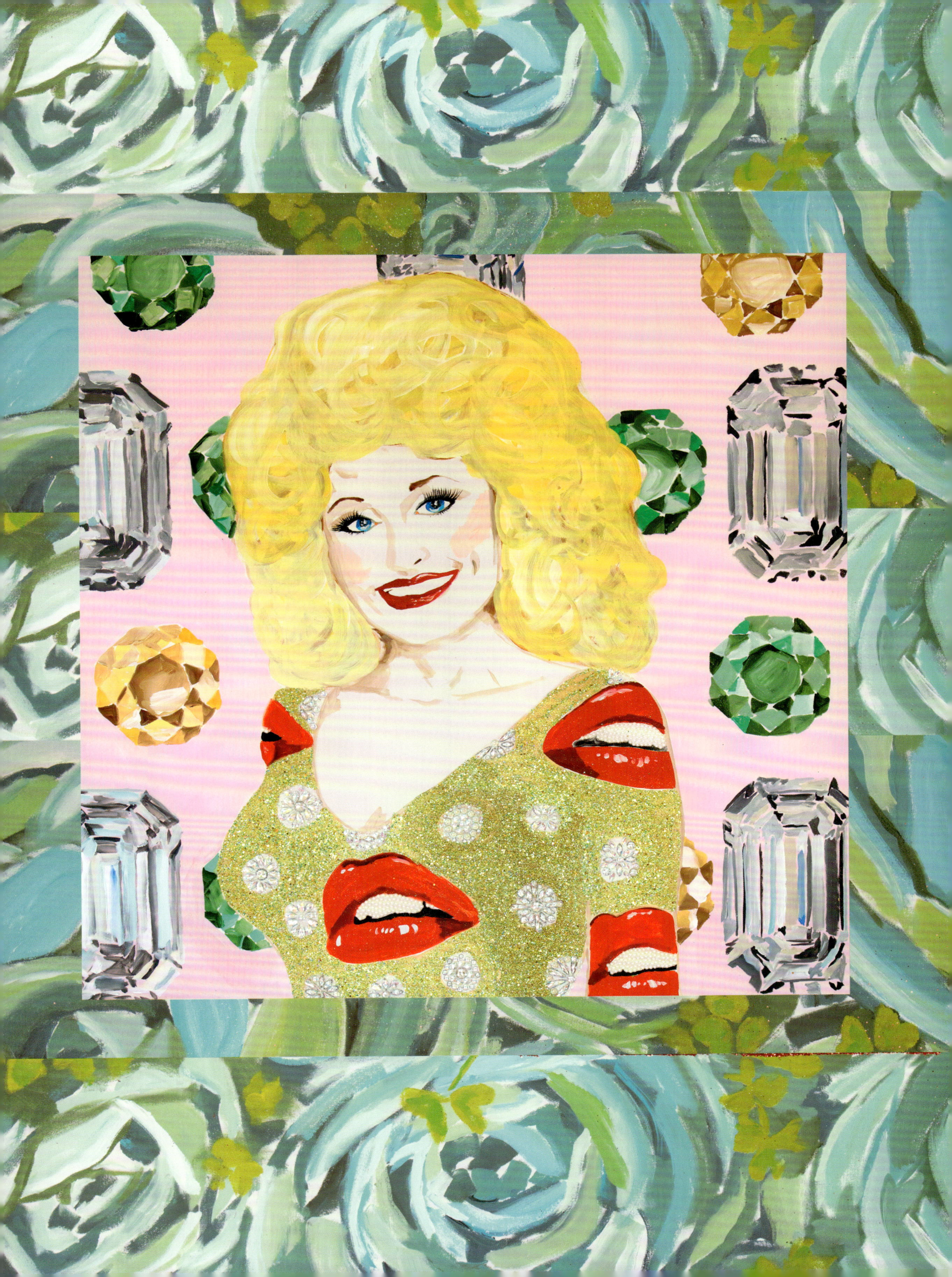

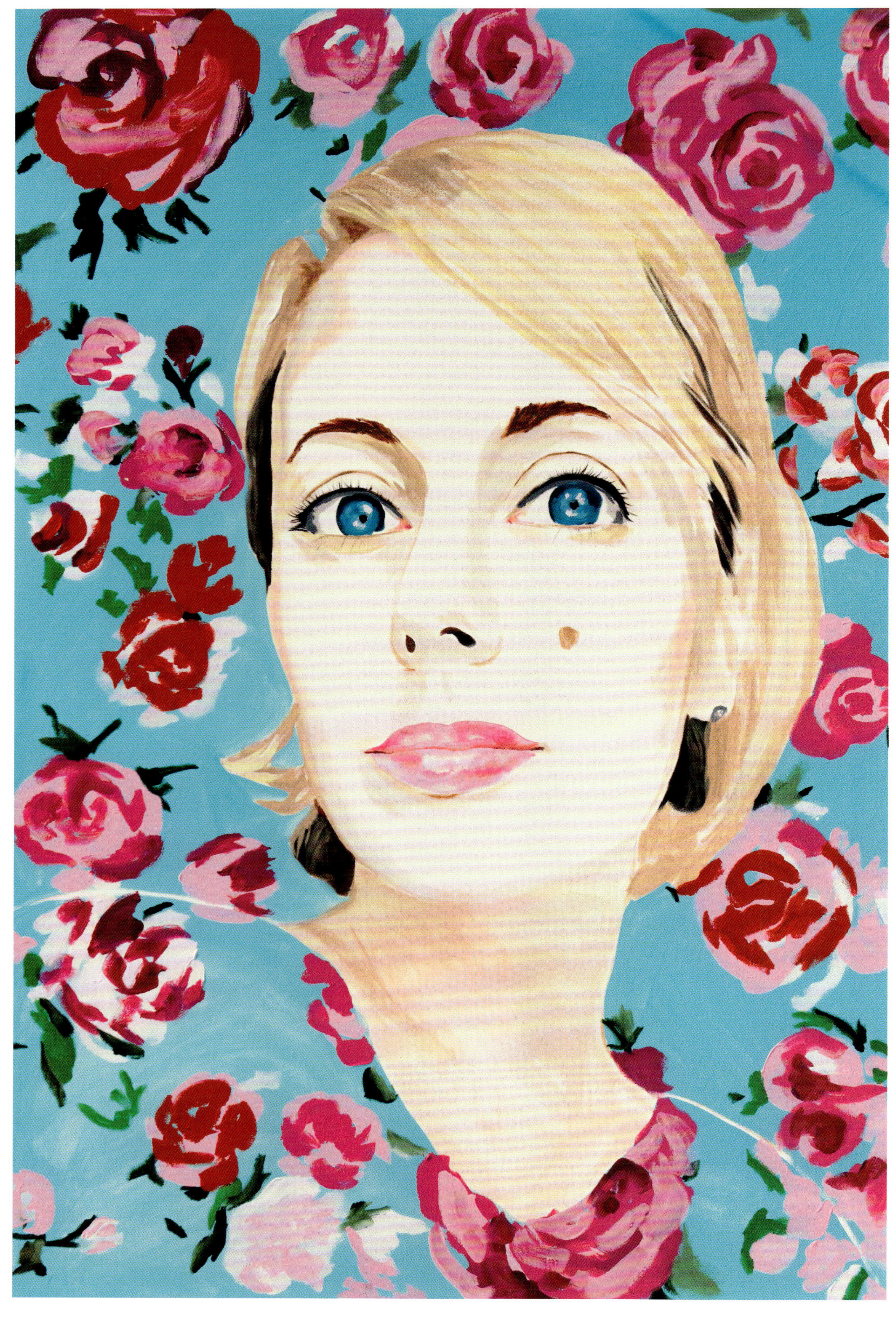

IN LOVING MEMORY OF MY BEAUTIFUL FRIEND ALIX MARTINEZ

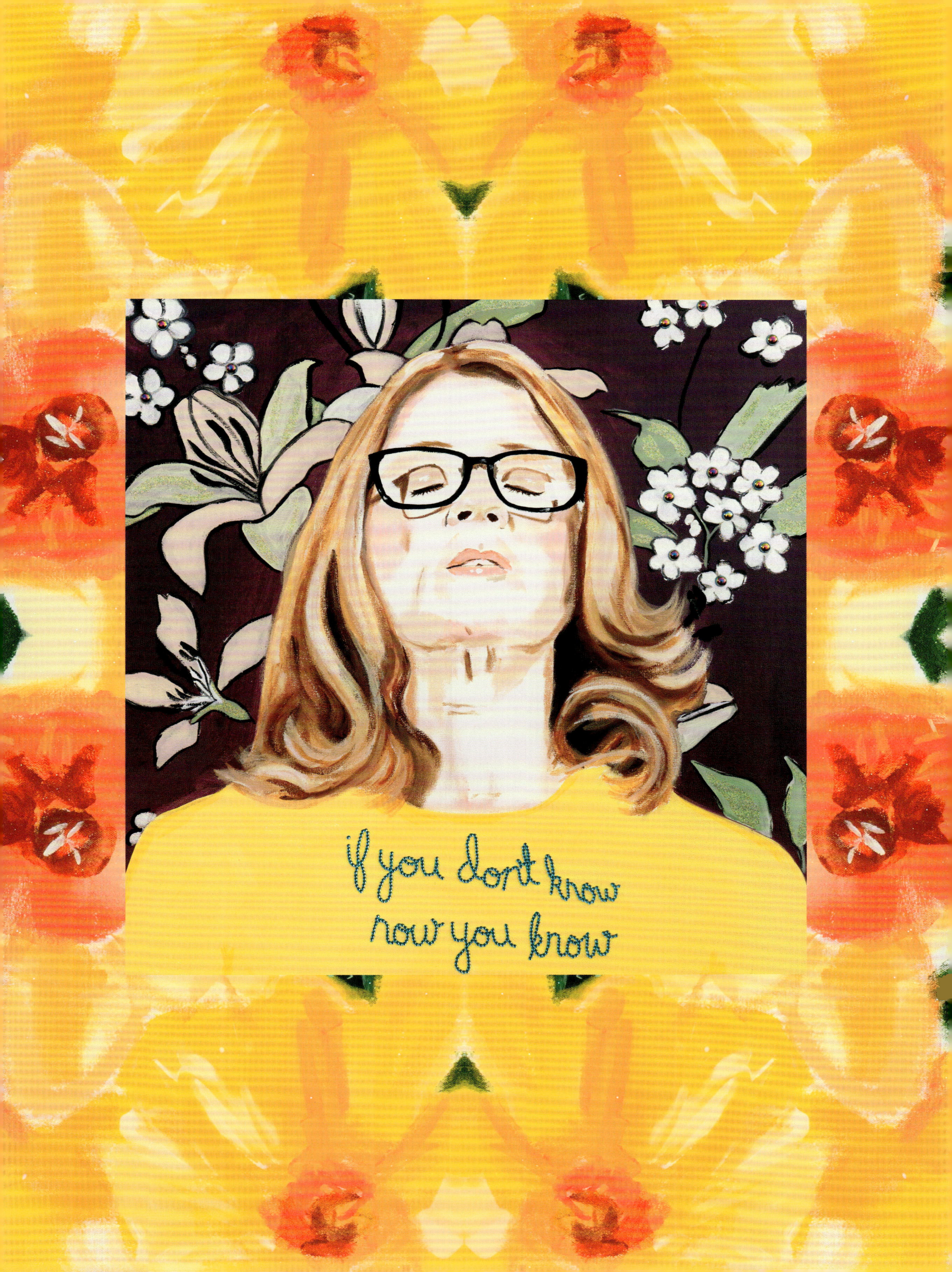
if you don't know
now you know

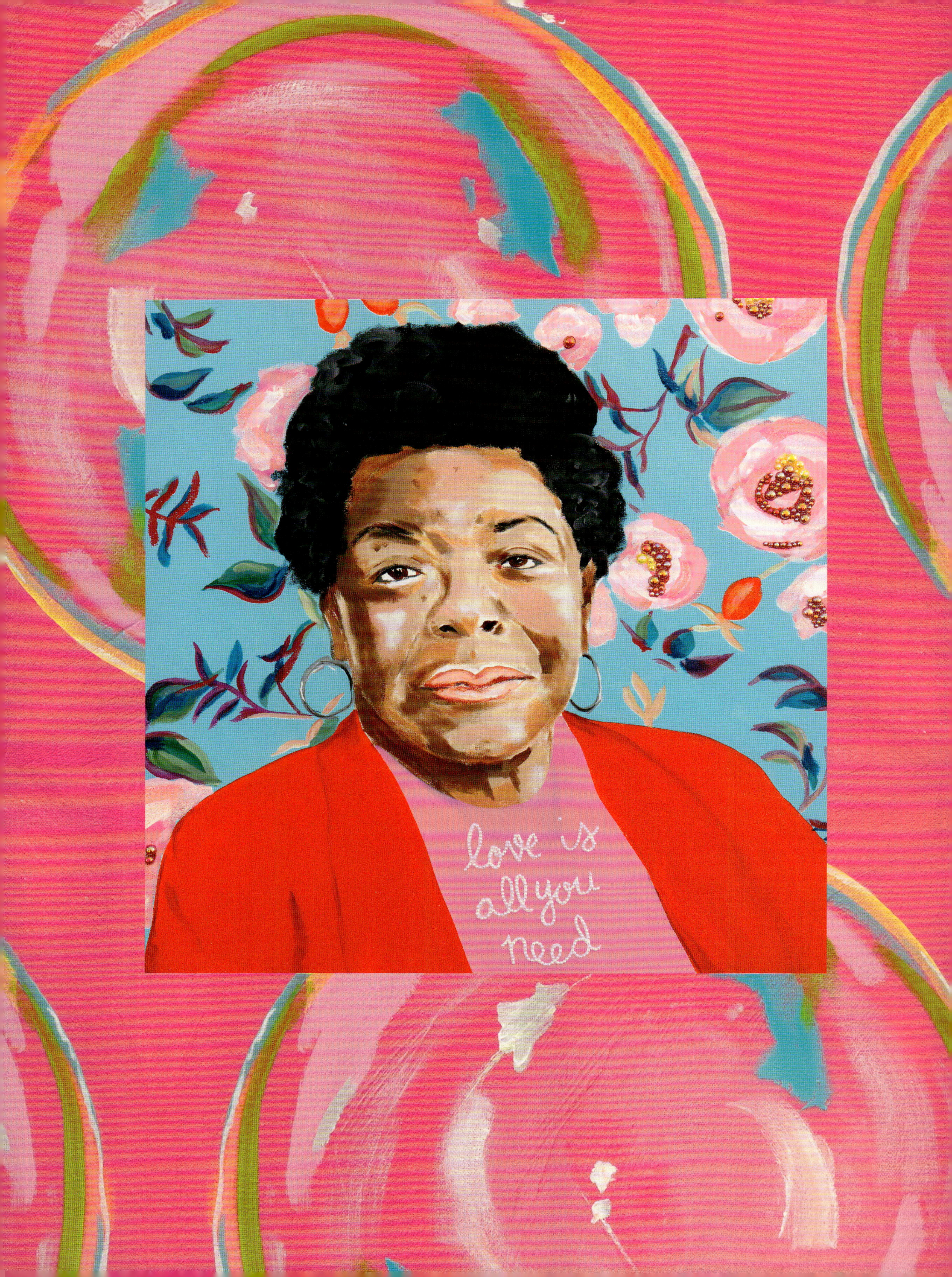
love is
all you
need

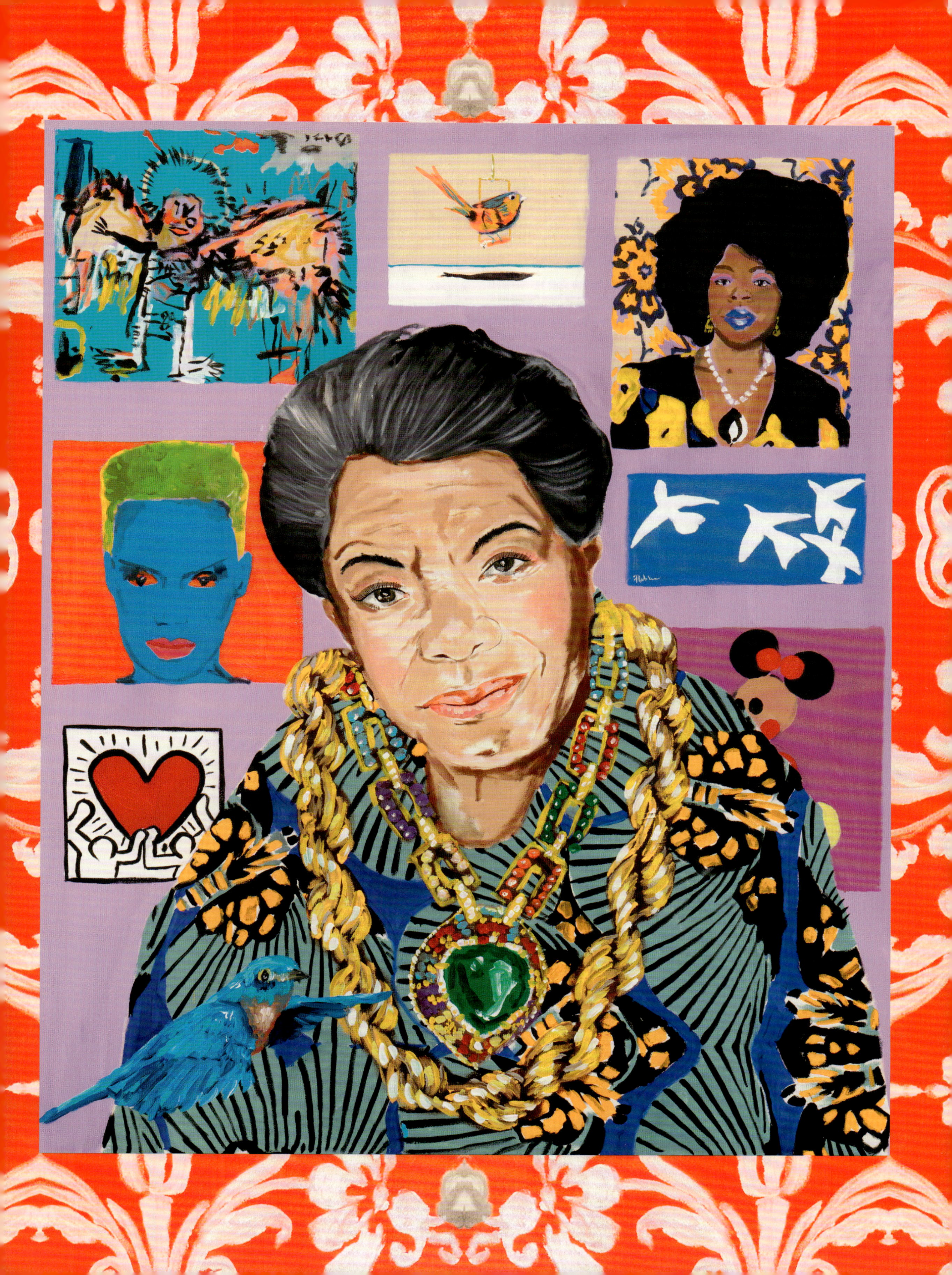

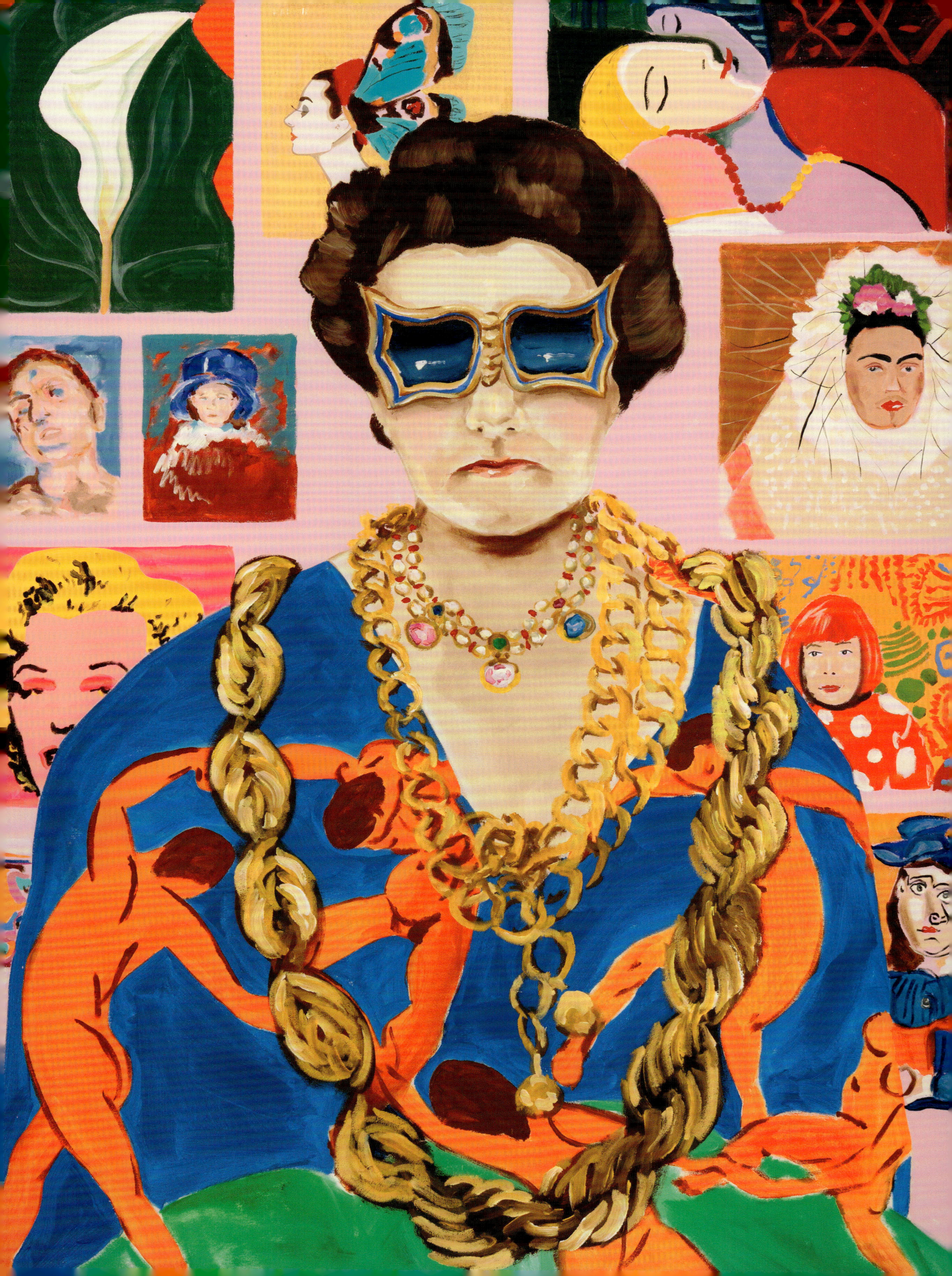

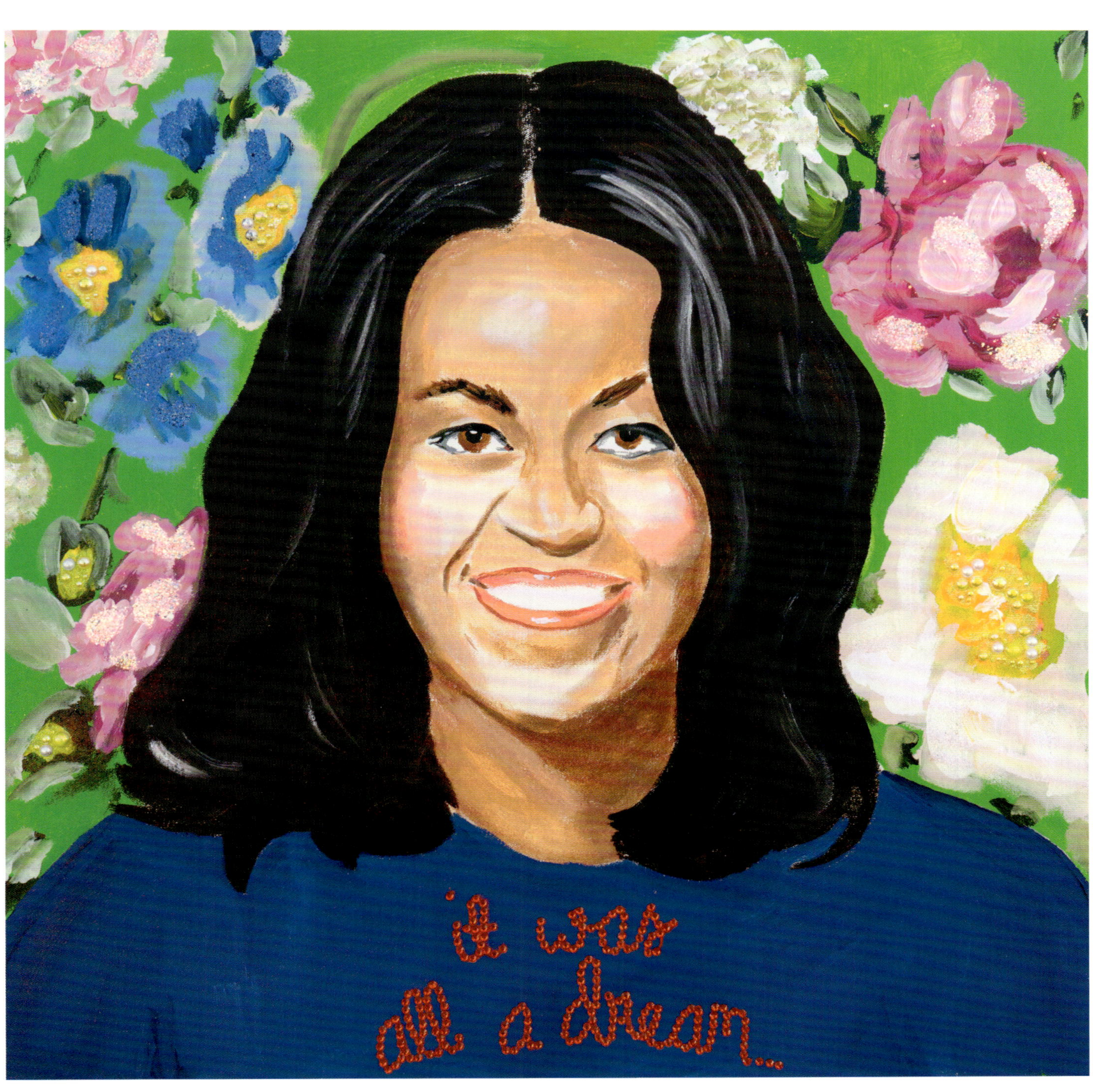
it was
all a dream...

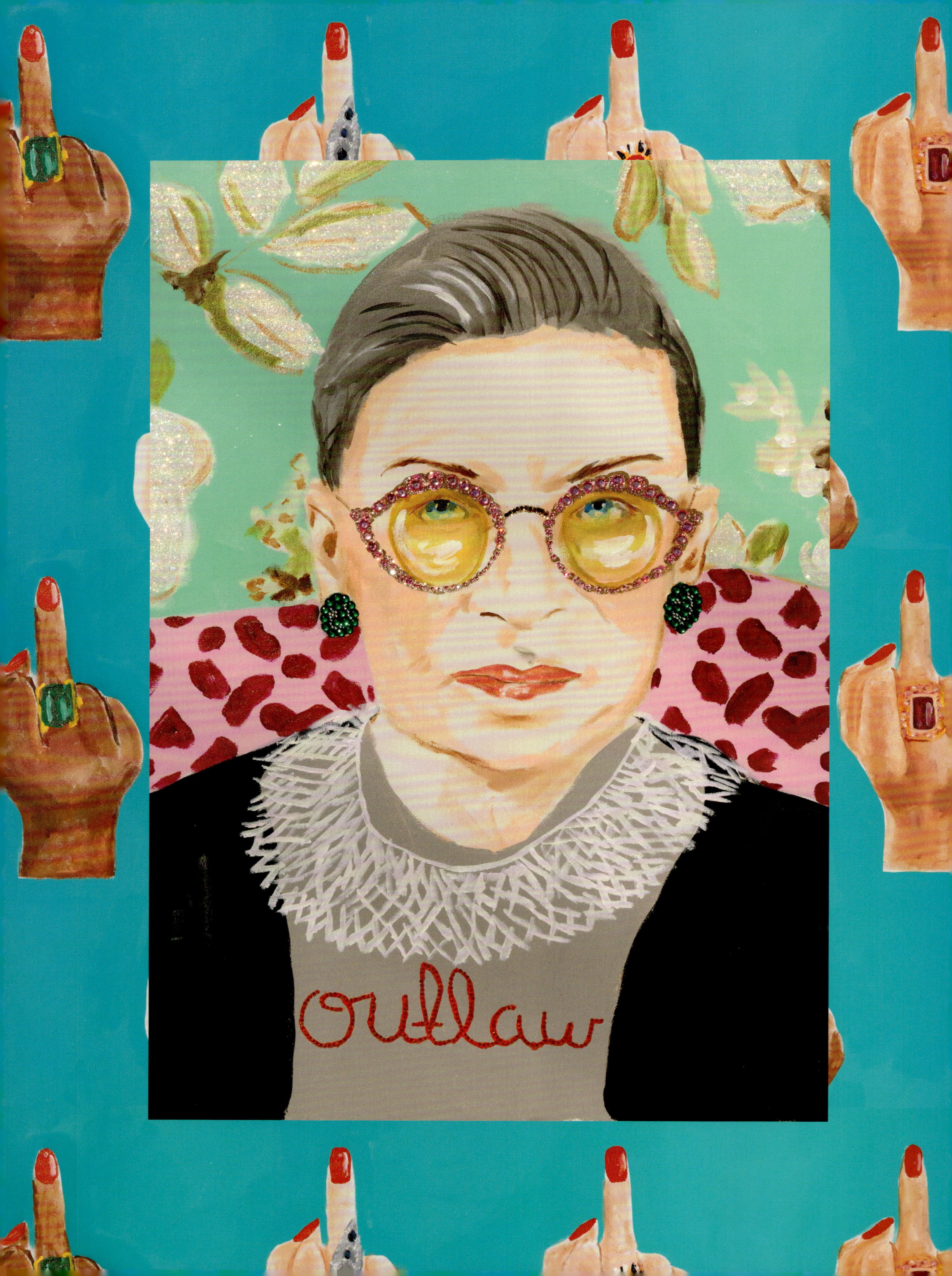
Outlaw

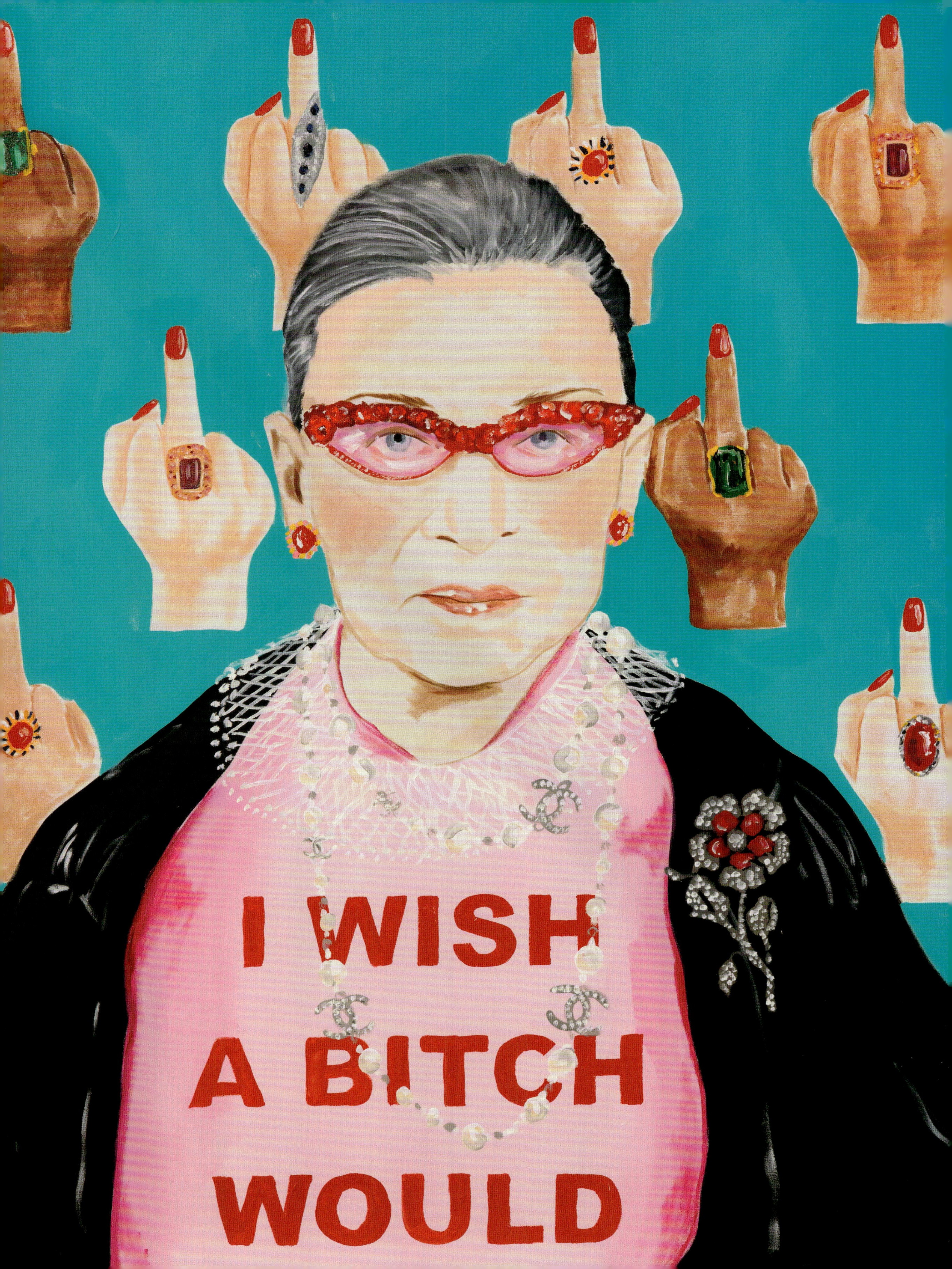
I WISH
A BITCH
WOULD

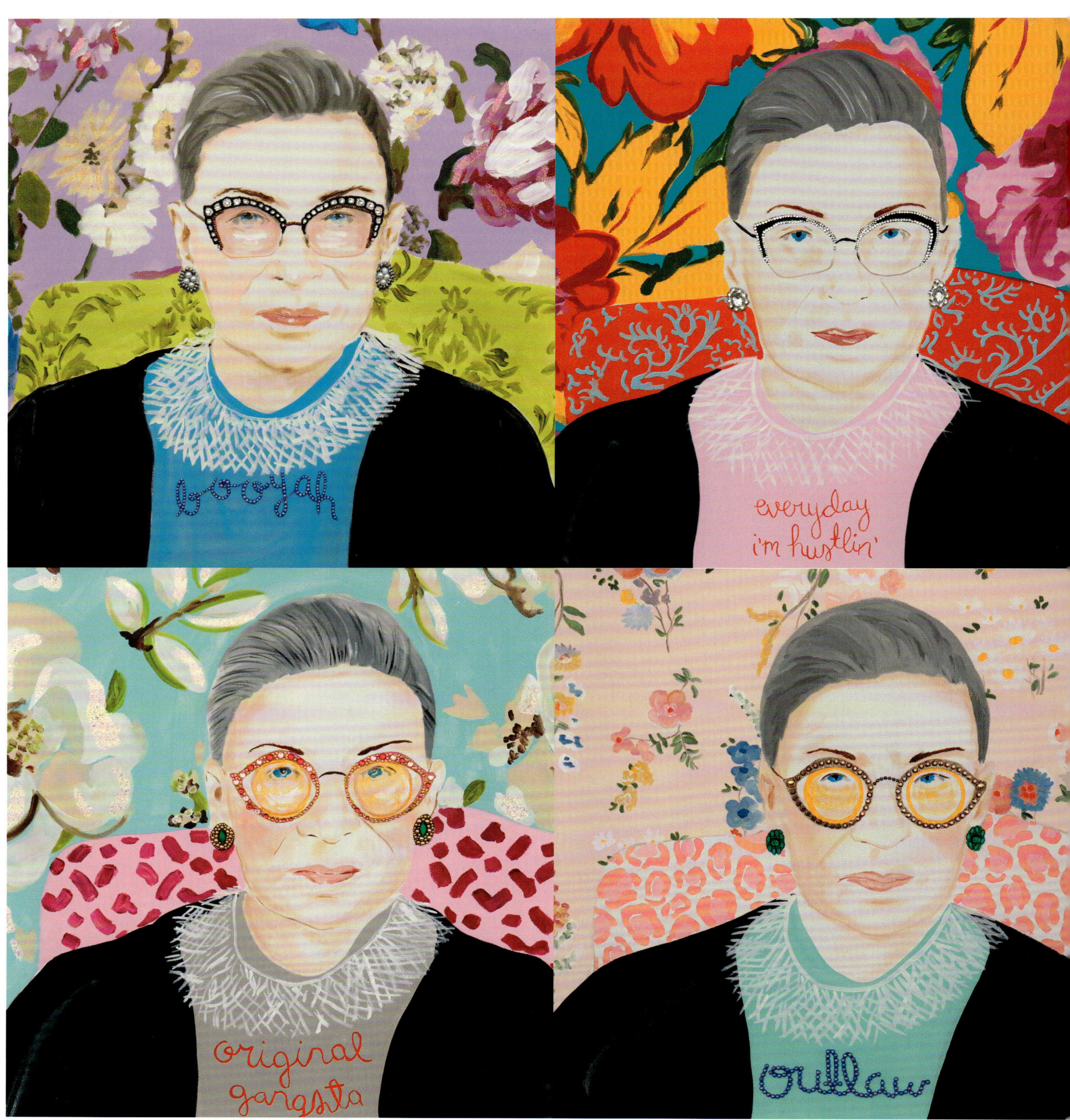
booyah
everyday
i'm hustlin'
original
gangsta
outlaw

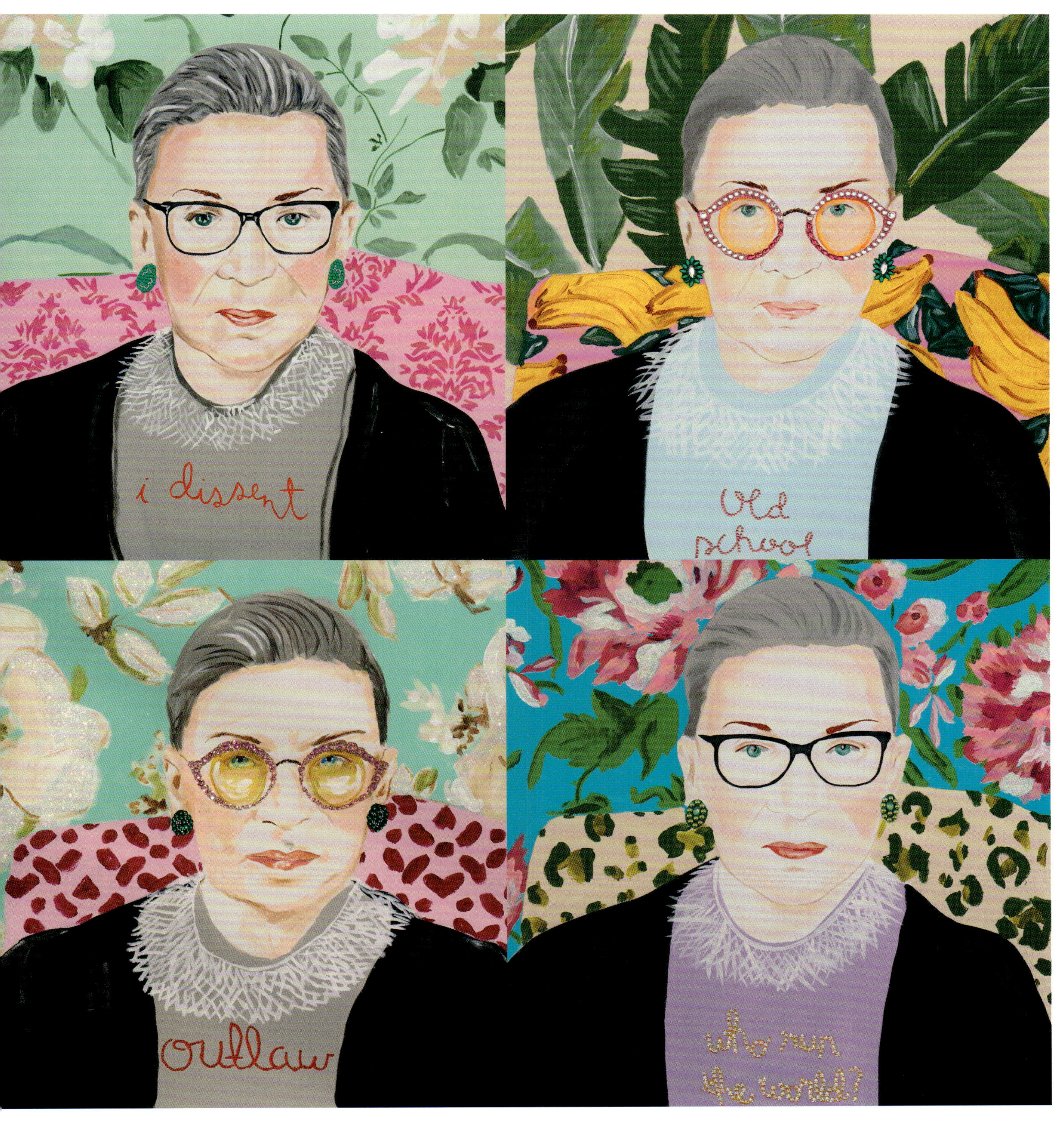

i dissent
Old school
outlaw
who run the world?

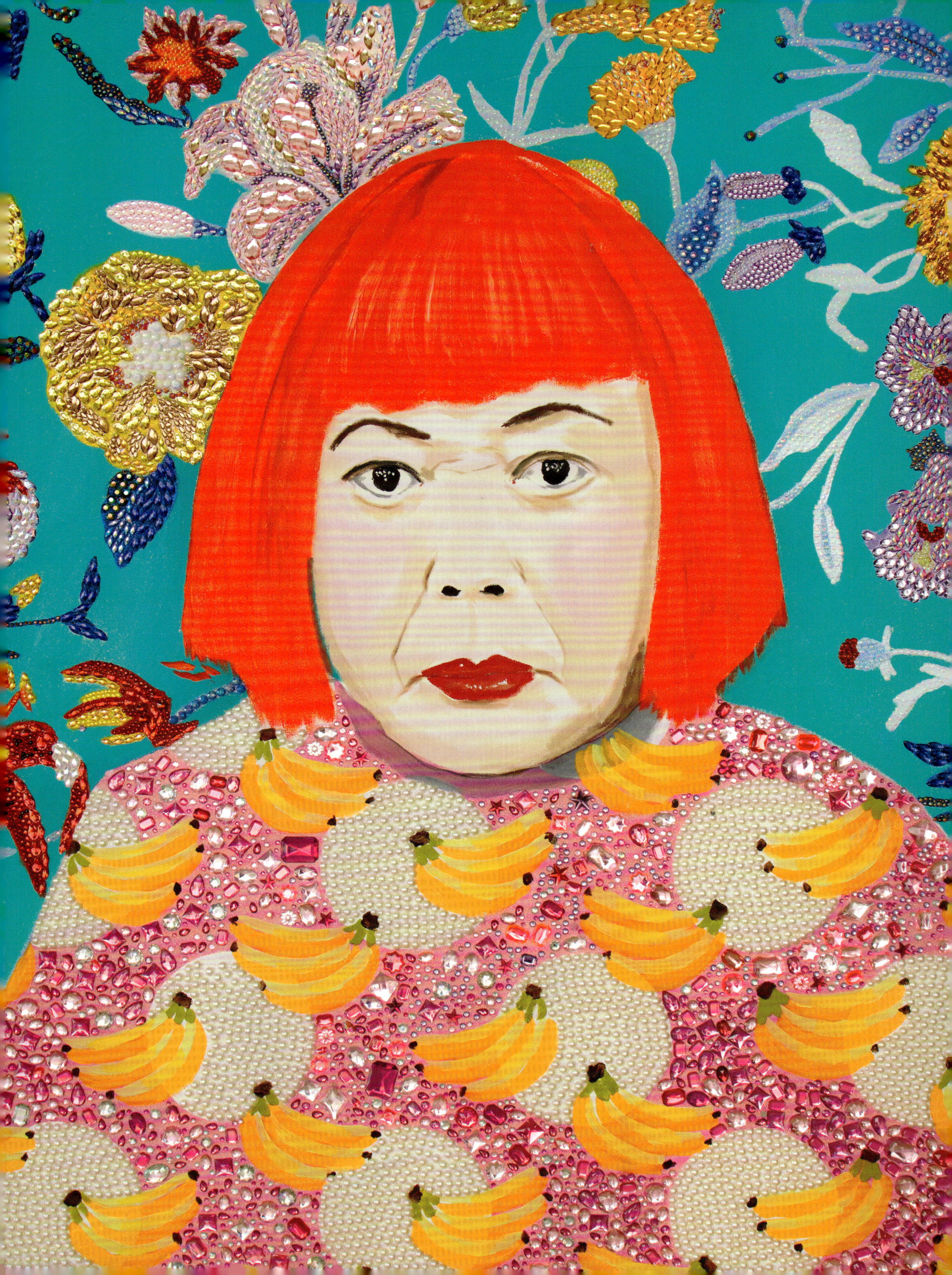

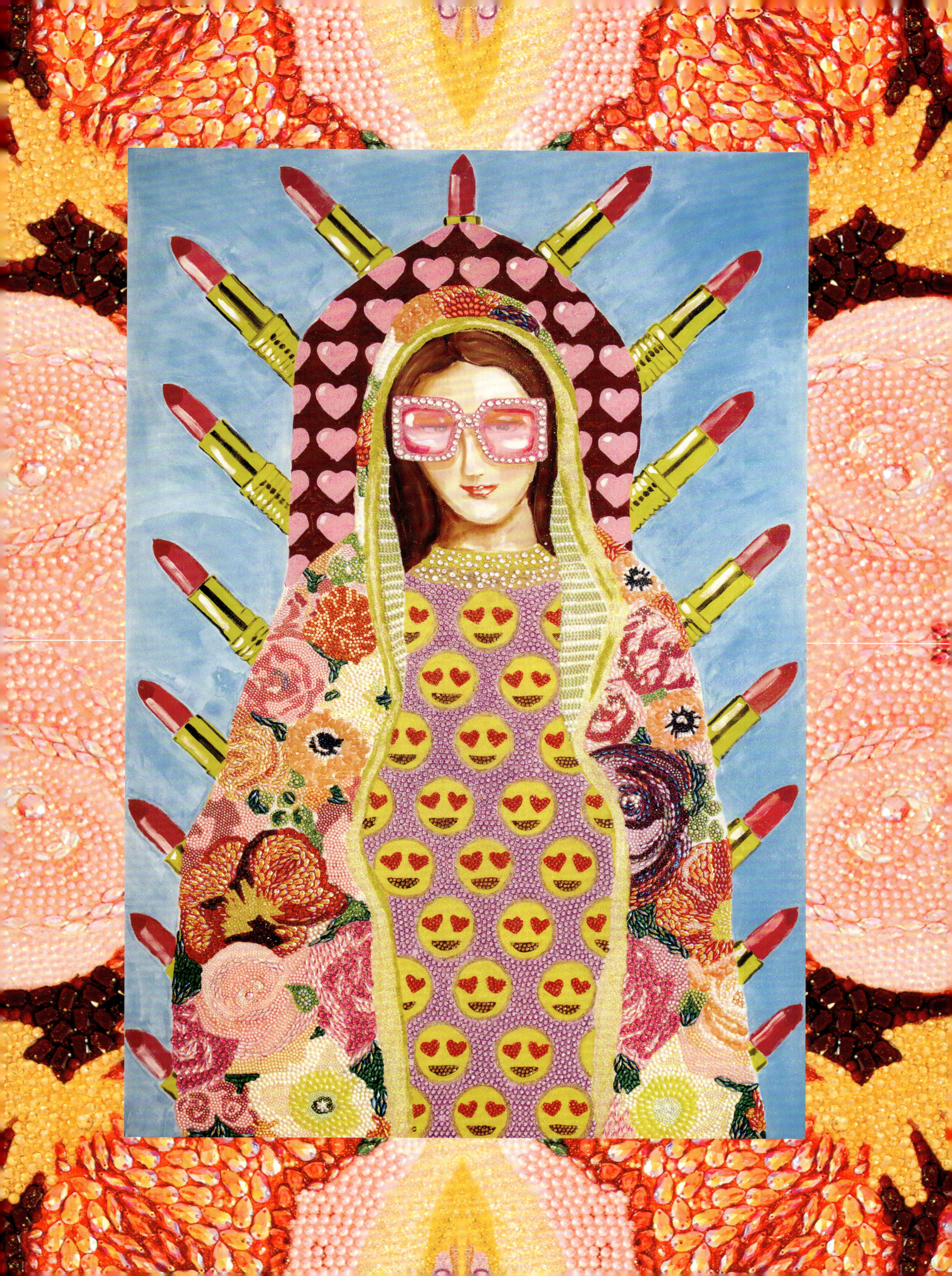

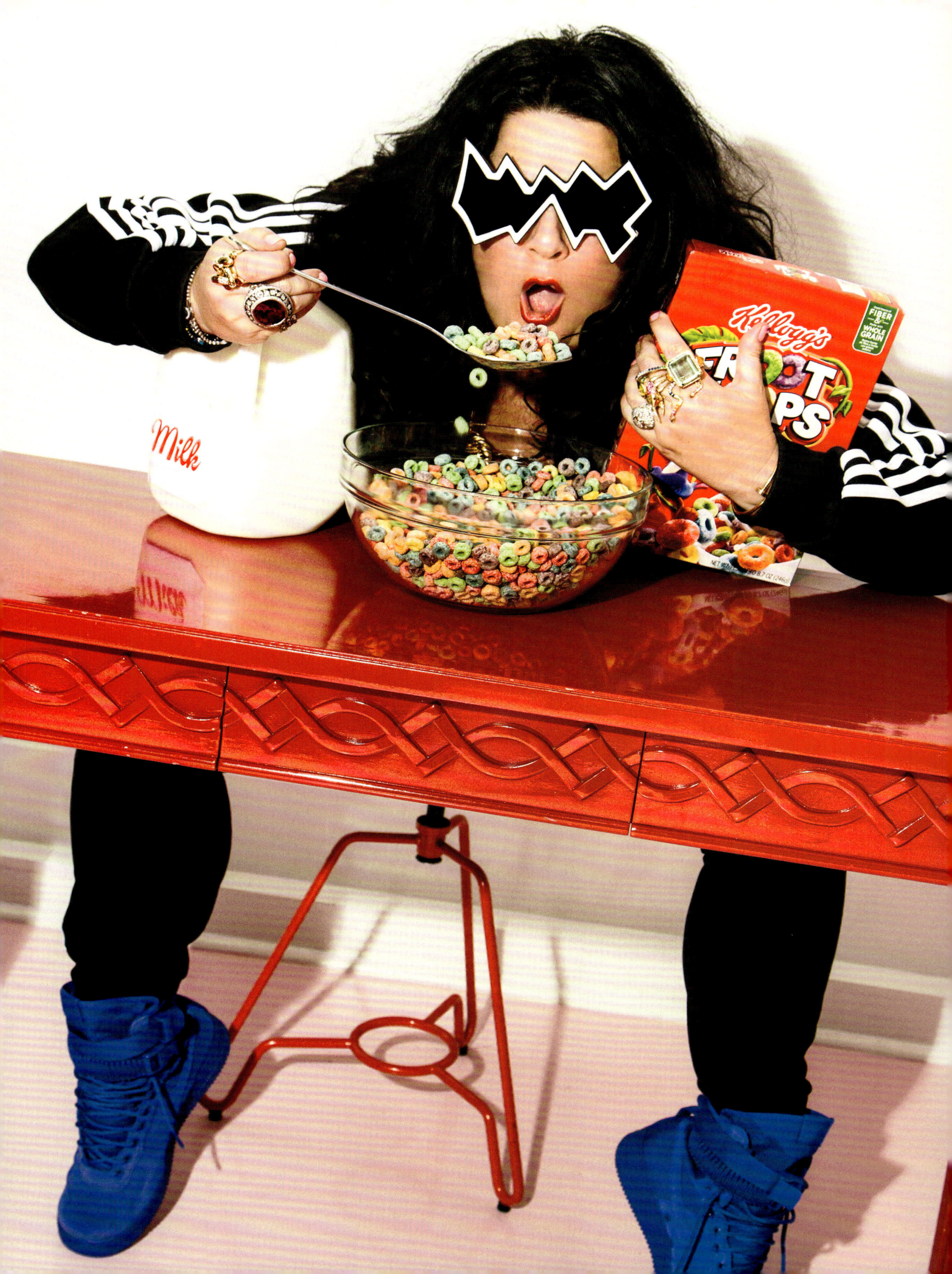
Milk
Kellogg's
FIBER
&
WHOLE GRAIN

BOOK CLUB

Little known FACT...

I HATE to read books...

I would rather watch NETFlIX or Mastutbate... or both

HARVARD BUSINESS REVIEW

Having The Cake, Eating The Cake, Making The Cake Your Bitch

A guide to cake acquisition and distribution

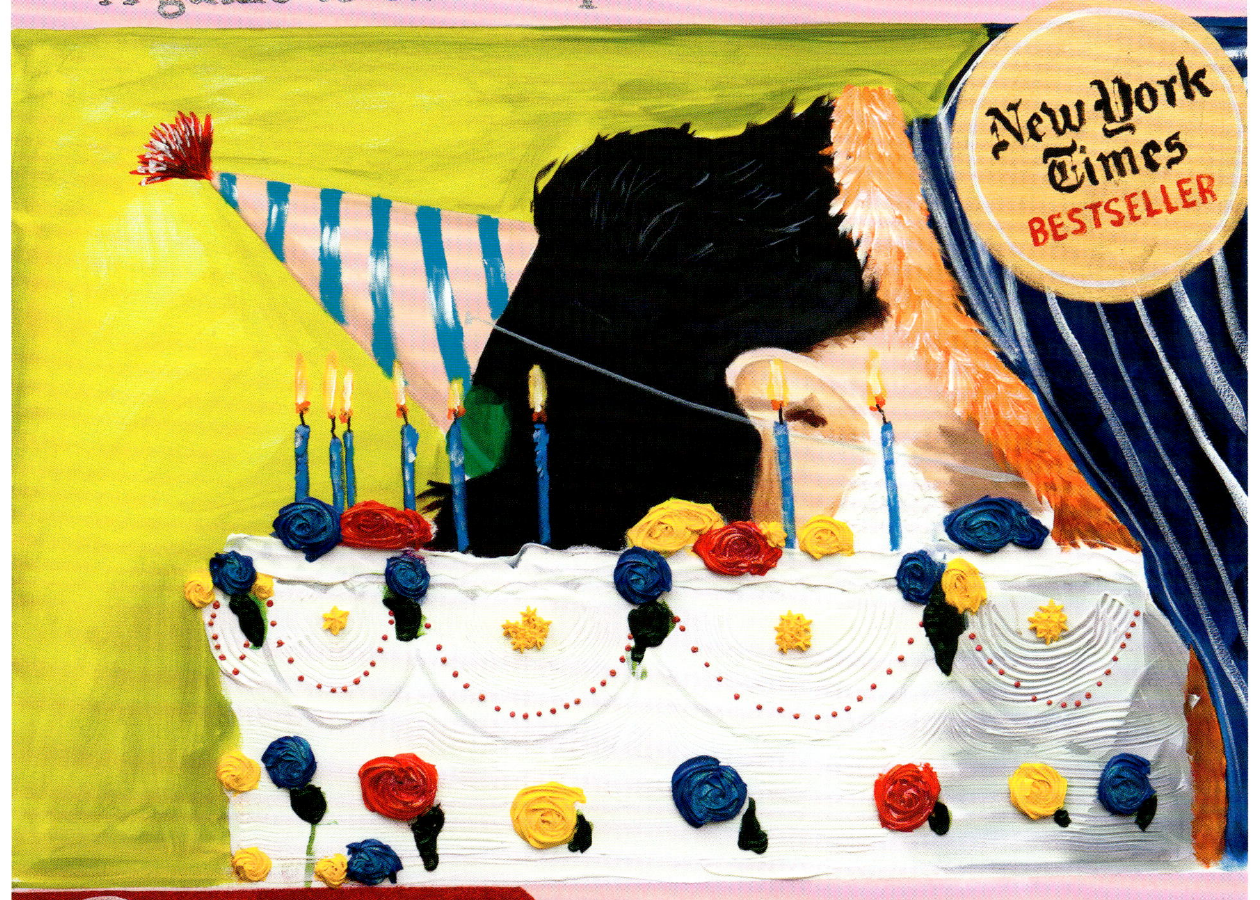

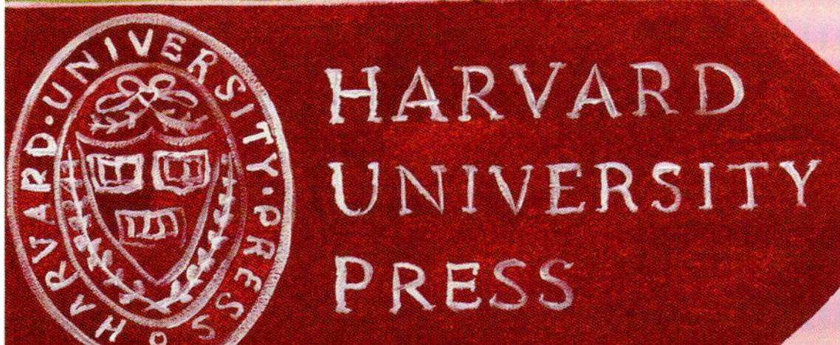

Ashley Longshore

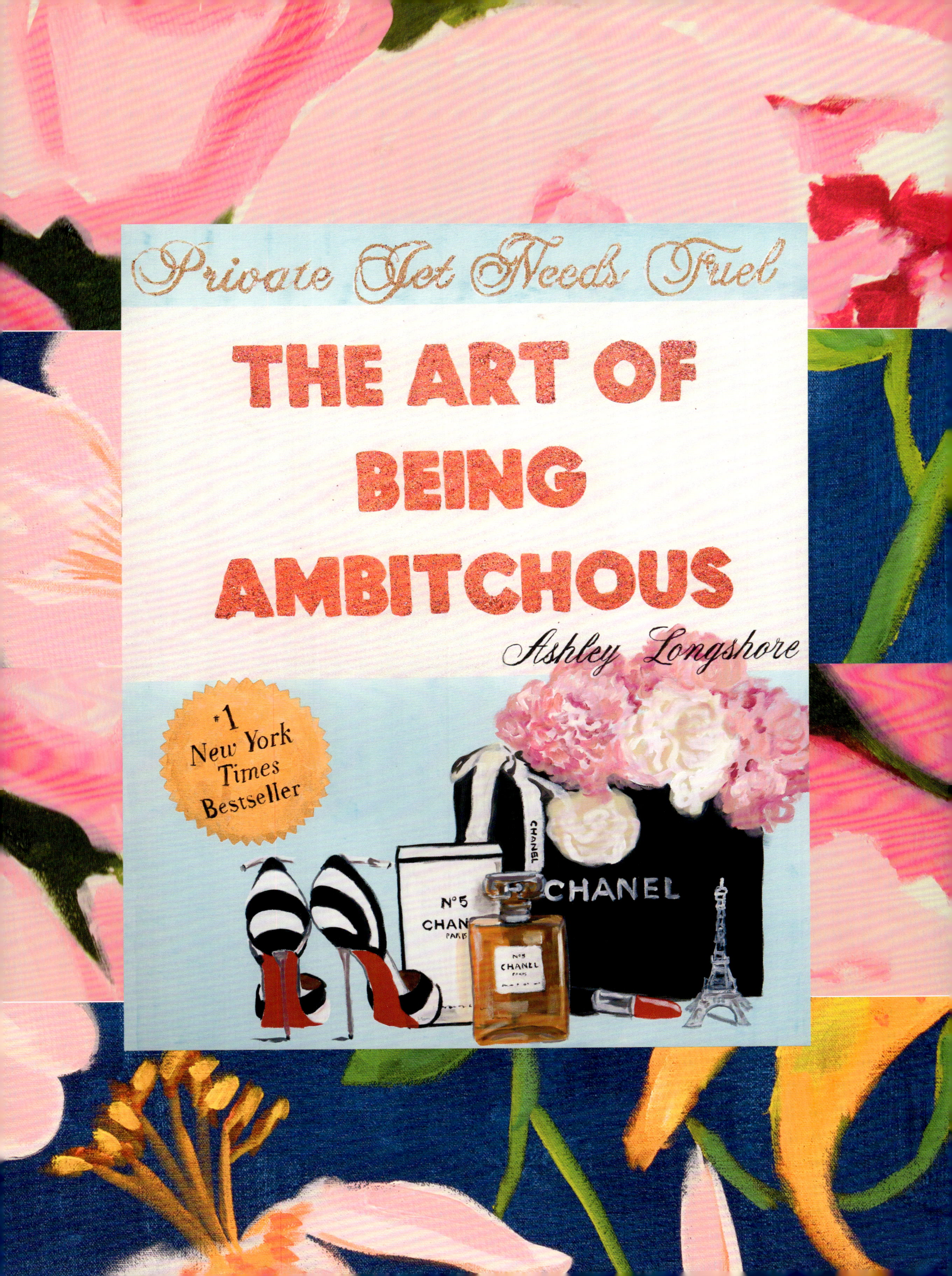
Private Jet Needs Fuel
THE ART OF
BEING
AMBITCHOUS
Ashley Longshore
#1
New York
Times
Bestseller
CHANEL
CHANEL
N°5
CHAN
PARIS
N°5
CHANEL

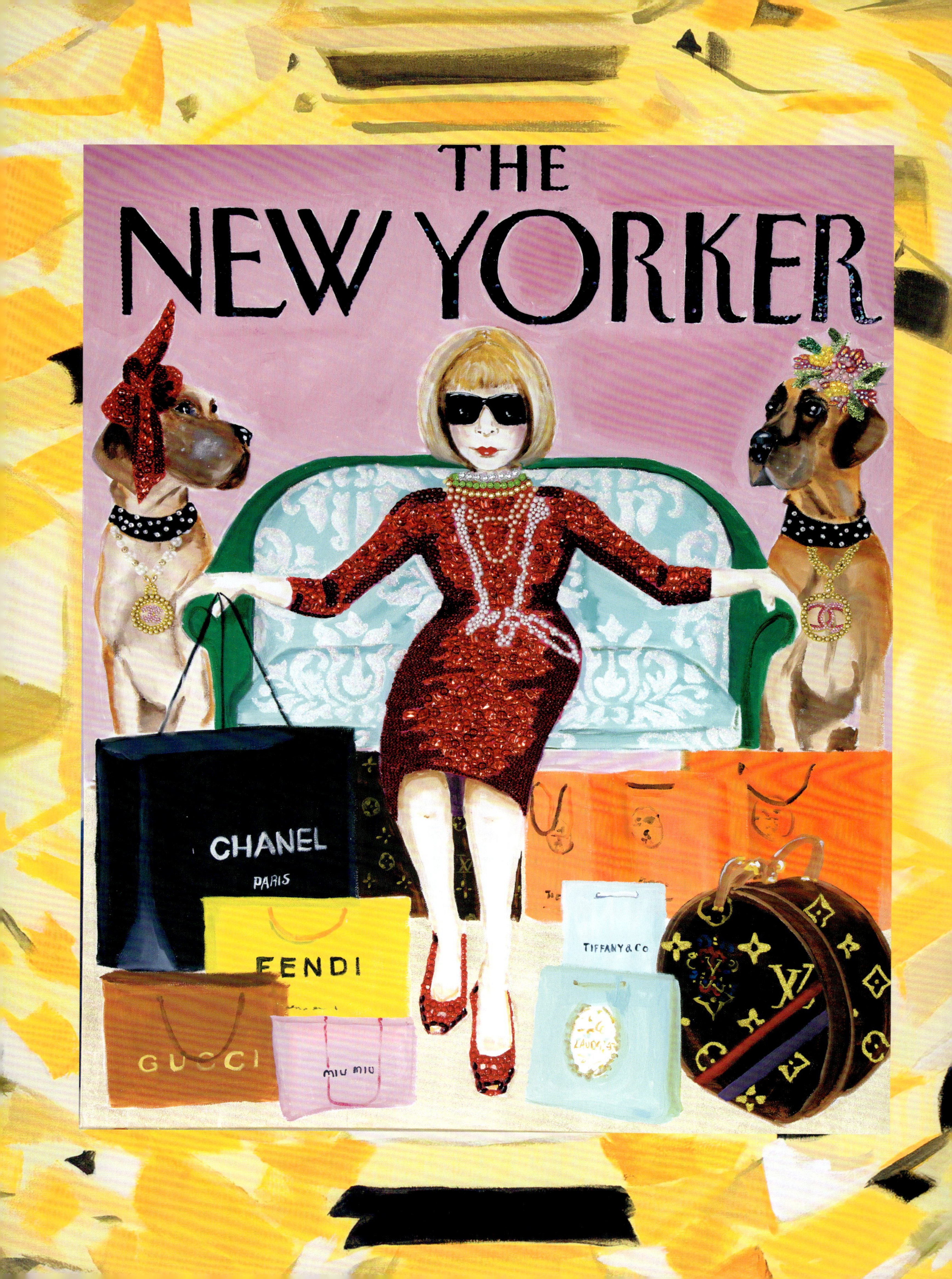
THE
NEW YORKER
CHANEL
PARIS
FENDI
GUCCI
miu miu
TIFFANY & Co

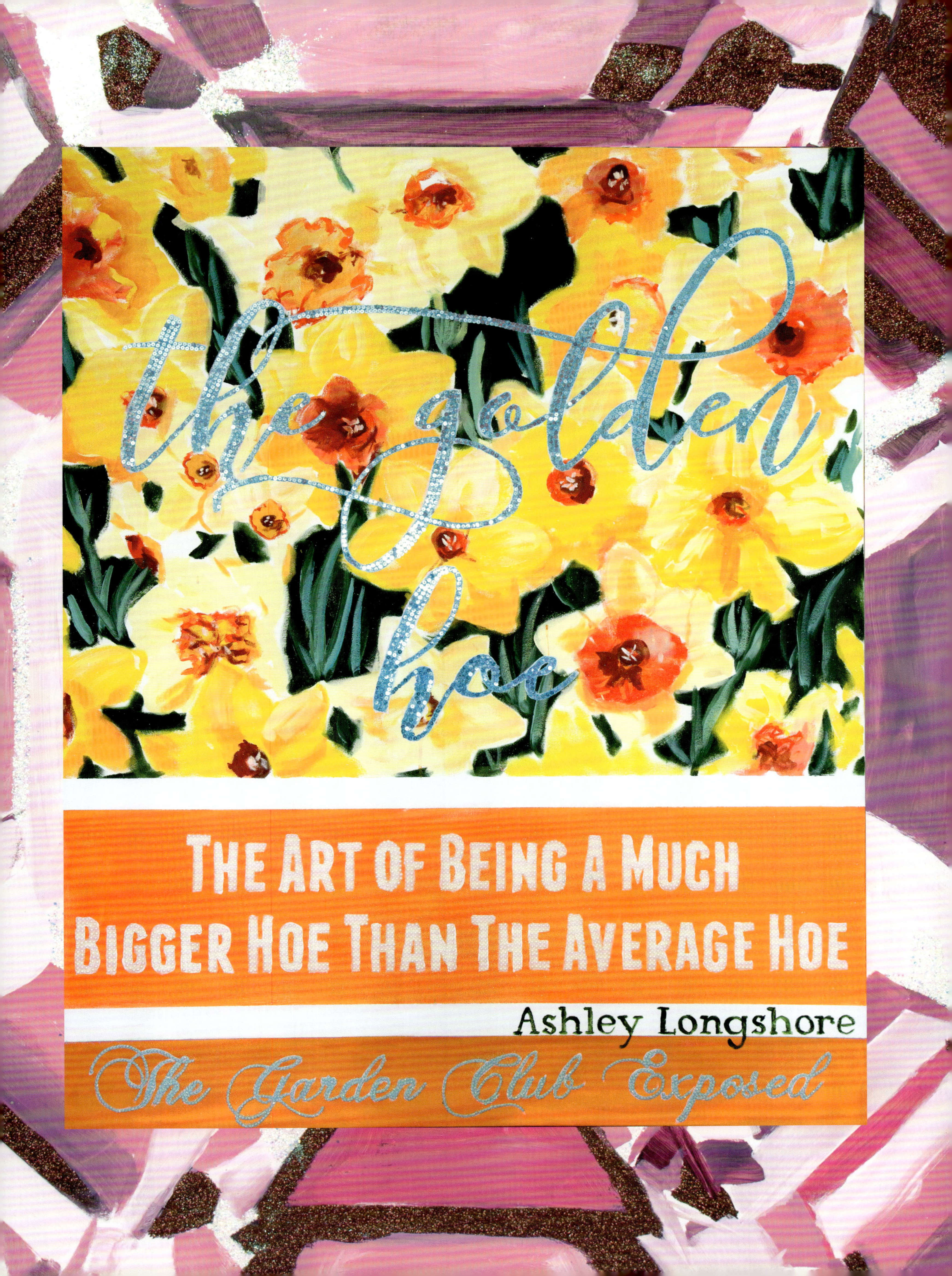
the golden hoe
THE ART OF BEING A MUCH
BIGGER HOE THAN THE AVERAGE HOE
Ashley Longshore
The Garden Club Exposed

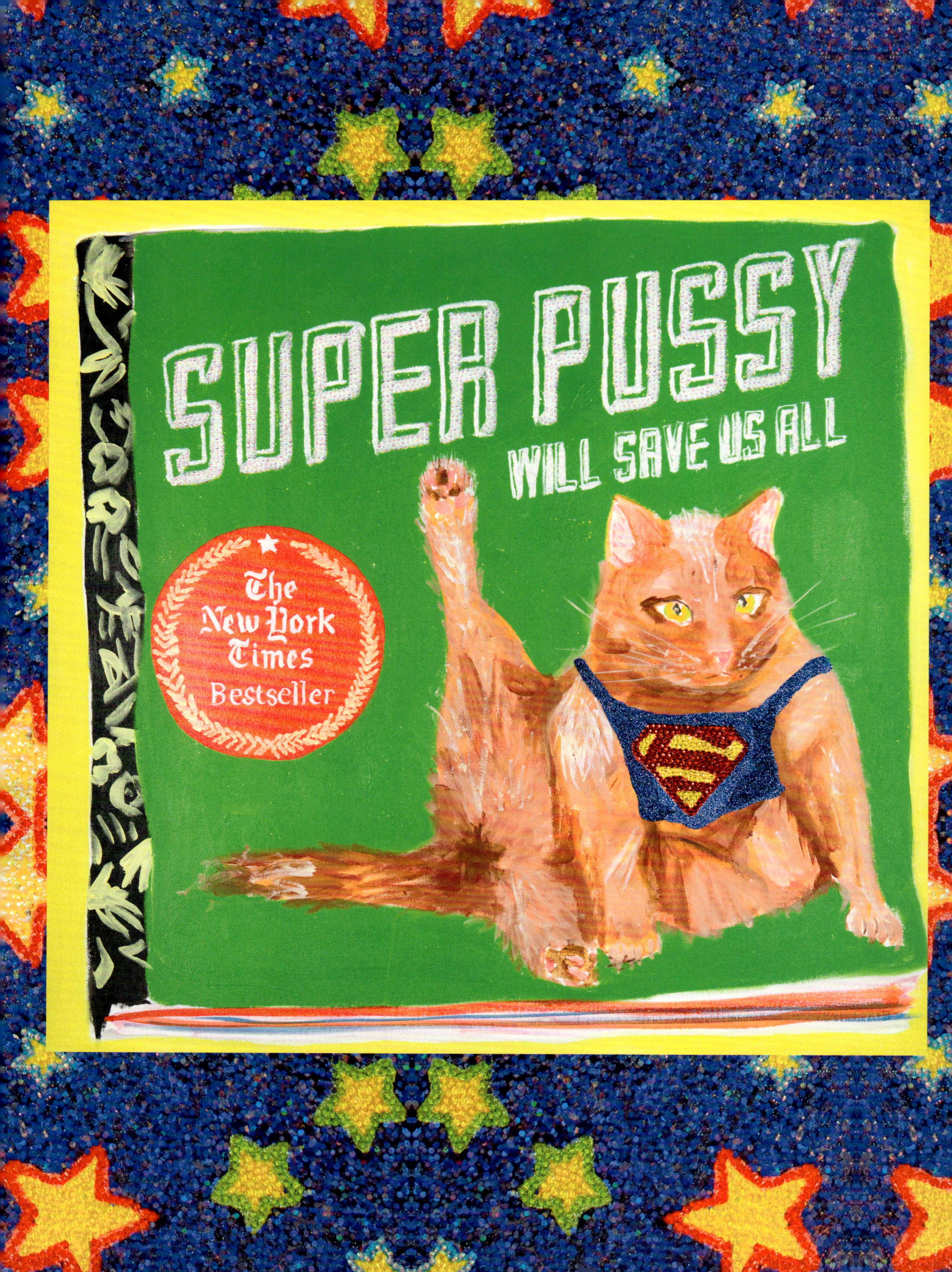

SUPER PUSSY
WILL SAVE US ALL
The New York Times
Bestseller

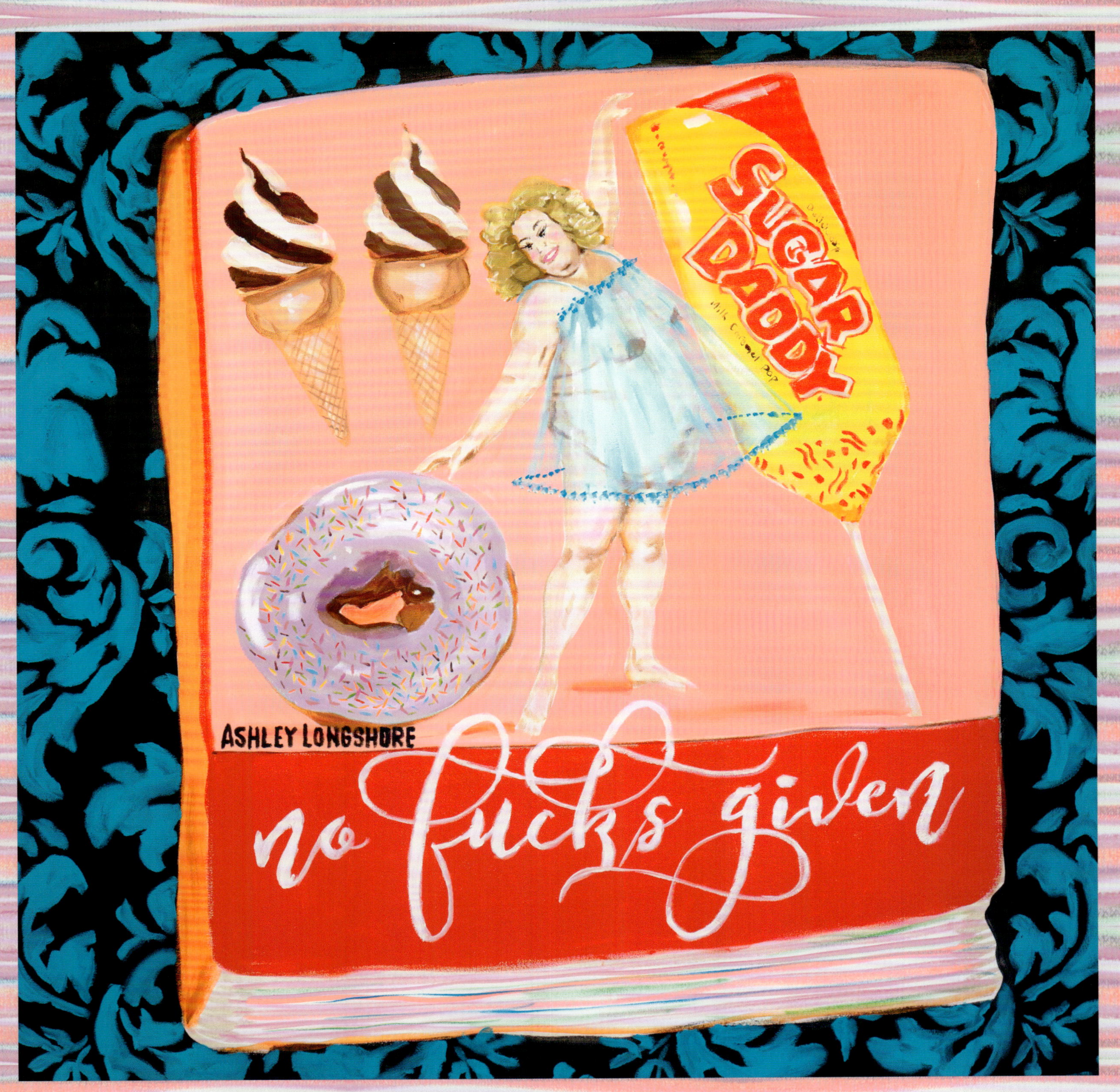
SUGAR DADDY
ASHLEY LONGSHORE
no fucks given

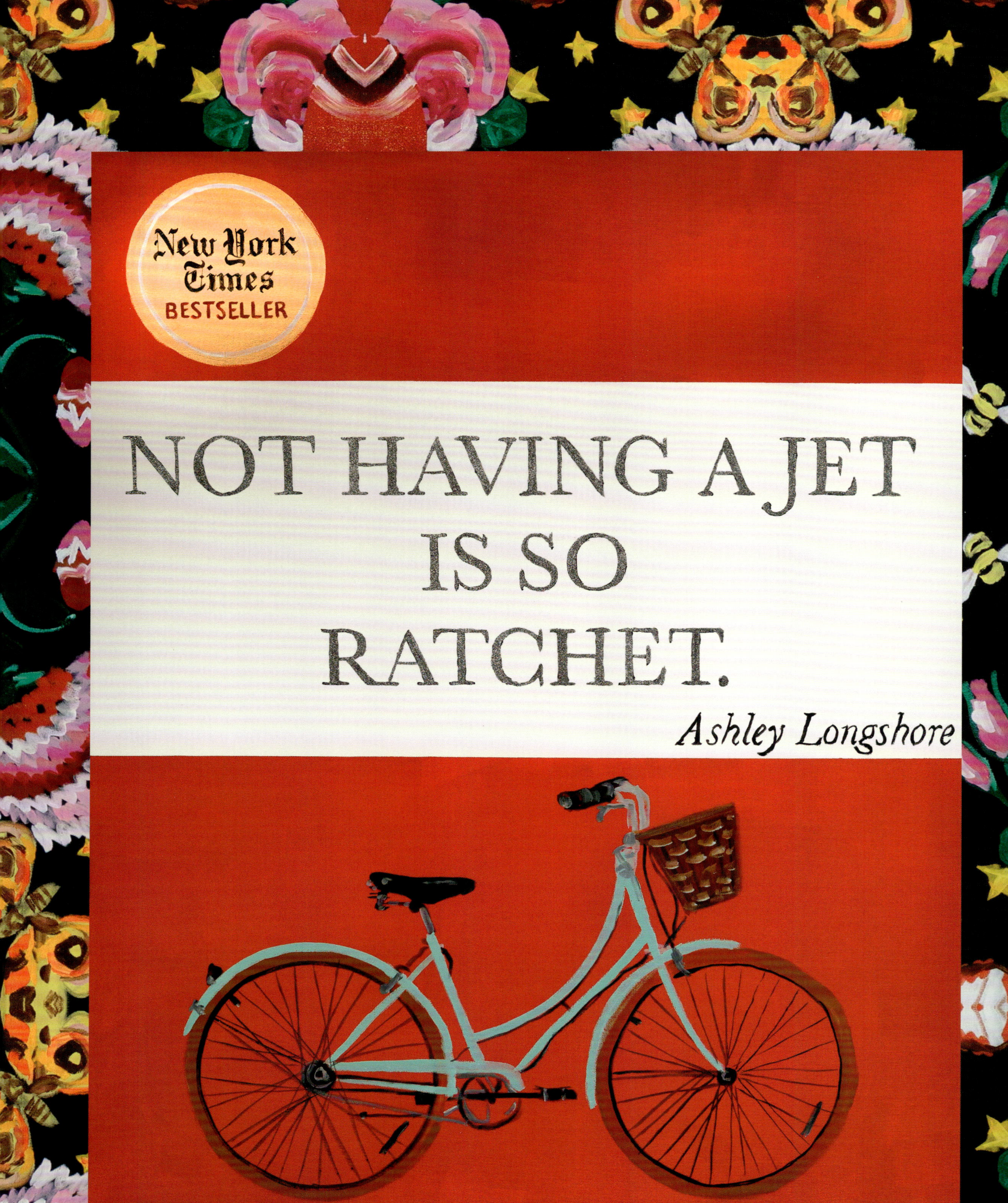
New York Times
BESTSELLER
NOT HAVING A JET
IS SO
RATCHET.
Ashley Longshore

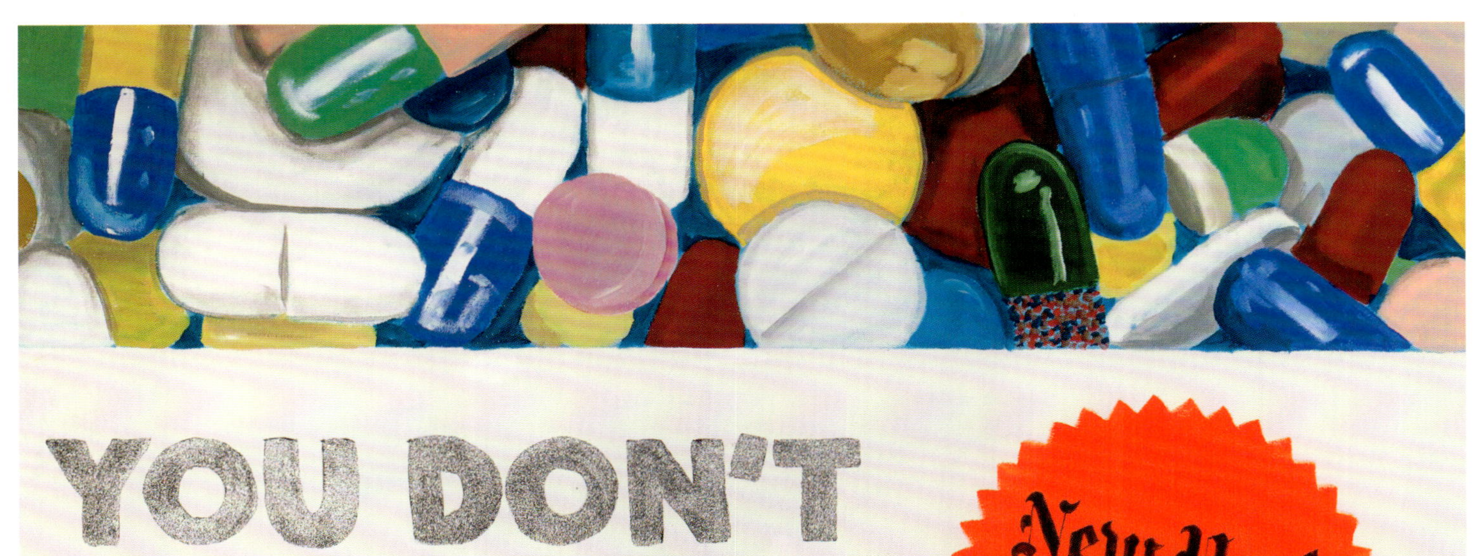
YOU DON'T
LOOK FAT
YOU LOOK
CRAZY

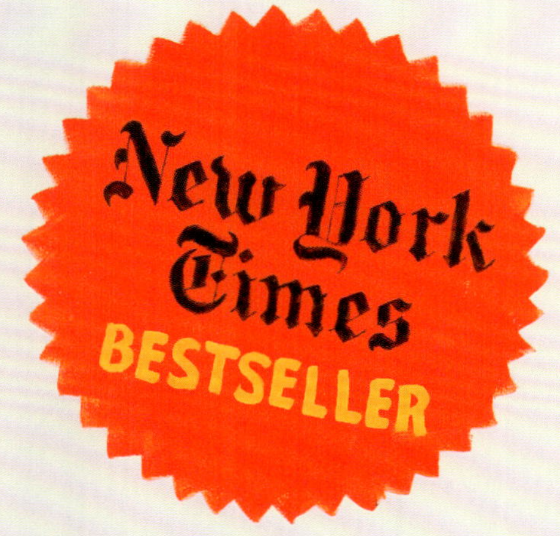
New York
Times
BESTSELLER
Ashley Longshore

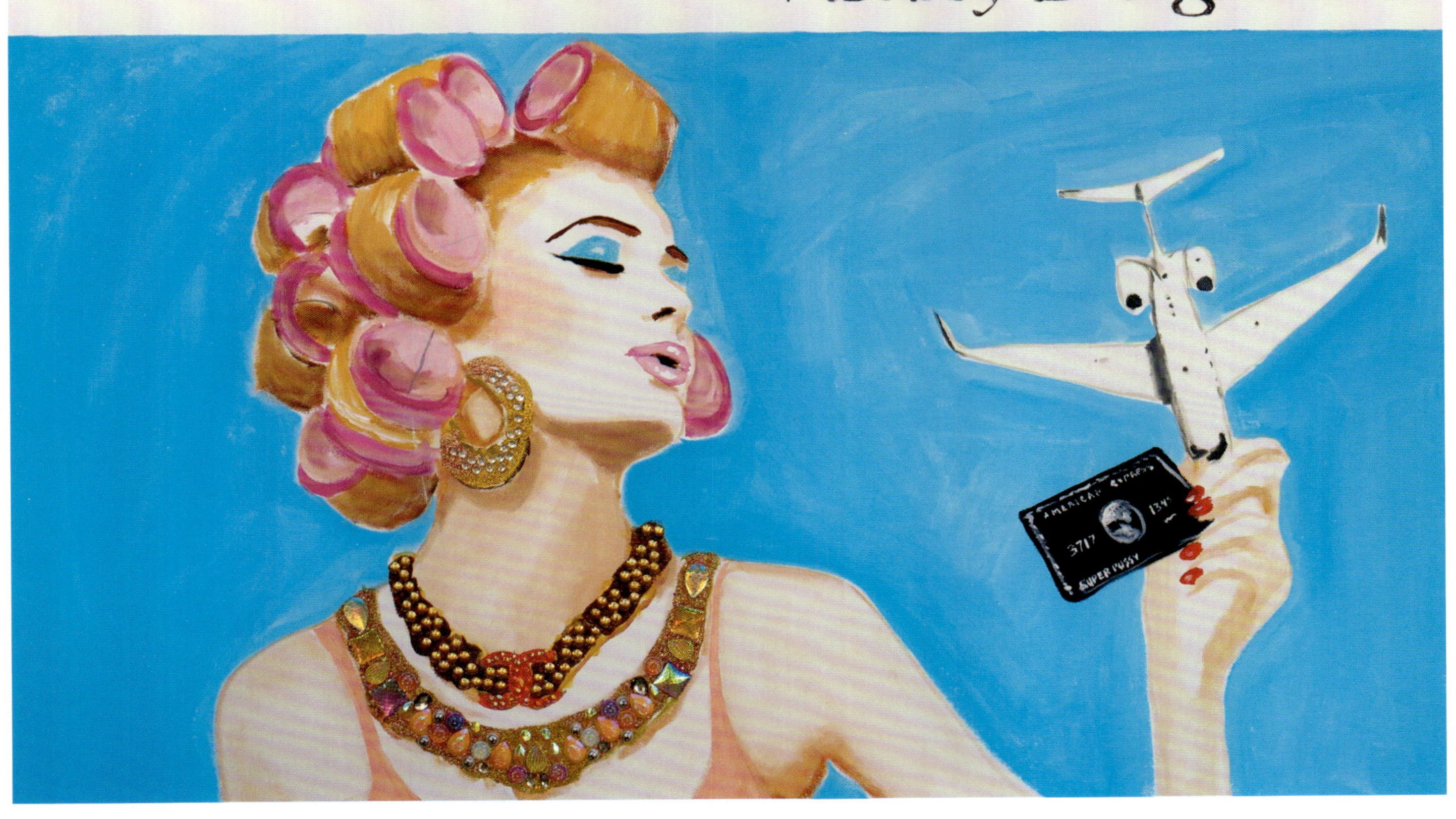

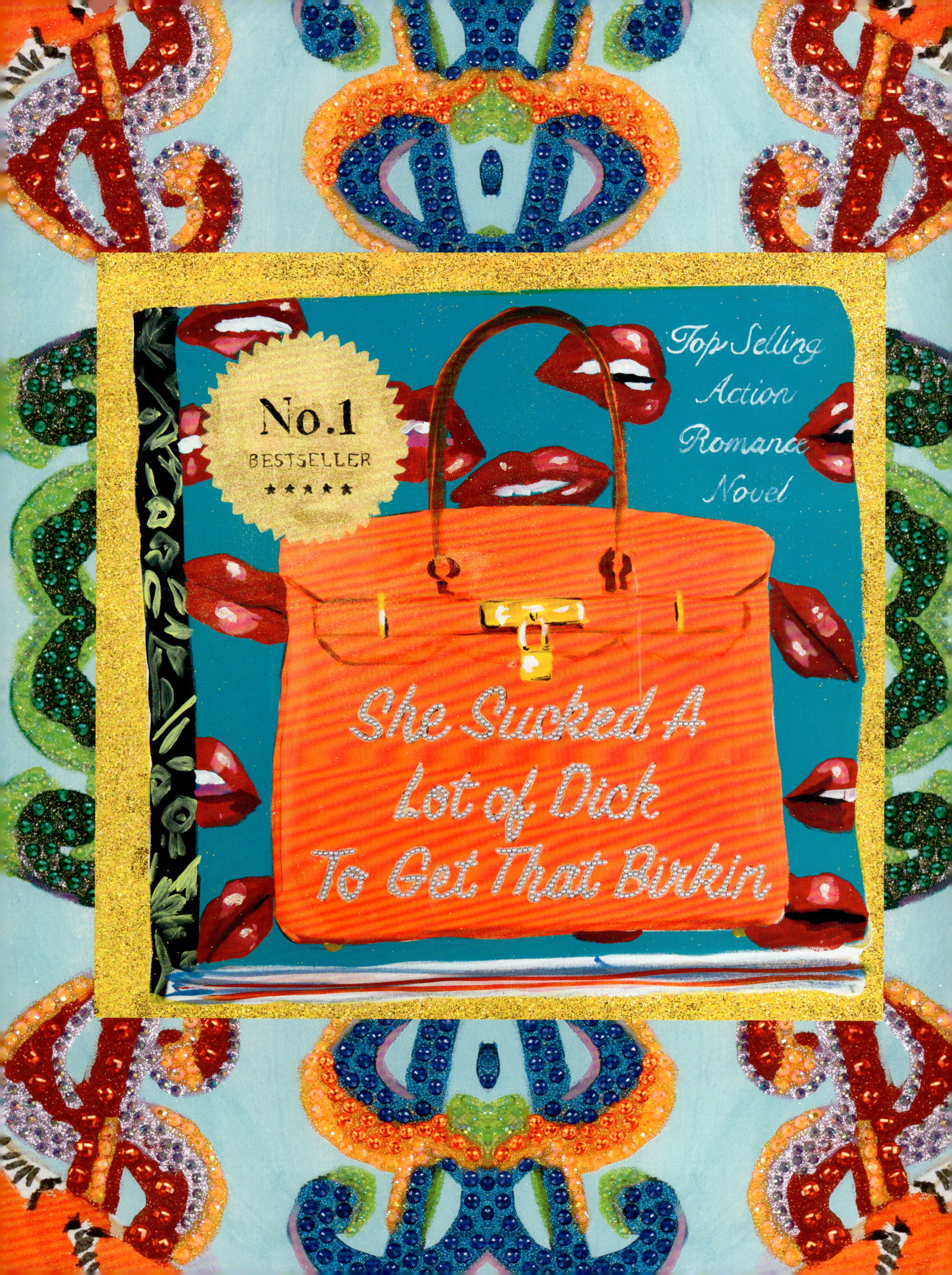
No.1
BESTSELLER
Top Selling
Action
Romance
Novel
She Sucked A
Lot of Dick
To Get That Birkin

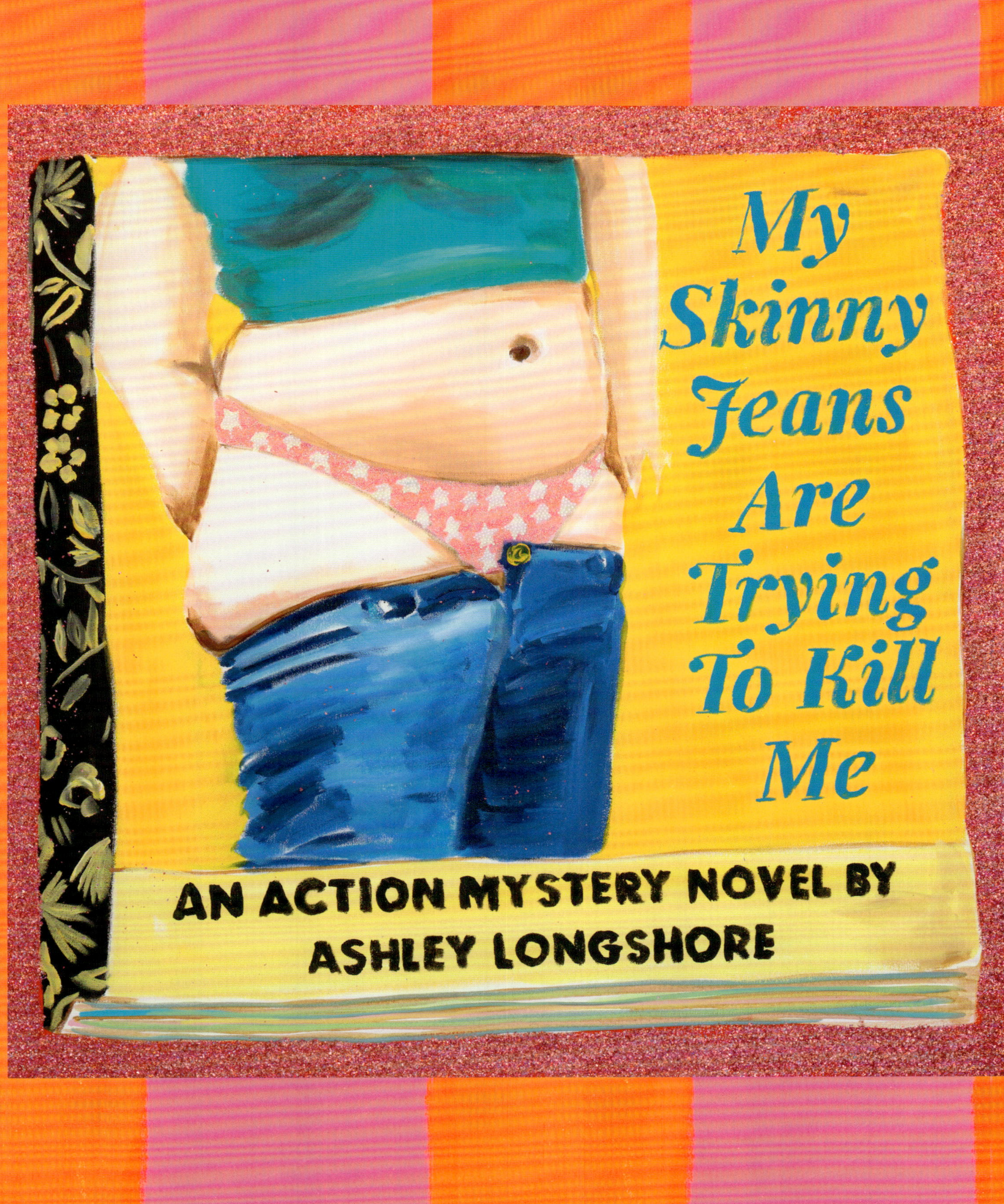
My Skinny Jeans Are Trying To Kill Me
AN ACTION MYSTERY NOVEL BY
ASHLEY LONGSHORE

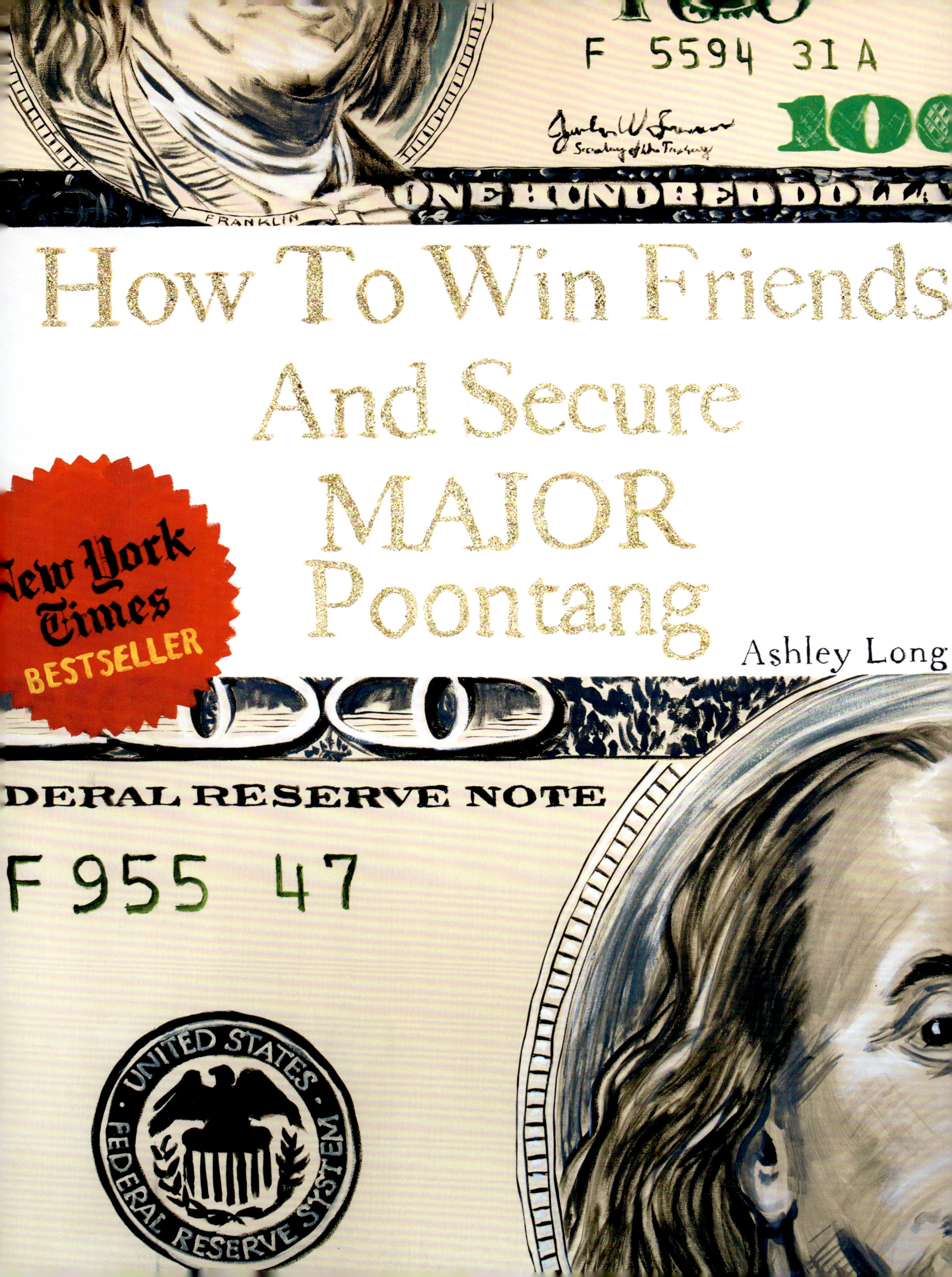
F 5594 31A
Secretary of the Treasury
100
ONE HUNDRED DOLLA
FRANKLIN
How To Win Friends
And Secure
MAJOR
Poontang
Ashley Long
New York Times
BESTSELLER
DERAL RESERVE NOTE
F 955 47
UNITED STATES
FEDERAL RESERVE SYSTEM

FRANKLIN

ONE HUNDRED DOLLARS

HUSTLE:

While you worried if the glass was half full or empty I SOLD IT

New York Times Bestseller

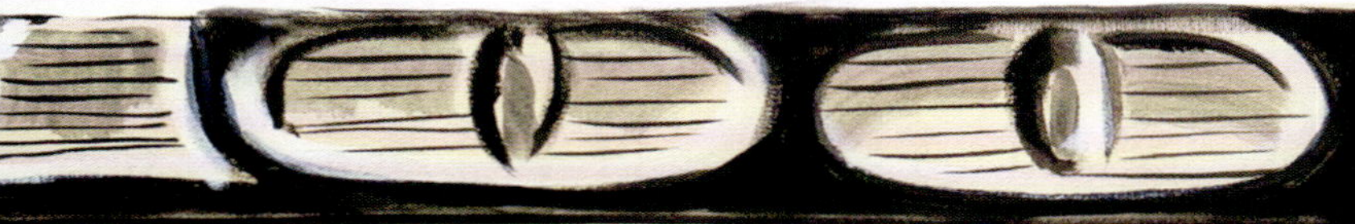

EDERAL RESERVE NOTE

J58232470A

J10

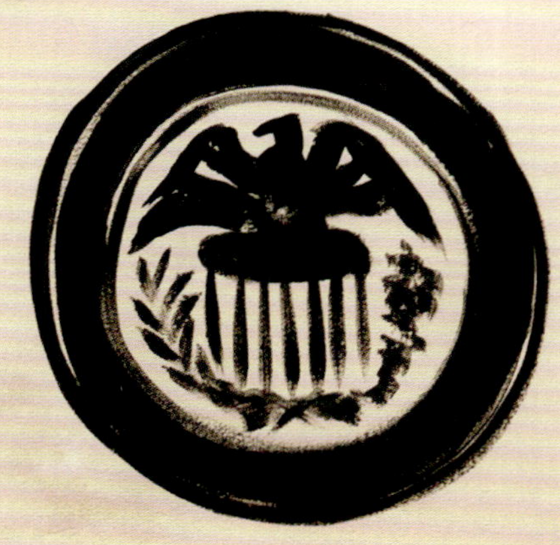

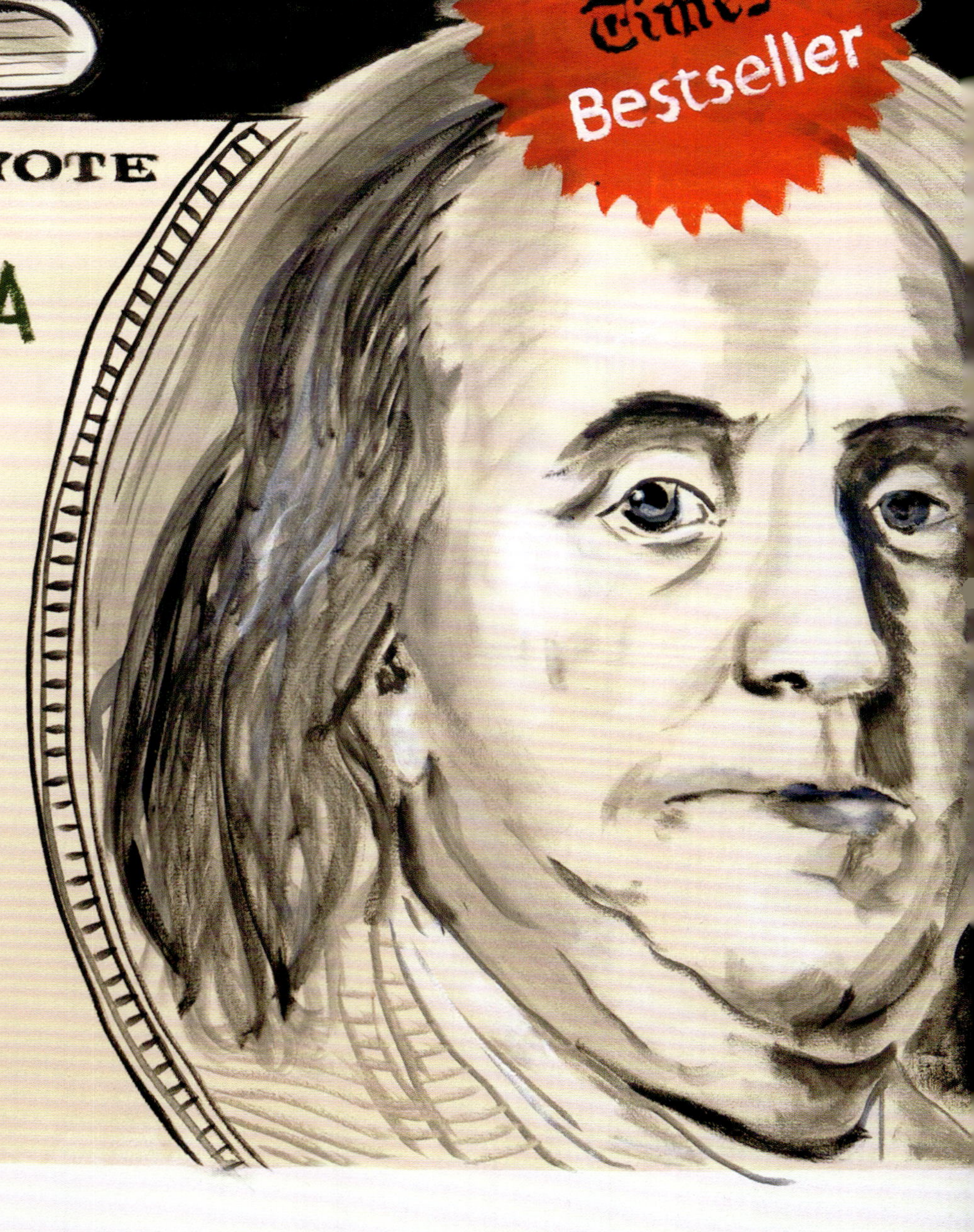

THIS NOTE IS LEGAL TENDER
FOR ALL DEBTS, PUBLIC AND PRIVATE

Treasurer of the United States

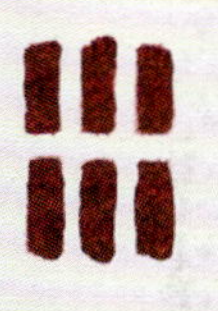

Ashley Longshore

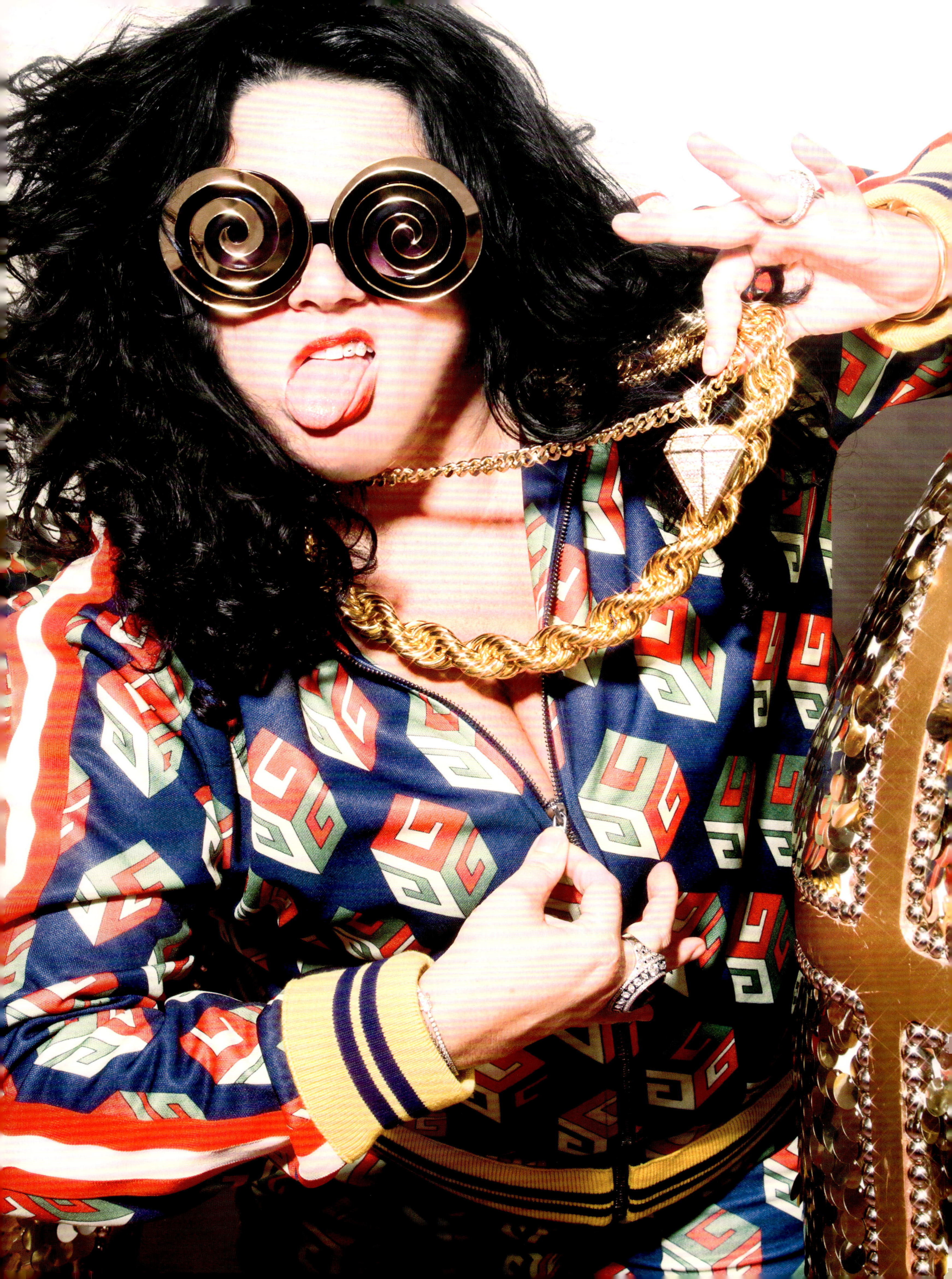

WAYNE

Pass it to the Left....

←

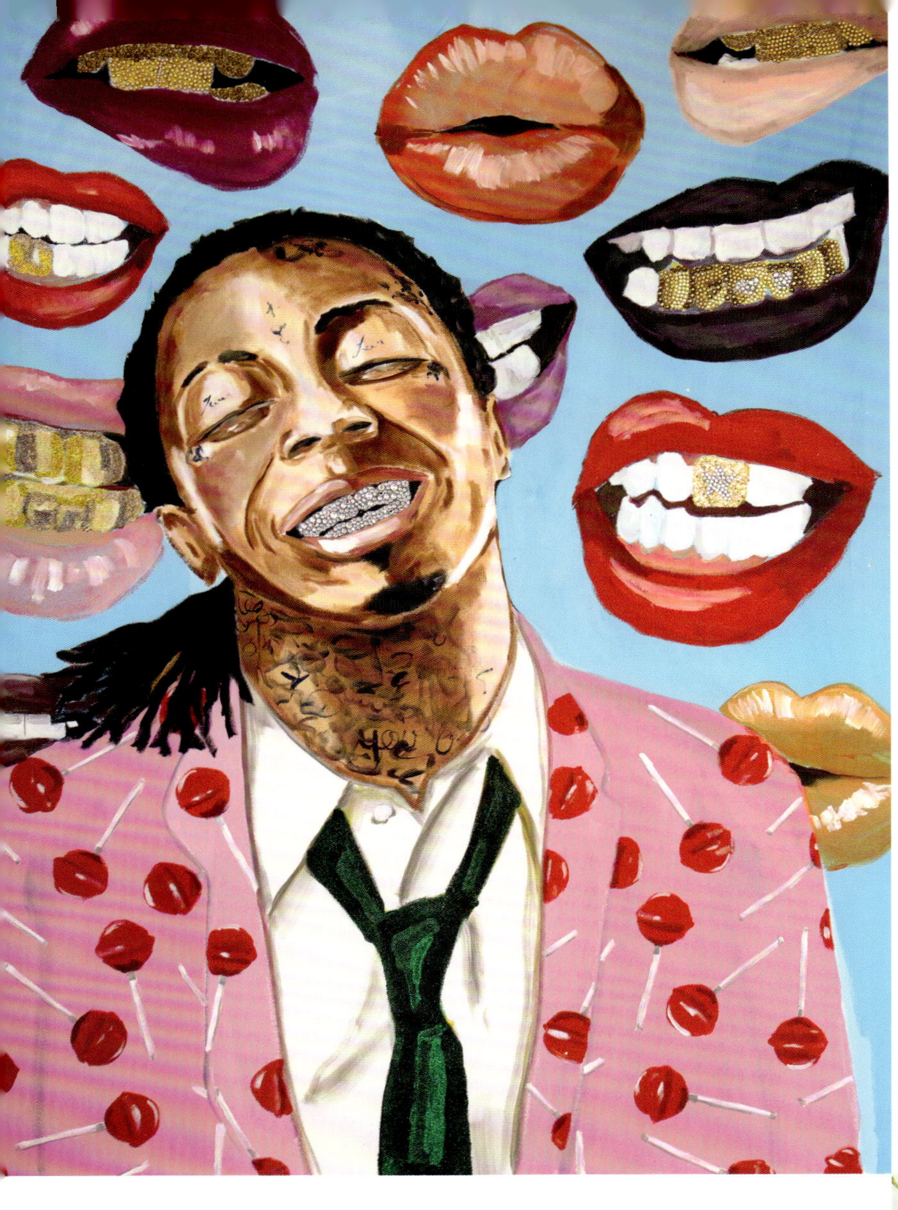

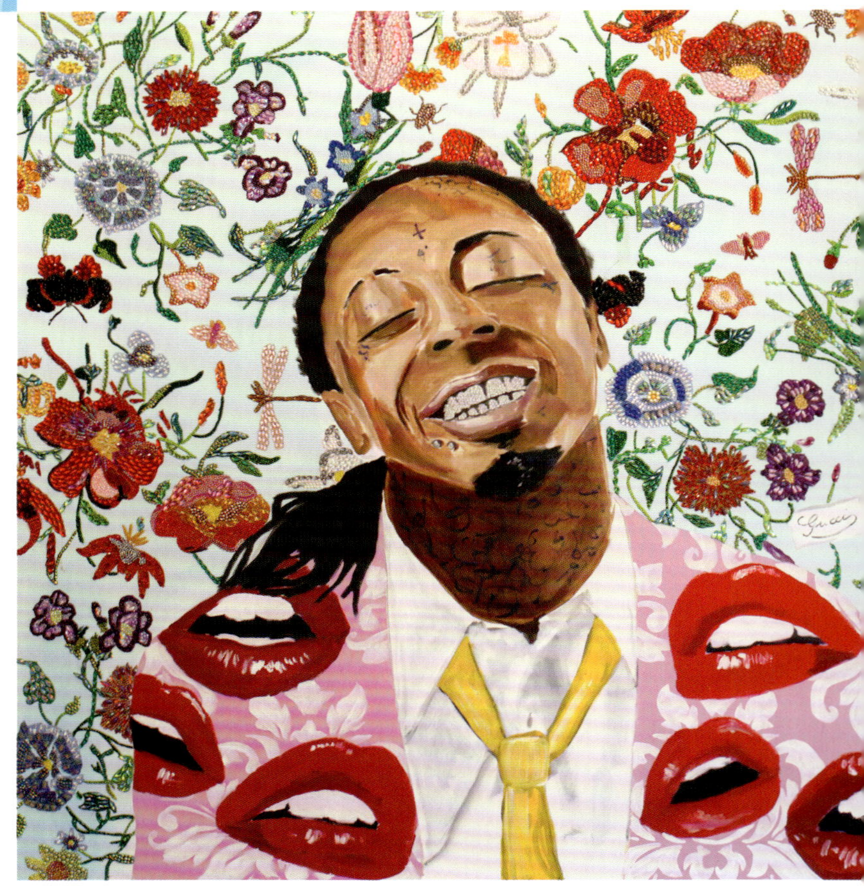

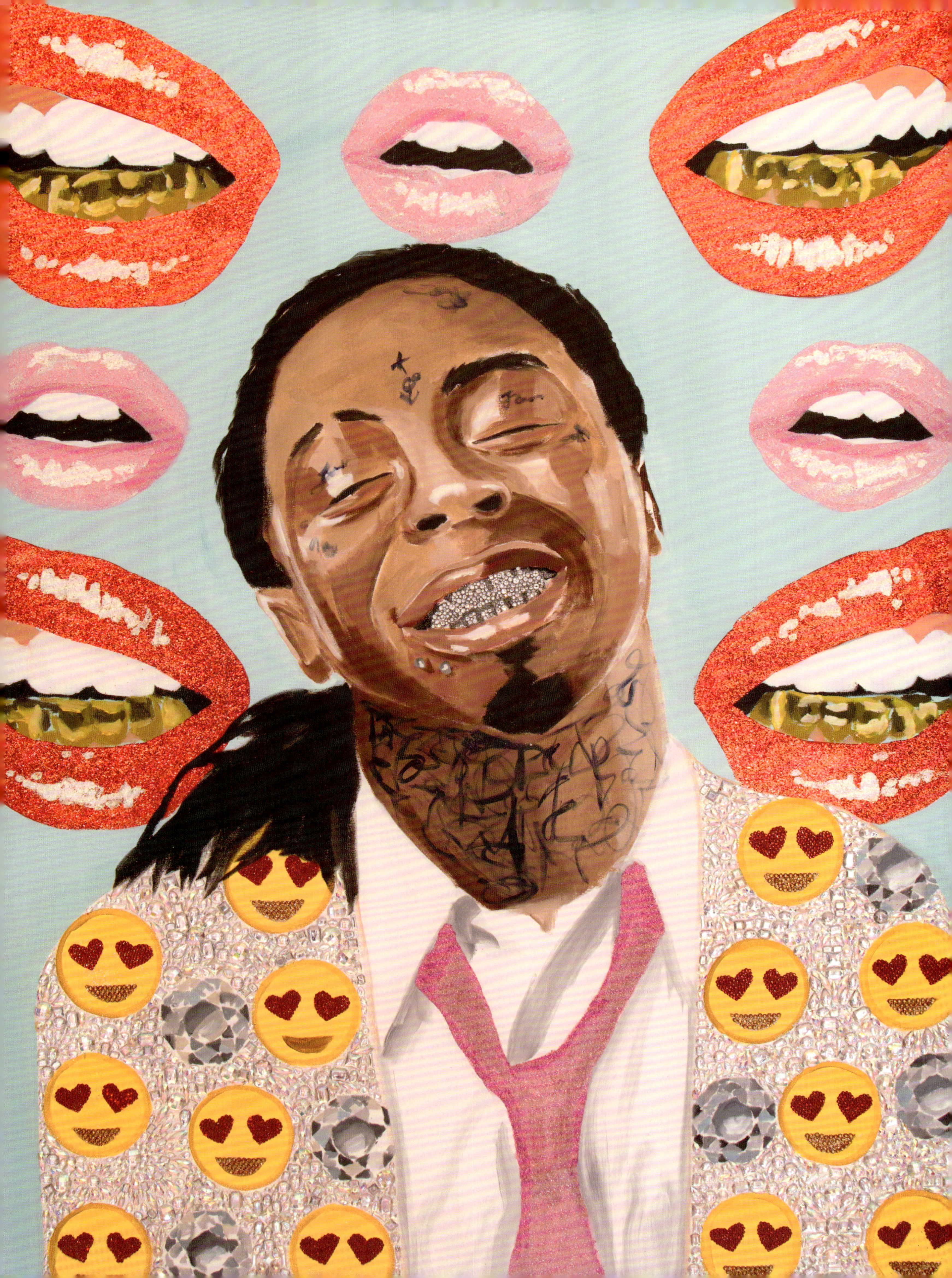

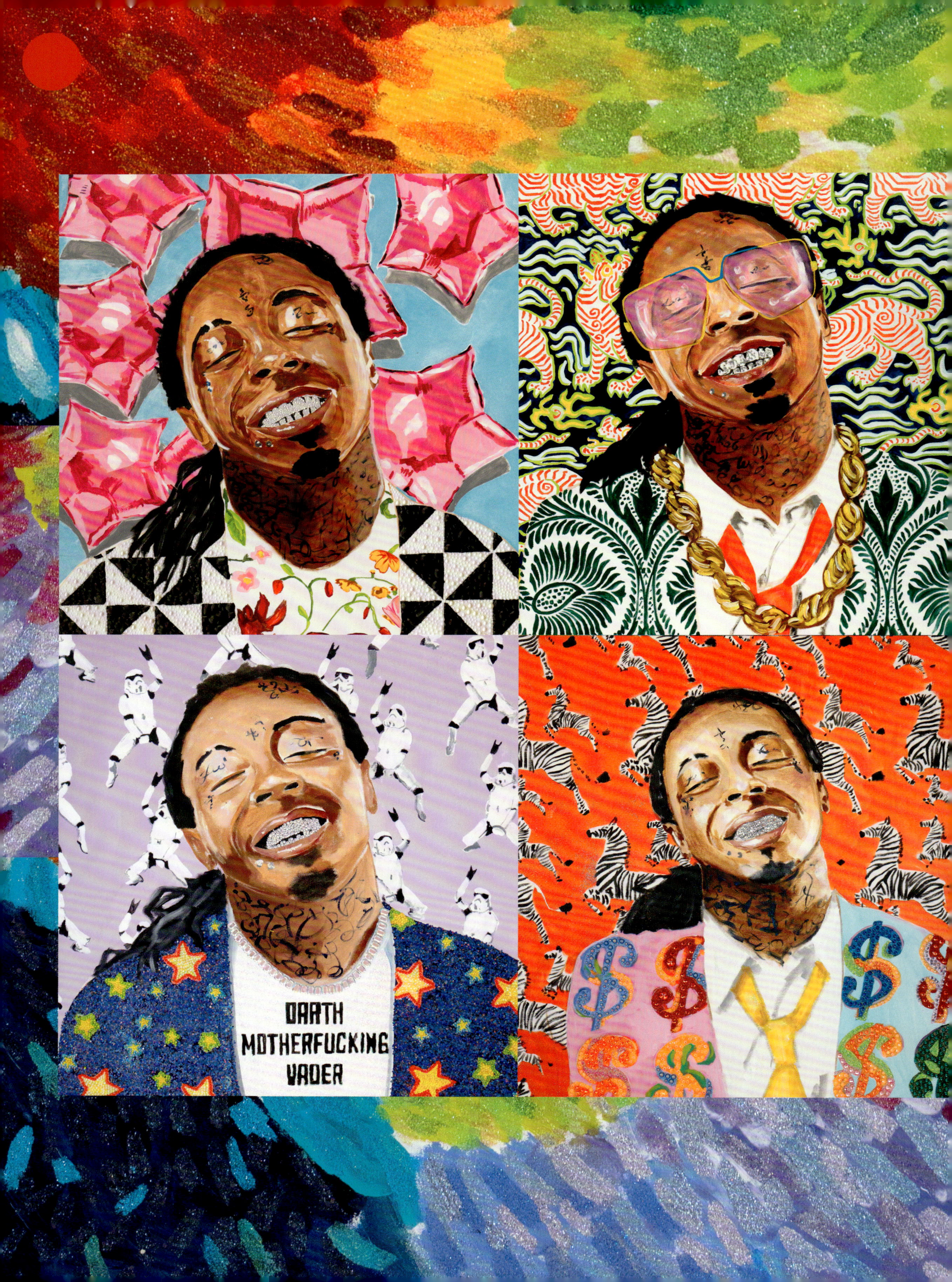
DARTH
MOTHERFUCKING
VADER

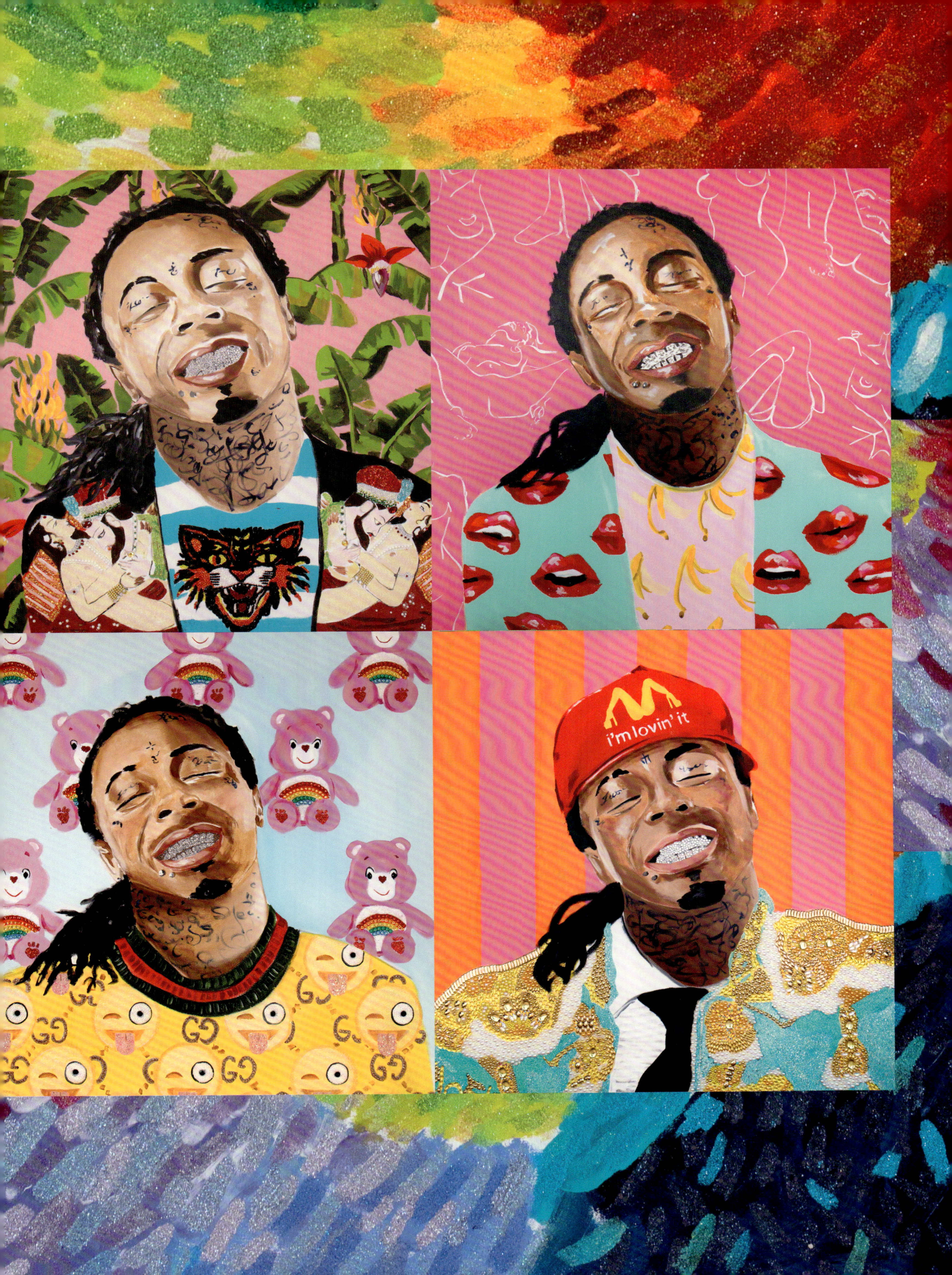
i'm lovin' it

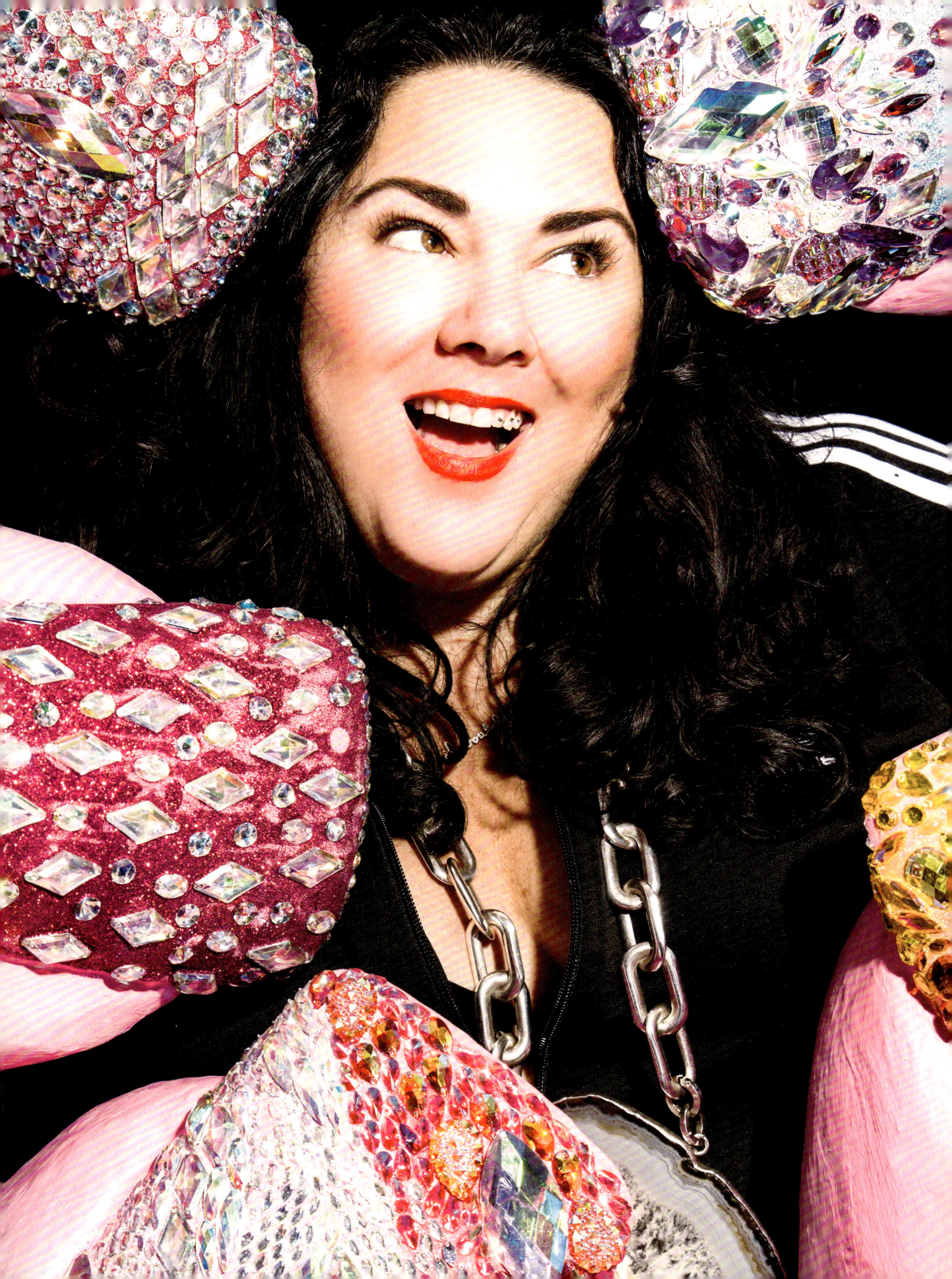

JEWELS

Sparkle Baby...
You are
a damn
Jewel!!

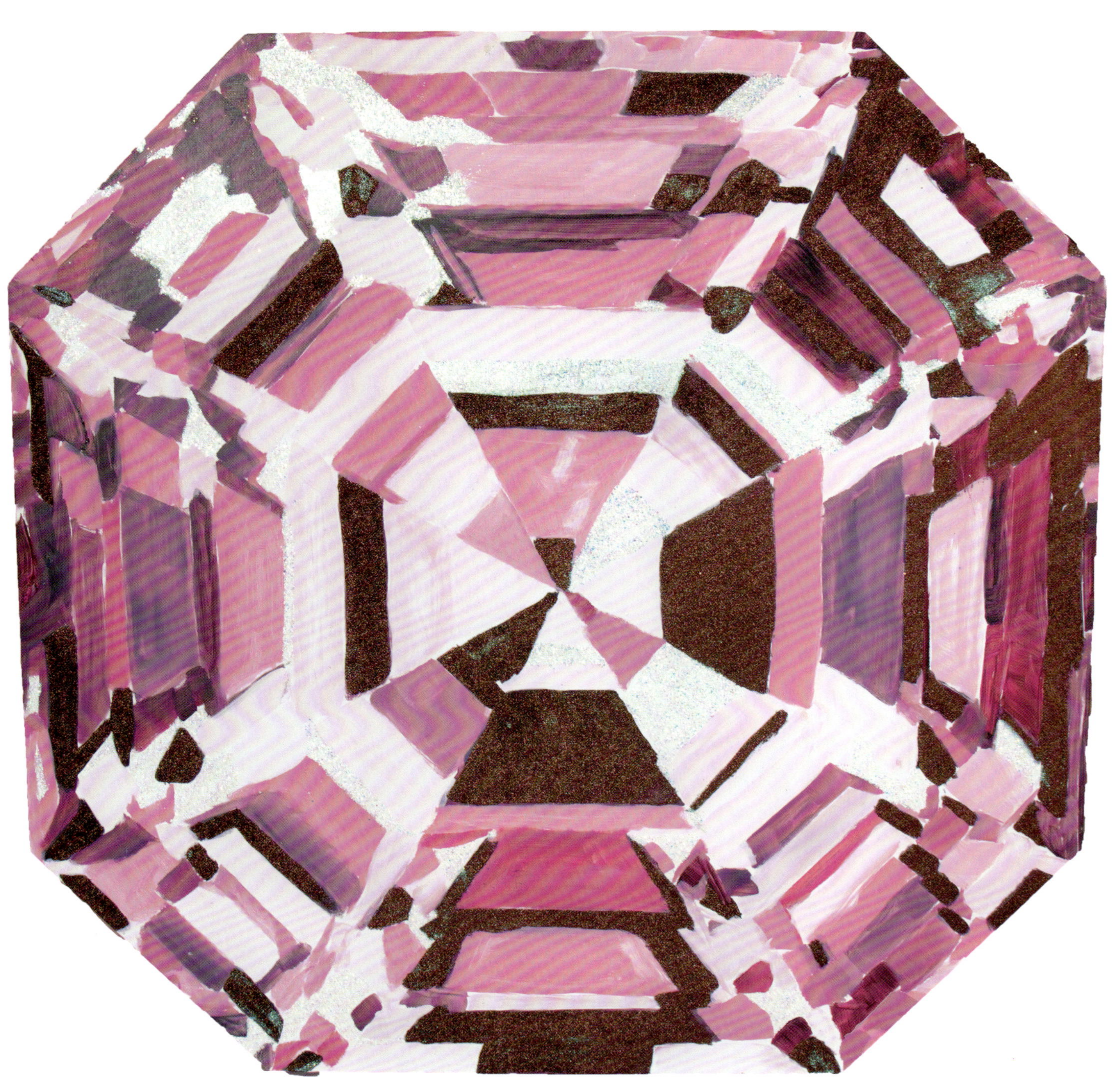

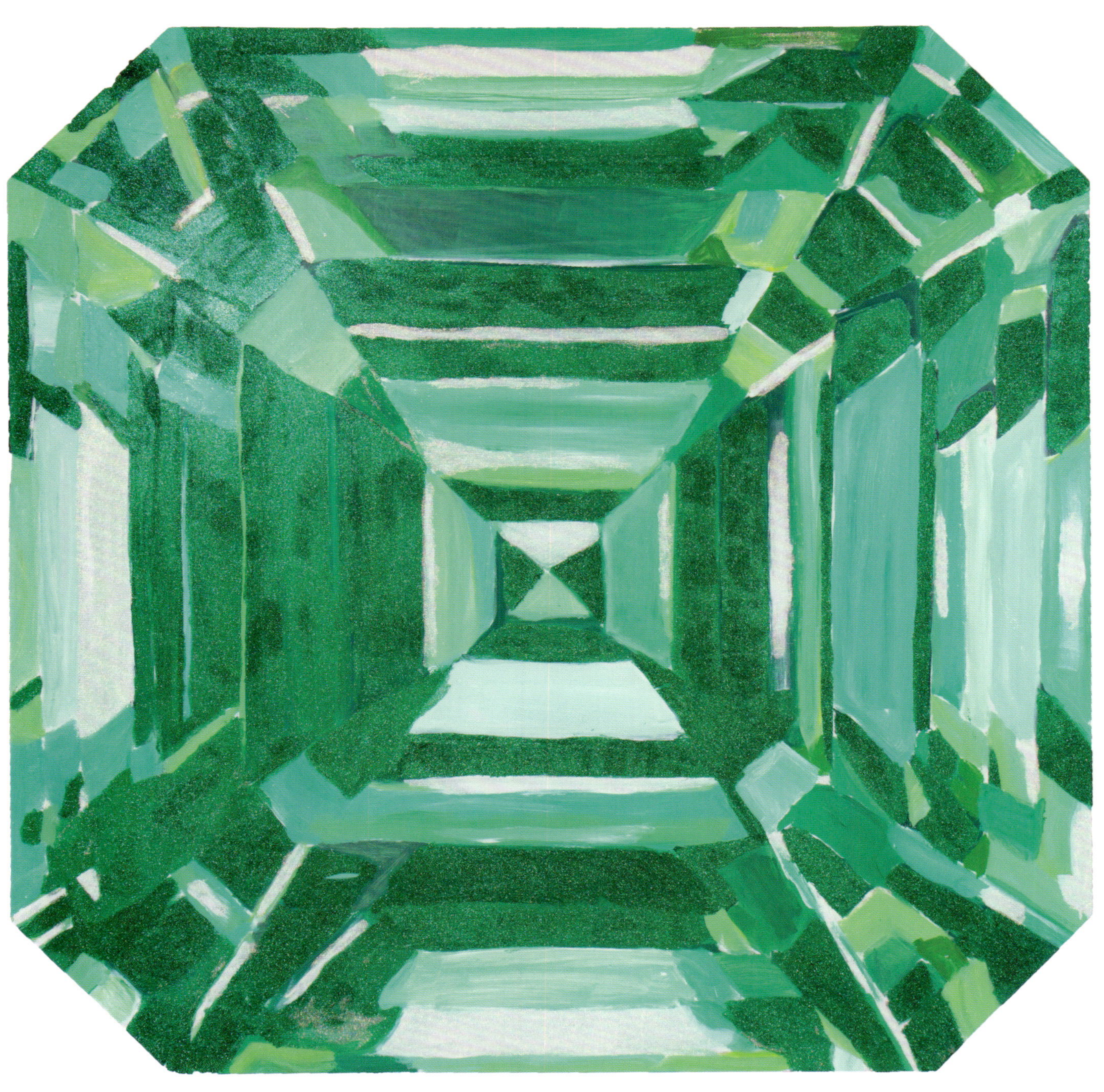

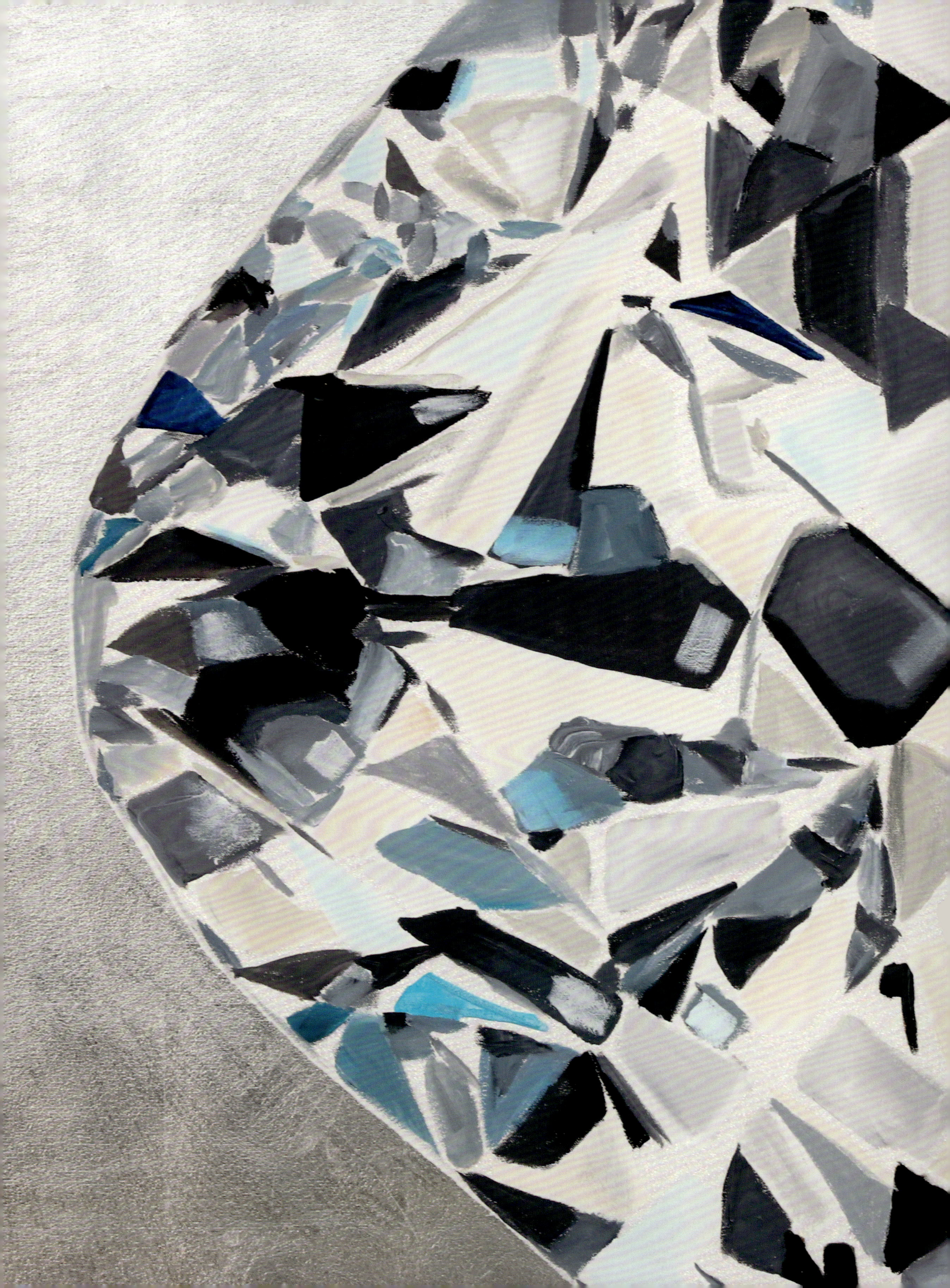

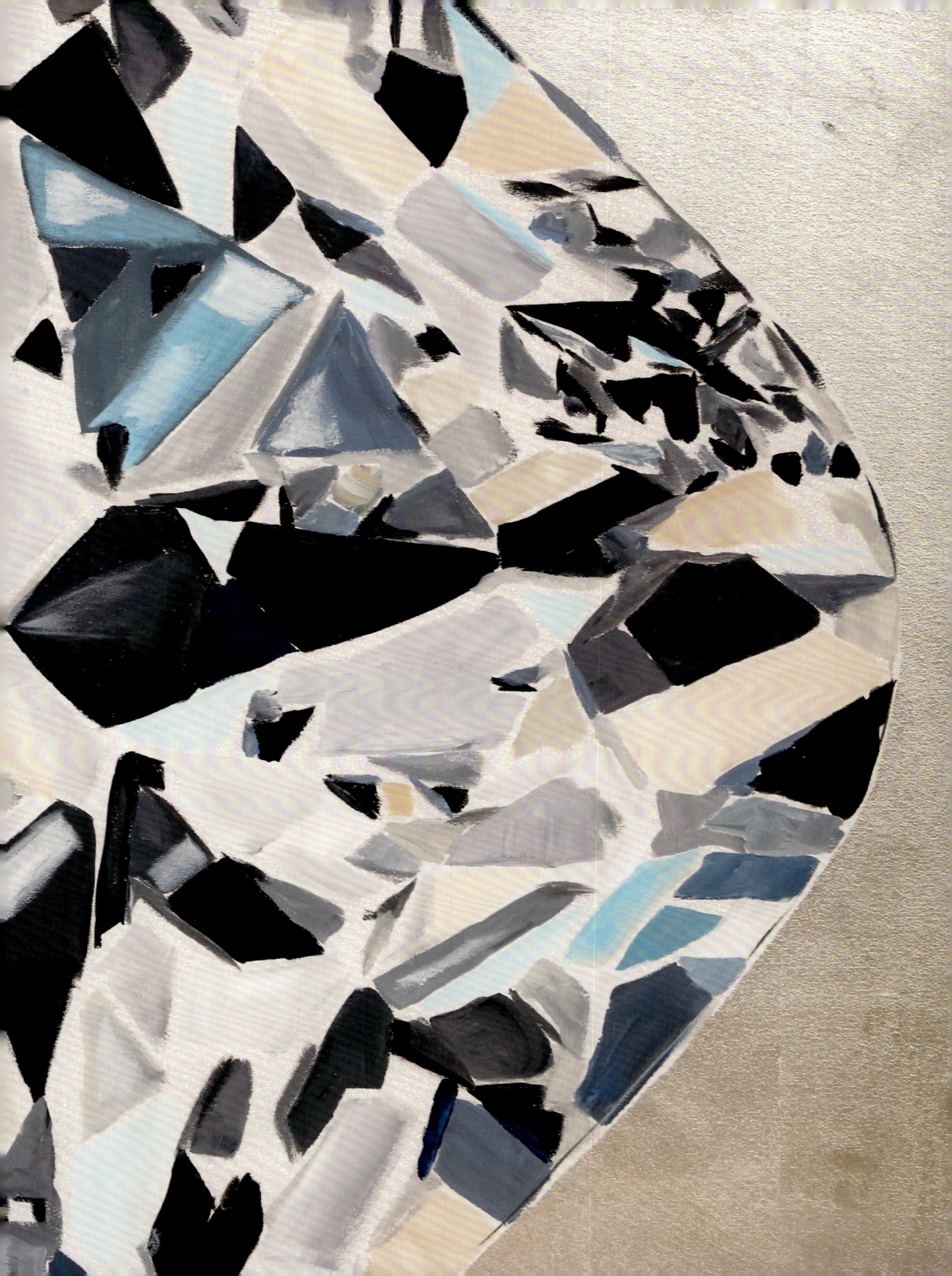

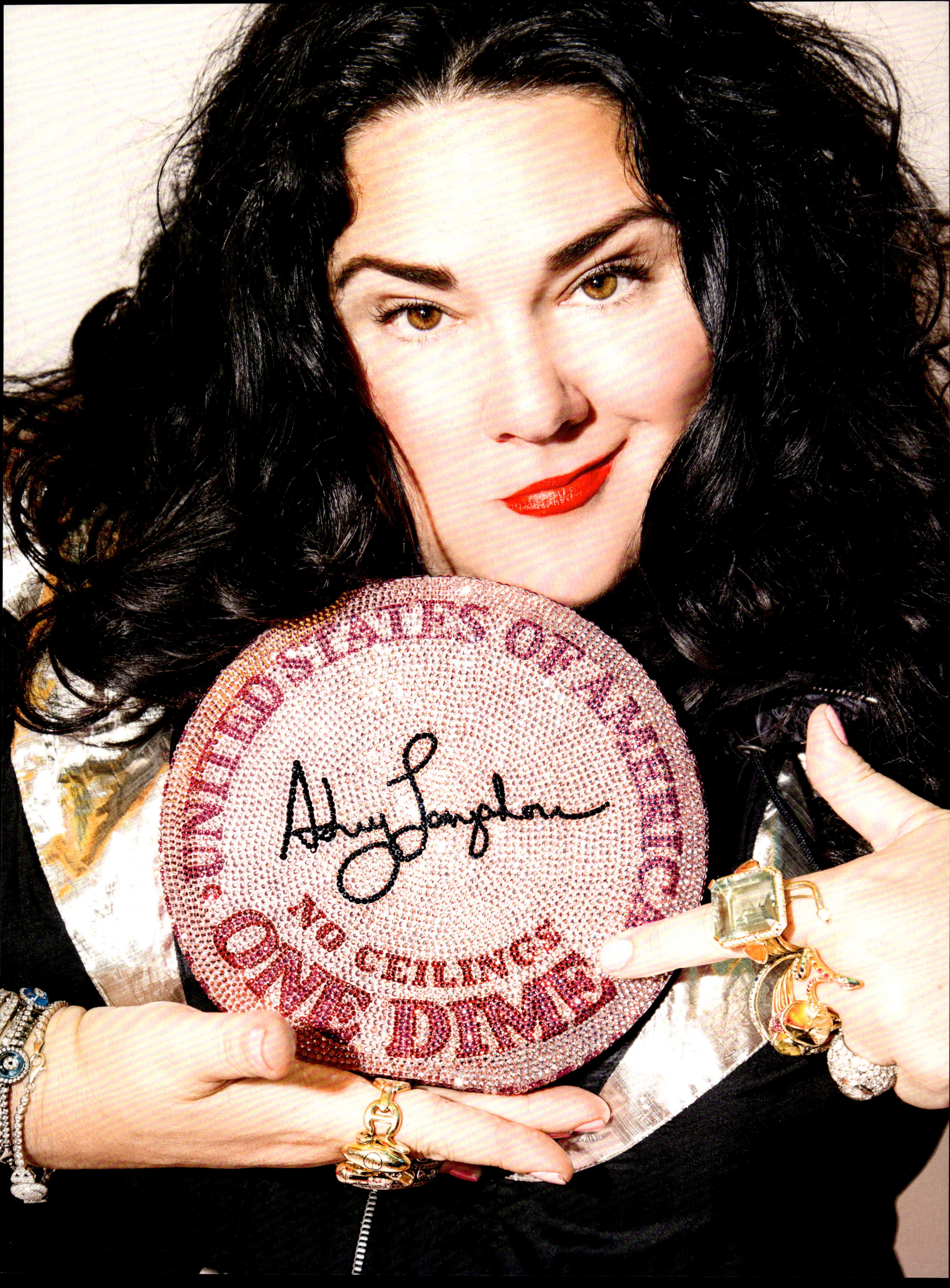
UNITED STATES OF AMERICA
NO CEILINGS
ONE DIME

PRESIDENTS

I pray to God
that in
my lifetime
I get to
paint a president
with a
VAGINA...
BYEEEE

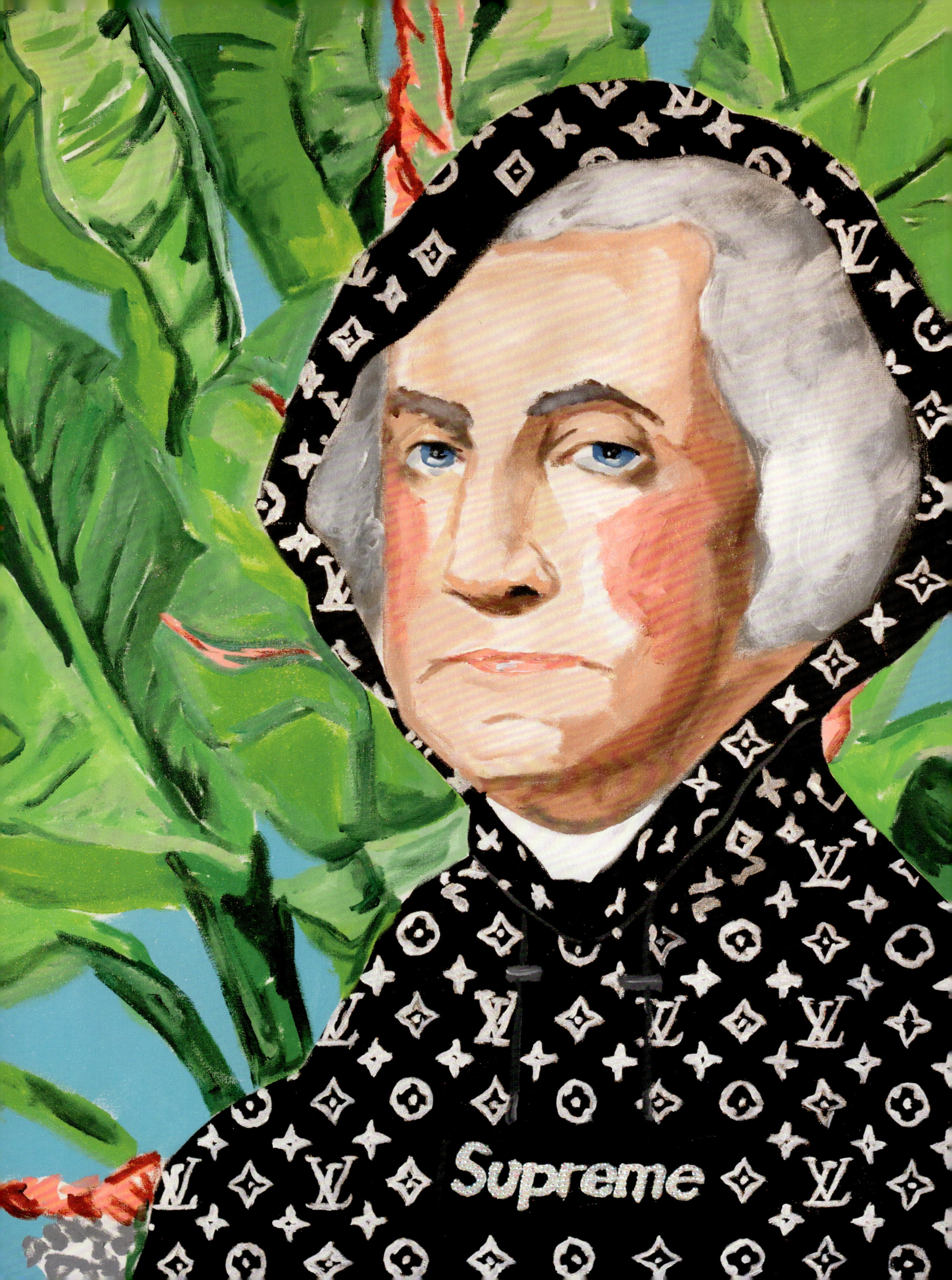
Supreme

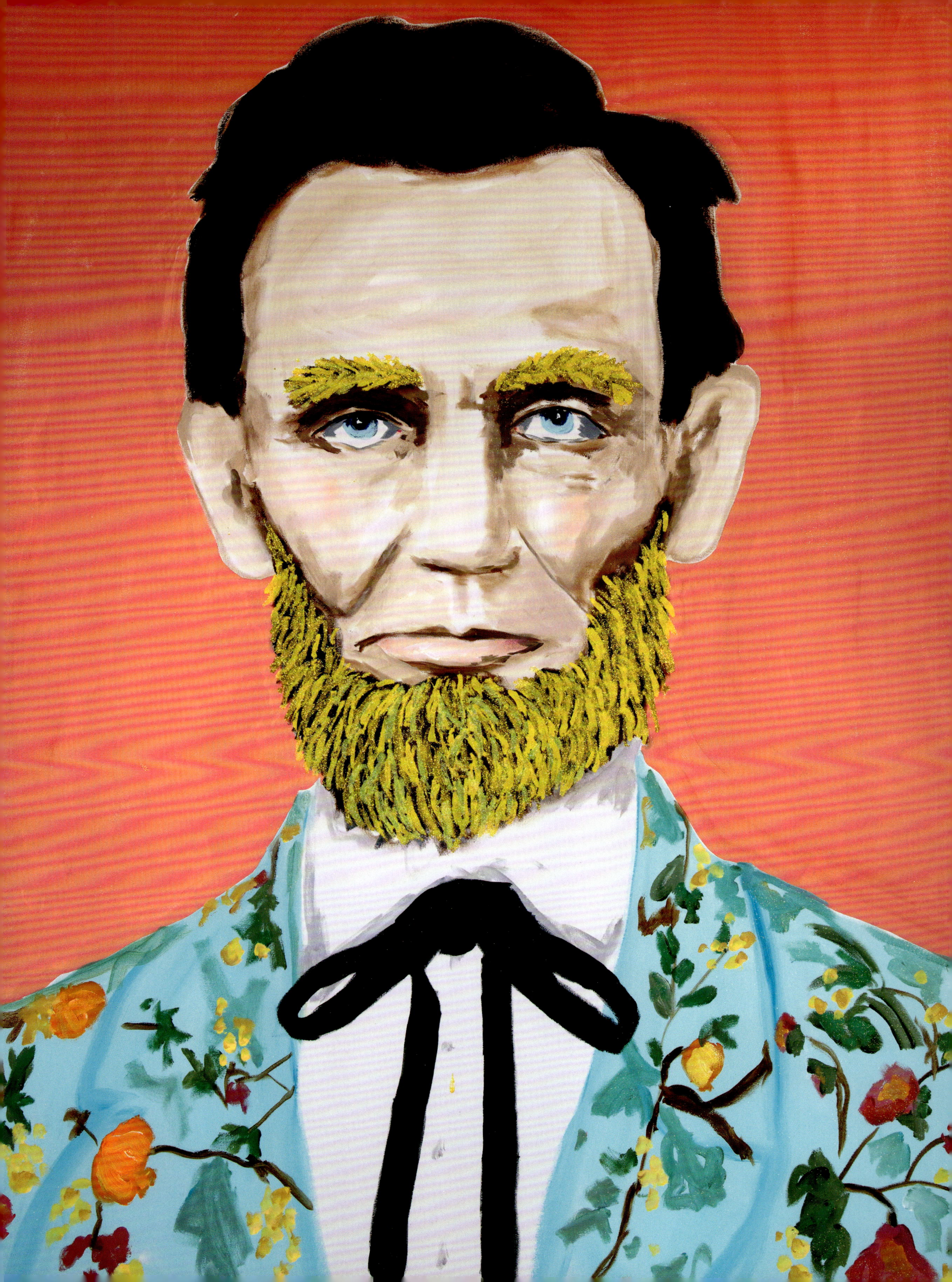

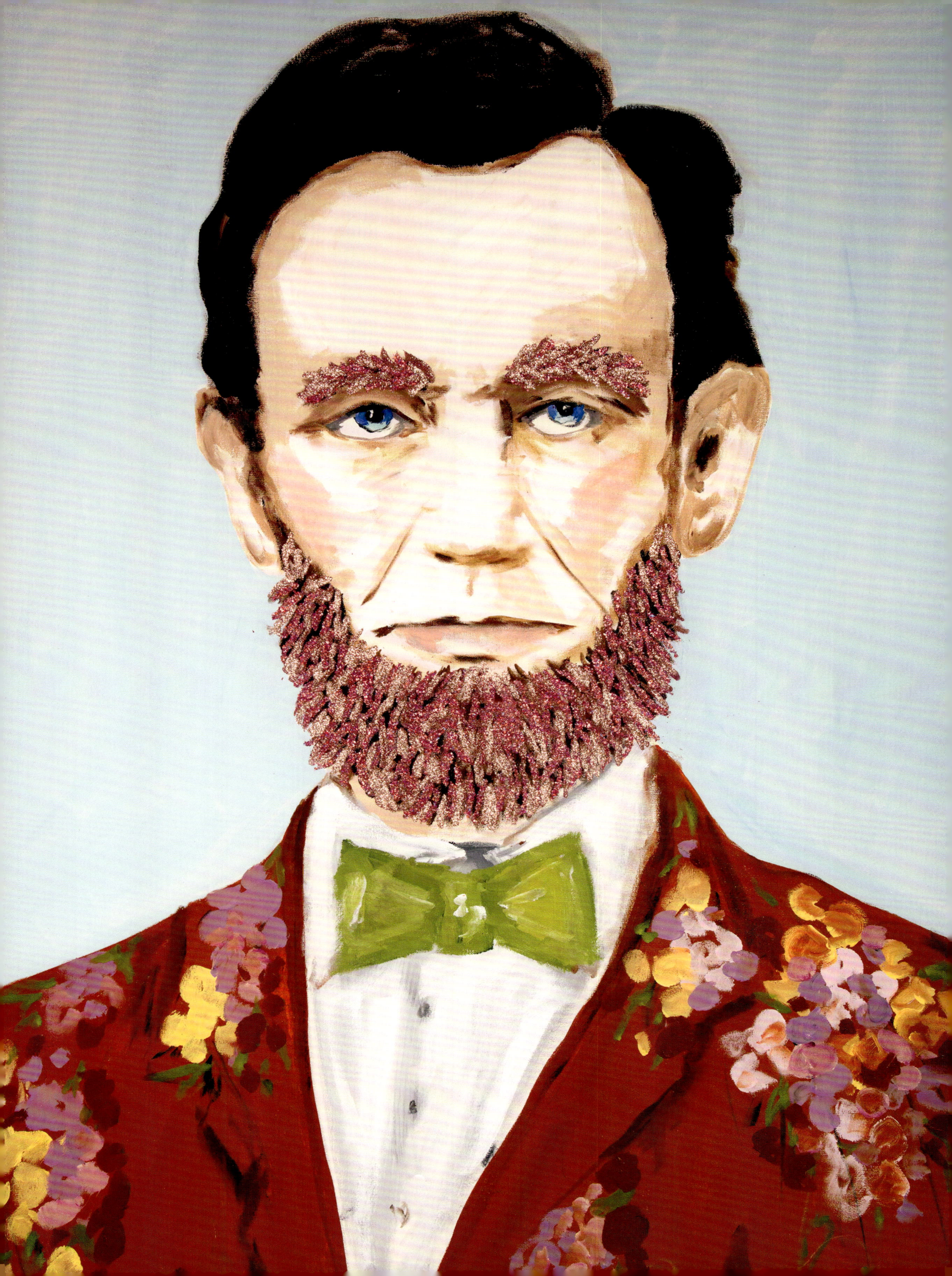

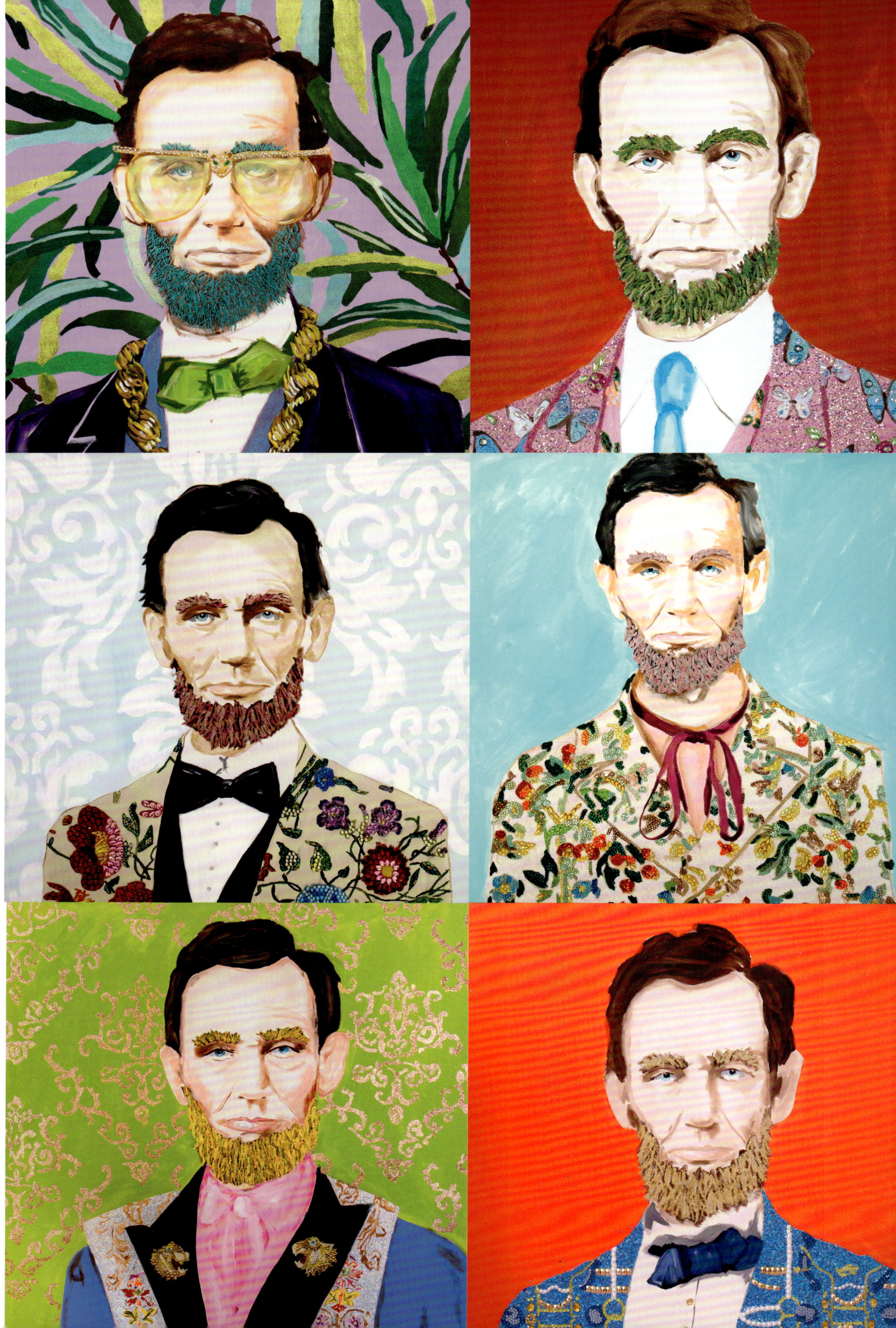

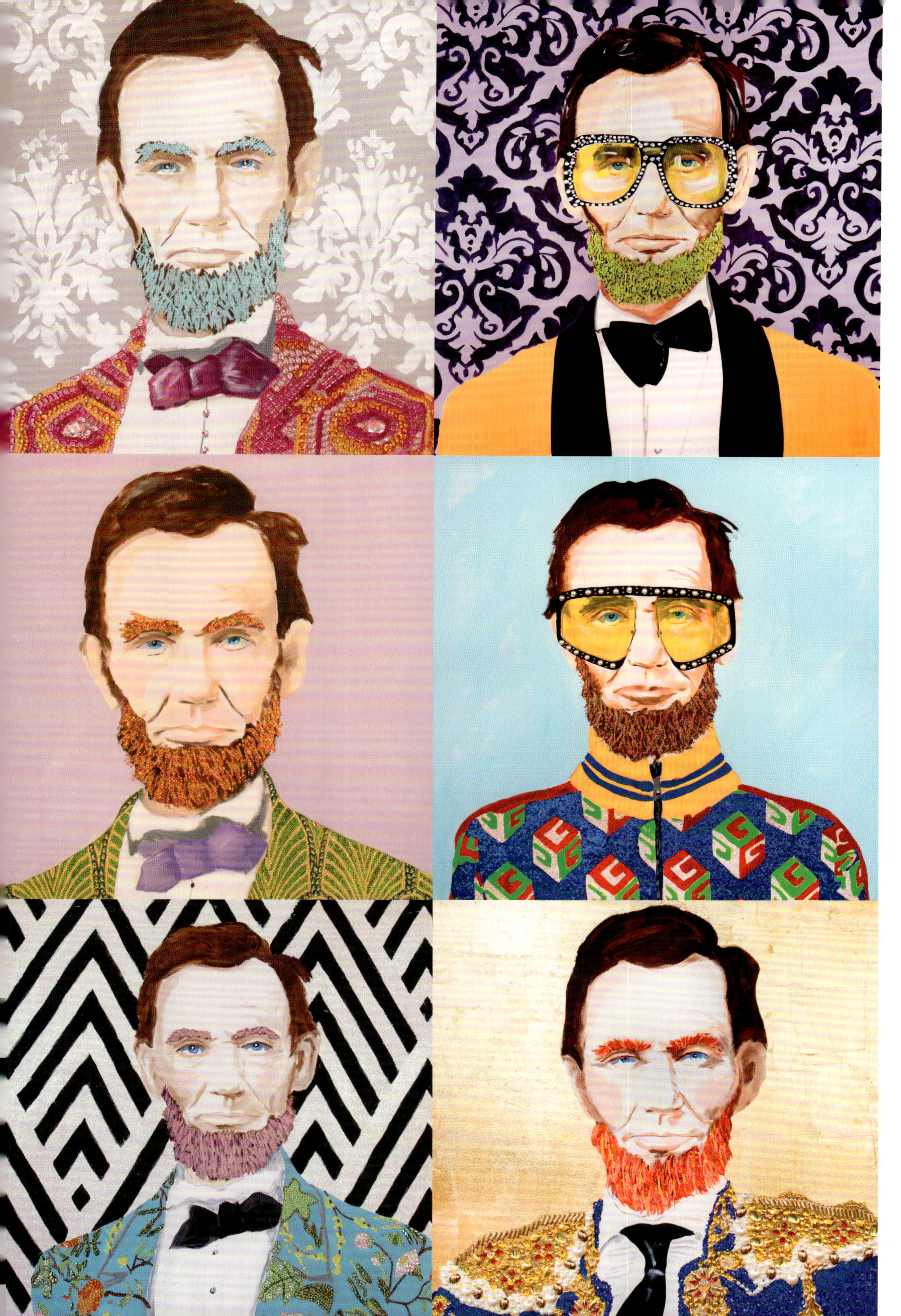

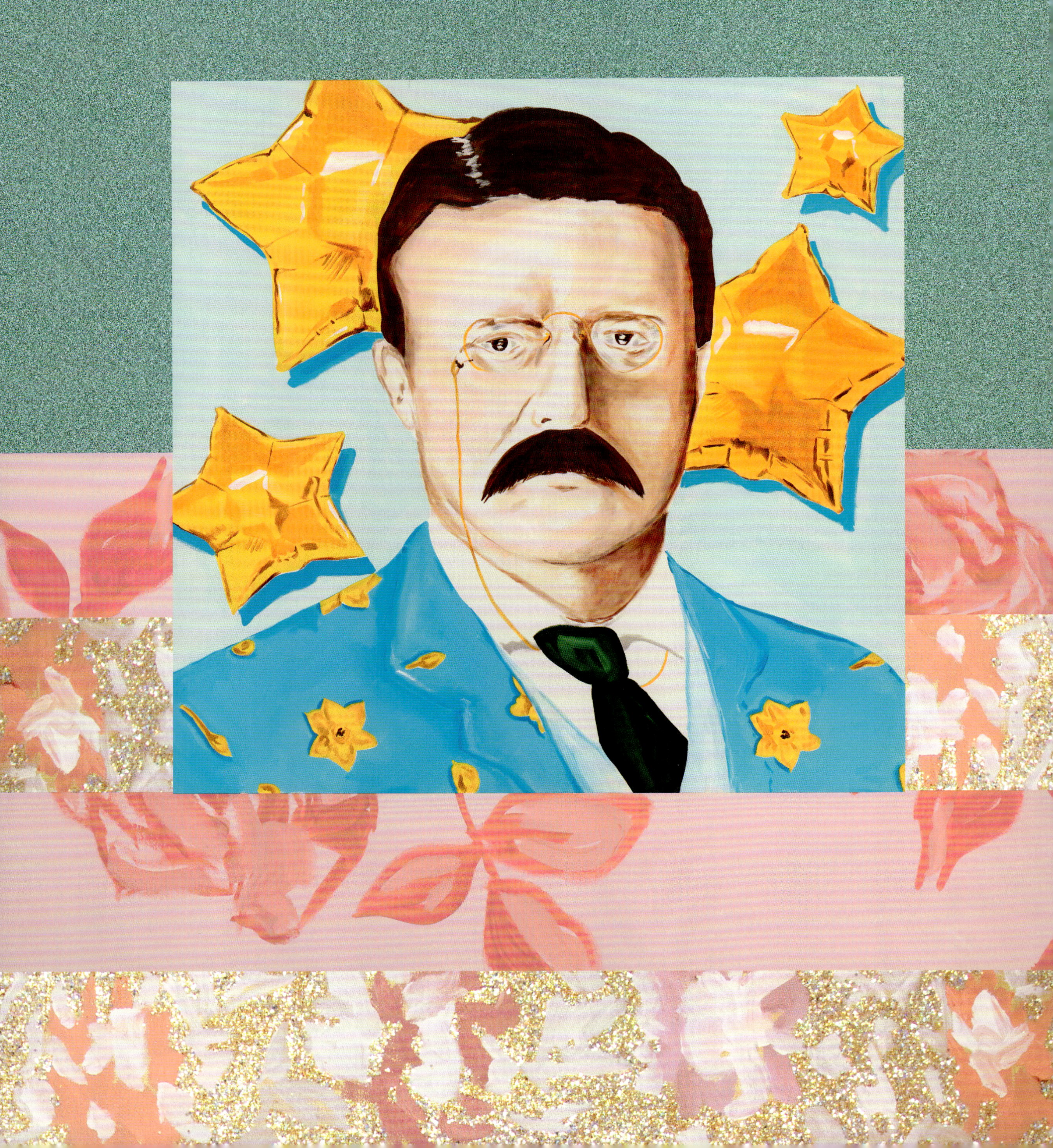

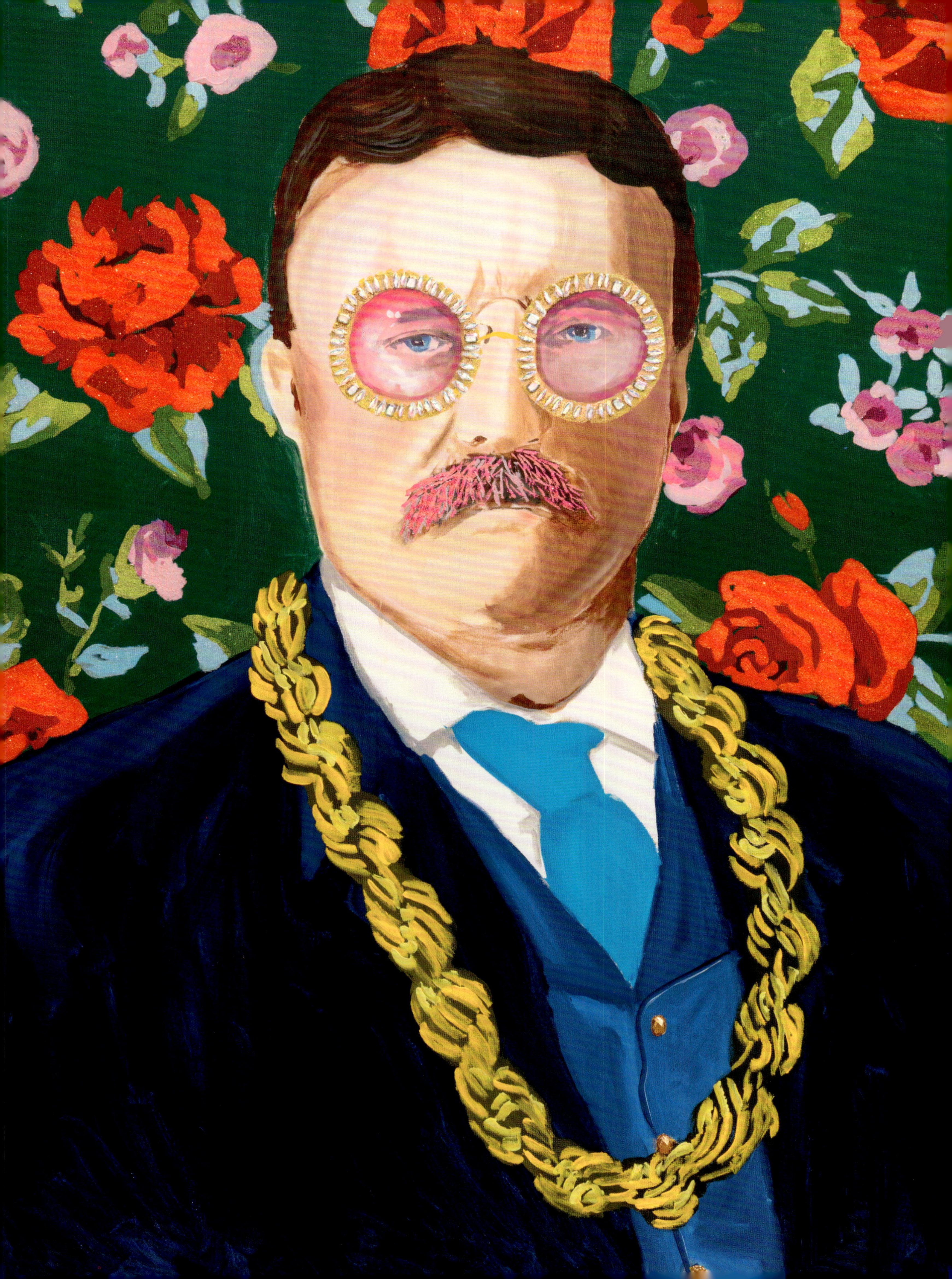

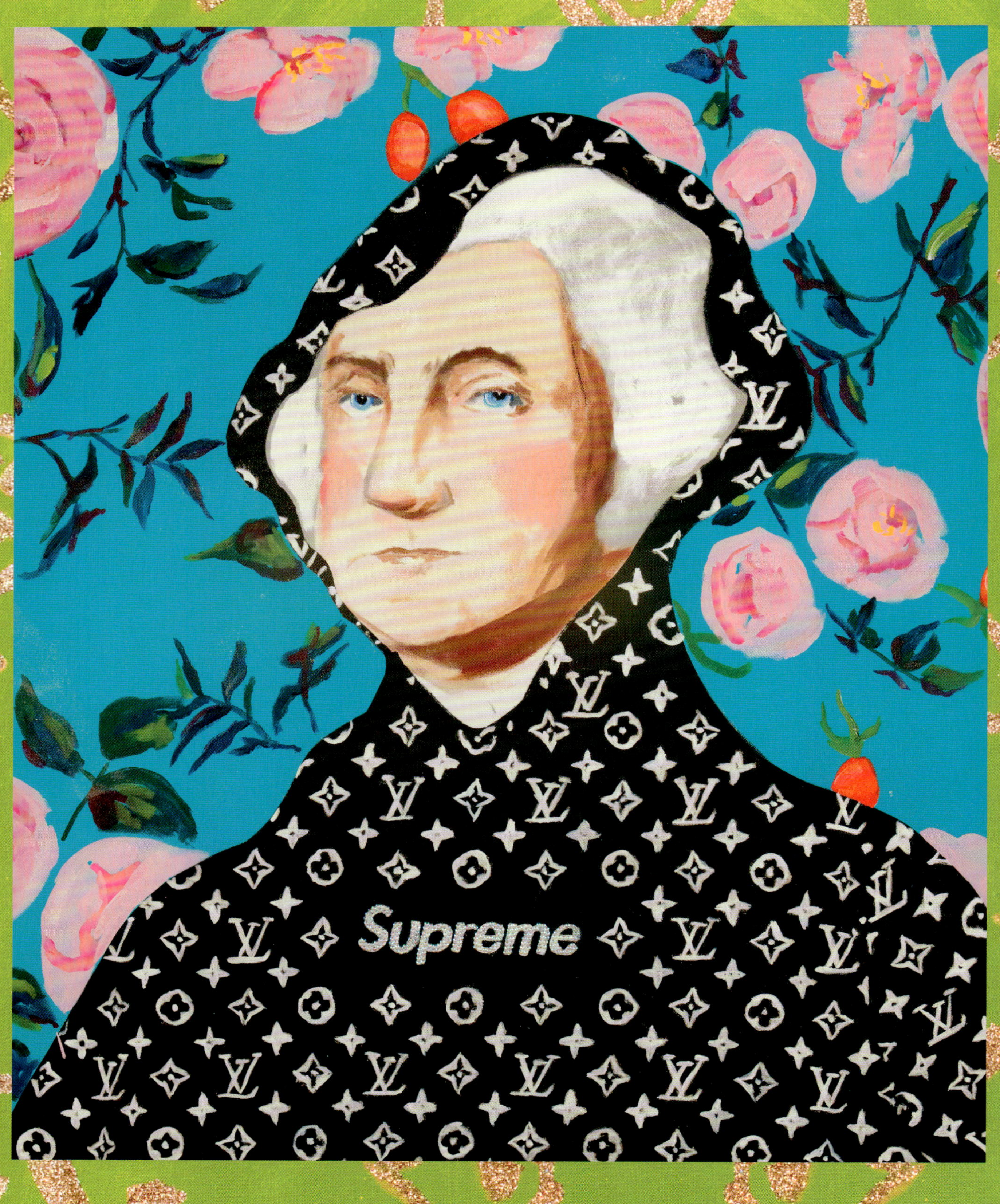
Supreme

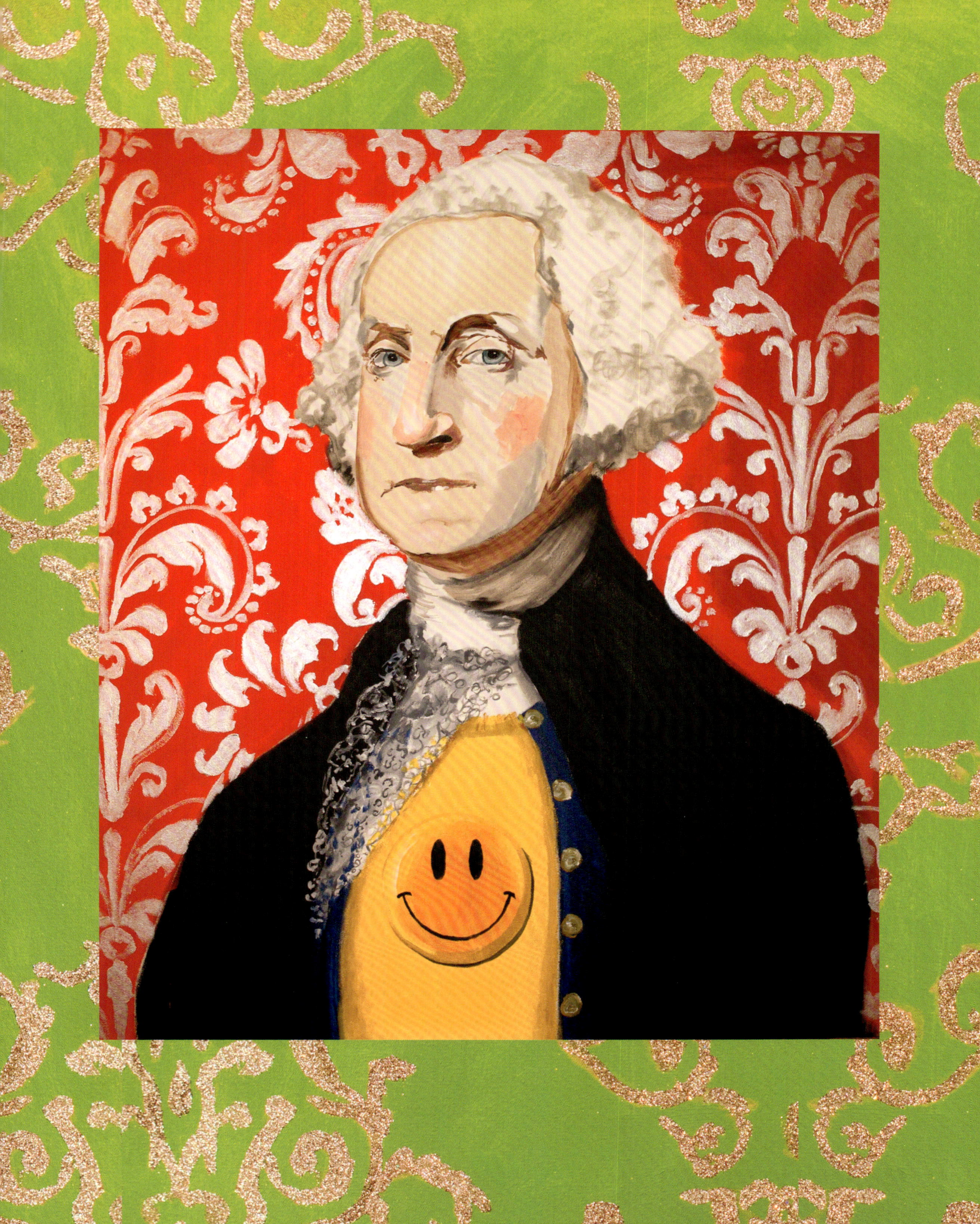

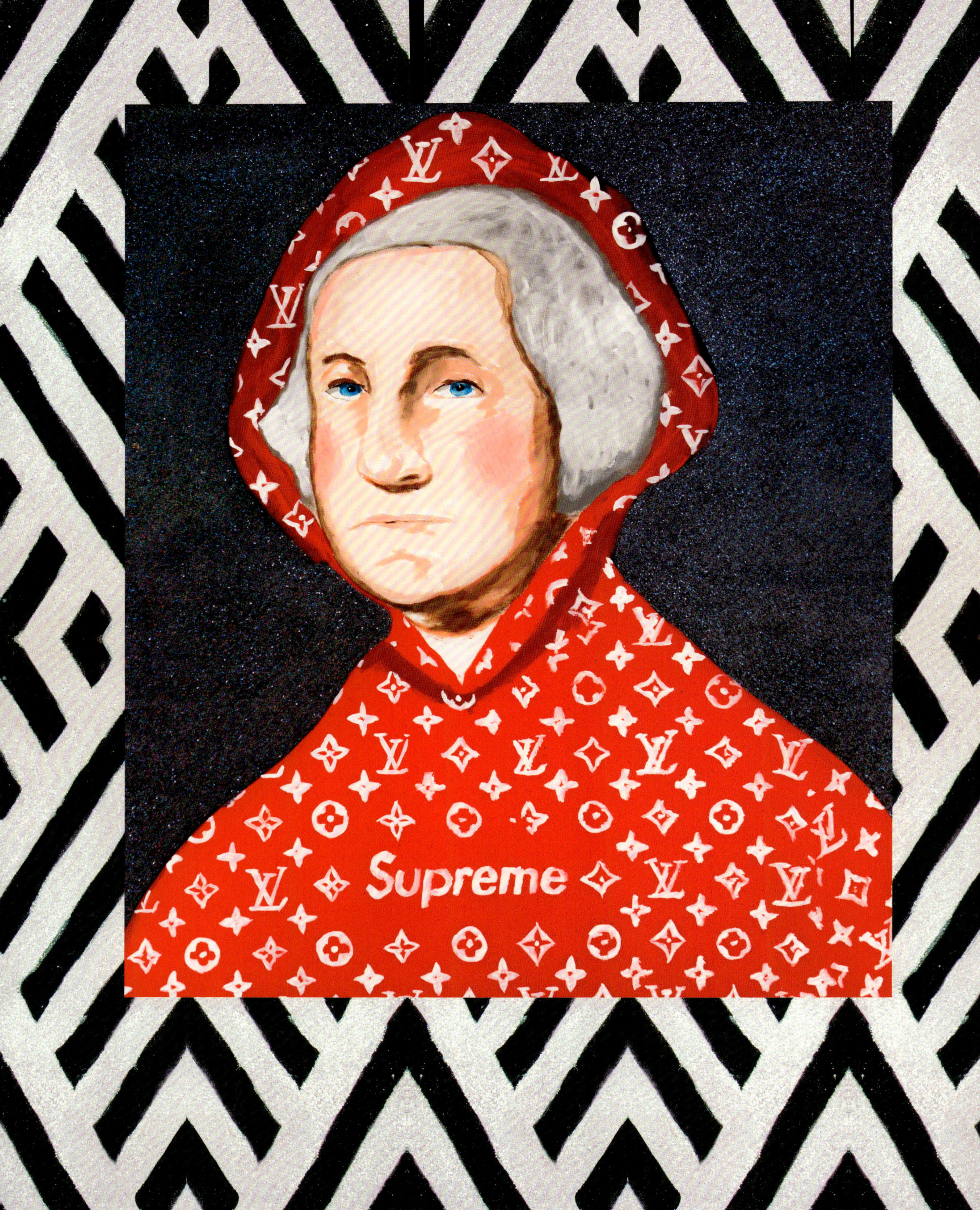
Supreme

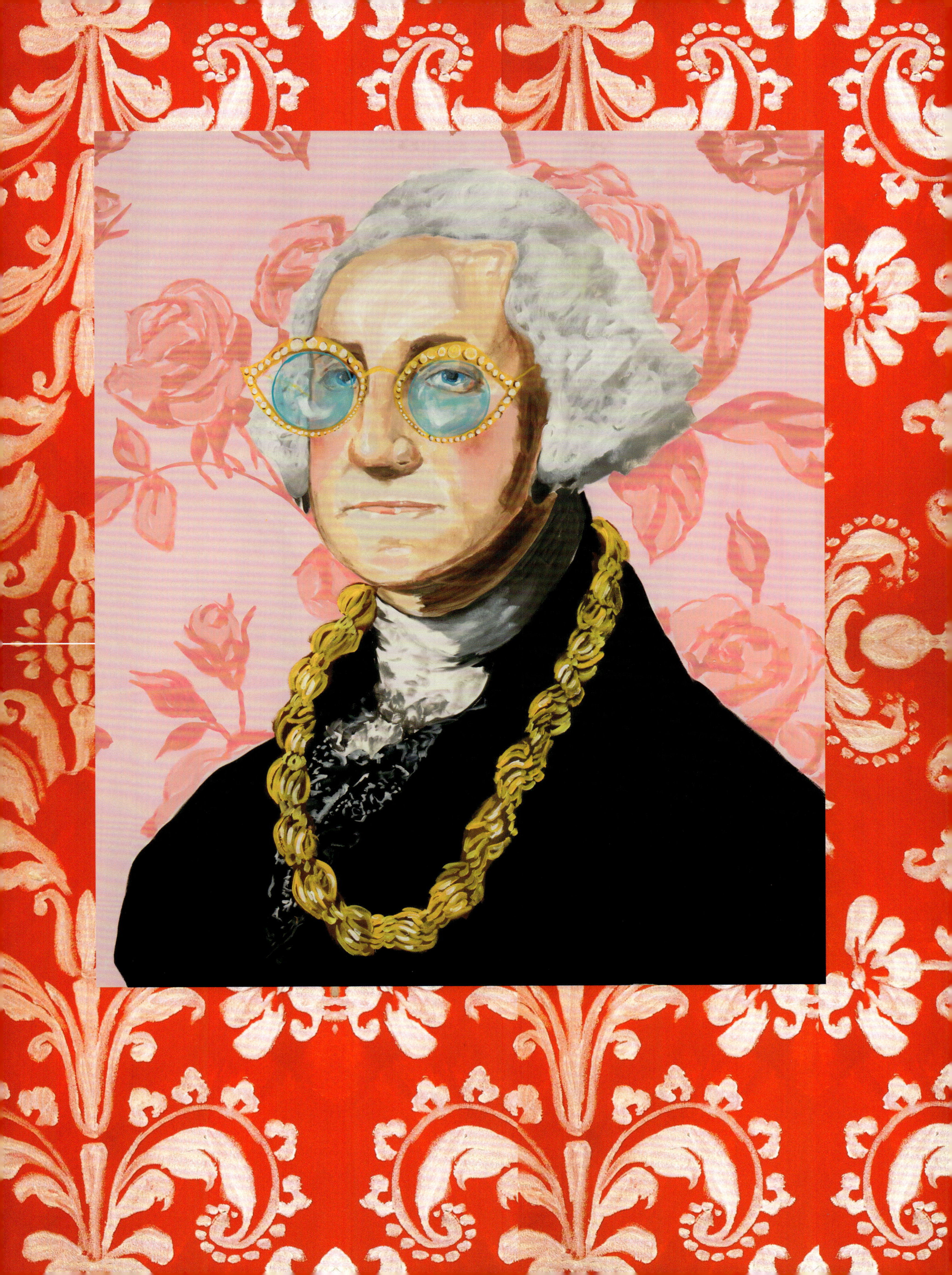

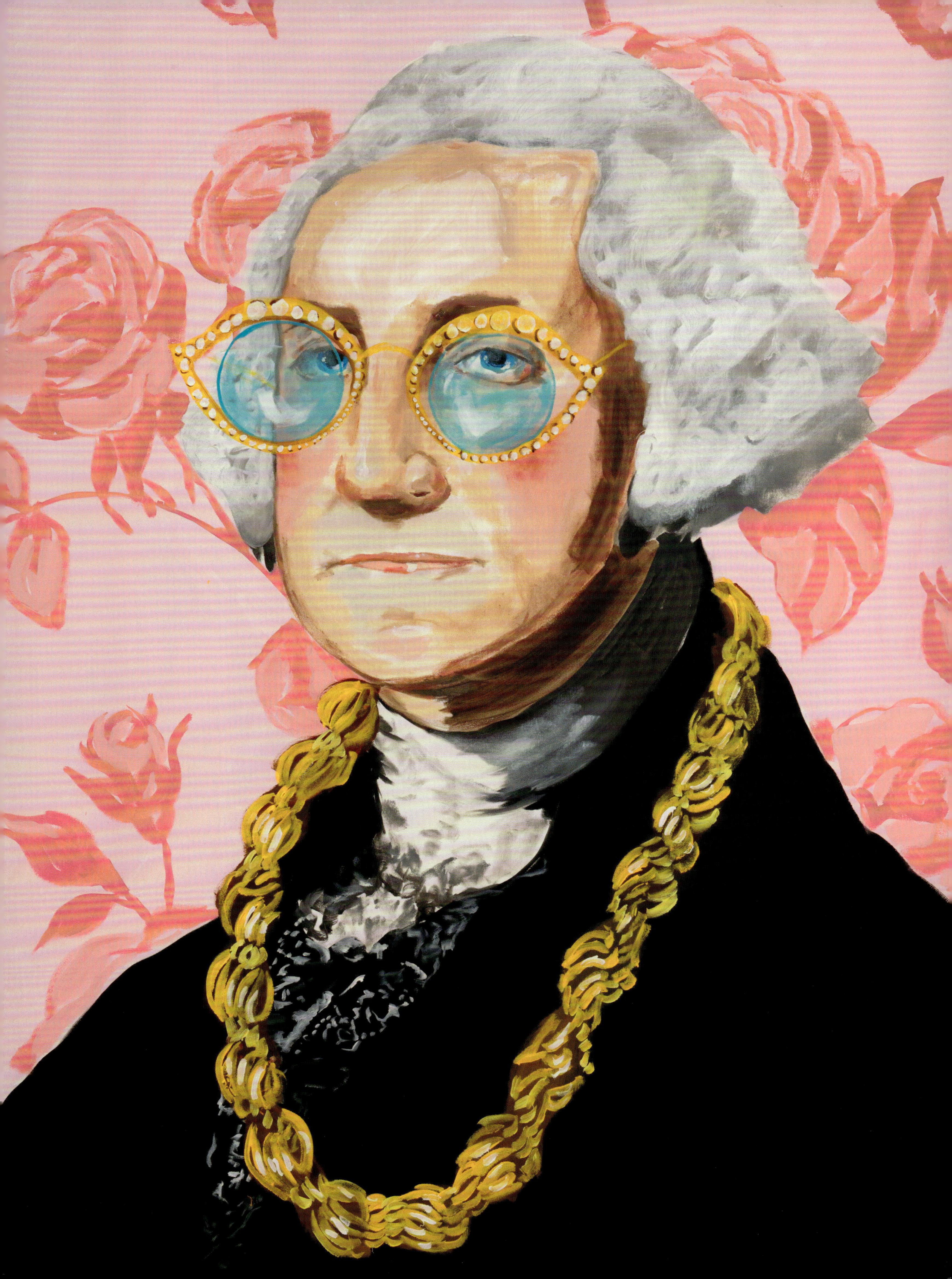

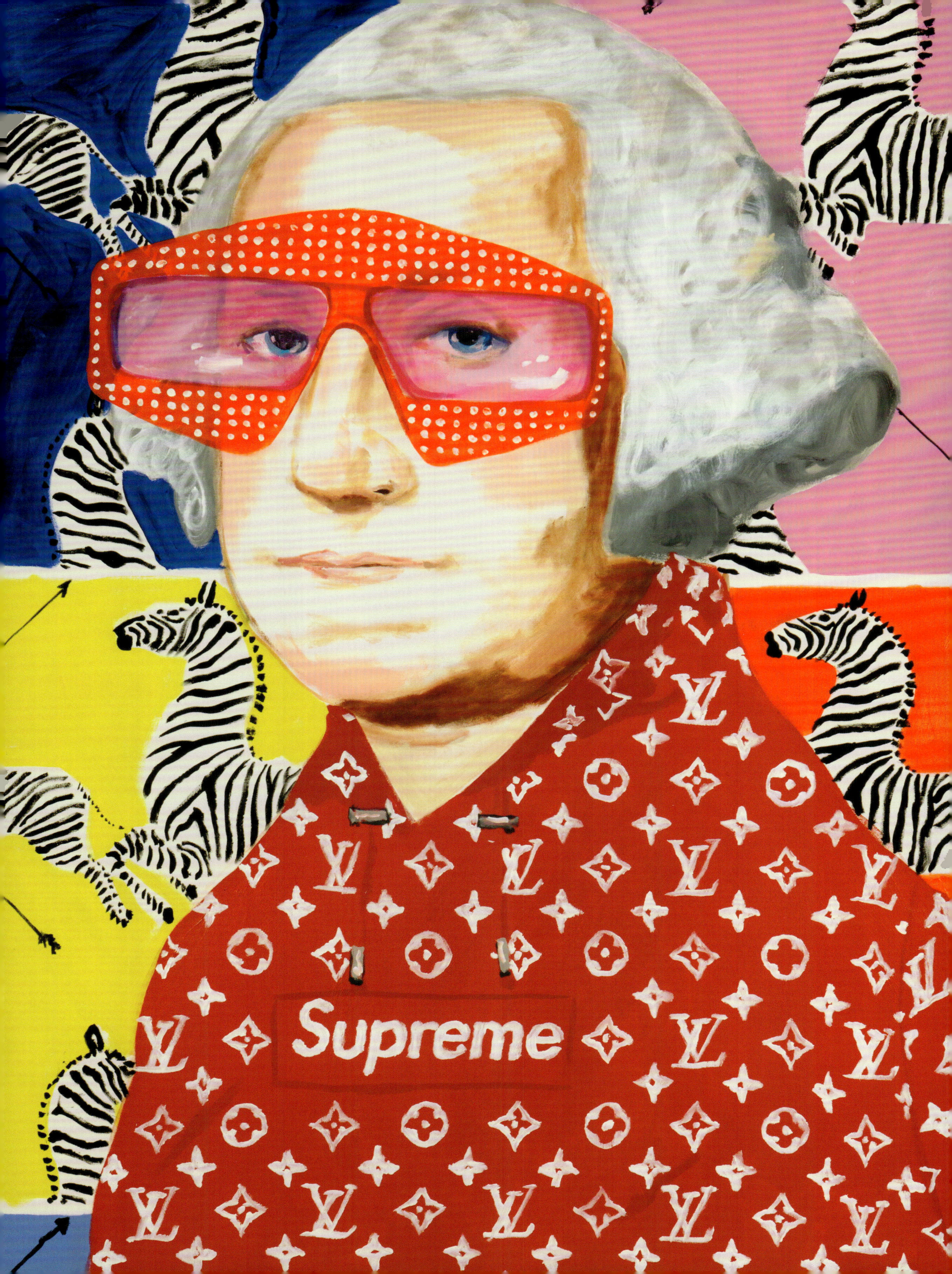
Supreme

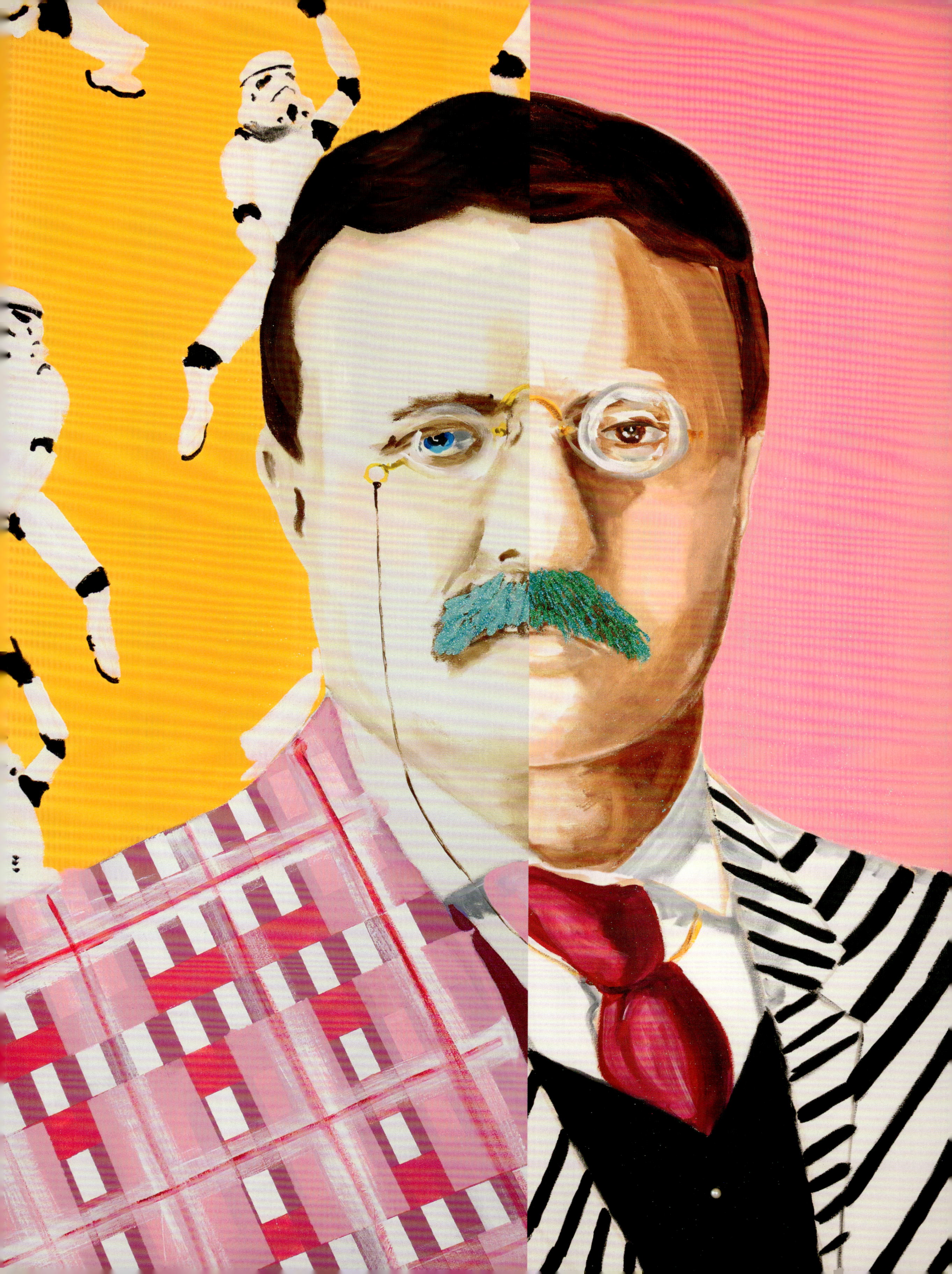

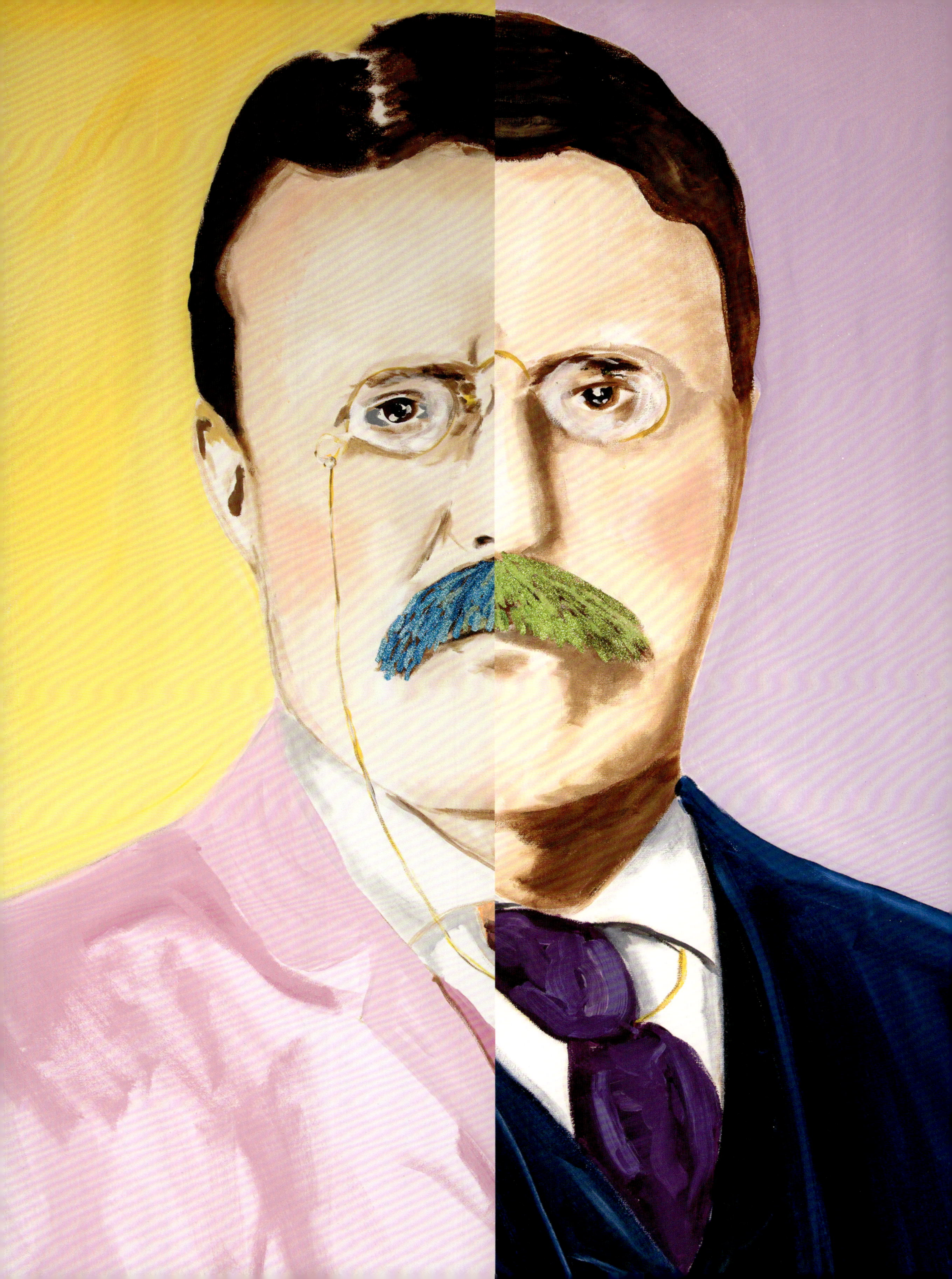

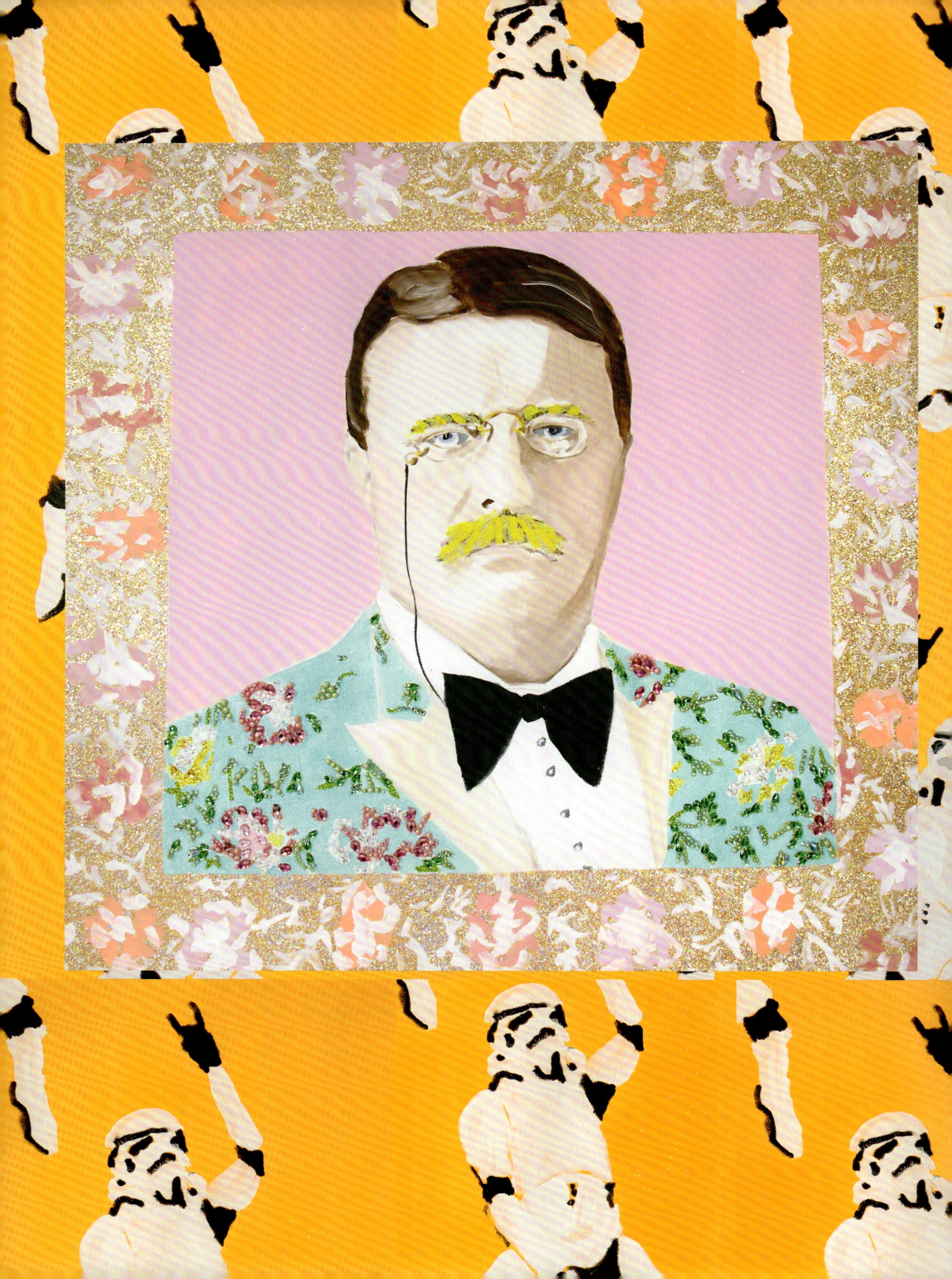

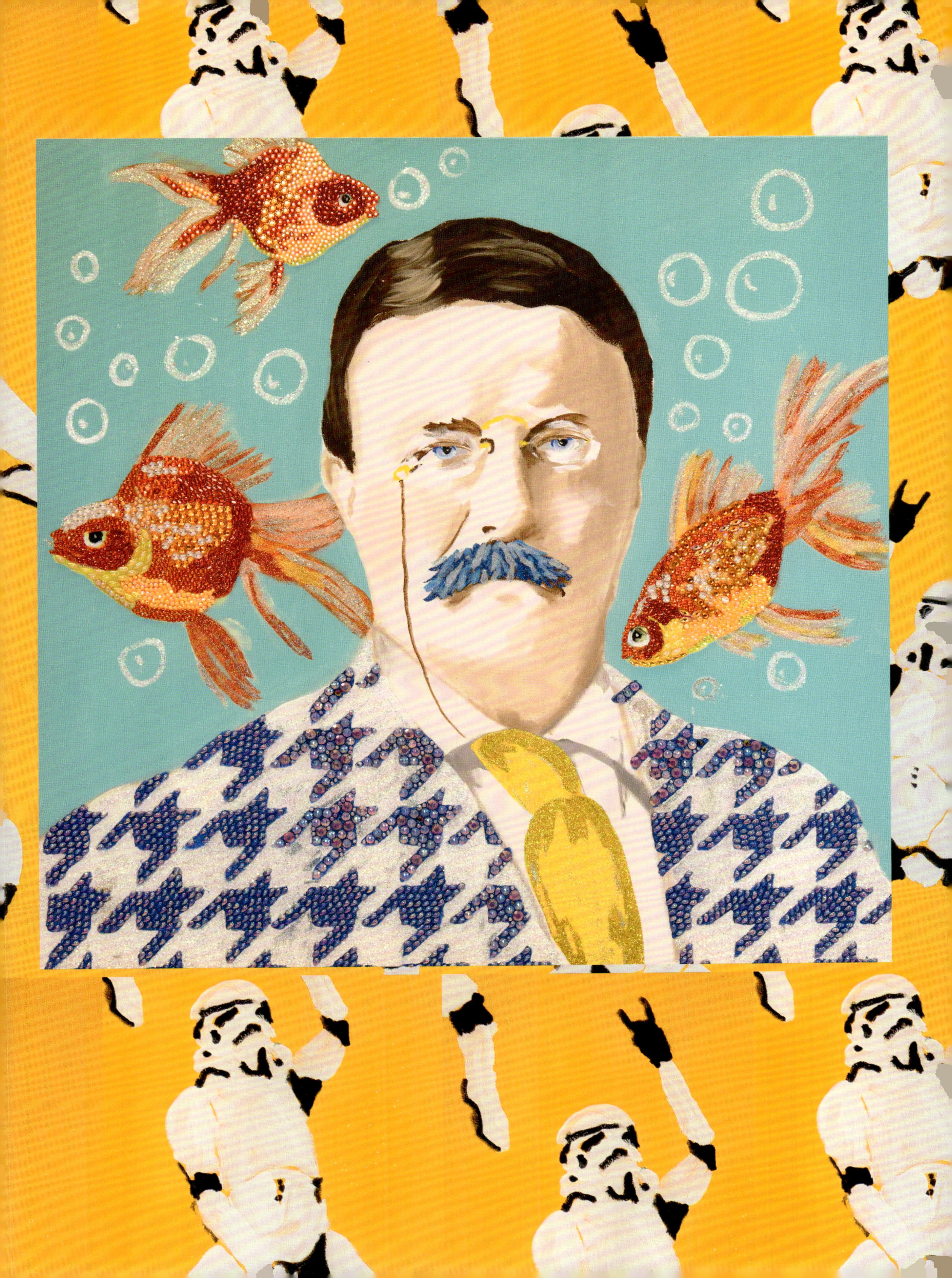

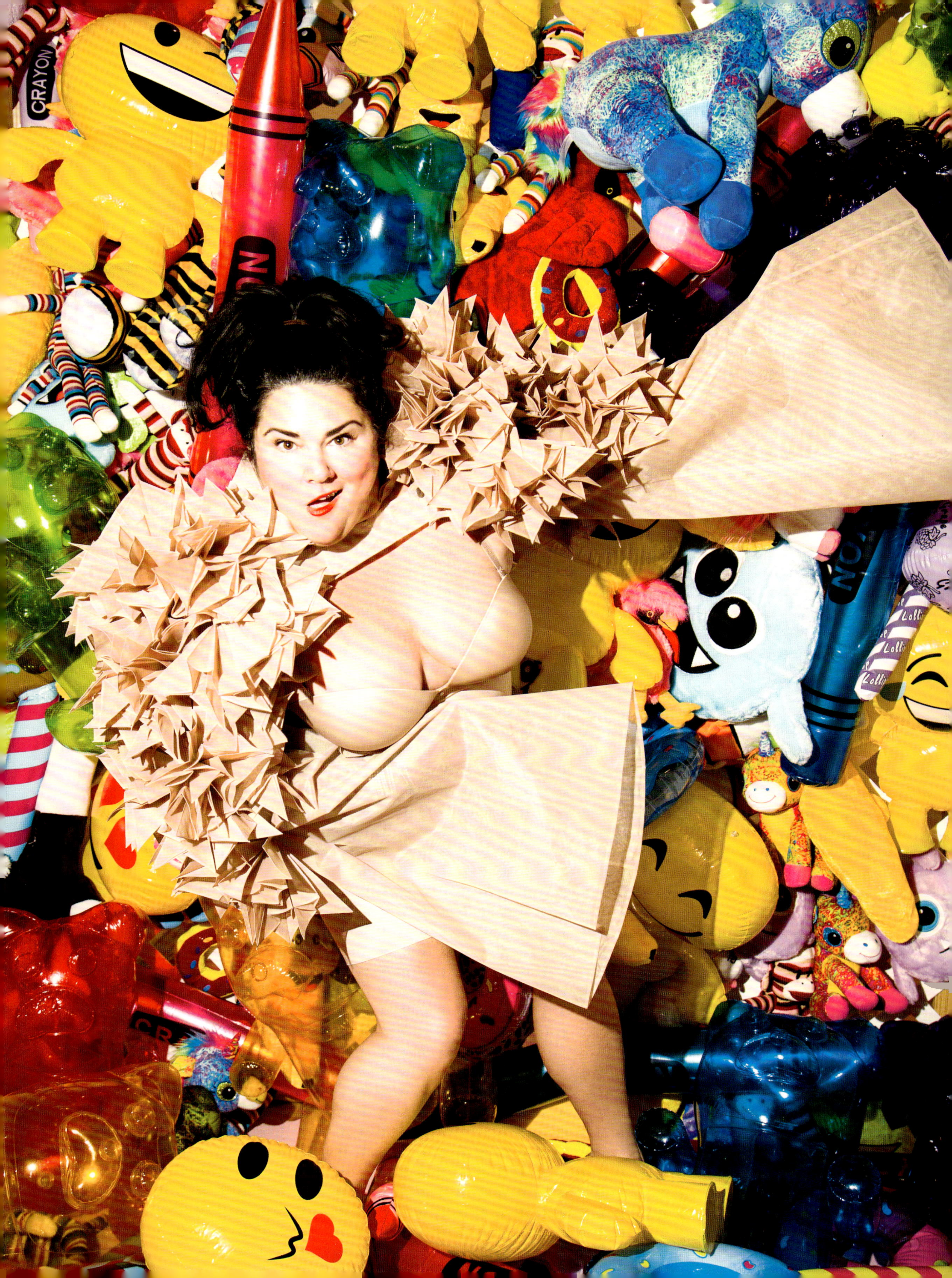
CRAYON

PORTRAITS

You are a living
Legend . .
Look in the
Mirror and
Scream . . .
"I would Fuck Me"
you deserve it .

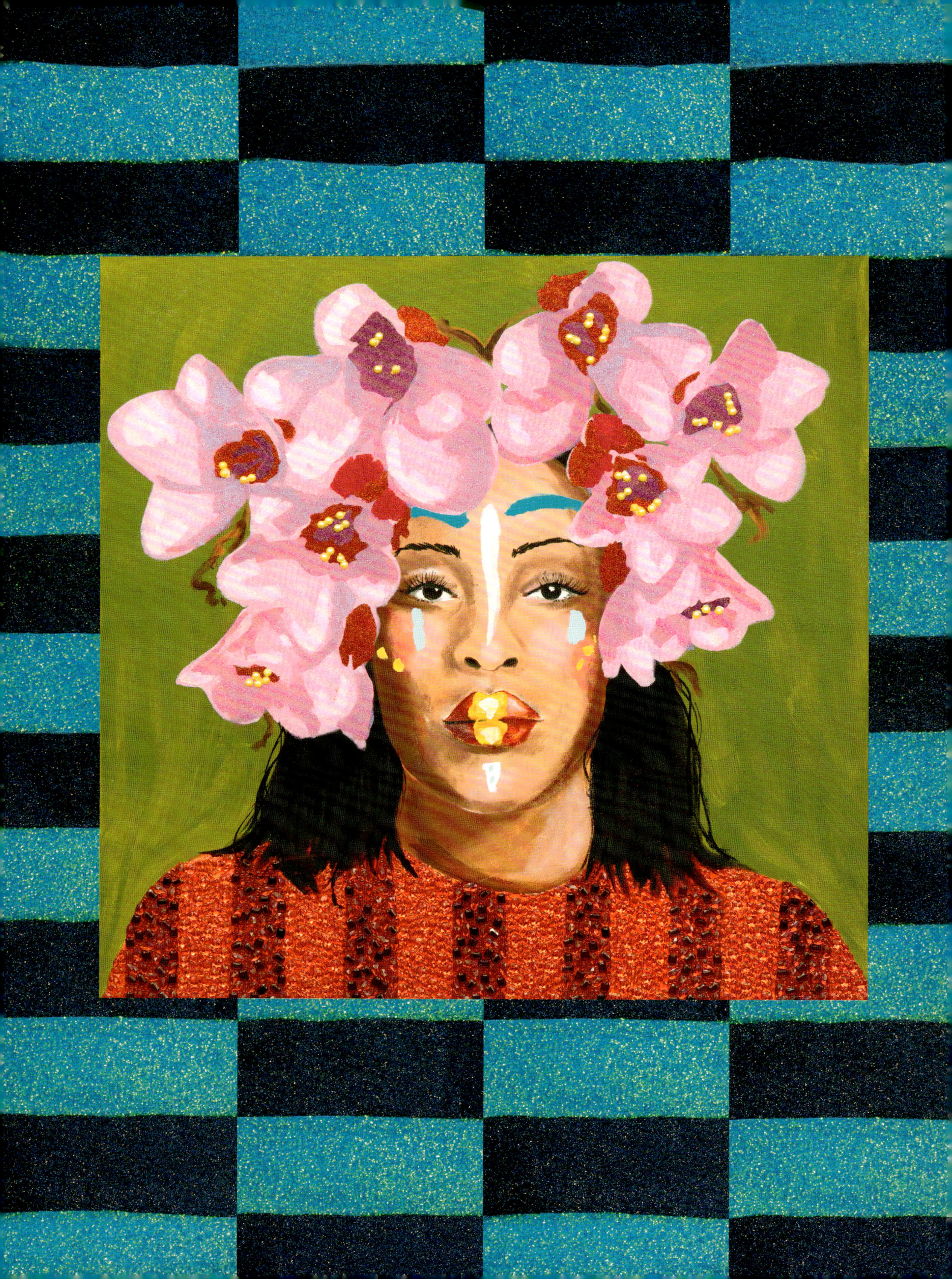

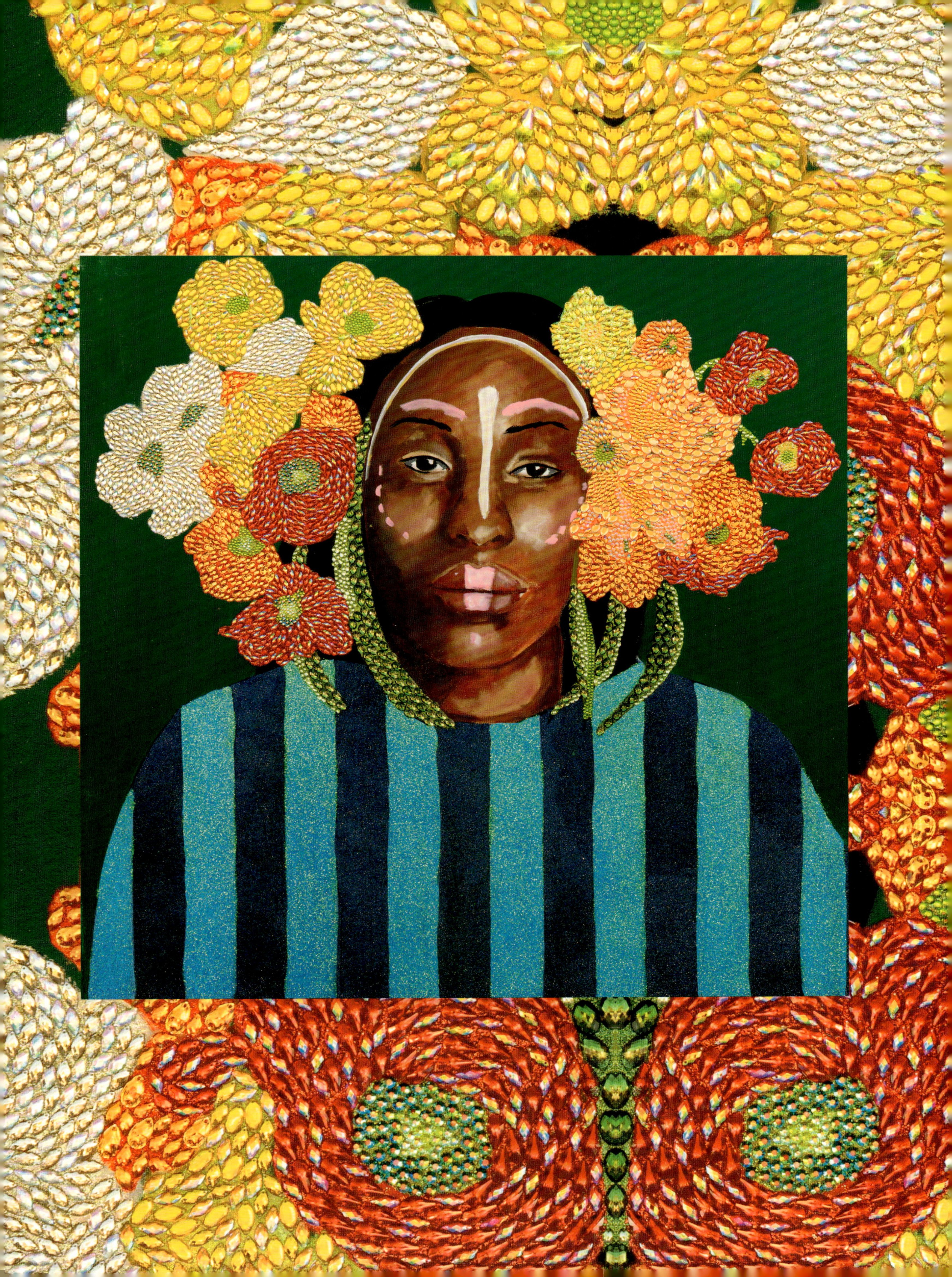

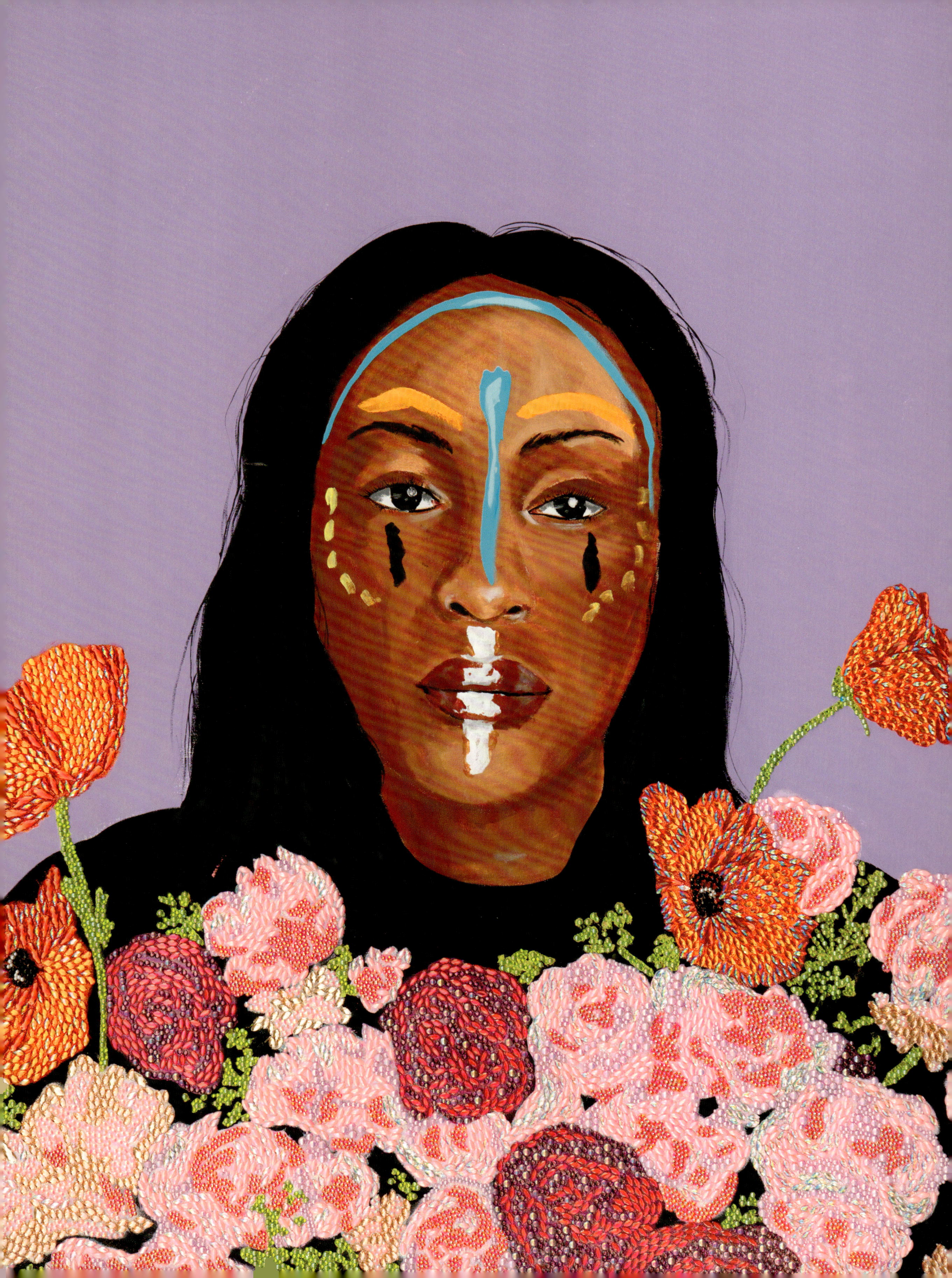

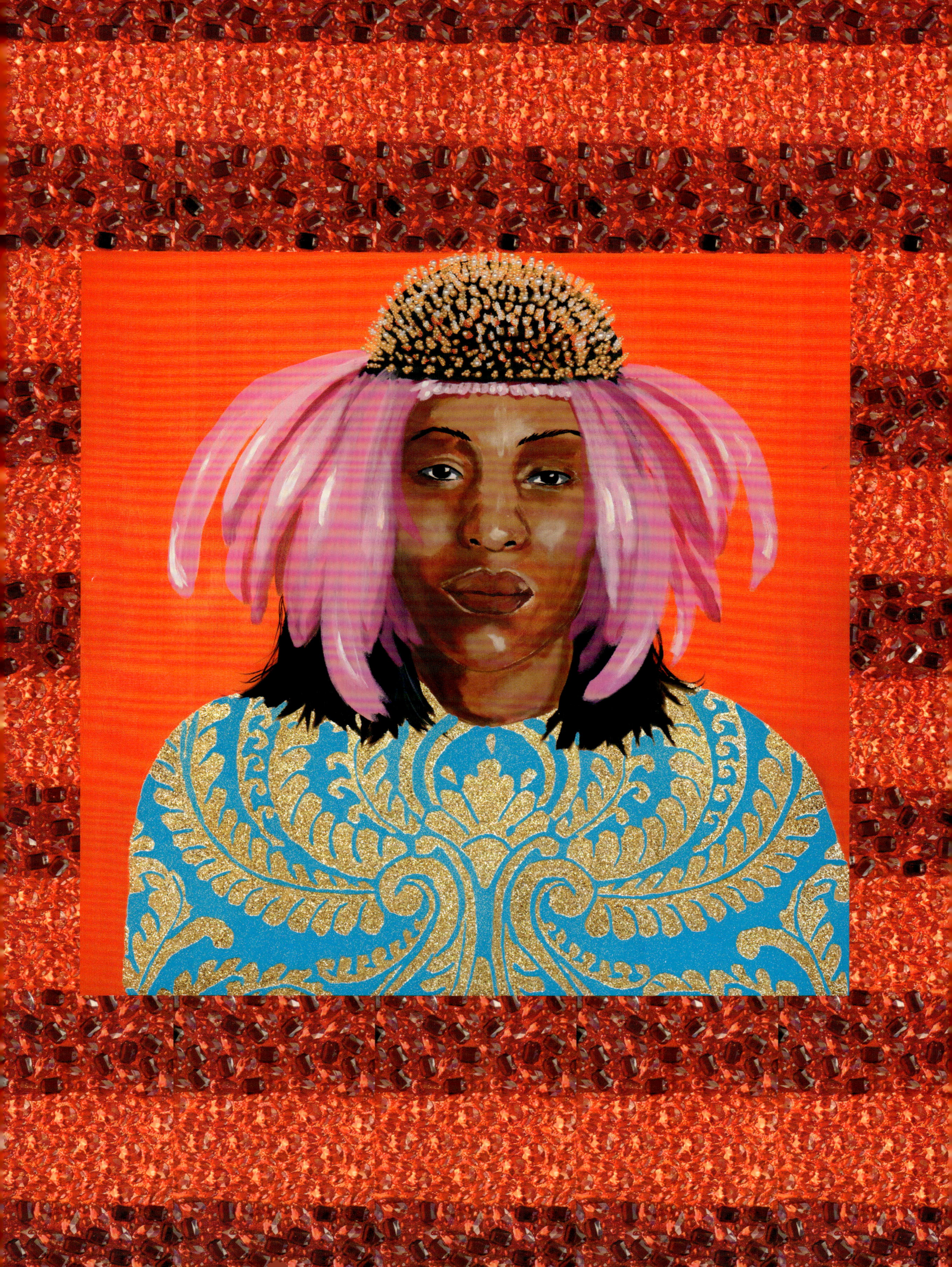

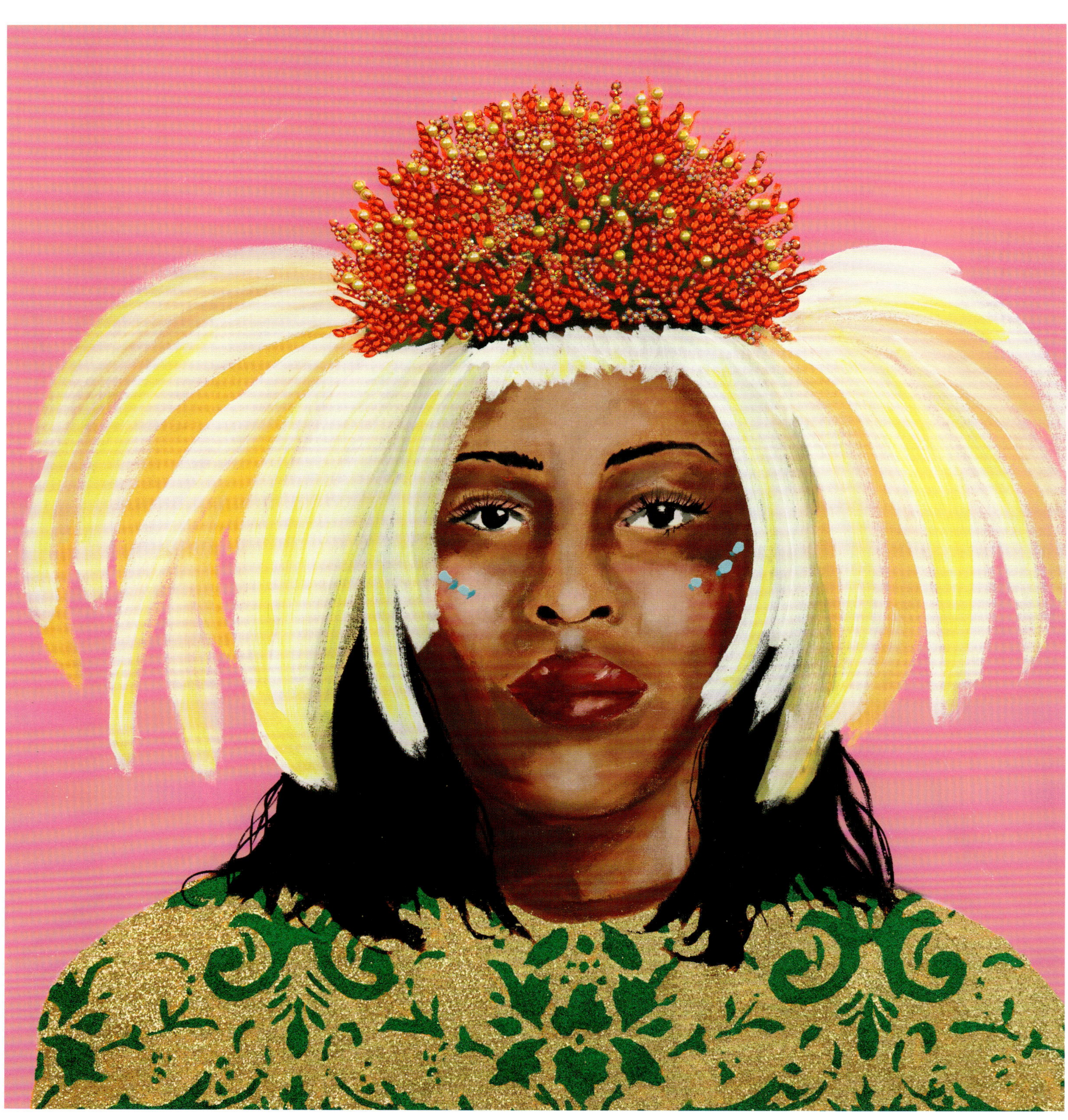

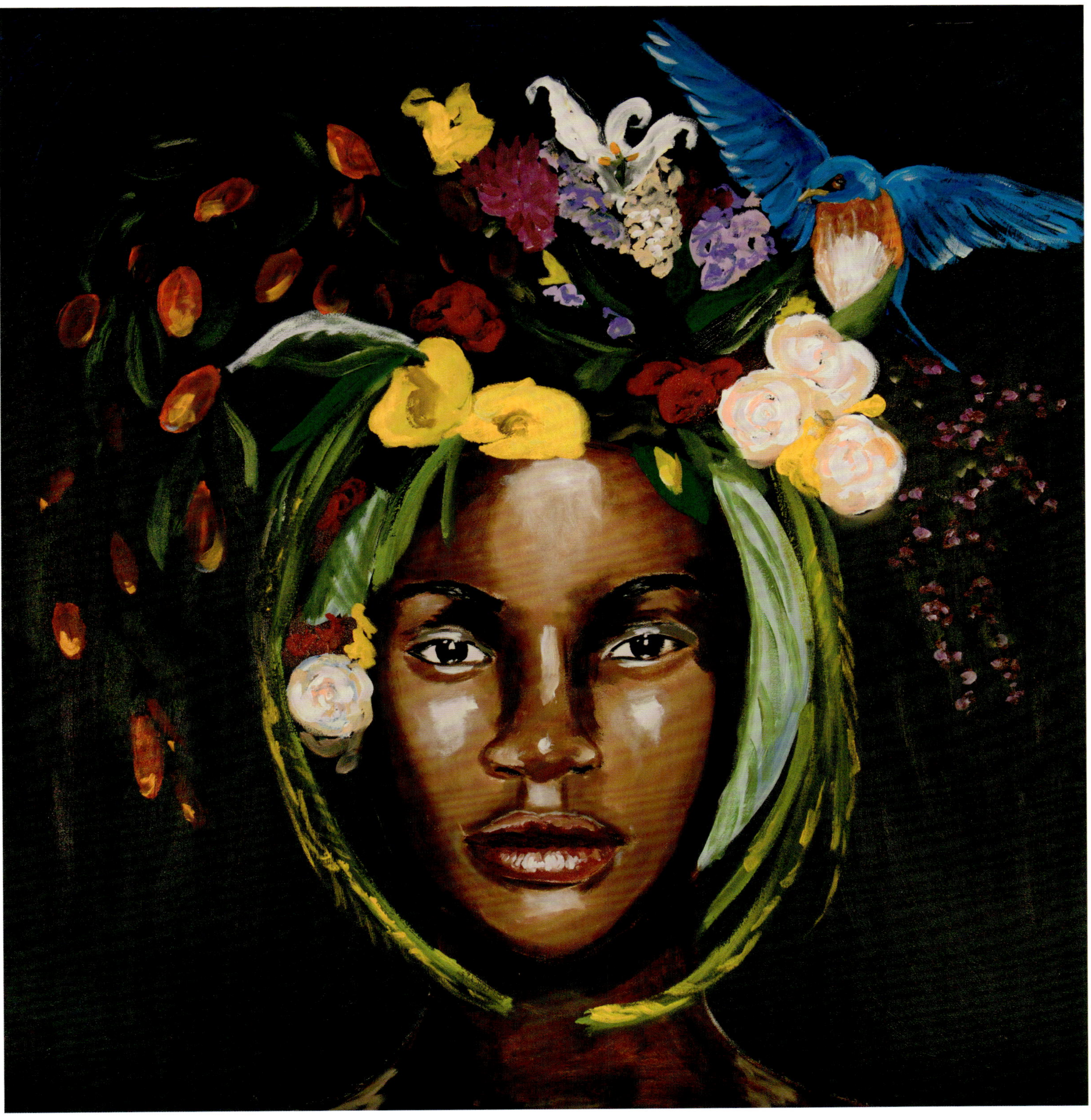

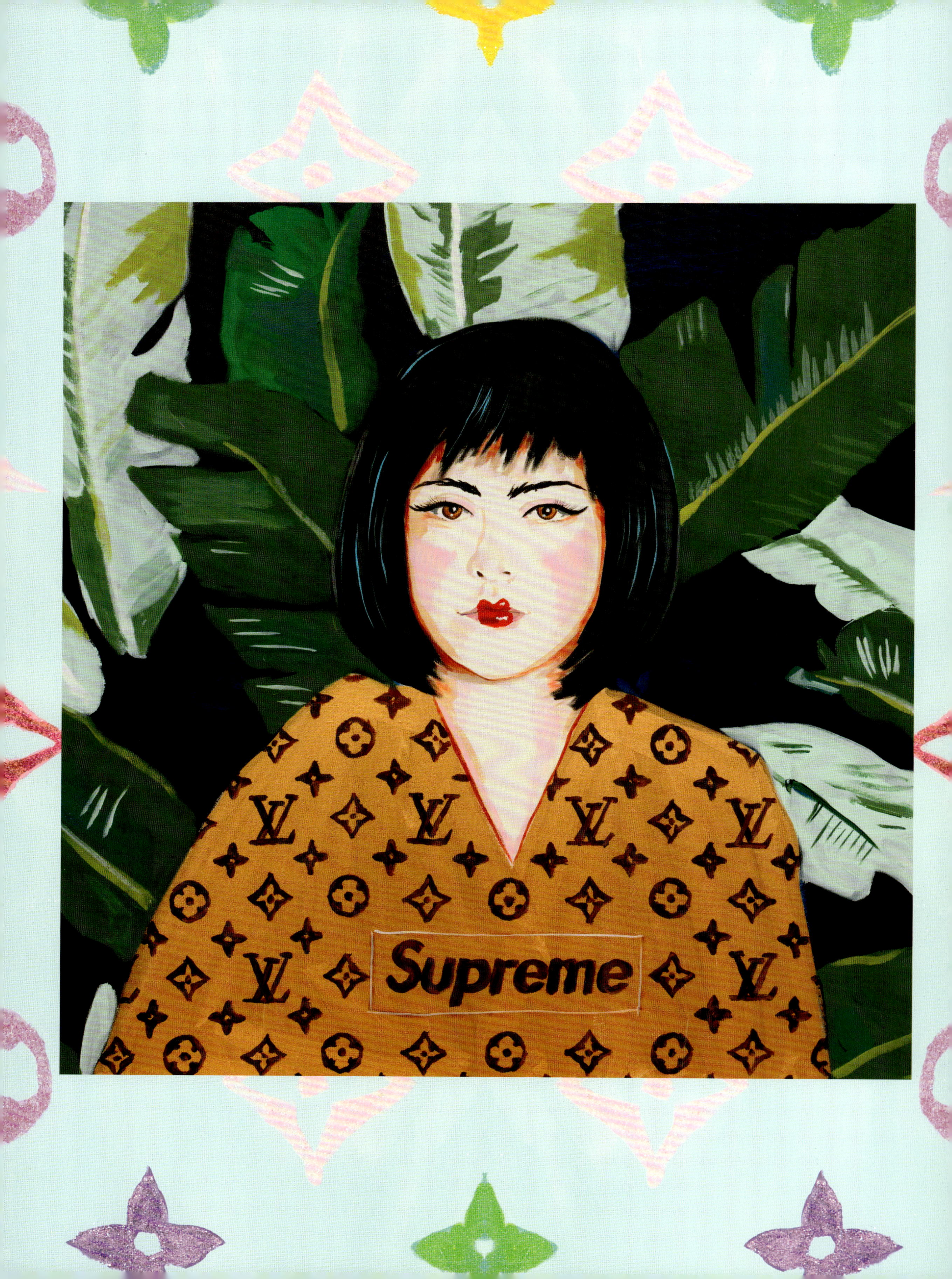

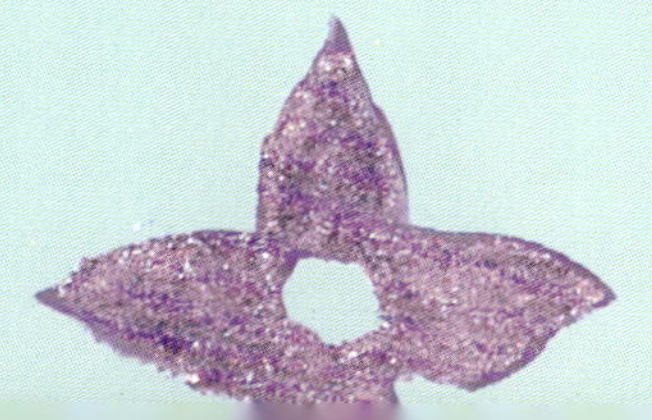
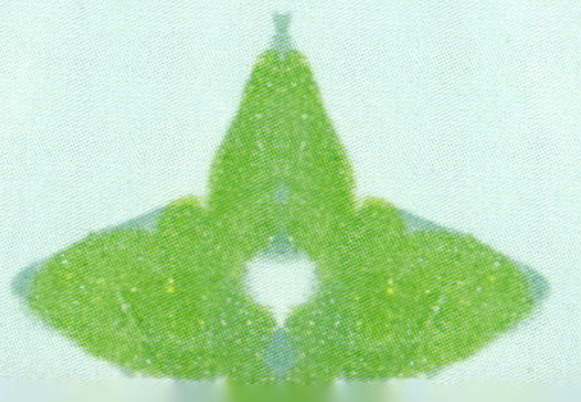
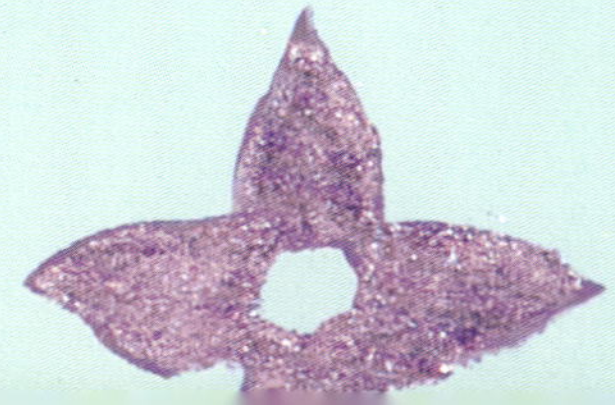

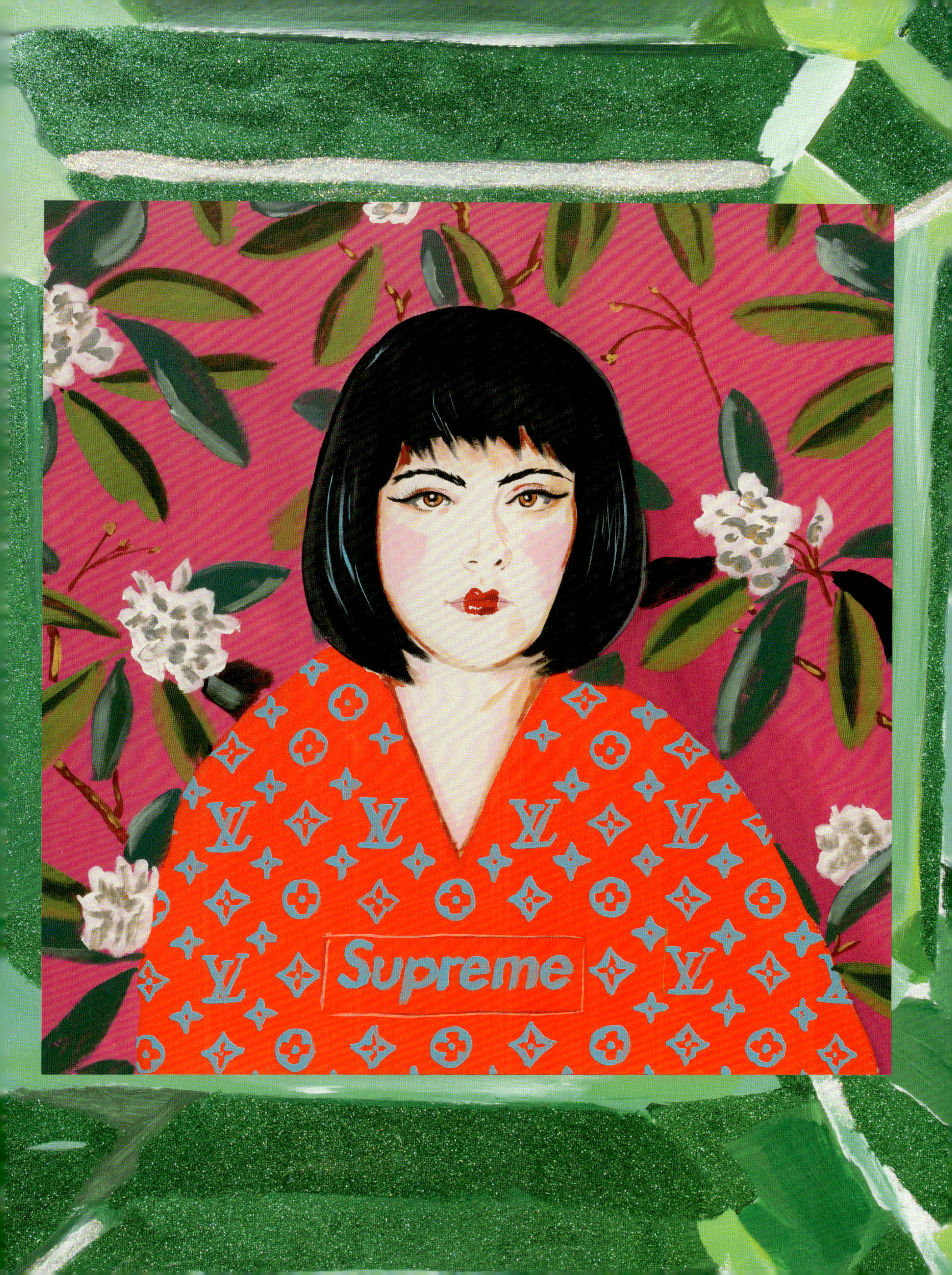
Supreme

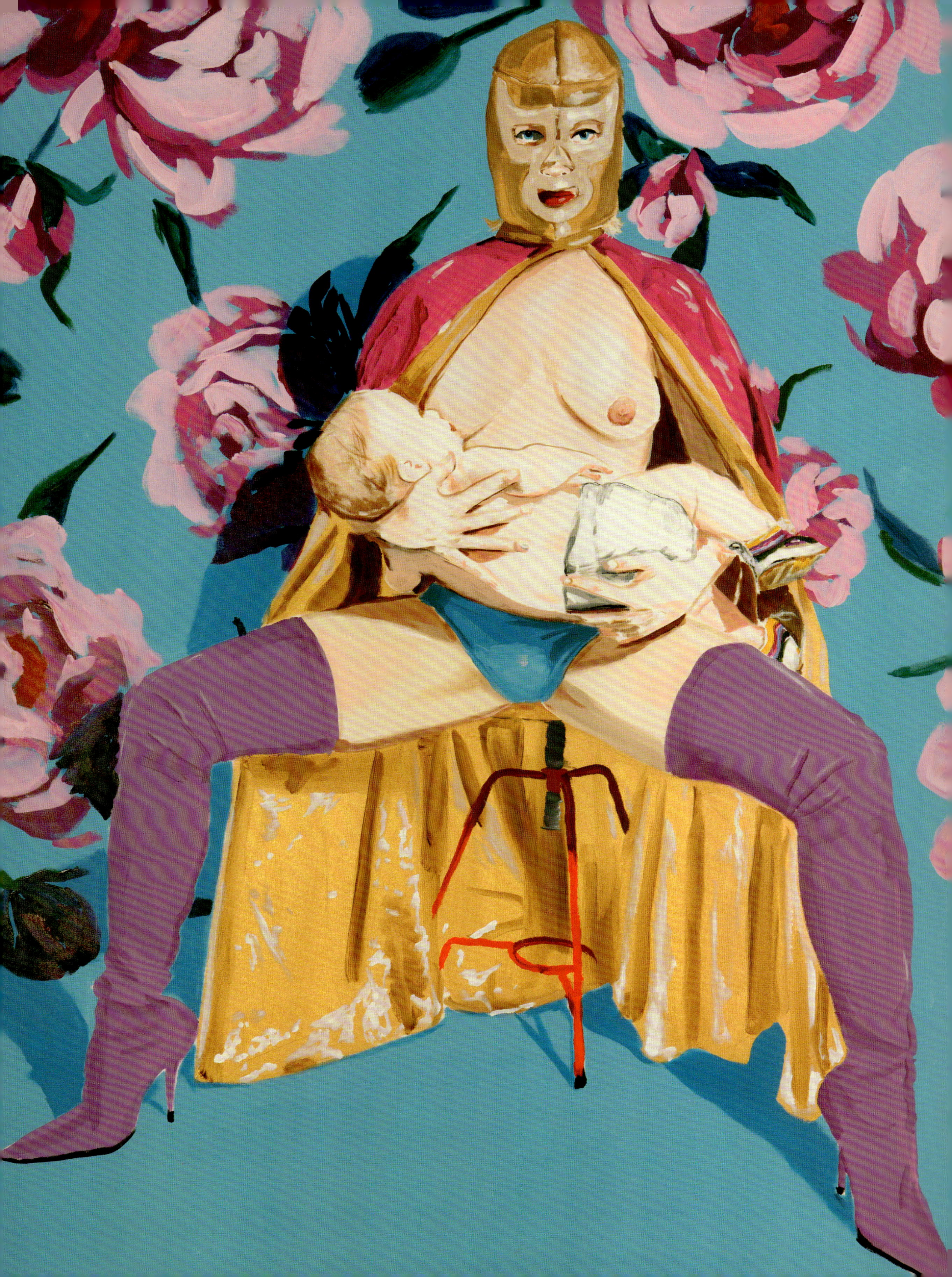

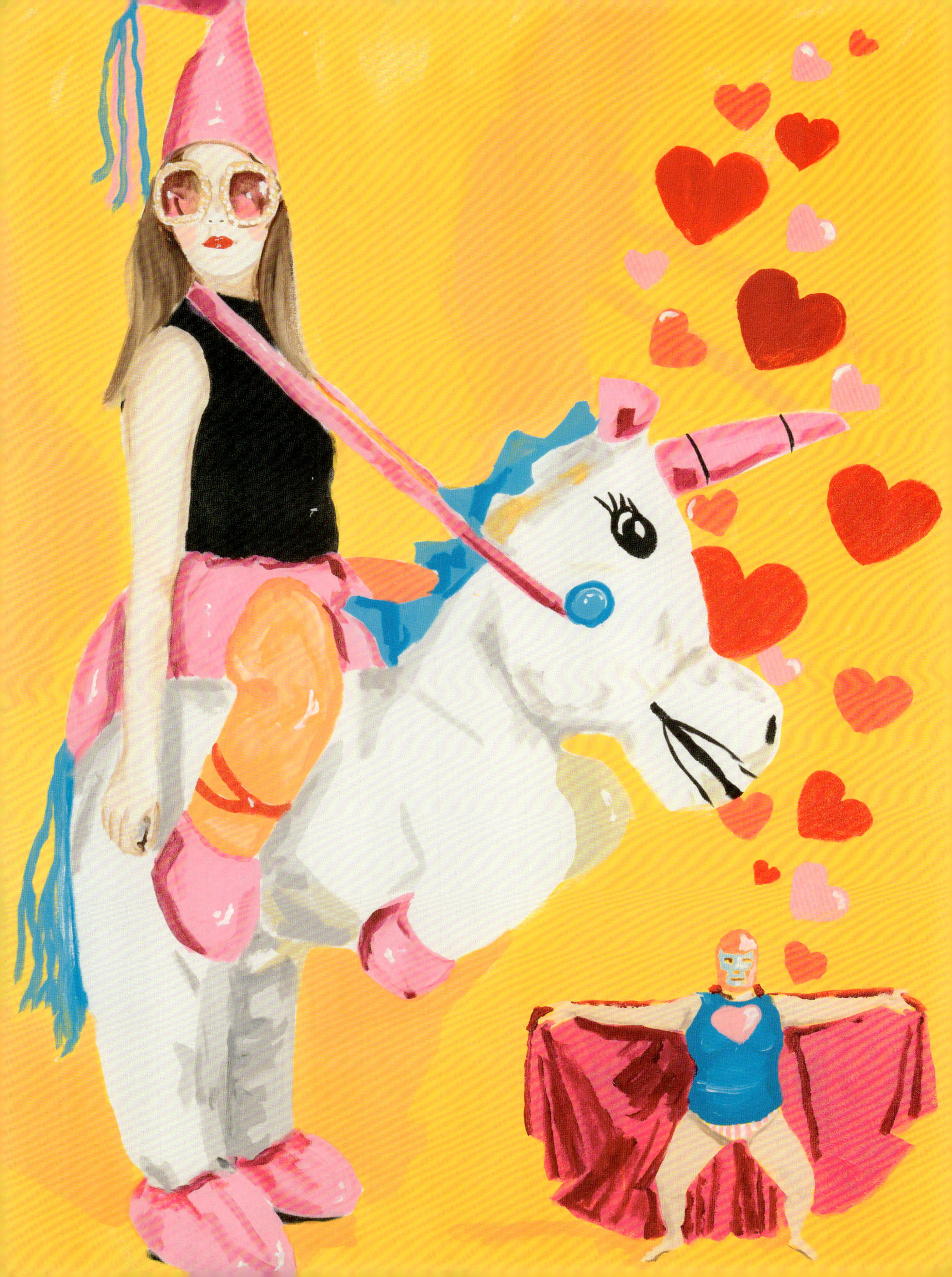

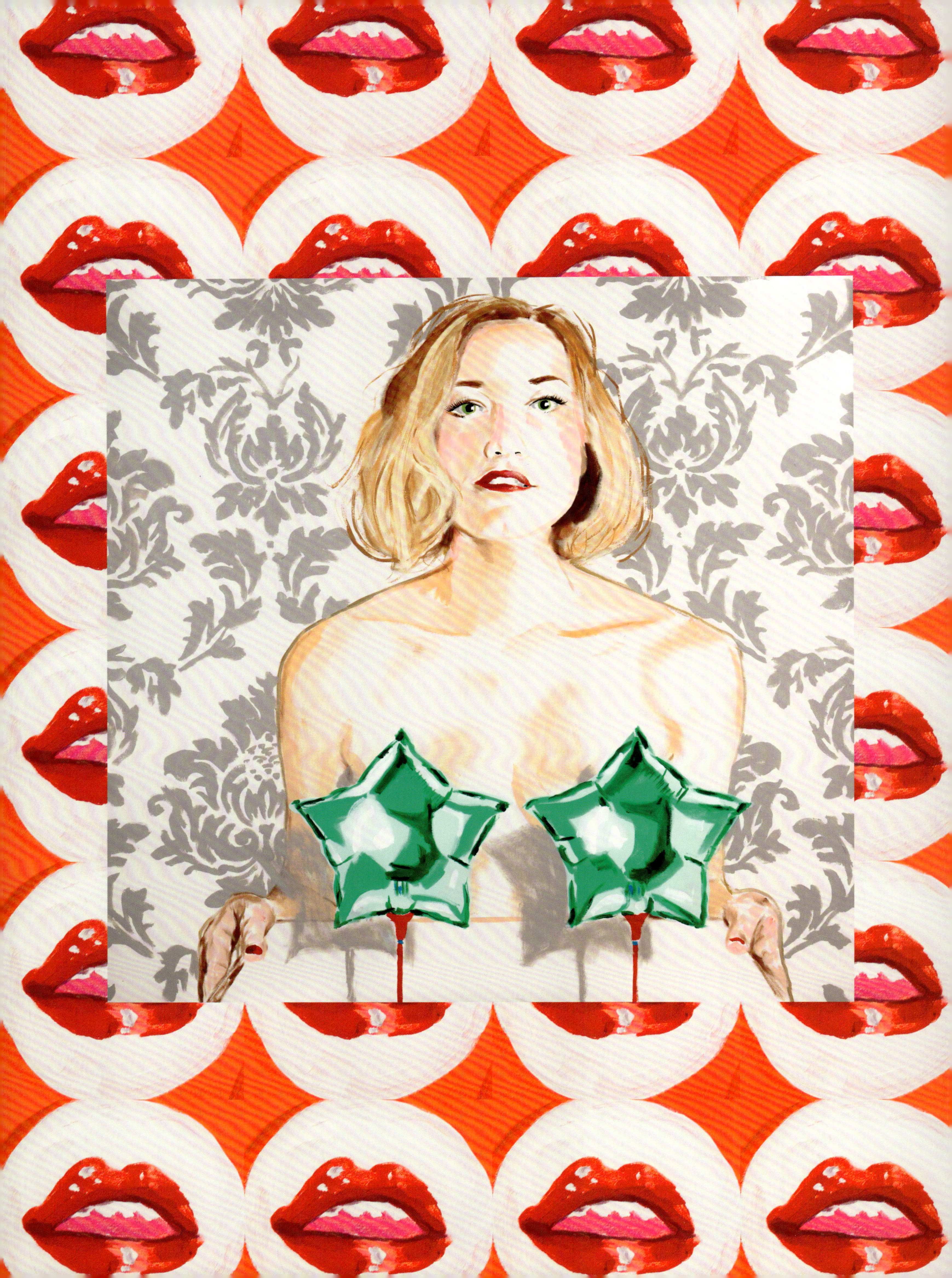

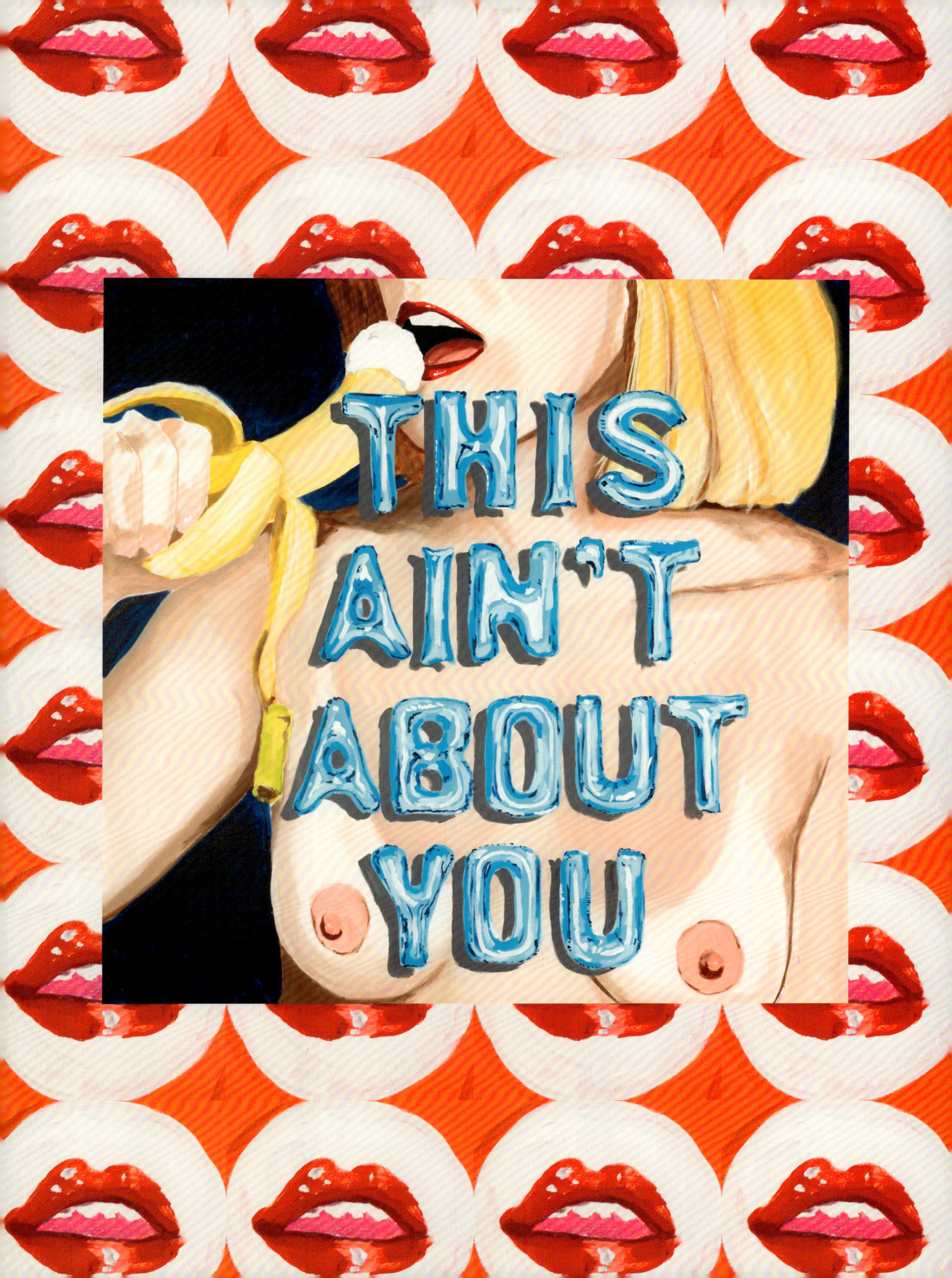
THIS
AIN'T
ABOUT
YOU

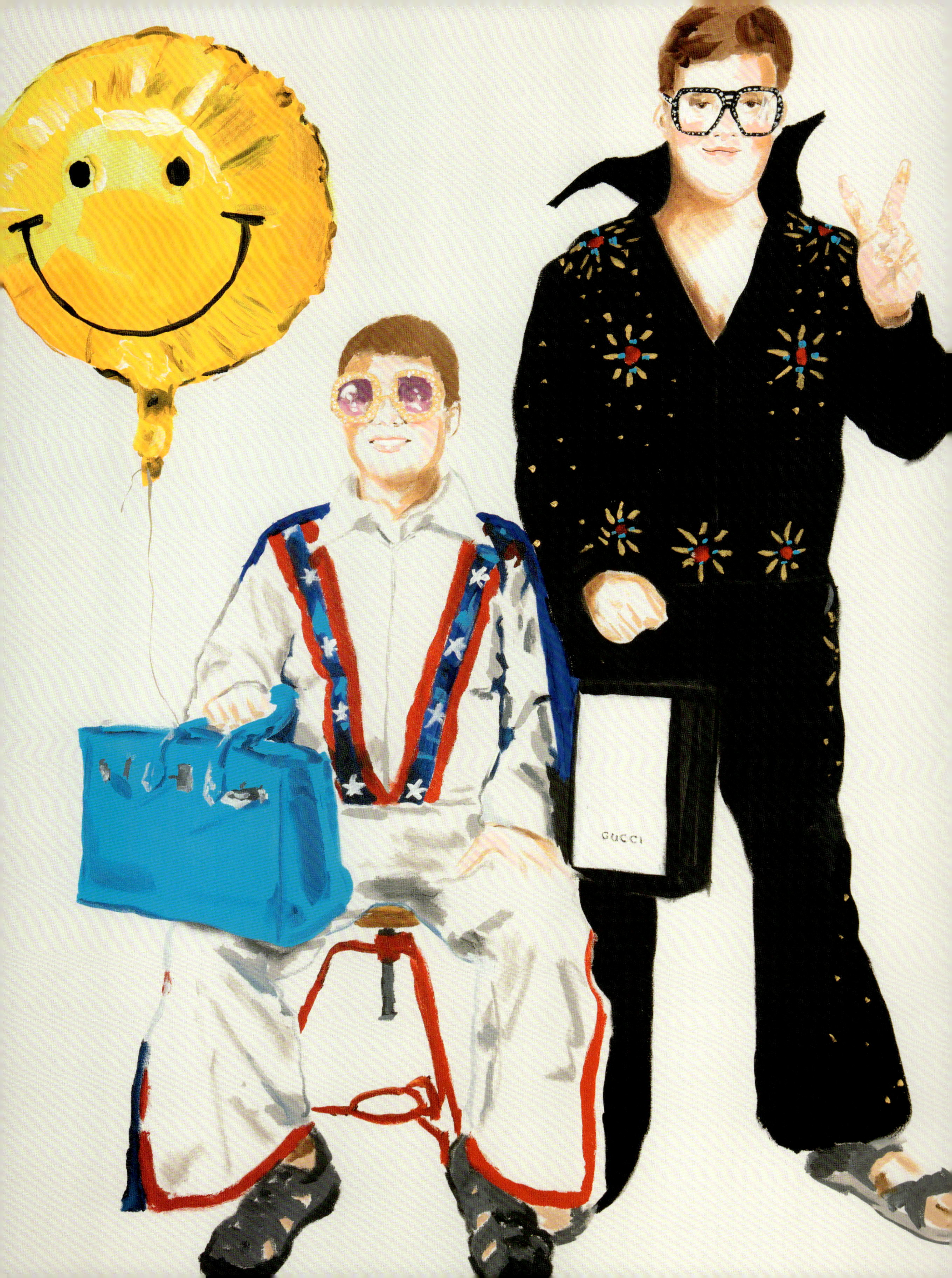
GUCCI

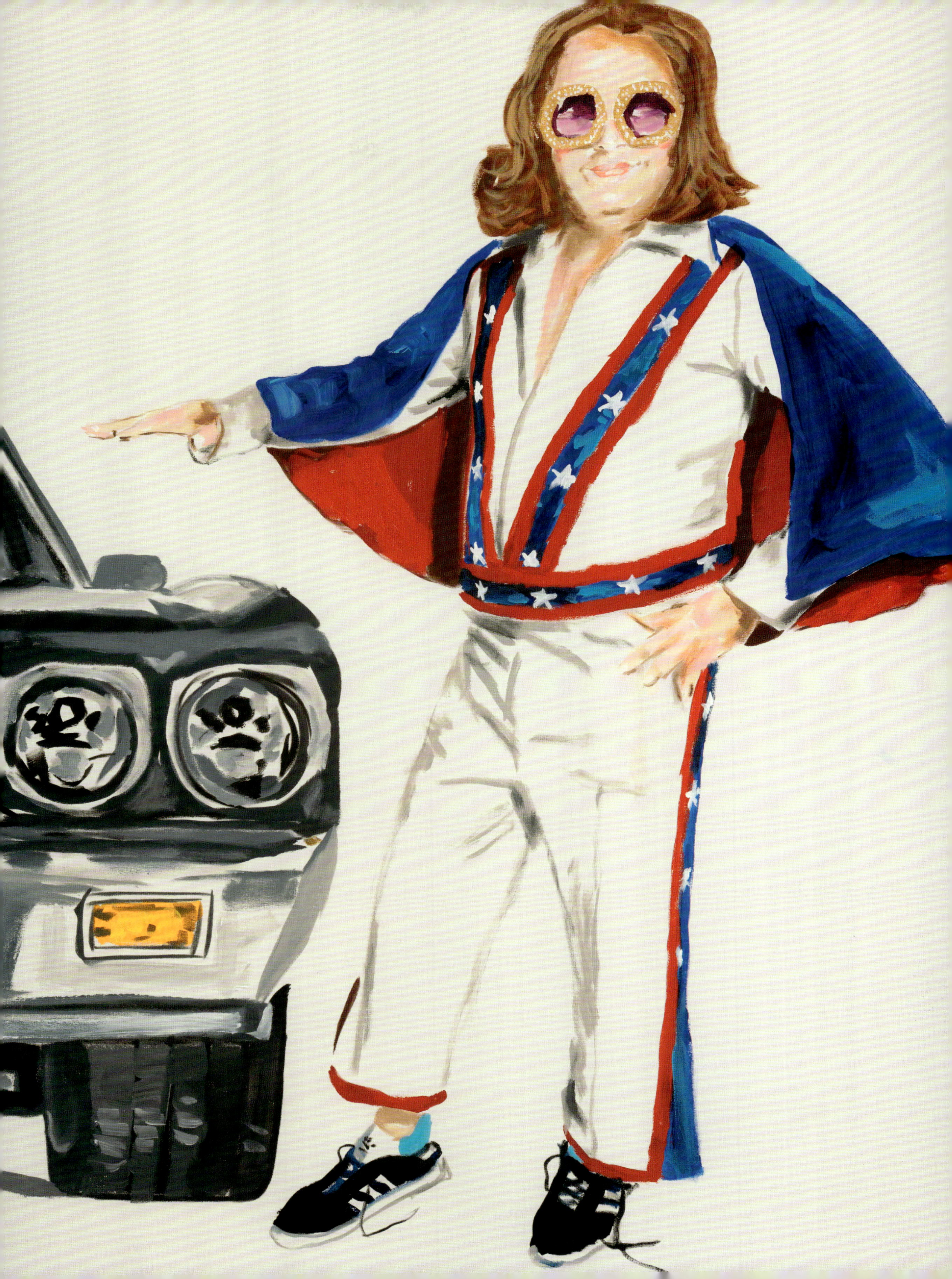

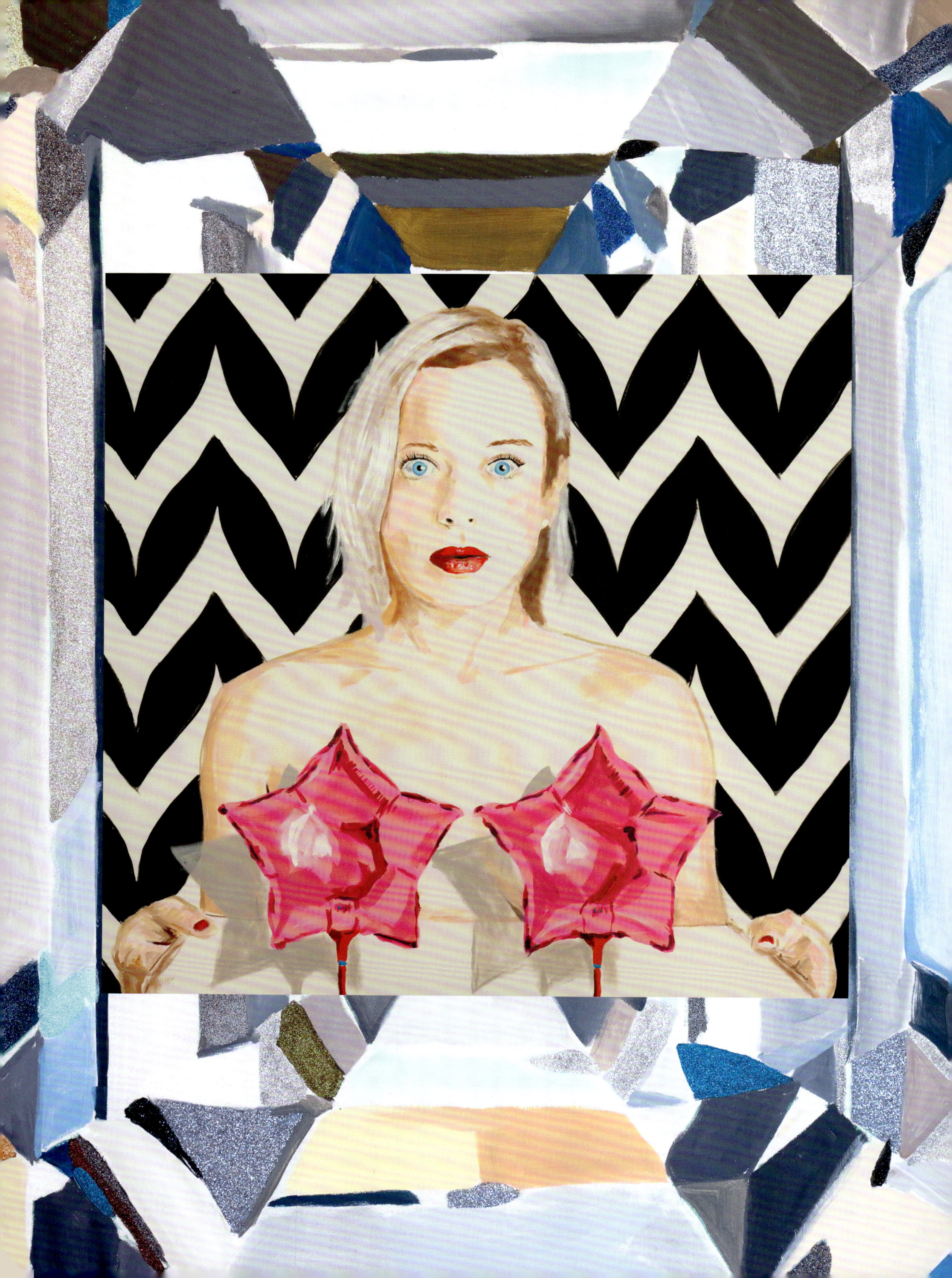

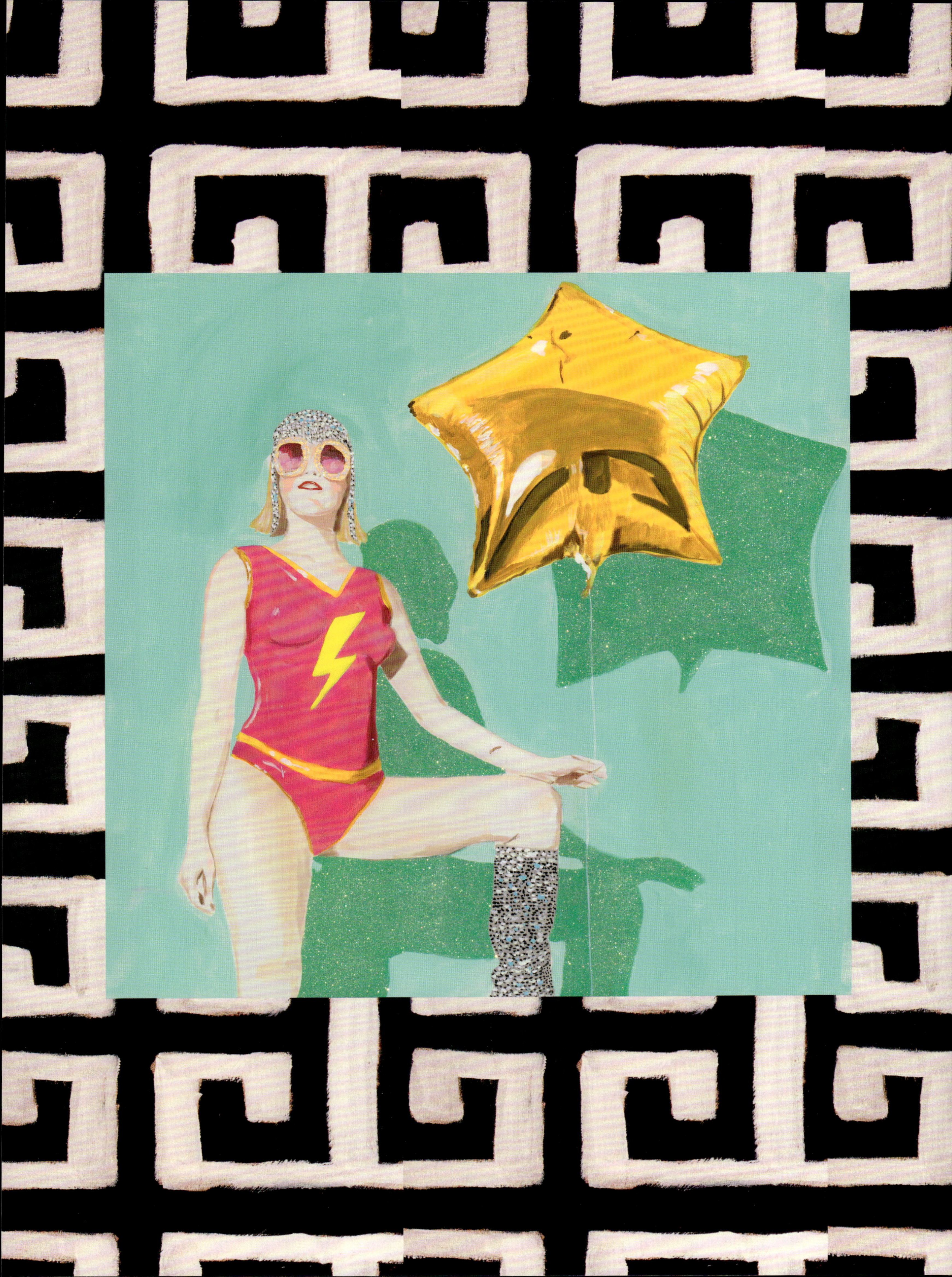

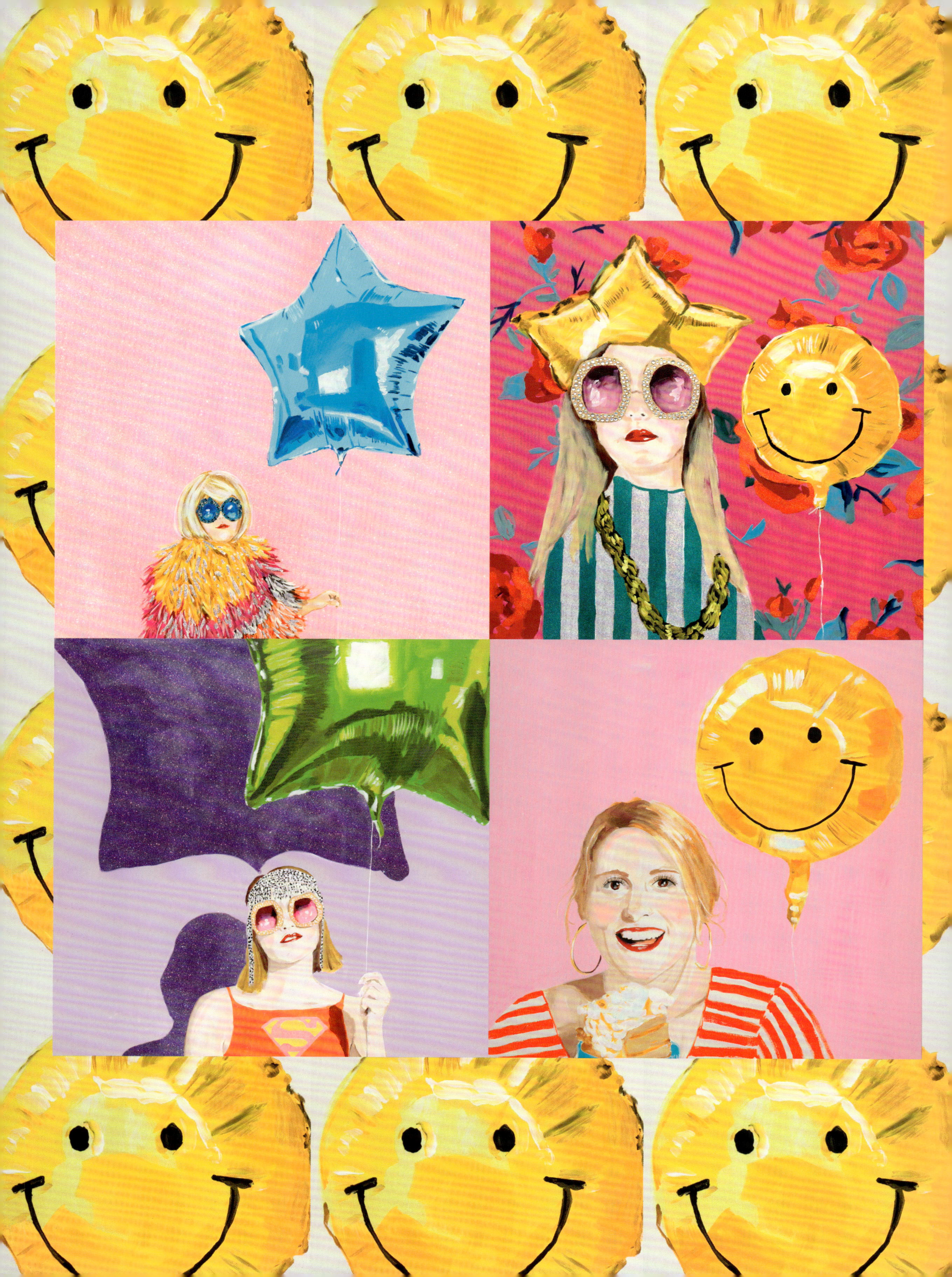

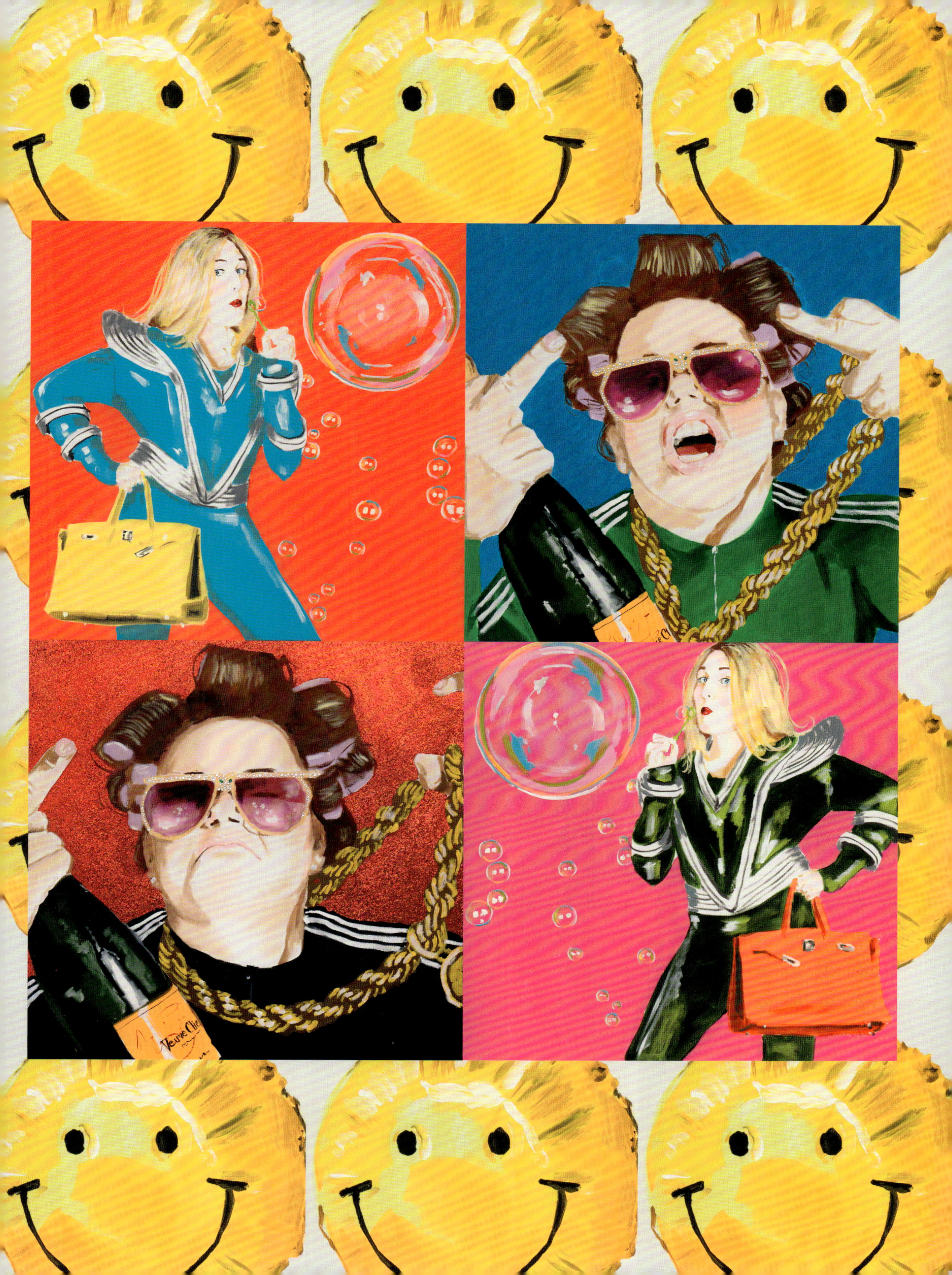

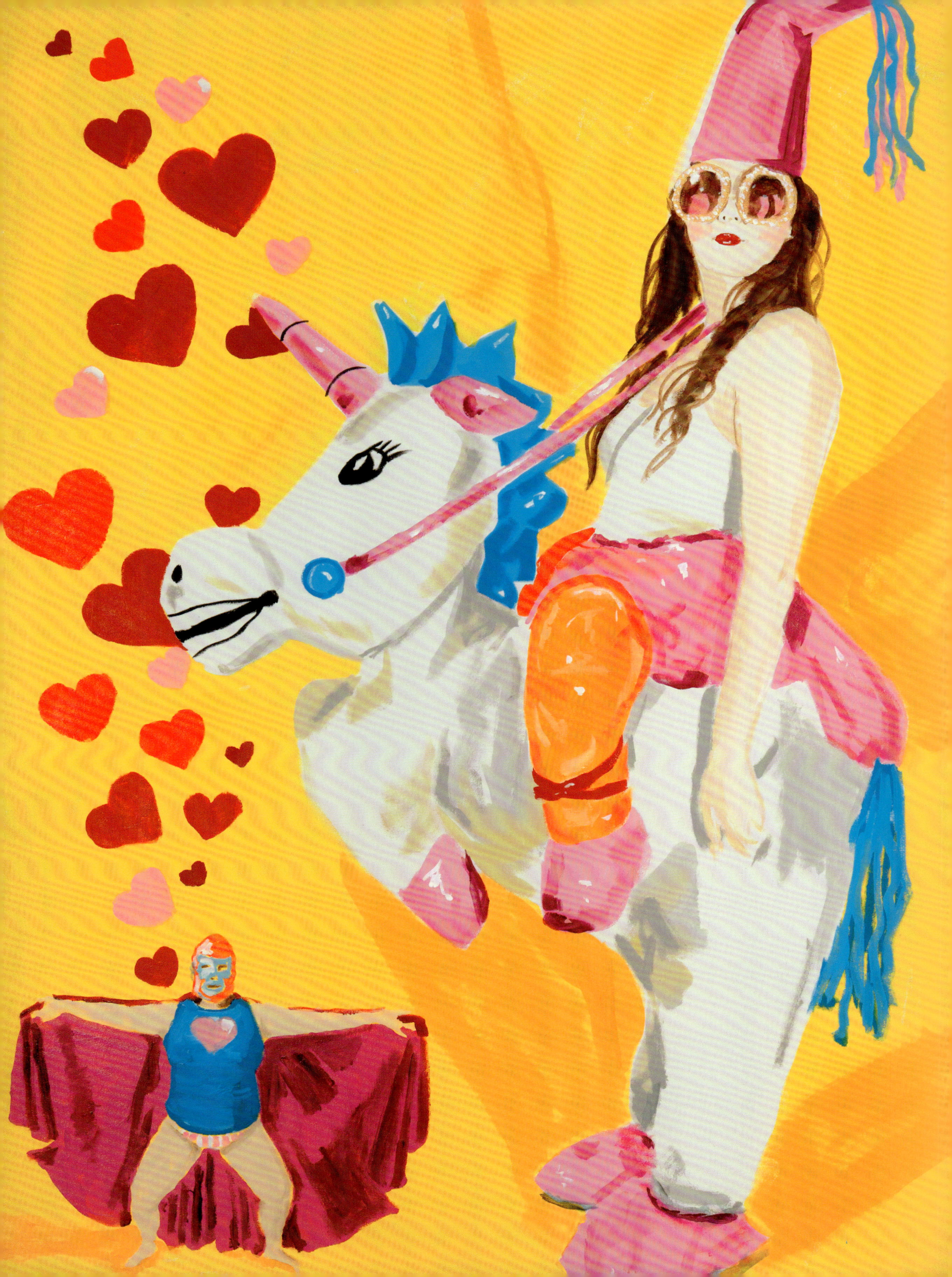

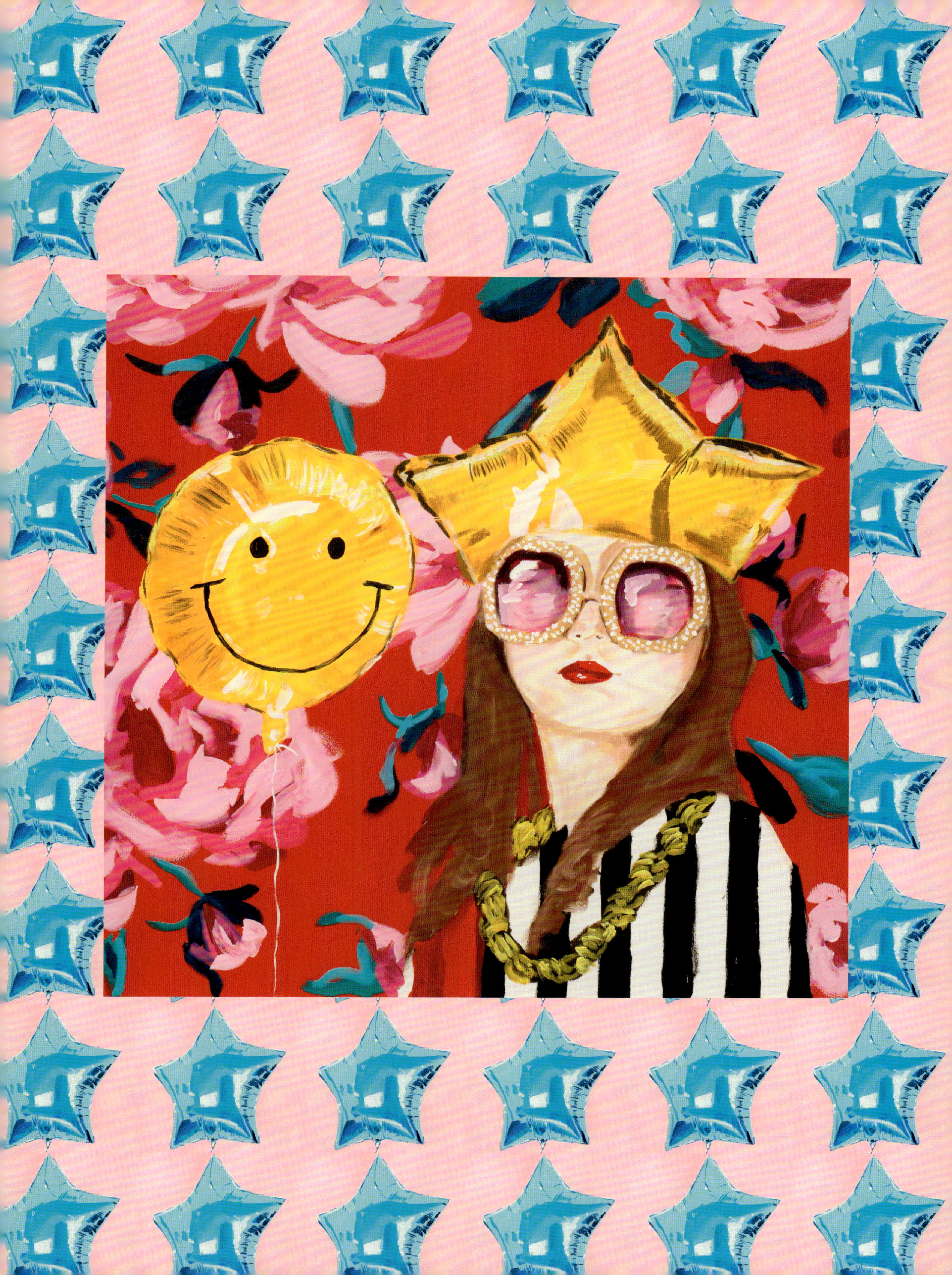

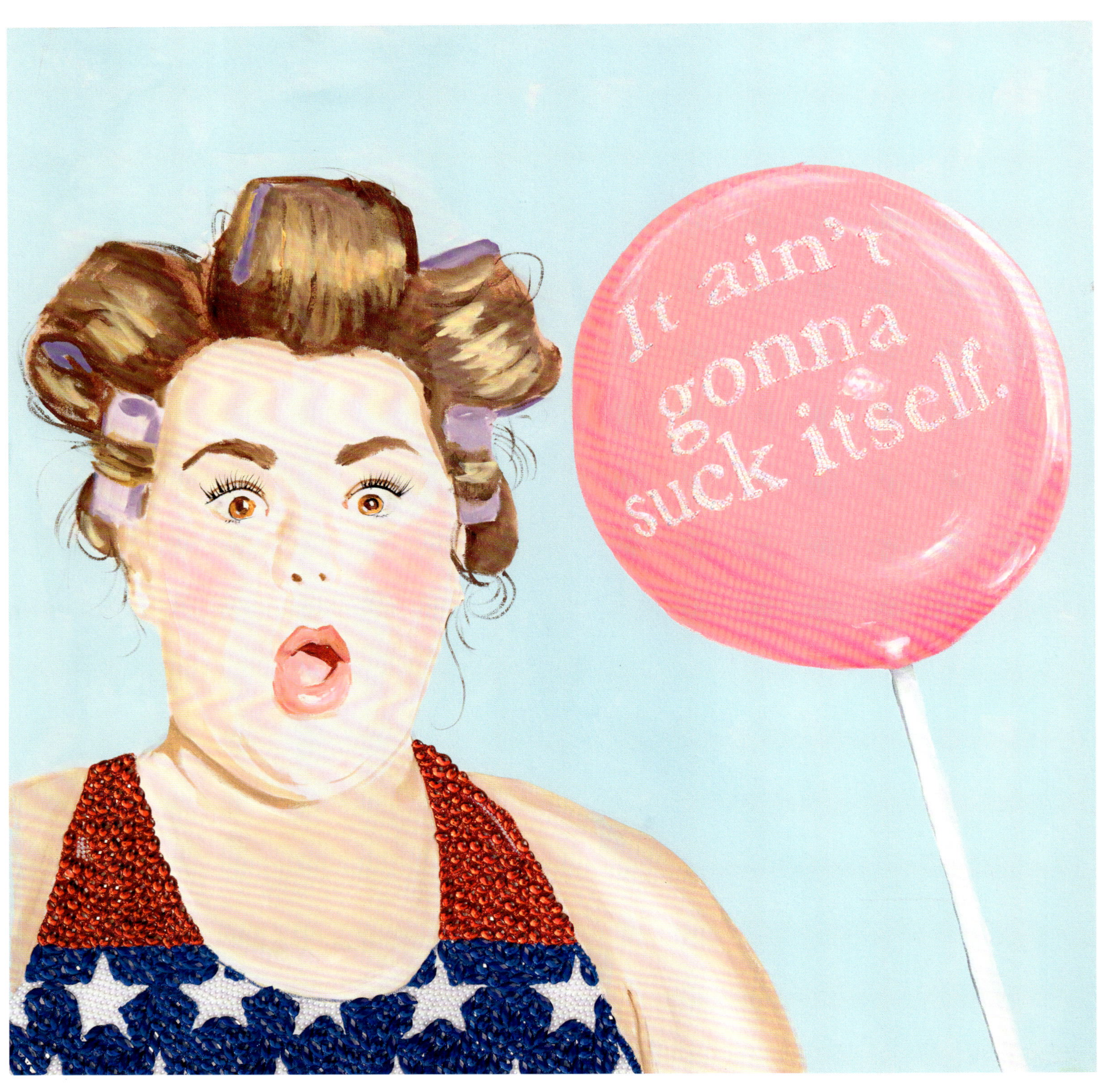
It ain't
gonna
suck itself.

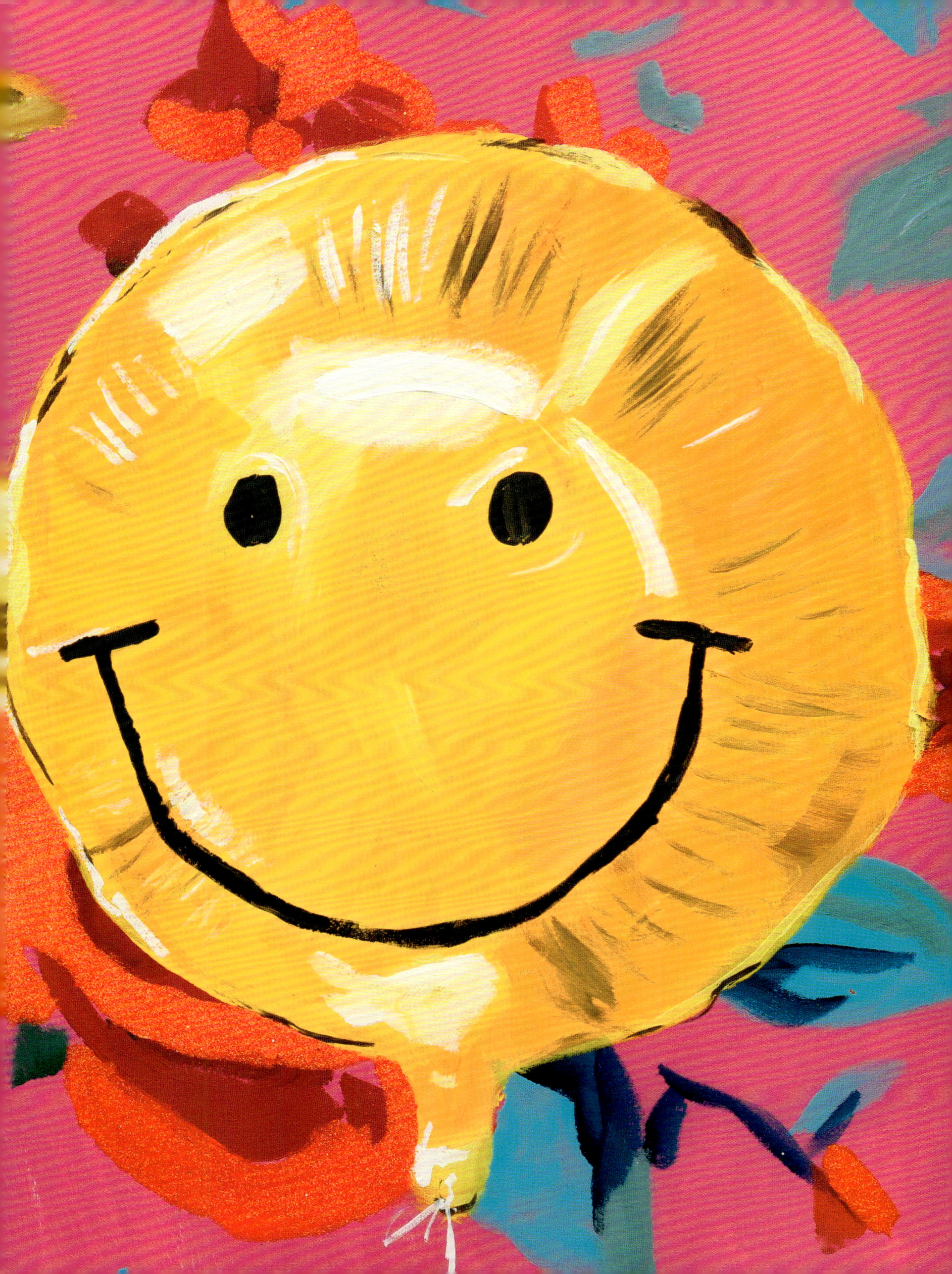

ACKNOWLEDGMENTS

I'd like to thank all of the fearless incredible women who have paved the road for me to be brave enough to be the woman I am. I'm an F-bomb-dropping, hard-working, unapologetic American woman . . . and I love that I have the freedom to say what I want. I also love that I have the liberty to make my own money and love who I want, buy what I want, and live where I want. My father nurtured me endlessly and made me believe that I could do anything. He taught me that I can always count on myself. His wisdom and nurturing has made me the woman I am today. And thank you to my Cindy, who takes care of and loves my Pappy! I love you so much. And my sister Allyson . . . I love you.

I also have the most incredible team on the planet. They are my logical family and I love them so much. I spend each day surrounded by incredible, strong, kind, brilliant individuals. Kate Grace, Shannon, Rachel, and Patri "heiress billionairess," my photographer James, Addy—you are my heart, all of my Bedazzlers and manufacturing team, I love you so much!

And to Michael, my love. You have been here since the beginning when we didn't have two dimes to rub together and easels stacked by the bed. I love you! Thank you for being so supportive and for being my love.

And to Nora and Emilie, I love you so much . . . my right hands.

And to my collectors, who have believed in me and supported me from the beginning. Your spirit is in everything I paint. You have enabled me to travel and follow my wildest art desires. You all have kept me in a studio with brushes and canvas. We are connected because we share a common zest for life, color, beauty, and humor.

To my sweet lifelong friends who have loved me for me always. I love you so much. And a huge thank you to my contributors! Diane, Tommy and Dee, Linda Fargo—I am so grateful that you believe in my spirit and wildness! Thank you for inspiring me to keep going for it!

I love life. I love every day even with the shit sandwiches and exhaustion and unpredictable fucking mayhem. Life is so short and I am very enthusiastic about what is next and very grateful for everything so far.

Thank you Rizzoli for making this book. Y'all are pretty fucking cool. I especially love making Charles blush in our meetings!

Rizzoli International Publications, Inc.
300 Park Avenue South
New York, NY 10010
www.rizzoliusa.com

Texts: Linda Fargo; Diane von Furstenburg; Tommy Hilfiger; Blake Lively

Publisher: Charles Miers
Editor: Jessica Fuller
Agency: Gio Chiappetta
Design Direction: Gio Chiappetta
Art Direction: Show Yoda, Emily Makarainen, Danielle Huthart
Production Manager: Kaija Markoe
Managing Editor: Lynn Scrabis

Printed in China

2023 2024 2025 / 10 9 8 7 6

ISBN: 978-0-8478-6646-5
Library of Congress Control Number: 2019940531

Visit us online:
Facebook.com/RizzoliNewYork
Twitter: @Rizzoli_Books
Instagram.com/RizzoliBooks
Pinterest.com/RizzoliBooks
Youtube.com/user/RizzoliNY
Issuu.com/Rizzoli

Photo Credits: Alexandra Arnold pp. 22, 28, 40, 84, 164, 178, 184, 194, 214; Flavor Paper 189, 190, 191, 192; Hunter Holder pp. 2, 3, 4, 5, 6, 7, 8, 10, 11, 12, 14, 17, 18; James Letten pp. 24, 26, 30, 31, 33, 39, 42, 43, 48, 50, 51, 55, 56, 57, 58, 59, 60, 62, 63, 67, 68, 69, 70, 71, 72, 74, 75, 76, 77, 78, 79, 86, 88, 89, 90, 92, 97 109, 112, 113, 114, 115, 116, 117, 118, 119, 120, 124, 125, 126, 127, 128, 129, 130, 131, 132, 137, 138, 139, 140, 141, 144, 148, 149, 150, 152, 153, 154, 155, 156, 157, 158, 159, 160, 161, 163, 170, 174, 182, 183, 196, 197, 200, 201, 202, 203, 204, 206, 207, 208, 209, 216, 217, 218, 219, 220, 221, 222, 223, 224, 225, 226, 227, 228, 229, 230, 231, 232, 233, 234, 235, 236, 237. Michael Smith pp. 26, 27, 31, 32, 34, 35, 36, 37, 38, 44, 45, 46, 47, 49, 52, 53, 54, 61, 63, 64, 65, 66, 73, 74, 75, 80, 81, 82, 83, 87, 91, 93, 94, 95, 96, 98, 99, 100, 101, 102, 103, 104, 105, 106, 107, 108, 109, 110, 111, 121, 122, 123, 133, 134, 135, 136, 142, 143, 145, 146, 147, 151, 162, 166, 167, 168, 169, 171, 172, 173, 175, 176, 177, 180, 181, 182, 183, 185, 186, 188, 193, 198, 199, 200, 201, 205, 210, 211, 212, 213; Jeenah Moon p. 21.

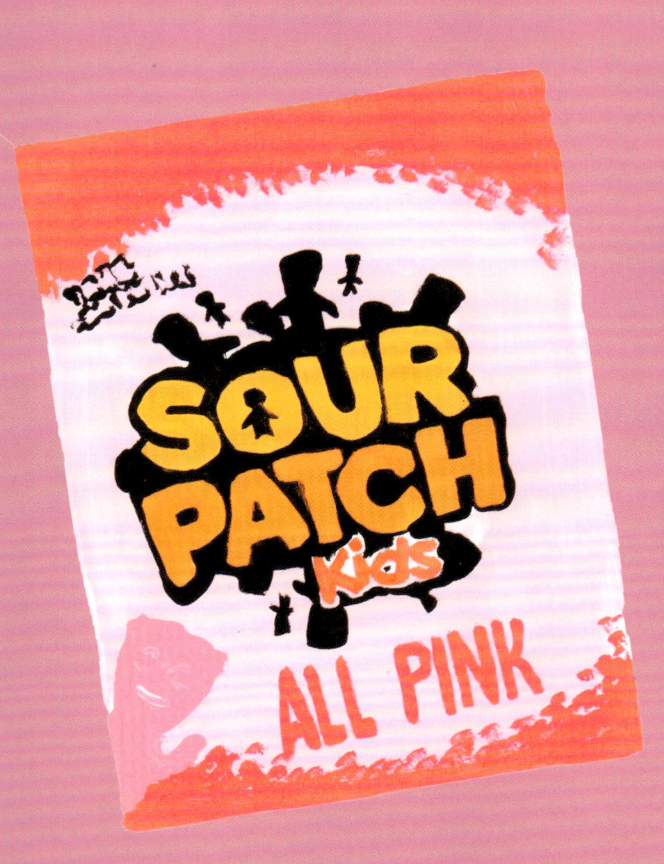

I'm a sour patch kid. I'll kick them in the BALLS and then giveum a Big HUG!